RICHARD ALDINGTON

RICHARD ALDINGTON

Novelist, Biographer and Exile
1930-1962

VIVIEN WHELPTON

Ⓛ
The Lutterworth Press

www.lutterworth.com
publishing@lutterworth.com

Paperback ISBN: 978 0 7188 9477 1
PDF ISBN: 978 0 7188 4550 6
ePub ISBN: 978 0 7188 4551 3
Kindle ISBN: 978 0 7188 4552 0

British Library Cataloguing in Publication Data
A record is available from the British Library

First published by The Lutterworth Press, 2019

In memory of Shelley Cox
(1948–2017)
Aldington scholar and enthusiast,
dear and generous friend

Contents

Part Three

THE RECLUSE

1951-1962

List of Illustrations

Acknowledgements

I wish to express my gratitude to the Estate of Richard Aldington and its agents, Rosica Colin Ltd, for the encouragement I have received since starting this project, in particular from Joanna Marston at Rosica Colin and from the late Catherine Aldington.

I wish to express further gratitude to the Authors' Foundation of the Society of Authors for a grant that covered the cost of a five-week research visit to the United States in 2016, enabling me to begin the task of writing this second volume of Aldington's life.

Excerpts from the writings of Richard Aldington, as specified below, are reproduced by kind permission of the Estate of Richard Aldington, c/o Rosica Colin Ltd, London:

Richard Aldington's memoirs, *Life for Life's Sake* (©Richard Aldington 1941, 1949, 1969); his novels, *The Colonel's Daughter* (©Catherine Guillaume 1931, 1958, 1986), *All Men are Enemies* (©Richard Aldington 1933, 1960, 1988), *Women Must Work* (©Richard Aldington 1934, 1935, 1961), *Very Heaven* (©Richard Aldington 1937, 1961, 1987), *Seven Against Reeves* (©Richard Aldington 1938, 1950, 1965) and *Rejected Guest* (©Richard Aldington 1939, 1947, 2005); his short story collections, *Roads to Glory* (©Richard Aldington 1930, 1958) and *Soft Answers* (©Richard Aldington 1932, 1935, 1949, 1959, 1967); *Artifex* (©Richard Aldington 1935, 1936, 1963), *Wellington* (©Richard Aldington 1943, 1946), *Pinorman* (©Richard Aldington 1954), *Four English Portraits* (©Richard Aldington 1948), *The Strange Life of Charles Waterton* (©Richard Aldington 1949), *Portrait of a Genius, But* ... (©Richard Aldington 1950, 1978), *Lawrence of Arabia* (©Richard Aldington 1955, 1957, 1969, 1971), *Introduction to Mistral* (©Richard Aldington 1956, 1960) and *Portrait of a Rebel* (©Richard Aldington 1957, 1985);

introductions to: *Selected Works of Oscar Wilde* (©Richard Aldington 1946, 1947, 1973, 1981), *Selected Works of Walter Pater* (©Richard Aldington 1948), the Chawton edition of the novels of Jane Austen (©Richard Aldington 1948), *The Religion of Beauty* (©Richard Aldington 1950), *The Trespasser* by D.H. Lawrence (©Richard Aldington 1950) and *Twilight in Italy* by D.H. Lawrence (©Richard Aldington 1950); articles and interviews originally published in: *Egoist, Nash's Pall Mall Magazine, Everyman* and the *Sunday Referee*; letters published and unpublished; unpublished essays and diaries; and the poems: *Life Quest* (©Richard Aldington 1935, 1962) and *The Crystal World* (©Richard Aldington 1937, 1965).

Extracts from various letters by Hilda Doolittle are reproduced by permission of Pollinger Limited on behalf of the Estate of Hilda Doolittle. Extracts from the letters and published works of Thomas MacGreevy are reproduced by kind permission of Margaret Farrington and Robert Ryan. Extracts from Irene Rathbone's letters and the poem *Was There a Summer?* are reproduced by kind permission of Nicholas Utechin. My thanks also go to David Higham Associates for permission to quote from the letters of Herbert Read. Extracts from *The Voyage Home, John o' London's Weekly* and an unpublished letter from Richard Church to Richard Aldington are reproduced by permission of Pollinger Limited on behalf of the Estate of Richard Church. Extracts from the letters of Ezra Pound are reproduced by permission of New Directions Publishing Corp. acting as agent © 2029 by Mary de Rachewiltz and the Estate of Omar S. Pound. Permission for use of extracts from Bryher's letters is granted courtesy of the Schaffner Family Foundation on behalf of the Bryher Literary Estate. The correspondence of Richard Aldington with Charles Prentice, Harold Raymond and Ian Parsons of Chatto & Windus, of Thomas MacGreevy, H.D. and Irene Rathbone with Charles Prentice and of Richard Aldington with Alexander Frere, Charles Seddon Evans and Arnold Gyde of William Heinemann, as well as correspondence between Alexander Frere, Harold Raymond and Ralph Pinker is quoted by kind permission of Random House Publishers.

Jennifer Aldington Emous kindly gave me permission to quote from her personal letters from Richard Aldington, while an extract from the unpublished work *The Early Life and Family History of A.S. Frere* by Jean Raulin Frere is reproduced by kind permission of Elizabeth Frere-Jones. The extract from Denison Deasey's article 'Lunch at the Villa' is reproduced by kind permission of Louisa Deasey. Simon Hewett kindly gave me permission to quote extracts from Richard Aldington's correspondence with Bertram Eskell.

I am indebted to the following libraries and institutions for permission to quote from or cite unpublished manuscripts in their collections:

Special Collections Research Center, Morris Library, Southern Illinois University, Carbondale: Richard Aldington Collection, Geoffrey de Montalk Letters from Richard Aldington, P.A.G. Aldington Letters from Richard Aldington, Selected Richard Aldington Correspondence, Alister Kershaw Collection of Richard Aldington Papers, Eric Warman Collection of Richard Aldington Papers, Henry Slonimsky Collection of Richard Aldington Papers, Ralph Pinker Collection of Richard Aldington Papers, Miscellaneous Richard Aldington Material from Eric Warman, Harry T. Moore Collection of Richard Aldington Correspondence, William Dibben Collection of Richard Aldington Correspondence, Alison Palmer Collection of Richard Aldington Correspondence, Richard Aldington Correspondence with Henry Williamson, Norman Gates Collection of Richard Aldington; also several vertical file mss and its General Photograph Collection.

Harry Ransom Humanities Research Center at the University of Texas at Austin: Richard Aldington Collection, Ezra Pound Collection, Brigit Patmore Collection, Nancy Cunard Collection, Edward Nehls Collection, Edward Dahlberg Collection, Richard Church Collection, David Garnett Collection, Frieda Lawrence Collection, T.E. Lawrence Collection and Charles Norman Collection.

Beinecke Rare Book and Manuscript Library, Yale University: Yale Collection of American Literature: Leonard Bacon Papers, H.D. Papers, George Plank Papers; General Collection: Richard Aldington Papers, Bryher Papers, Louise Morgan Theis Papers.

Special Collections Department at the University of Victoria: Herbert Edward Read Fonds, Charles Doyle Fonds.

Special Collections at the University of Reading: Chatto & Windus Archive.

Penguin Random House Archive and Library, Rushden, Northamptonshire: William Heinemann Archive.

Manuscripts and Archives Research Library, Trinity College Dublin: Thomas MacGreevy Collection.

Special Collections at the Brotherton Library, University of Leeds: Bonamy Dobrée Collection.

Special Collections at the Bancroft Library, University of California, Berkeley: Frederick Schiller Faust Papers.

Special Collections, Houghton Library, Harvard University: T.S. Eliot Editorial Correspondence 1904-30.

Special Collections at the Charles E. Young Research Library, University of California, Los Angeles: Alvin George Manuel business correspondence with Richard Aldington, 1940-1956.

Special Collections at the Library of the University of Illinois at Urbana-Champaign: H.G. Wells Papers.

Archives and Manuscripts Department, British Library: Schiff Papers; Letters of Richard Aldington to Netta Aldington.

Henry W. and Albert A. Berg Collection of English and American Literature: Richard Aldington Collected Papers.

My thanks go to the staff of these institutions for all the assistance I have received, in particular to Aaron Lisec of the Morris Library, Richard Watson of the Harry Ransom Center and Catherine Flynn of the Random House Archive and Library, whose patience and helpfulness have been unstinting and invaluable.

While every effort has been made to obtain permission from holders of copyright material produced herein, the publishers would like to apologise for any omissions and will be pleased to incorporate missing acknowledgements in any further editions.

A number of individuals have given me invaluable help. Anne Williamson kindly provided me with information about the friendship between Richard Aldington and her father-in-law, Henry Williamson, while Lynn Knight (editor of the 1989 Feminist Press edition of Irene Rathbone's *We That Were Young*) and Nicholas Utechin, Rathbone's grand-nephew, have similarly helped me to build up a picture of the relationship between Rathbone and Aldington, and Sylvain Kershaw has helped me enormously with information about his father, Alister Kershaw. My contact with Louisa Deasey, whose research into her father's life was published in 2018 as *A Letter from Paris*, helped me to an understanding of the nature and importance of the friendship between Deasey and Aldington, and Louisa has been generous with information, photographs – and encouragement.

Elizabeth Frere-Jones gave me helpful information about her father, Alexander Frere, and access to her sister-in-law's unpublished biography of him, while Andrew Harrison, Director of the D.H. Lawrence Research Centre in the School of English at the University of Nottingham, read my chapter on *Portrait of a Genius, But* . . . and offered me rigorous and helpful criticism. Susan Schriebman, Professor of Digital Art and Culture at the University of Maastricht, has helped me with information about Thomas MacGreevy and with access to his photograph collection.

The community of Aldington scholars and enthusiasts has, as always, been my principal support line. In particular, I wish to thank

Simon Hewett, Andrew Frayn and Elizabeth Vandiver for reading and commenting on particular chapters, and Simon and his wife Marjorie for welcoming me to New York and making his Aldington archive available to me. Simon, along with Michael Copp and the late David Wilkinson, has been a constant encouragement and source of ideas and information.

Beyond the 'Aldington community', my grateful thanks go to my friend, the clinical psychologist Desmond King, whose professional insights and comments, in particular in relation to chapters 8 and 9, proved enormously helpful, and also to two other friends, the military historians Peter Simkins and Brian Bond, who kindly reviewed my chapter on T.E. Lawrence and my references to Basil Liddell Hart, whom they both knew well.

I shall never forget the kindness and generosity of the late Shelley Cox and her partner, Bob Thomas, during my research visits to Carbondale, and I am grateful to Melinda Thomas, Bob's daughter, for providing me with the files of the Aldington bibliography on which Shelley had been working for many years. It was work that, sadly, she had to give up when her mobility became a problem for her, but those files represent years of work and travel and will be of enormous interest to Aldington scholars.

Throughout the project I have received information and encouragement from Jennifer Aldington Emous and Tim Aldington, whose enthusiasm at the prospect of a new biography of their uncle was motivated by their memories of his kindness to them in their youth.

I wish to express my gratitude to Adrian Brink, Director at Lutterworth Press, for commissioning both volumes and for his supportiveness throughout. My thanks go also to Dorothy Luckhurst, my copy editor for this volume and to my editor, Debora Nicosia for her patience and understanding.

I conclude with gratitude to my husband, Barrie Whelpton, who has once more been a rigorous and constructive critic and without whose support I could not have completed this work.

Introduction

Volume One of this biography covered eighteen years of Aldington's adult life, ending with the publication of *Death of a Hero*, his novel of the First World War, in 1929. During those years he was a founder member of a new poetic movement and the literary editor of a modernist journal. He went on to serve as an infantryman on the Western Front and, when the war ended, to endure a decade of post-traumatic stress – at the expense of his marriage to the American poet H.D., his subsequent relationship with Dorothy Yorke, and many friendships, such as those with Frank Flint, John Cournos, T.S. Eliot, Harold Monro, D.H. Lawrence, Bonamy Dobrée and Herbert Read. He published five collections of poems and three long poems as well as being a major contributor to several anthologies;[1] he worked as a reviewer and critic for several prominent journals; and he published over a dozen translations as well as selections of his essays and critical writings and a literary biography of Voltaire.[2]

Death of a Hero was a departure – in several respects: it was his first novel; it signified the end of his 'poetic' persona (although he would publish two more long poems); and, with its withering contempt for his native land, it launched him on the expatriate existence and the combative relationship with the English literary establishment that would characterise his later life. For now, his passionate relationship with Brigit Patmore and the enthusiasm with which he flung himself into a volume of war stories and a second novel, into travel and into a number of new friendships were indications of a renewed vitality. 'In the autumn of 1929,' he wrote later, 'it seemed to me that I could accept the remainder of life with a certain amount of confidence and cheerfulness.'[3] There were more short stories to come, as well as six more novels, some of them as disquieting as *Death of a Hero*. More controversially still, there were memoirs and biographies: of Wellington; of the nineteenth-century naturalist and eccentric, Charles Waterton; of D.H. Lawrence; of Charles Prentice, Pino Orioli and Norman

Douglas; of Robert Louis Stevenson; of the Provençal poet Frédéric Mistral; and, most contentious of all, of T.E. Lawrence, the man Aldington began by admiring but for whom he came to feel contempt.

Inevitably, there were other lovers. Other struggles. Other fraught relationships – and several fulfilling ones. There was the joy, as well as the anxiety, of parenthood, particularly when it became, as it did from 1950, single parenthood. There was the return into his life of H.D. and, more surprisingly still, of her partner, Bryher.

Aldington's dysfunctional upbringing and his war experience continued to influence his personal life and behaviour (and, in the case of the war, his physical health and well-being too). They were also played out in novel after novel; but so were his love of nature and the physical world and his passionate beliefs in individuality and in the power of love between a man and a woman. The public image of him for the last sixty years or more has been of an isolated and embittered figure, an image which many attribute to the appearance of his 1955 biography of T.E. Lawrence and the fury with which it was received by the political and literary establishments. Yet that reputation began much earlier, as can be seen from remarks made by C.P. Snow in the booklet he wrote to accompany Heinemann's reprinting of six Aldington works in 1938:[4]

> The bitterness is there all right. But it only predominates in one or two books, and in them is accompanied by much else. In everything he has written we ought to find many qualities far different and far more important. In order to get all we can from him, we need to understand the 'bitterness', put it in its place, and see beneath it the particular conception of life, the particular kind of passion and sensitivity, of which it is only one result . . . [5]

As we set about evaluating Aldington's later life and work, we might do well to bear in mind Snow's advice about how to read his complex personality.

Part One

THE WANDERER

1930-1936

1. A Sociable Life
Travel, Friendship and Patronage
1930-1931

In 1930 travel was still a novelty, a privilege won by the success of *Death of a Hero* – and Aldington's gift to Patmore. They spent the first two months of the year in North Africa. Aldington had asked Henri Davray to use his contacts with the French government to arrange passes, travel and accommodation in Tunisia and Algeria.[1] They were thus able to tour both countries freely and cheaply by car and train. He had also arranged to write an article about each country for *Nash's Pall Mall Magazine*.[2]

In Tunisia they based themselves in the capital but spent a fortnight covering some 850 miles of the interior by train and car, travelling by train to Kairouan and then south-west and inland to the oases of Nefta and Tozeur, then by car across to the coast at Gabes and on to the island of Jerba. Their return train journey took them north along the coast to Sfax, inland to El Djem (where Aldington admired the Roman amphitheatre, 'standing up immense in the twilight against a huge, bare plain'), then back up to the coast at Sousse and on to Tunis.[3]

Anthony Clarendon, the protagonist of *All Men Are Enemies* (1932), is unimpressed by the art, architecture and culture of Tunisia, but overwhelmed by the natural landscape: on the night train from Kairouan to Tozeur he is electrified by the sight of the desert in the hours before dawn, 'the dome of the sky clear and vast, filled with the white of the moonlight which shone over a great sea of lion-coloured sand'. He is standing on a siding as dawn finally breaks: 'The light shone on a desolation, but its silence was majestic.' It is this silence which moves him: 'The silence, the space, the limitless on and on of the desert were intoxicating ... the almost ecstatic peace which gradually occupied your whole nature as you rode in the sunlight over the sand in the brisk scentless air.'[4] In a throwback to George Winterbourne's adulation of the fighting infantry in *Death of a Hero*, Tony also admires 'the dignity and self-possession ... the complete poise and self-harmony [of] the men coming in from the desert wrapped in their burnous'.

In February Aldington and Patmore moved on to Algeria, where they made a round trip of over 900 miles, crossing the border at Gardima and travelling west to Constantine, then south to El Kantara and Biskra, and pushing down into the Sahara Desert at Touggourt before turning north to head for Algiers. After the barrenness of Tunisia, Northern Algeria surprised them with its 'flowery landscape, wooded hills, trees coming into bud, blossoming fruit trees and grass meadows ... the almond gardens in full bloom, the olives and cypresses, the vineyards and young wheat'. In Constantine it was again the men that impressed Aldington, with 'the physique and somewhat vacant hauteur we have learned to associate with warriors'. Further south, he was appalled by the tourism of Biskra but liked Touggourt where, once more, it was the people, with 'their quiet satisfaction in living', and 'the spaciousness and silence of the desert' that made an impact upon him.[5]

* * *

Nancy Cunard and Brigit
Patmore, 1930

Back in Paris, the couple continued to see the friends they had made there: Nancy Cunard and her current lover, the black musician Henry Crowder; the Irish writer Thomas MacGreevy, no longer lecturing at the École Normale Supérieure but surviving on odd jobs of translation work; and Walter Lowenfels, the American poet, and his wife, Lilian. However, the relationship between Lowenfels and Aldington soon began to unravel – and that with Cunard would not last much longer.[6]

Flush with money and success, Aldington attempted to sponsor other writers through the institution of two prizes. He and Cunard arranged for the Hours Press to offer £10 for the best poem in English on the theme

Samuel Beckett and Thomas MacGreevy in London in the early 1930s

of time. By the deadline, 15 June, little of any merit had been submitted; but that night Samuel Beckett's poem *Whoroscope* was slipped under the door of the Hours Press shop in the Rue Guénégaud. Both Cunard and Aldington recognised at once the extraordinary talent at work.[7] (Beckett, hard-up though he was, spent the prize money on a meal for MacGreevy, Aldington, Patmore and himself at the Cochon de Lait.)

Meanwhile the other prize had become contentious. Edward Titus, owner and editor of the expatriate literary journal *This Quarter*, had agreed to institute a 'Richard Aldington Award' for 'the ablest young American poet'.[8] Aldington would provide an annual prize of 10,000 francs, 5,000 from his own pocket and the remainder from other sponsors. His favoured candidate for the first award was Lowenfels. However, not content to let events take their course, Lowenfels started to harry Aldington. On the latter's return to Paris Lowenfels threatened to call a press conference for American journalists and announce the result. In a reference to Lowenfels' father's manufacturing business, in which the poet had worked for some years – and would be forced to work again on his return to the States in 1934 – Aldington commented tartly to MacGreevy: 'You can't bring the morals of the butter business into literature.'[9]

The affair dragged on for months. Lowenfels tried to cause trouble through an anonymous letter to *This Quarter* suggesting that *The Imagist Anthology*, which Chatto & Windus were about to publish, was a hoax. Titus sent the letter to Chatto for comment and Charles Prentice consulted Aldington, who had no doubts about the identity of the writer. He told Prentice: 'Walter . . . has become the egocentric and egomaniacal raté – a most unpleasant form of the genus artist, which abounds in wet purlieus of Montparnasse.'[10] At the end of the year he wrote to Titus from Italy to ask what was happening about the award.[11] It says much for his integrity that he still favoured Lowenfels, arguing that Titus's preferred candidate, e e cummings, already had an extensive reputation. Not until the following summer was a compromise hammered out (and only after Titus had dispatched an envoy to the south of France to act as mediator): cummings and Lowenfels would share the prize. Announcing the award, Titus referred to Aldington's 'iron fist within a velvet glove'.[12] It was an early indication of how intransigent he could be. There was to be no further award: Aldington had only 5,000 francs to spare in 1932 and *This Quarter* ceased publication.

Most of his attempts to support aspiring writers were more private and more successful. He had first corresponded with James Hanley in 1929, in response to the latter's praise of his poetry, and he was swift to offer to obtain a typewriter for him from 'a wealthy friend' (probably Henry Church) as well as to read Hanley's manuscripts.[13] He also sent him money and advised him about pursuing a career in journalism to finance his creative writing. He wrote the introductions to two of Hanley's first three novellas, *The German Prisoner* and *The Last Voyage*, mounting an impassioned defence of the writer's habit of grim realism; and he used his column in the *Sunday Referee* to recommend Hanley's subsequent work. James Reeves also received encouragement, after sending Aldington in May 1930 a proof copy of his review of *A Dream in the Luxembourg* for the *Cambridge Review*. Reeves, then a twenty-year-old undergraduate at Jesus College, visited Aldington in Paris that June. Aldington and Patmore had taken a three-roomed apartment in the Rue des Ursulines (their first and only attempt at home-making in Paris). Reeves found Aldington 'kind, pleasant and interested in the ideas of a young unknown man concerned with literature'.[14] Later in the year Aldington attempted (unsuccessfully) to place with Chatto an anthology of young Cambridge poets, including Reeves, as well as advising the young man on his attempts to gain a foothold in reviewing. Beckett, MacGreevy's friend and fellow countryman and his successor at the École Normale Supérieure, was another beneficiary, and not only through the Hours Press publication of *Whoroscope*; he was commissioned at Aldington's instigation to write a monograph on Proust for the Chatto Dolphin imprint, Aldington's brainchild.[15]

The writer on whose behalf Aldington dedicated most of his efforts was MacGreevy.[16] He gave him financial support and had him to stay at his rented villas in the south of France in the summers of 1930 and 1931, as well as financing MacGreevy's visits to himself and Patmore in Venice in November 1930 and in Florence in February 1931, from where they spent two months together touring Italy and travelling through Austria, Germany and Switzerland back to France. Aldington would later write that 'there never was a more good-humoured fellow-traveller or one who gave more by communicating a fine appreciation'.[17] The main intention behind these arrangements, however, was to enable MacGreevy to write and

Thomas MacGreevy, 1930

to help him establish a working routine – always a priority for Aldington himself, wherever his travels took him and in whatever accommodation he was housed.

He persuaded Prentice to commission MacGreevy for two of the Dolphin monographs on contemporary writers, one on T.S. Eliot and the other on Aldington himself.[18] At times, however, he despaired, writing to him from North Africa in January 1930: 'You're a lazy man Mr M'Greevy, Sir. You have about three times as much ability as I have, and you wrap your talent in a napkin. Beware of Judgement Day.'[19] At the end of the year he told Alexander Frere Reeves of Heinemann: '[Tom] got quite a kick out of Venice, and went off full of beans and good intentions. . . . I think [he] is determined to get away from his present scratch as scratch can existence, but we shall have to keep him up to it.'[20] He was probably right to recognise his friend's natural laziness but perhaps wrong to assume that MacGreevy should be taking the same path as himself; 'If you can pull off a novel, you will find that everything becomes plain sailing,' he told him.[21]

Although the two never fell out, the friendship faded as Aldington perceived that the novel was never going to be completed and that MacGreevy was reverting to 'scratch as scratch can'. By the end of 1933 MacGreevy was in London, supporting himself on reviewing and translating, and a disappointed Aldington wrote to Frere Reeves: 'What I object to in Tom is that he acts as if his poverty were our fault instead of his own.'[22] He would reflect in *Life for Life's Sake*:

Tom MacGreevy had all the gifts of a writer, except the urge to
write ... [H]e hadn't in him that aggressive daimon who after
each failure to reach to imagined height drives a man back to
his desk to try again. His creative impulse was satisfied by the
undoubted influence his talk had on a sympathetic audience; and
that is the danger of having the gift of conversation.[23]

MacGreevy, although in Paris between April and November of 1933,
was not invited that year to the villa Aldington had taken on the Côte
des Maures, and the correspondence between them became intermittent
for the remainder of the decade, although they probably met up when
Aldington was in London, where MacGreevy eventually established
himself as a prominent art critic. It was Aldington's disappointment in
MacGreevy's failure as an imaginative writer, not their differences of
personality – or belief (MacGreevy was a devout Catholic) – that drove
them apart.

Aldington's relationship with Cunard soured quite soon and she remained
bitter towards him for the rest of her life. On their return to Paris in 1930
Aldington and Patmore had continued to see her regularly, although her
lifestyle was more chaotic than their own and Patmore remained wary of
Cunard's predatory behaviour towards men. For all her hedonism, Cunard
was serious about the Hours Press and Aldington agreed to give her what
would be 'positively [his] last war story'.[24] Entitled *Last Straws*, it came out
in January 1931 and was sold out before publication.[25] However, it was
the direct cause of their estrangement. Cunard had departed with Crowder
for the south of France, leaving her friend Wyn Henderson as temporary
manager of the Hours Press. Henderson dispatched a cheque for advance
royalties to Aldington, now in Florence for the winter, but he returned the
cheque, saying that he had given the story to Cunard, not to a 'manager'
and that any communication should come from Cunard herself.[26] At first
Cunard did not realise the intensity of his anger; she wrote a warm, friendly
letter in early March, giving news of herself and Crowder and suggesting
that, 'Later, you and I if you will, can do more serious things. There *must* be
Time here.'[27] However, Aldington had already written to Patmore (visiting
London to see her sons):

Still not a word ... about my story and not a penny of money.
How foully dishonest! She goes and spends on niggers & saphs
the money she owes me. To hell with her. I am finished as far as
she's concerned. When I get my cheque from her – *fini, mais fini*.
Rotten little beast.'[28]

The casual homophobia is characteristic; the racism is not. Indeed, in her memoir Cunard recalled: 'To see Richard and Henry laughing together, to hear them talk about America, especially about the ironies of the race and colour question, was very worthwhile.'[29]

The exchange escalated until Aldington resorted to a letter of complaint to the Society of Authors. That organisation pointed out that both individuals were Society members, but offered to arbitrate. By now Cunard had folded up the Hours Press, all her efforts for the next four years being devoted to her new project, *The Negro Anthology*. Aldington received no satisfaction and in July 1931 he resigned from the Society.

Given his savage satire of Cunard in *Soft Answers* a year later and their battle over the reputation of Norman Douglas in 1954, her lasting hostility towards him is understandable but in her memoir, written shortly before her death in 1965, she acknowledged his 'generosity of spirit' in the days of their early acquaintance, instancing his support for Hanley and, particularly, his loyalty to D.H. Lawrence. She also expressed her lasting admiration for *The Eaten Heart* (which she published in 1929) and remarked of *Last Straws*, the grim tale of three war veterans which had been the cause of the rift between them: '[A]lthough the story upset several of the critics, it was convincingly written; it was meant to be bitter, and bitter it was. What is wrong with that?'[30]

2. A Sociable Life
France
1930-1933

Paris in 1930 afforded its amusements: the company of Aldington's old friend John Halcott Glover and his wife, Etta, visits to Henry and Barbara Church at Versailles, a lunch with Michael Arlen, a dinner at Olga Rudge's apartment when Pound was visiting Paris in April, and even visits from Frank Flint and James Gould Fletcher. Patmore told H.D. that she loved 'swinging into circles and out again'. However, she refused to see Flint because of his past 'disloyalty' to Aldington and, while she was charmed by Pound on the occasion of their reunion, telling H.D. that Rudge was 'good for him', she soon found cause to be irritated when he called round one afternoon and was rude to another visitor.[1]

However, Aldington found Paris and their tiny apartment inimical to work. At the end of June, having completed the set of war stories that would be published in September as *Roads to Glory*, he moved to the Villa Bouquet at Aiguebelle on the Côte des Maures three miles east of Le Lavandou. He stayed for three months, writing to advise Herbert Read to follow his example:

> [T]his bit of coast ... is much finer and less spoiled than the 'Bloomsbury bit' i.e. between Marseilles and Toulon.[2] This is far less accessible, between Hyères and St Maxime, served only by a sort of dilapidated decauville [narrow guage railway line] and a road which makes a car bump like a pea on a drum. There is a huge land-locked, or semi land-locked, bay, extending from Le Lavandou to Cavalière, with numerous beaches of white sand. The finest is Cavalière (about 2 kms from here) where the beach must be a mile long. There are big capes to east and west and the islands of Port Cros and Le Levant between them. Consequently, the water is scarcely ever rough, even in a gale. The country behind (les Maures) is mysterious. There are big hills, rather like the country behind and beyond Rapallo

in shape, but much more wooded. What is mysterious is that it is practically inaccessible. There are no roads and no footpaths. I have tried to explore it though the climbing is pretty stiff, but could not get through the thorns and brush.

Here he adds, one veteran to another: 'Rather like trying to get through a series of barbed wire entanglements.'[3]

It was the first of three villas he would rent in the locality over the next few years. In 1931 it was the Villa Koechlin at Rayol-Canadel, which he took from May to late September. He boasted to Read:

I was very lucky to get this villa, which is bang in the middle of the finest bay in the best section of this coast. It is about five miles to the east of the villa I had last year and better in every way. Private bathing beach and company's nightingales laid on.[4]

He told his literary agent, Ralph Pinker, that since it belonged to an artist, the villa was 'not only furnished simply and tastefully but arranged with the greatest practical common sense'.[5]

In 1932 he could not afford a villa, but he was back in 1933, from April until mid-September, at the Villa Devos in Pramousquier, halfway between Aiguebelle and Rayol-Canadel, this time sharing the cost with Frere Reeves, who was married at the villa that summer. It was, he told Bonamy Dobrée, a place he had wanted for a long time: 'There are two terraces and a half-wild garden going steeply down into a tiny little sand and rock beach all on their own.'[6] It was another opportunity to let the *Criterion* circle know how successful he was.[7]

The routine that he had first adopted at Fabrégas in 1929 suited him perfectly: rising early and working in the morning, then a swim before lunch. By the end of his first month at the Villa Bouquet he had written

Brigit Patmore and H.G. Wells in the south of France, early 1930s

20,000 words of a new novel. Nevertheless, some of his time was taken up with social visits (facilitated, from 1931, by the ownership of a car). The Côte d'Azur was occupied – in some cases year-round – by prominent literary figures: those of the older generation, like H.G. Wells, who had built himself a home with his lover, Odette Keun, at Grasse,

Aldous Huxley, 1931

and Somerset Maugham in his palatial mansion on Cap Ferrat; and those of Aldington's own generation: Michael Arlen near Cannes and Aldous Huxley at Sanary-sur-Mer on the other side of Toulon. In his novel *The Rock Pool* (1936), Cyril Connolly jokes:

Brigit Patmore and
Michael Arlen in
the south of France,
early 1930s

All along the coast from Huxley Point and Castle Wharton to Cape
Maugham little colonies or angry giants had settled themselves:
there were Campbell in Martigues, Aldington at Le Lavandou,
anyone who could hold a pen in St Tropez, Arlen in Cannes, and
beyond Monte Carlo and the Oppenheim country.[8]

There were other celebrities to be visited too: Natalie Barney at
Beauvallon near Saint-Tropez, where Aldington and Patmore also met
Colette, along with Barney's long-term lover, Elisabeth de Gramont; and
another Elizabeth, the novelist Elizabeth von Arnim, Countess Russell,
famed for *Elizabeth and Her German Garden* (1898), whose home, Mas des
Roses, was at Mougins, north of Cannes. Then there was Noel Coward at
Saint-Tropez: Aldington told H.D. that he had liked Coward more than he
had expected, finding 'a genuine vein of humanity' in him.[9]

Huxley was the one figure with whom we might have expected Aldington
to develop a close friendship. He told Read that Huxley was 'still a bit
Bloomsbury and inklectual [*sic*], but a likeable fellow and a good talker'.[10]
He admired Huxley's work and felt drawn to him for his iconoclasm and for
his loyalty to D.H. Lawrence; he also respected the writer's independence
of any literary clique, a contrast with Read's fraught but unwavering ties
to the *Criterion* circle.[11] Ultimately, he was probably in awe of Huxley's
intellect, although it was Huxley's predominantly ascetic nature and his
rejection of hedonism and sensuality that set them most apart.[12] For
Michael Arlen, another candidate for friendship, he felt warmth and
affection; he told Read how much he liked Arlen: 'He's extremely modest
and good-tempered and really rather witty, and as good-hearted a fellow
as you could hope to meet.'[13] Arlen's life, however, was extraordinarily
self-contained – and perhaps Aldington did not consider him a completely
serious writer. He had told Prentice, on first meeting Arlen in Paris in
1930: 'I like [him] extremely; he is totally uneducated of course, but an

Halcott Glover in 1914-1915,
when serving for the American Red Cross in France

amiable and warm-hearted man.'[14] These social interactions occupied only a small portion of the long summers on the Riviera; for Aldington, work and the routine it demanded were always his first priority; others were the simple pleasures of good – but not over-expensive – food and wine, walking, exploring the countryside and nearby villages, and swimming. His chief pleasure, however, was acting as host to those who were now his closest friends: Glover, MacGreevy, Frere Reeves and Prentice.

Only Glover and MacGreevy were writers, and neither was having much success. Glover had been a moderately successful playwright when Aldington had met him in the early 1920s but he had found little reward in recent years and was now trying his hand at the novel. MacGreevy was also attempting to write a novel, but in 1931 his main task, successfully accomplished, was to produce the Dolphin monographs on Eliot and Aldington. Prentice and Frere (who dropped the 'Reeves' in 1929) were highly successful publishers, the former senior partner at Chatto & Windus, the latter a director at Heinemann. They had both met

Aldington in 1929, Prentice when Donald Friede, Aldington's American publisher, had suggested Chatto as the British publishers for *Death of a Hero*, and Frere when he came to Paris to meet up with Lowenfels, whose poems Heinemann were publishing. Aldington and Patmore felt great affection for Prentice; the former valued his scholarship, and his wisdom and tact as a publisher, while they both appreciated his kindness and integrity: 'A man utterly without affectations . . . of simple dignity and straightforward utterance; so considerate of others as to seem almost diffident; so generous that one was always trying to restrain him; and at the same time full of laughter and appreciation of a good thing said.'[15]

Frere was very different, in tastes and temperament more like Aldington himself. Whereas MacGreevy and Prentice had had stable childhoods, in Ireland and Scotland, respectively, Frere's upbringing had not been easy. His father had left shortly after he was born and he and his mother were forced to live with relatives in Southampton. When he was thirteen years old, she left him to set up home with a new partner in Wiltshire, where she gave birth to a daughter. In an unpublished account of Frere's life his daughter-in-law, Jean Raulin Frere, wrote that 'whatever his movements during his teenage years [these being hard to establish] Frere seems never to have lived in a conventional domestic environment that offered stability and love'.[16]

Richard Aldington, Brigit Patmore, Thomas MacGreevy and Alexander Frere (pointing) in the south of France, early 1930s

Having served in the East Kent Yeomanry before the war, Frere was sent to Gallipoli in October 1915, and thence to Egypt. Commissioned in 1916, he transferred to the Royal Flying Corps the following year but in April 1918 was seriously injured when his Sopwith Camel crashed. He received intermittent hospital treatment for two years, including considerable periods at the Maudsley Military Neurological Hospital. He went up to Cambridge in 1919 and in the 1920 summer vacation travelled to Switzerland to catalogue Elizabeth von Arnim's library. He became her lover for nearly twelve years, although she was nearly thirty years his senior.[17] Indeed, Frere, who worked as a reporter on the *Evening News* after leaving Cambridge, owed his opening with Heinemann to von Arnim, since in 1925 she persuaded her friend, the American publisher Nelson Doubleday, to employ him, as a result of which he was offered the job at the British publishing house which Doubleday had recently acquired. His always-turbulent relationship with von Arnim came to a stormy end in March 1932 but they would subsequently become close friends – and he would visit her frequently at her home on the Riviera. He had been briefly and unsatisfactorily married in 1927 and was then married for the second time – to the daughter of Edgar Wallace, the crime writer – at the Villa Devos in June 1933.

Perhaps because he sensed in Frere deep-seated tensions not dissimilar from his own, Aldington confided in him more than in his other friends. In a 1934 letter he advised Frere:

> There is much truth in the old tag: Resist not evil . . . in the sense that by making too much of an effort against what is evil, one becomes negative. I have wasted so much time kicking against the pricks (not to mention cunts) that I want to save you from the same waste.[18]

He would tell Read, when arranging for him to meet with Frere in 1934:

> Just one word of warning. He crashed badly in 1918, and occasionally suffers from appalling headaches in consequence. At such times he is moody and apt to say things he doesn't mean. He's been much better in the past two years – in fact since he divorced and took up with Pat Wallace – but these head pains do take him sometimes. At such moments the wisest thing is to say nothing and clear out.[19]

There are other hints in the correspondence amongst the group of friends that Frere's behaviour could be unpredictable.

Aldington would always have more time for publishers than for fellow authors, partly because of his respect for Prentice and Frere but also because he knew that publishers were his 'bread and butter'. 'My settled opinion,' he wrote in his memoirs, 'is that the professional author's best friend can be and should be his publisher. Apart from the author's own family, nobody is so deeply interested in the success of a book.'[20] None of this, however, would prevent his relationships with both Chatto and Heinemann from becoming stormy in later years.

The mainspring of his affection for Glover, MacGreevy, Prentice and Frere was their shared war service. He had retained no friendships from that period of his life: in 1916 and 1917 he had been a middle-class infantryman with little in common with his fellow soldiers; in 1918 he had been so preoccupied with the free-fall status of his marriage that he had socialised very little with his fellow officers. On his return from war, however, he had felt alienated from his fellow writers, the older ones 'so hopelessly out of date, so unaware that earth's foundations had trembled and that nothing would really be the same again', while he bitterly resented those of his own generation who had not fought.[21] The years had not softened this instinct and it lay behind much of his antipathy towards Eliot and others amongst the *Criterion* set.

With MacGreevy, Prentice and Frere, all around his own age, he felt himself to be a cherished member of a different kind of club. (Glover, who had served with the Royal Flying Corps, was some fifteen years older.) He wrote to Prentice in May 1931:

> When I think of what we silly buggers went through, and how we were betrayed, and have nothing but each other, and yet can utterly trust each other, and know we're just as much side by side as if we were in the line – well, I won't try to express it.[22]

'If we got nothing else out of this bloody War, we at least got the affection of men like Frere and Charles,' he told MacGreevy.[23] These 'unforgettable bonds' strengthened his combativeness when he encountered opposition: '[I]t's antiseptic to be alone. We held the world on our bayonets, and, by God, we'll hold it on the point of our boots,' he told Prentice when his next novel was facing the hostility of reviewers and booksellers.[24]

As for MacGreevy, twice wounded in the war, Gerald Dawe argues that not only his poetic output (some 50 poems) but also his monograph on Aldington show him 'work[ing] through the personal and political effects upon himself of his involvement in World War One'.[25] If Aldington found himself alienated from postwar Britain, how much more must MacGreevy,

Brigit Patmore
in the south of
France, early
1930s

a Catholic Irishman who had served as a British officer, have felt himself to be stateless on his return to an Ireland at war with Britain? In *Richard Aldington: An Englishman*, he addresses the legacy of the war long before he introduces Aldington's name:

> If you have been placed suddenly on the other side of the grave and left there for months and years, you do not forget it. And you do not forget those you left there when you came back. Sometimes you bring back not only a darkened spirit but a maimed body from there, and that reminds you.[26]

Shared leisure, however, brought the group great joy. Prentice wrote to Aldington in January 1931, 'I spent a heavenly evening with Frere on Thursday. He is a champion; one of the most delightful men I ever met'; and, after his visit to the Côte des Maures that summer: 'I couldn't have been happier than I was with you and Brigit at Canadel; now it is like looking back on a dream.'[27] However, there were also Patmore's two sons, now in their early 20s, to be accommodated during those summers, as well as a variety of other visitors. In 1930 Aldington confided in Prentice, 'I had planned it out with great skill, but everybody changes his mind and date', and 'There have been so many guests at Le Bouquet that I haven't progressed as rapidly as I might.'[28] The following year he would confess: 'I have been a little bothered by people.'[29] Some of these people were well-meaning 'outsiders' who did not appreciate that his days were circumscribed by his need to be at his desk each morning. A visit from Malcolm Hilbery, his high-flying lawyer friend from his boyhood days, prompted the complaint: 'Like all good bourgeois, they imagine books are the product of complete idleness, and we (Tom and I) have to fight for our mornings.'[30]

Another visitor was Aldington's sister Margery. Since Padworth days her life had been hard. Employment for a singer in London in the late 1920s was mainly casual and intermittent. Eventually, she had joined a Variety group touring India, and in Delhi she had met and fallen in love with an expatriate official on the Indian Railways, a man whose wife had left him to bring up their two children in England. With a family to support and aware that he had little to offer Margery, he had encouraged her to return home at the end of her tour. However, she had later returned to India and become pregnant. Again, he had persuaded her to return home and to have an abortion, which, because of her debilitated condition, she had no difficulty in obtaining. She remained in London for three years, living with Olive Salter, the long-time friend with whom she had shared a cottage in Berkshire, only returning to India in late 1933.

She and her lover were finally married in India in 1937, by which time she had written an autobiographical novel, *Pavane for an Unborn Child*. Never published, it is a heart-rending account of the many tragedies of her life. How much of what had transpired in India she revealed to her brother during her enforced stay in England we cannot know, but she visited him at the Villa Koechlin and developed a warm friendship with the kindly Prentice. Aldington would write to Prentice from Portugal in 1932: 'You were very sweet and kind to take Margery to lunch. I'm afraid the English winter does weigh on her, but I don't quite know what can be done about it. I wish she could get to India as she wants.'[31] Describing her to one correspondent, he referred to her 'tendency to want to do good to others, without being able to do good to herself'.[32] In 1931 she was trying to do good to their younger sister, Pattie, who had escaped from their mother but who had no qualifications and was unable to support herself. Again, it was Prentice to whom Aldington turned for help.

The Côte des Maures, with its sun and sea, gave Aldington a base, even a home, to which he could welcome his friends. For the first three years of the decade, however, it was Italy, the remembered paradise of 1913, to which he was drawn and to which we shall now turn.

3. A Sociable Life
Italy – Further Friendships
1930-1932

In 1930 and 1931, as the sun and sea lost their sparkle and the Riviera emptied, Aldington and Patmore gravitated to Italy – for its culture and climate and for its personal associations for Aldington. In 1930 they set off at the end of September, with the object of giving Patmore her first encounter with Venice. After five weeks there they moved on to Lecce, in the 'heel' of Italy, from where Aldington once again wrote to Read.

Although his acquaintance with Read had begun in the immediate aftermath of their military service – and would persist for the rest of their lives – it had become a relationship marked by wariness and mistrust. Aldington was acutely aware that Read had Flint, Eliot and the rest of the *Criterion* set at his elbow and he was keen to remind them all of his professional and personal success. He had also been hurt by Read's response to the proofs of *Death of a Hero*, which he had sent him for comment 'as an old friend and fellow officer'. Read's comments, Aldington informed Prentice, had amounted to 'four pages of oblique but positively vindictive denunciation'.[1] Read was equally critical of *Roads to Glory*, objecting to a lack of 'restraint' in some of the stories.[2] This issue had been aired frequently between them over the years, as an aspect of the polarity which Aldington felt their work represented between intellect and feeling, with Read – and the Eliot school – on the side of intellect.

When he heard of Read's appointment to the Chair of Fine Art at Edinburgh University in the summer of 1931, Aldington was, however, quick to congratulate him; and it was to Aldington that Read wrote for advice in January 1933 when he felt stifled by the academic life – although he appears not to have revealed that his marriage had also fallen apart and that he was in love with the young Margaret Ludwig. Aldington's advice was clear – and characteristic:

Herbert Read, 1934

First, you must decide . . . whether the life of your creative instinct and its expression in literature is really more to you than anything else. Second, if you do decide in the affirmative, your next step is to go straight as an arrow for the way of living which you believe most likely to attain that end. You may make mistakes (who doesn't) but you'll live.[3]

It was the route that he had taken – and it was the route Read would take that June, when he resigned his post, left his wife and son and fled Edinburgh with his lover. Aldington sent him congratulations: 'This will be an enormous release, and you'll go like a race-horse now.'[4] He even sent Read a poem, entitled 'Life Goes On'.[5]

He was also quick to offer practical help: he was resigning as reviewer on the *Sunday Referee* and would recommend Read for the post. Nothing came of this but in London in December 1934 he was able to be of greater service, persuading Frere to publish Read's novel, *The Green Child*, which Faber had rejected, and to take Read on as a literary adviser.[6] Aldington left London two months later, having received no word of thanks from Read. He returned in the autumn of 1935 and a letter to Read dated 25 February 1936 begins: 'I'm very glad you wrote because it clears up a misunderstanding,' and continues: 'I felt your silence was rather hard on me, since I had worked loyally on your behalf. ... At any rate I got the impression that you didn't care about keeping in touch, and that there was nothing to be done about it.'[7] In this letter he proposes a meeting and we can only guess whether this took place.

There is an intriguing postscript to this tale of misunderstanding. Read's contribution to *Richard Aldington: An Intimate Portrait* comprises a detailed review of his letters from Aldington in which he asserts that the correspondence ceased (for eleven years) 'for no apparent reason' with Aldington's letter of 31 December 1934.[8] James King, Read's biographer, reflects:

> Read's uncharacteristic mendacity about the existence of the February 1936 letter reveals an unwillingness to deal with his harsh behaviour towards an old but frequently difficult friend. ... He may have thought that he had wronged Aldington and wanted to keep the matter from scrutiny. Read was always careful to maintain the facade of a relatively untroubled, generous person. In this instance, his scrupulous regard for public opinion demonstrates the insecurity behind the mask.[9]

Read was under the influence of the *Criterion* set and specifically of its leader: the outward life had to be sober and conventional. That he recognised this as a problem is apparent in his once remarking to Richard Church (also a member of the *Criterion* group): 'Eliot has been rather like a gloomy priest presiding over my affectionate spontaneity.'[10] Both he and Aldington offended against the rules but, whereas Aldington had left England to escape being an outcast, Read found himself an alternative support group in the Modernist artists amongst whom he and his new partner came to live in 1933 and whose principal advocate he became.[11] Nevertheless, he maintained the sober and conventional demeanour and was soon back in the *Criterion* fold. 'Affectionate spontaneity' was not Read's *forte*: he would tell Church: 'You Londoners will never understand the Yorkshire nature, which has to be controlled because it is fundamentally so emotional.'[12]

We might find other factors to account for this reserve. Aldington and Read were both damaged by their war experience and had spent the 1920s in a state of numbness. In a revealing review of *All Quiet on the Western Front*, Read wrote: 'For these men the war lasted too long to be an adventure; it withered something in them that had never come to full growth.'[13] Additionally, both had had difficult childhoods, particularly Read, who had been torn from an idyllic rural existence at the age of ten by his father's death from a fatal accident, and sent to an orphanage. They had much in common – but contrasting temperaments and different coping mechanisms. Read's reserve and his wariness of Aldington meant that the relationship between these two men could never be close.

Aldington, however, imported to Italy the members of his own support group. During their five-week stay in Venice in 1930, he and Patmore were visited by both MacGreevy and Prentice. After leaving Venice, Prentice wrote: 'You are the dearest people. I don't think I ever had a more adorable time. It was a most painful wrench to leave.'[14] In January 1931 Patmore told MacGreevy, 'Richard and I decided that you and Charles are the gifts from life in these last two years', a message that MacGreevy delightedly passed on to Prentice.[15] When he and Patmore reached Florence in December 1930, Aldington summoned Frere from Cannes – although not purely for the purposes of companionship: Frieda Lawrence was visiting the Italian publisher Giuseppe ('Pino') Orioli, and Aldington was keen for Heinemann not only to publish Lawrence's letters and the posthumous work, but to buy back all Lawrence publication rights from Martin Secker.[16]

In February of 1931 MacGreevy was back with them in Florence, his fare paid by Aldington. The latter had meanwhile purchased a second-hand Ford car and, having passed his driving test, took Patmore and MacGreevy on an eighteen-day round trip between Florence and Rome, visiting about twenty towns in the provinces of Siena, Perugia, Terni and Viterbo. From Rome, they also made a trip to the Amalfi coast. Aldington wrote to Prentice:

(above) Thomas
MacGreevy and
Richard Aldington
at the Temple of
Paestum, 1931

(left) Thomas
MacGreevy and
Richard Aldington's
Ford car, 'Romolina',
Italy, 1931

(opposite) Brigit
Patmore and Thomas
MacGreevy at the
Temple of Paestum,
1931

We have seen more of Italy in five days than could be seen in five weeks in the ordinary way, and we have seen it more cheaply, taking picnic lunches in the car, and avoiding the big hotels. . . . I have kept careful account of all our expenses. . . . I have never had a more delightful trip in all my life.[17]

On their return, Prentice joined them in Florence for a week, on his way to Greece. As soon as he left they were off again, taking MacGreevy with them – this time for a longer journey, driving east and north to Ancona, Rimini, Ravenna, Ferrara and Mantua before travelling the length of Lake Garda and through the Brenner Pass to Innsbruck, Salzburg and Munich and thence to Lyons and Marseille, via Switzerland. (Some achievement for someone who had only just passed his driving test!) In November they came back to Florence, driving there via the French and Italian Rivieras.

The travelling project for the spring of 1932, influenced by Norman Douglas's 1915 book *Old Calabria*, was the mountainous region that formed the 'toe' of Italy, followed by Sicily.[18] Meanwhile, Aldington had become extremely ill with Vincent's angina, a severe form of tonsillitis and pharyngitis, which started in mid-December and left him still weak in early February. He tells us in *Pinorman* that Frieda Lawrence, who was in Florence again for Christmas, 'cheered everyone up by remarking in her optimistic way that I looked very much as Lorenzo did before he died'.[19] The *Sunday Referee* had to explain a two-week gap in January 1932, announcing: 'It is regretted that Mr Richard Aldington is still not well enough to contribute his usual article.'[20]

Nevertheless, the party, consisting of Prentice, Orioli, Patmore and Aldington, set off in mid-February on a three-week trip via Rome and Naples and then down the west coast. From Calabria they crossed over to Messina and visited Cefalù, Palermo, Segesta, Selinunte, Agrigento and Siracusa. Aldington was disappointed in Calabria:

> What we found were dirty villages which stank, earthquake-shattered ruins, mere dens of dwellings, a neglected and barbarous population . . . the landscape is wild enough and often beautiful, but so far as moments of the great past are concerned you must see nearly all of them with the eyes of historical memory and take them on trust. On your map you see a great name in history; in fact you see a desolate marsh or a few shapeless broken stones or a malaria-smitten village.[21]

He may have been influenced by the 'desolately wintry' conditions of their journey, involving cold winds, heavy rain – and several blizzards.[22] On the mountain pass of Campo Tenese, at 3,000 feet, the car broke down and they had to wait for several hours in a road-mender's cottage to be rescued. Only as they worked their way west and south in Sicily did the signs of spring begin to appear.

However, the trip was a merry one, and Prentice, who left the party at Reggio Calabria to return by train to London, wrote: 'What a time you gave me . . . what would we have done without your stout and obstinate driving I really don't know – and your directing mind and B's pots and pans and darling Pino and all the good cheer. We were a marvellous party.'[23] Aldington, in turn, reported to MacGreevy: 'Brigit was really marvellous, enduring hardships and difficulties with complete cheerfulness. Charles was as dear and charming a travel companion as yourself, which is the highest praise I can give. Pino was high-spirited and amusing, but sometimes a little too drunk.'[24] Looking back ten years later, and after much more extensive travels, he called the trip 'the most amusing and adventurous journey' he had ever made.[25] He was certainly hurt when Orioli published an account of an almost identical trip he made in the spring of 1934 – this time by bus, train and taxi – with Douglas, Prentice and Ian Parsons (another partner at Chatto & Windus), his only references to the earlier trip with Aldington being an exaggerated account of the breakdown at Campo Tenese and a passing mention of visiting Tiriolo 'with a friend in his car'.[26]

It was Orioli – both in December 1930 and in November 1931 – who found accommodation in Florence for Aldington and Patmore, the first time a suite in the Gran Bretagna Hotel, overlooking the Arno, the second

Norman Douglas, Florence, 1935

time a luxurious apartment at 12 Piazza Santa Croce, where they stayed for six months and which was really beyond Aldington's means. When they came to Florence from Lecce in December 1930 it was in order to meet the 62-year-old Norman Douglas. In *Life for Life's Sake*, his 1941 memoirs, Aldington explained that draw:

> I had read most of his books, and found in them a man with a sane, intelligent view of life, wit and high spirits, an astonishing variety of interests, and a fund of valuable and unusual knowledge. Here was somebody, I thought, who had not allowed life to push him around, but had forced life to give him what he wanted and had wanted many different things. A masculine adult mind and a writer of almost classical proportion.[27]

His only comment on the darker side of Douglas's lifestyle was: 'It did not trouble me in the least that I differed very strongly from Douglas on certain points of human conduct, wherein I did not and do not approve either his theory or his practice.' Describing Douglas as 'a man of the world', he compared him to Somerset Maugham, seeing both men as 'not to be imposed on by fads and pretences' and as possessing an extensive knowledge and understanding of European literature.[28]

Giuseppe (Pino) Orioli, Florence, 24 June 1935

The reader may well think of another similarity between these two men, their rampant, preying sexual drive, in Douglas's case towards pre-adolescent boys. By the time Aldington came to write *Pinorman*, after Douglas's death in 1952, this was an aspect of the writer's conduct that did trouble him and he was prepared to spell out the details, as well as to question the standing of Douglas's creative *oeuvre*, while still expressing admiration for the 'natural dignity' of his 'truly classical prose'.[29]

Douglas was in Paris for dental treatment when Aldington and Patmore arrived in Florence, and they were entertained by Orioli until his return towards the end of December. Aldington had known Orioli since pre-war days, when he had first visited his bookshop in Florence. In *Life for Life's Sake* he refers to him as 'a kind of Boccaccio junior', telling us: 'He is an immensely entertaining companion, always alert, witty and observant, and above all intensely alive. . . . No man has ever given me more of the priceless gifts of laughter and good fellowship.'[30] Derek Patmore, in his introduction to his mother's memoirs, describes Orioli as playing the part of Sancho Panza to Douglas's Don Quixote, but he also explains his importance to Douglas: 'It was Pino who organised the material side of Norman's life [and who] by publishing Norman's books in expensive limited editions in his Lungarno Press series, provided his friend with enough money to live modestly in Florence.'[31]

Once Douglas returned, Aldington and Patmore lunched or dined with him regularly, especially while Orioli accompanied Frieda to London for talks with Heinemann. They found his conversation full of good sense and wide-ranging knowledge. It seems to have been during this period that the eight friends – Frere, Douglas, Frieda Lawrence, Orioli, Patmore, Aldington and, in their absence, MacGreevy and Prentice – formed the 'Canterbury Literary Society', to cock a snook at the élite literary circles of the day – like the *Criterion* set. Prentice was already known to Douglas and Orioli and an admirer of Douglas's writing; during that first winter in Florence Aldington wrote to him: 'We see Douglas and Orioli nearly every day. They speak of you with a warmth which wins our hearts.'[32] He told MacGreevy: 'Pino and Norman are dying to meet you.'[33]

However, there is no doubt that not only Douglas's amoral outlook and sexual conduct, but also his conversation, had palled by the end of Aldington's and Patmore's second winter in Florence. As early as February 1931, when Patmore had briefly returned to London to see her sons, Aldington wrote to her that he had:

> dined with Norman and Pino, and had quite a quarrel with them (see what happens when you go away!) because they are cynical and say one should only live for oneself. I said that we should think of people who will live 20 million years after us. But they don't understand. They don't care! I am rather proud of us because we do care and keep up the fight.[34]

A year on he was writing to MacGreevy: 'Norman looks well, finishing a book, drinks little, but there are other bothers you can guess. I marvel at Pino's constant skill & tact in staving off awkward situations,' and he told Prentice not to encourage Douglas to join them on their trip to Calabria: 'If he does, we shan't see anything but pubs and boys, for nothing else interests him now. It is very dreary, but alas, it is so.'[35]

Mark Holloway, Douglas's biographer, remarks that:

> Food, drink and sex became more and more the chief preoccupations of his existence; intellectual activities occupied less and less of his time; life in general, as it will in middle-age, became more mechanical and less spontaneous. ... In this Florentine period Uncle Norman – rather portly, rather inflamed of countenance – was characteristically encountered in a restaurant autocratically overseeing the production of the food

Osbert Sitwell and Richard Aldington
at Castello di Montegufoni, Florence, 1931

he was about to eat, treating the waiter as his personal servant, exacting lieutenantship from Orioli, his personal Fool, weighing the wine, and letting nothing pass that did not meet with his absolute approval. It became a sight that all who were interested were determined to see; and those who succeeded in seeing it were often rewarded, alas, by Uncle Norman performing as required.[36]

There were other social and literary acquaintances, some of them part of the Douglas circle, such as the ageing Reggie Turner, devoted friend of Oscar Wilde, and the young Anglo-Italian aristocrat and writer Harold Acton.[37] Aldington and Patmore also visited Osbert Sitwell, whose family's Italian seat, the Castello di Montegufoni, lay 20 miles south of Florence; in Venice they dined with Clive Bell and with Nancy Cunard, her cousins Victor and Edward, and Dolly Wilde; in Rome, on their way from Lecce to Florence, they met up with Edward Storer, whom Aldington had known from pre-war years.[38] Aldington also began a lifelong friendship with the American poet Leonard Bacon, a future Pulitzer Prize winner, who lived with his family in Florence from 1927 until 1932 – and who lent Aldington his car and chauffeur when he was learning to drive.

However, as early as December 1930 Aldington was complaining to H.D.: 'The only drawback is that so many people ask us out, and we want time to write and look at things.'[39] There is some showmanship in the remark, but work was always his priority, to be sustained throughout his travels, both his weekly reviewing for the *Sunday Referee* and his own creative work. In Venice in October 1930, despite a heavy cold which laid him up for several days and the visits of MacGreevy and Prentice, he wrote three *Referee* articles, the short story *Last Straws* for Cunard and 7,000 words of *The Colonel's Daughter* (the novel he had begun on the Riviera in July) as well as coming up with the idea for another volume of short stories – which would become *Soft Answers*. Having completed the final third of the novel in Lecce, he wrote to tell Prentice that, although he had promised himself a month off, he was too fired up with the idea for this satirical collection of stories. He had written the first in Florence by the end of the year and would write the remainder at the Villa Koechlin in the summer of 1931.

The following winter his illness severely curtailed his work, and he had to complete eight *Referee* reviews in the first three weeks of February 1932, before setting off for Calabria. He had been preoccupied all winter with the editing of D.H. Lawrence's *Last Poems* and writing an introduction for *Apocalypse* for Secker, and he wrote to MacGreevy:

I can't tell you how much I have been moved by these last poems
& how glad in my deepest heart I am that in the end there was
no more carping or hating, but the grandeur and dignity of a real
man, the real L. whom I could not help loving.[40]

By May of 1932 he was discussing with Prentice his plans for his third
novel. He knew that he could not write it in Florence. 'In the early stages
of a book I am more nervous than a pregnant woman, and outside people
upset the whole structure so I have to begin again from the beginning,'
he told Prentice.[41] He intended to go to London, but a short trip to Capri
while Derek Patmore was visiting changed his plans. He had once again
visited the Pensione del Lauro in Anacapri, where he and H.D. had spent
an idyllic five weeks in 1913, and he decided on impulse that this was
where he should write his romantic novel. Giving up his contract with
the *Referee*, he returned to Capri, renting two rooms on the upper floor
of the pension ('looking over the quiet garden and up to Monte Solaro')
from the original proprietress, Maria di Tommasi.[42] He and Patmore were
glad to have a quiet, settled (and inexpensive) existence for which they
did not require a car, their Ford, 'Romolina', having been written off in an
accident shortly before they arrived. It was here over a period of eleven
weeks that more than half of *All Men Are Enemies* was written, its pages
regularly dispatched to the approving and delighted Prentice. Visitors
only came in the last two weeks of their stay – in the shape of Hal and
Etta Glover – and it was with the Glovers that they sailed from Naples to
Toulon in the first week of August.

We might wonder why Aldington left Capri before his novel was
completed. Certainly, he would usually have taken a villa on the Riviera for
the summer, but the 1932 financial crash and his own depleted resources
made that impossible; he had not even been able to invite MacGreevy to
Capri and had advised him that his best option in the current economic
crisis was to go home to Ireland and write his novel. However, Frere was
keen to meet up and Aldington did not want his hard-pressed friend to
have to come all the way to Capri. Furthermore, the island was filling up
with summer tourists, progress on the novel had slowed – and Aldington
had had a series of the stomach upsets to which he was prone.[43] He had
completed 90,000 words and had another 50,000 or 60,000 to go. Prentice
was bound, with Parsons, for a walking tour of Austria with Orioli and
Douglas. It seemed the moment to pause.

Life for Life's Sake offers us another reason for Aldington's departure
from Italy in 1932 – his increasing distaste for the Fascist regime: 'I was
miserable and oppressed by the sight of so much misery and oppression

Charles Prentice and Norman Douglas in Florence, 22 June 1935

in the name of a pretentious national glory and power far beyond the country's real capacity and contrary to the real interests of the people.'[44] He told MacGreevy: 'Italy is so spoiled and one gets so weary of Fascist brag and interference. They've killed the old Italy – one more sweet benediction of that blessed War. Those Italians in power now are shits, real shits, and a most disturbing force in Europe.'[45]

4. The Public Face
Critic and Satirist

The nature and reception of Aldington's second novel, *The Colonel's Daughter* (1931), and of his short-story collection *Soft Answers* (1932) allow us to become acquainted with both his literary persona and his public standing in this period.

While he had exiled himself from the literary world of London, and the *Criterion* set in particular, he was physically present in the capital for quite extensive periods: only a couple of weeks in 1930 and no more than a month in 1931 and in 1932, but in each of the four years from 1933 to 1936 he and Patmore spent between three and six months at a time in London. As Florence palled, for political and personal reasons, London became the default winter substitute, a surprising choice given his susceptibility to bronchitis. Patmore's desire to be near her sons was one of the motivating factors; another was his need to be in touch with his publishers and his literary agent, Ralph Pinker; but most of all, the recession had made the Continent a less practicable solution to what were increasingly straightened circumstances.[1]

He also needed to be in the public eye. Stephen Steele reminds us that: 'In contrast to Joyce, Eliot and Pound, Aldington did not benefit from the private patronage that enabled those others to compose highly esoteric works.'[2] He did not want to compose 'highly esoteric works': he despised them; but producing popularly marketable books was a financial requirement as much as a creative choice. Steele even argues that economic necessity was behind his 'drift' from poetry to prose in this period. This view is persuasive, although it fails to acknowledge his seriousness of intention: his choice of the novel, certainly as exemplified by *Death of a Hero*, *The Colonel's Daughter* and *Women Must Work*, was because he wanted a vehicle for social criticism.

However, he had found a profitable audience with *Death of a Hero*, one he wished, as well as needed, to cultivate; but he had also discovered the constraints that this audience imposed upon the writer and which he found difficult – if not impossible – to accept. The asterisks of *Death of a Hero* had been his protest against these constraints but he would have to find more subtle responses. Acquiring a literary agent who knew the middle-class audience well – and numbered popular novelists such as Bennett, Galsworthy and Maugham among his clients – was a particularly adroit move. Reaching out to that audience – and educating and informing them – in his role as a reviewer for the *Sunday Referee* was another calculated strategy, as well as a source of income.

The Colonel's Daughter is the story of a fifteen-month period in the life of a young middle-class woman in a Home Counties village in the aftermath of the First World War. Her genteel poverty, limited intelligence, plain appearance, dutiful conduct and unquestioning acceptance of the values that have been imposed upon her deny her the opportunity to escape her humdrum existence, even by marriage. For Aldington it was a huge irony that the very values which he attacked in the novel would come into play in the attempts to suppress it. His biggest problem was the subscription libraries. Few middle-class readers purchased books; instead they subscribed to the circulating libraries – Boots Booklovers Library, Mudie's, W.H. Smith's, The Times' or Harrod's. The libraries were by far the biggest purchasers of fiction and the gatekeepers of this middle-class readership.[3] The refusal of Boots or W.H. Smith to stock a book would have a massive impact on its sales. Justifying its decision to withdraw *The Colonel's Daughter* from circulation, Boots told Chatto that its customers wanted a book which encouraged them to see 'the worthwhileness of things, not the sordidness of life'.[4] Meanwhile, W. Roy of W.H. Smith, which had refused to stock the novel in the first place, wrote: 'There are probably three, and certainly two, scenes in the book whose details are not to be excused by any artistry or by any requirement of the plot or movement of the story.'[5]

The response of the booksellers and stationers was similar.[6] The most hostile were the Cambridge bookshops – Heffers, Bowes & Bowes, and Deighton, Bell & Company – who cited their responsibility to protect the young people who were their chief customers as their reason for cancelling their orders. There were some positive voices among the booksellers. Oxford seems to have been more enlightened than Cambridge, the Blackwell's buyer commenting as he ordered 50 copies, that he had found the book 'so human and full of humour'.[7] In general, however, booksellers had to be circumspect. Alfred Wilson of Ship Tavern Passage, Gracechurch Street, London, for example, appreciatively described the novel as 'a witty and caustic picture of modern tendencies as they encroach on the old standards of country life', but regretted that: 'For many of my subscribers I am afraid that it is a little too coarse in places, as I have a number of clergymen and middle class ladies on my lists.'[8]

While pre-publication sales to the libraries and bookshops accounted for a huge share of the first printing, reviews were crucial to the maintenance of the sales figures after publication. Not belonging to any of the established groups which divided up the London literary world – and the journals – Aldington could not hope for any 'log-rolling'.[9] Indeed, he feared quite the reverse.

He could at least count on the support of Hayter Preston, literary editor at the *Sunday Referee*, who announced that, while he had no desire to question the commercial or critical right of those booksellers who had banned *The Colonel's Daughter*, 'Readers who have for the past year enjoyed Mr Aldington's weekly critical reviews of current literature in the *Sunday Referee* will doubtless form their own opinions as to his high-minded regard for truth and his sincerity of purpose.'[10] Reviewing the novel in the same issue, Edward Crickmay grasped both why it caused widespread offence and why it was, nevertheless, important:

> If at times one's conventional literary conscience – for that is all it is – is shocked by Mr Aldington's vigorous expression one becomes used to it before the end of the book is reached. . . . Unlike most of his contemporaries, he believes in something and his beliefs at once barb and justify his assaults.

Even the *Daily Mail* reviewer, Douglas West, was able to make this distinction, commenting that the novel was 'disfigured by one or two needlessly brutal passages which will cause offence to the majority of readers' but calling it 'a bitter though impressive book, which strips English life since the war of what the author considers its dangerous shams and hypocrisies'. West said that the novel revealed Aldington as 'a vigorous satirist' and added that it was 'enlivened by a great deal of wit and adorned by gleams of genuine beauty.'[11]

Given the broad base of his middle-class readership, Aldington needed favourable reviews from both the 'popular' and the 'serious' dailies and Sunday press. Unlike the *Daily Mail*, the *Daily Express* was dismissive, calling the novel 'tiresome' and its characters 'futile'.[12] Amongst the 'serious' newspapers, *The Manchester Guardian* was the most disapproving, remarking that Aldington, 'like a victim of disease', had become 'obsessed' and saw everything 'in terms of deformity,

excrescence, spiritual sickness'. *The Morning Post* was enthusiastic, while
the *Times* reviewer was more measured, remarking that, 'Now and again
some brutality of phrase or suggestion makes one wince', but noting
'the liveliness and colour of the narrative, shot through with gleams
of beauty when he turns from men and women to Nature'.[13] Ralph
Straus in *The Sunday Times* similarly found 'life and colour and a curious
strength' in the book despite its 'lapses in good taste'. Rounding up 'The
Year's Books' in December, Straus would write: 'Richard Aldington may
have shocked the Puritans with *The Colonel's Daughter*, but of its high
literary merits there can be no possible doubt.'[14] Howard Marshall in the
Daily Telegraph found both 'an honest fury' and 'a sense of pity' in the
novel but concluded that 'Mr Aldington ... will do better when he has
cooled down a little', and expressed his concern about the occasional
'unnecessary and stupid coarseness'.[15]

It was the journals that Aldington feared, since several of them had
become the fiefdoms of the *Criterion* set and their connections. However,
Dobrée's review in *The Spectator* was encouraging. He found the novel
'vividly and expertly written, with an admirable command of phrase and
allusion'. There was a reservation, however: '[E]very now and then his
pungent satire descends to sneering. ... [Y]ou cannot cleanse without
love, and great satire is essentially humane.'[16] Aldington could not let a
Criterion man get away with this and wrote to Dobrée, telling him that
he had missed 'all the major intentions and implications' of the book:
'Because I laugh at the human comedy, you assume I have no compassion.'
'[D]oesn't Georgie ... suggest to you,' he asked, 'that even an ugly,
ordinary, stupid girl may possess almost heroic qualities, and though
utterly defeated in the search for happiness still retain a real moral
dignity?'[17]

Other reviews focused almost entirely on the 'sneering'. Frank
Kendon in *John O' London's Weekly* remarked that '[a]s an exhibition of
unnecessary (though entirely literary) cruelty, *The Colonel's Daughter*
leaves a bull-fight nowhere'. 'From the secret recesses of the souls of his
creatures,' he continued, 'Mr Aldington draws out, with bitter laughter,
their wriggling vices, their vicious stupidities, their unspeakable desires.'
Yet he conceded that the character of Georgie 'did awaken much curiosity
and not a little sympathy'.[18] Desmond McCarthy's *Life and Letters* called
the novel, 'a book full of personal hatred, without idealism, without
hope, in which no one circumstance and no one character ever comes to
fulfilment'. In the violent language that the novel seems to have provoked
amongst reviewers, he remarked that 'each incident ... seems like a dead
child aborted by a callous vivisectionist'.[19] St John Ervine in *Time and*

Tide called the book 'ill-written, ill-natured, vulgar and venomous' and expressed incredulity at the favourable reviews in *The Morning Post* and *Punch*.[20] ('You will recognise the light touch of the Prince of Bullshitters!' Aldington wrote to Prentice, no doubt recalling Ervine's damning review of *Death of a Hero* in 1929.)[21]

David Murray in *The Times Literary Supplement* (*TLS*) did perceive Aldington's 'wry pity' for his heroine and one or two other characters, but regretted that 'there does not seem to be anybody in his book for whom he has affection or respect' and objected, like other reviewers, to 'details and phrases of a rawness that makes us wonder . . . whether Mr Aldington has any taste at all'.[22] The *New Statesman* reviewer also recognised the 'veiling pity' in Aldington's handling of his heroine, that 'makes her both real and moving', but felt that the novel otherwise fell back on 'stagey caricature types' and that 'an overweening sense of dreariness and triviality and blague' vitiated much of the writer's satiric intention.[23]

Punch went completely against the trend. 'The Colonel's Daughter,' the reviewer declared, 'is not, in the village sense of that epithet, a "nice" book, but I venture to think it is a great one because of its humanity.' He even went on to compare the character of Georgie Smithers with Hardy's Tess.[24]

Aldington's letters revealingly apply metaphors of war to this controversy. He apologised to Harold Raymond, Prentice's other partner at Chatto that he and Parsons had 'got all the front-line strafe', while he and Prentice 'were in HQ dugouts'.[25] He told MacGreevy that Prentice had gone back to London 'determined to fight to the last ditch' and lamented that the whole situation was 'Cambrai 1917 – we broke the line but the reserves weren't there'.[26] In mid-May, as sales of the novel slowed down, he told Prentice: 'Very few books could have survived the barrage poor Georgie has been through since the 30th, and it would have been surprising indeed if she had come through without casualties.'[27] He estimated that the Smith's and Boots' ban had lost Chatto at least 2,000 sales.[28]

Sydney Schiff, who had written enthusiastically about the novel to Aldington, was told that, in response to the 'intensive campaign against the book', *Everyman*, which had earlier offered Aldington some work, must have 'taken alarm'.[29] Malcolm Hilbery had written to tell Aldington that he had found nothing shocking in the novel, but did not respond to a request that he write to the press to say so. Aldington had also had a 'charming letter' from H.G. Wells, he told Read, but Wells had 'not said the fifty words in public that would have sent Boots-Smith off with their tails down.'[30] '[A]ll these people are either lazy or cowards,' he told Prentice. 'We must feed the guns ourselves.' However, he mentioned an enthusiastic letter from the Glovers, 'backing us to the last ditch'.[31] He was hurt by the lack of public support from fellow writers. 'Even when we dislike each other,' he told Read, 'we ought to stand up for one of the trade against an outside attack'.[32]

For him this was a battle – perhaps a campaign (and one that, to an extent, he relished, as his correspondence demonstrates) – in two senses. First, he was up against both the snobbery of the literary élite and the prudishness of the middle-classes. A letter to Prentice in early June, as the furore died down, encapsulated his views:

> There is a legend about me among the highbrow and reviewing sets, i.e. bad temper &c &c. And a lot of them disliked my early work and prophesied that I should never do anything; so they have to stick to their prophecies. Notice that only with Georgie has the legend ceased that I cannot write a novel and cannot construct character. Further there is the inner jealousy felt by the unsuccessful writer (which is what most reviewers are) for the writer who gets a public. Aldous, Strachey, even Osbert suffer from this. But they all have an aura of inherited respectability. What is intolerable is that a poor man should emancipate himself from the drudgery of reviewing. Again, I championed writers like Joyce and Lawrence, who are now admittedly masters, at a time when all the reviewers were trying to knock them down. Further there is some moral society which tries to get books suppressed. I judge that the Dame Gwynne episode and the library ban might very likely be traced to their activities. ... That is the extent of the 'conspiracy'. Certainly it is not 'organised', but I notice a similarity of terms of disparagement among the *Criterion* set, and another set of terms among the old Liberal hacks. The reason we get the best reviews from Conservative papers is that their reviewers are really more independent than either the highbrows or the Lib-Lab lot. I mean they judge for themselves and not by group gossip.'[33]

The criticisms of tastelessness, sneering and cruelty had hurt him, although he had clearly heard the notes of approval too. He identifies here four sources of the hostility: jealousy, snobbery, his past support for Joyce and Lawrence, and the existence of a moral crusade. He was probably correct on all counts, although his defensiveness and the degree to which he personalised all criticism was unfortunate; he might have identified those critics who had no axe to grind and paid them closer attention, or even attempted serious consideration of some of the criticisms of the novel, regardless of their provenance. That Prentice was so supportive was a limitation in some respects. Aldington was to be plagued throughout his career, and ultimately with very harmful personal and professional consequences, by an inability – or unwillingness? – to temper strongly felt emotion with any degree of authorial detachment.

The other sense in which the controversy was embattled – at least on the writer's side – is that the novel itself was effectively a continuation of *Death of a Hero*, a further onslaught on the Victorian and Edwardian values which lay behind the war and which continued to plague Britain in the 1920s. He told Reeves that it dealt with 'the prolongation of pre-war mentalities into the post-war world'.[34] In the tenth volume of the *Oxford English Literary History* Chris Baldick notes: 'the pervasion of the satirical impulse across the range of literary genres, movements and schools' in the aftermath of the First World War.[35] He maintains that: 'it was a mark of literary modernity to discard as a feature of "Victorianism" all false respect for the old idols of Home, School, Nation and Empire, and likewise to subject the old virtues, whether of patriotic heroism or of domestic respectability, to what was now called "debunking"'. However, Baldick goes on to argue that the more adventurous prose satirists of the 1920s and 1930s attempted the bigger challenge of 'setting out to map the "waste land" of modern civilisation and to caricature the hollow men and women who peopled it'. He cites Lewis, Huxley, Isherwood and Evelyn Waugh as the key figures in this project.[36] *The Colonel's Daughter* attempts this very task. While it debunks the 'old virtue' of domestic respectability which dooms his heroine to a life of non-fulfilment, it mounts an equally powerful attack upon the intelligentsia and a yet more savage one upon the forces of modernity, the amoral, self-indulgent youth of the upper middle-class and the capitalists who were the true victors of the war.

Modern readers are unlikely to be offended by the passages which attracted the censure of the subscription libraries, but we might agree that at times the satire descends into sneering and find the farcical portrayals of the low-life characters and the novel's self-consciously mock-heroic epilogue heavy-handed. (Prentice, never one to impose his judgements, knew that the epilogue – originally planned as a prologue – was clumsy.)[37] Nevertheless, several characters are treated with some sympathy, even compassion, most of all Georgie herself. The venom of the novel is directed at the genuinely malicious, insensitive or self-serving.

We might feel less inclined to be critical of Aldington's depiction of 'Georgie' than of the insensitivity with which he made use of his real-life source. That the novel is closely modelled on the inhabitants of Padworth in the 1920s, in particular on Aldington's landlord and near-neighbour Brigadier-General Mills and his family, with whom Aldington and Yorke had enjoyed social contact, can be seen as an act of tastelessness, even unkindness. Georgie Smithers' story – including even the flirtation with a local clergyman, but most especially the circumscribed nature of her existence – is completely accurate. Aldington's estimations of the limitations of her appearance and intelligence are cruel and his account of her sexual longings intrusive. That she is portrayed as a kindly creature who excites the reader's pity can have been little compensation for the humiliation that the real-life Georgie, Helen Mills, must have experienced as she – and most of the village of Padworth – read Aldington's novel.

That the experience was distressing for her is confirmed by the research of David Wilkinson, whose investigations into the real-life origins of *The Colonel's Daughter* have been published.[38] Jessie Capper, who witnessed Helen Mills's embarrassment, was inclined to be charitable:

> The 'heroine' was drawn truthfully, sparing nothing, but she was drawn with great sympathy. She 'lived'. It was cruel of him to write it under his own name, for the subject of the book actually read it, and I could see how much it hurt her. But all the same, it was an artistic portrayal, and it was done with sympathy, though she wasn't likely to be able to see this.[39]

In some respects, however, Aldington's familiarity with Home Counties village life is the strength of the novel. This is true not only of its detailed, if satiric, social observation but also of its realisation of the natural landscape in all seasons, although even the pastoral is folded into the ironic vision of the novel as the final description of it is given to the self-satisfied Purfleet:

> He spent some little time trying to determine exactly how to classify the scene he was looking at. It was obviously English landscape school between 1770 and 1840, and probably a water-colour, for only water-colour could 'get' those very damp-looking white clouds with darker borders and the rather mottled look of the distance. Turner was too obvious, too much a martyr to the picturesque. Constable perhaps? Yes, very much Constable in a way, but there was a touch of Bonnington in the handling of the middle-distance, and quite a Crome-ish bit in the foreground.[40]

While the actions of the circulating libraries, the moral crusade against the novel and disparaging reviews undoubtedly affected its commercial success, by August 1931 a respectable 8,500 copies had been sold. Aldington had meanwhile turned his satirical aim on targets closer to home. Baldick notes that, 'the temperature of modern satire tends to rise when it seeks its targets among the author's private enemies'.[41] Aldington had already demonstrated the truth of this in his portraits of Pound, Ford, Eliot and Lawrence in *Death of a Hero*. The personal lampoons of his *Soft Answers*, however, reached a new level of rancour, particularly 'Stepping Heavenward', his satirical 'biography' of Eliot.

Such lampoons were rife in literary London and were driven as much by personal resentments as by literary ideals. *The Georgiad*, Roy Campbell's mock-heroic poem attacking the Bloomsbury Group (along with Robert Graves, Laura Riding and Humbert Wolfe) was chiefly motivated by Campbell's fury over his wife's affair with Vita Sackville-West.[42] The most venomous portraits in *The Apes of God*, Lewis's attack on the dominant literary groups of the day, were of those who had been his patrons, such as the Sitwells, the Schiffs, Dick Wyndham and Edward Wadsworth. (Lewis could never forgive those to whom he had been indebted; 'A friend who does him a favour is doubly his enemy,' Aldington told Schiff.)[43] Aldington hugely admired *The Apes of God*, telling Read: 'It has more energy and concentrated scorn and superb writing than anything I've read for a long time.'[44] However, he did concede that the book was too 'intellectual' and didactic for a novel, and 'could be immensely improved by being cut down by a third'.[45]

In his *Sunday Referee* column he identified the main problem: 'Mr Lewis has superb intellectual courage. . . . [*Apes of God*] is a great display of ferocious knight-errantry, but I was disappointed that our St George came home with a bag of lizards and worms, instead of one or more of the numerous dragons which infest the landscape.'[46] His review of Osbert Sitwell's *Dumb Animals and Other Stories* a few months later gives us a clearer notion of his own understanding of the satirical mode:

> His satire is witty rather than fierce or indignant, but it is one of his most effective methods. It is the satire of a generous-hearted man who is revolted by cruelty, stupidity and humbug. It has power, because Mr Sitwell is not afraid of his feelings, and it gains immensely in effectiveness by contrast with his sense of beauty.[47]

In the five short satires that Aldington grouped under the title *Soft Answers*, Eliot is the subject of 'Stepping Heavenward' and Cunard of 'Now Lies She There', while 'Nobody's Baby' is about Pound; 'Yes,

Aunt' and 'A Gentleman of England' are more generalised satires about representative figures whom Aldington despised – a dilettante amateur writer, and a war profiteer, neither of whom enlisted in 1914-1918.[48] Tellingly, the latter theme runs across the collection, the failure to serve in the war being highlighted in the cases of both Eliot and Pound. Sexual politics, another Aldingtonian theme, figures in all five stories. The original intention was a collection of short tales entitled *Wives of Great Men*, and the merciless scrutiny of a marital relationship remains at the centre of four of them.[49]

'Now Lies She There' clearly had its roots in his recent falling-out with Cunard but perhaps also in her earlier rejection of him as a lover. It shares with 'Nobody's Baby' a framework that is deceptively informal and relaxed, involving an observer-narrator and an acquaintance, through whose meetings and conversations the protagonist's story is pieced together; but the portrait of the heroine is penetratingly cruel in its social and psychological analysis and the narrative outcome savage – although its power to shock the modern reader may lie in its correspondence with the tragic circumstances in which Cunard's life was to end 33 years on.

This narrative framework works even more effectively in 'Nobody's Baby' since this story is the pursuit of a puzzle, the parentage of the child produced by 'Charlemagne Cox' and his wife 'Ophelia' (Ezra and Dorothy Pound).[50] The tale is a satirical romp and the portrayal of Pound is shrewd, exuberant and entertaining; but the representation of Ophelia is poignant, the narrator finding her, some years after the war, to have become a 'husk of a woman . . . emptied of life' . . . suffering from 'a kind of premature withering like an apple left too long on a fruit-dish . . . a kind of virginal pathos in her fragility, in the thin hands and wrists, and the legs which seemed too long for so tiny a trunk'.[51]

The pitiless portrait of a marriage is repeated – more cruelly – in 'Stepping Heavenward':

> Adèle became more and more unhappy. It is always *rather* unpleasant to live with a genius, but quite awful when he is a Cibber. . . . [He] considered [marriage] as an inviolable legal contract, implying none but social obligations. . . . Cibber invariably stood up when she came into the room, and their quarrels were conducted on coldly intellectual lines.

Given the dismal state of the Eliot marriage, which would end in formal separation in 1933, the description seems particularly intrusive. The rejection of Eliot the poet is more understandable – and of long standing.

Aldington had told Eliot back in 1919 that he thought his poetry 'over-intellectual and afraid of those essential emotions which make poetry'.[52] That view never changed.

Nevertheless, the lampoon, taking the form of an obituary purporting to present 'a cool unbiased account of this celebrated life in its private rather than public aspects', is savage. Aldington told Prentice that he would not mind if the latter advised against publication, but Prentice told him: 'Cibber is devastating, it is masterful ... such cold and controlled ferocity I have never seen before.'[53] In February 1931, with Chatto's permission, Orioli published a limited edition of the story, and Chatto issued it as a Dolphin later in the year (prior to including it in *Soft Answers* in the spring of 1932). At this point Geoffrey Faber (Eliot's publisher) – apparently unaware of the prior existence of the Orioli edition – wrote to ask Chatto to withdraw it. Faber claimed that Eliot knew nothing of the story, and Aldington told Schiff that if Eliot had written to him personally, he would probably have withdrawn it; as it was, there was no further communication on the subject.[54] Patmore, who had once been quite a close friend of Vivien Eliot, thought the satire 'too cruel' and even Aldington admitted to H.D., when he told her of the imminent publication of *Soft Answers*, 'I don't much like the book . . . never want to see it again, but I suppose it rounds off certain grouches.'[55] 'Rounded off' perhaps, but they would never be abandoned; as late as 1957 Aldington would tell the literary critic John Atkins:

> I do think that Eliot managed to cash in on the work done by Ford, Lewis, Pound and myself, because Ford, Lewis and I did three years in the army, and Pound cleared out in 1919. Eliot sucked up to the bishops and the dons and the editors and the reviewers – and got his reward. Well, I'd rather be in the discard with Lewis and Campbell.[56]

The book had a print run of about 2,500 copies and a smattering of reviews. Some were approving. Crickmay, of the not-disinterested *Sunday Referee*, thought the collection 'one of the most remarkable comments on the last decade that has yet been written', arguing that it placed Aldington alongside some of the best satirists in English literature, and proved him to be 'without a peer among his contemporaries'.[57] Straus was also encouraging: 'He may irritate you, but he never ceases to demand your attention. For my part I found the book engrossing, and, at the end of it, was wishing, like Oliver, for more.'[58] However, Orlo

Williams of the *Criterion* camp, writing in the *TLS*, was critical of the way in which Aldington still carried around 'emotional relics of the War': 'It is impossible,' he argued, 'to get a proper view of the world today, even artistically, with the eyes of ten years ago.'[59] The *Times* reviewer also felt that Aldington's indignation seemed to be 'too exclusively nourished from his War complex'.[60]

That Aldington was not finished with the war and the bitterness would be evident in his next project, but it would not be a work of satire.

5. The Public Face
Elegist and Romantic

The 'war sketches' that make up *Roads to Glory* were written over the course of the year immediately following the completion of *Death of a Hero* in May 1929.[1] 'I must clear up the odds and ends of the experience, before I go on to anything more hopeful,' Aldington wrote to Prentice in August.[2] Frere begged, with Prentice's agreement, to have one story to publish; two more went to Elkin Mathews; and five appeared in *Nash's Pall Mall Magazine*, acting as 'kite-flyers', the reception of which encouraged Chatto to bring out the full collection of thirteen in September 1930, a year after the appearance of *Death of a Hero*.[3] Covici, Friede, Aldington's American publishers, struggling to survive in the wake of the Wall Street Crash, were reluctant to publish the stories until Aldington had given them another novel; Pinker advised a move to Nelson Doubleday, Frere's patron.[4] The book was dedicated to Frere. Aldington wrote one more war story, not included in the collection: 'Last Straws' he had promised to Cunard, the arrangement which led to misunderstanding, acrimony and the termination of their friendship.

The finest of the stories are those which not only draw closely on Aldington's own war and postwar experience but which are filtered through the consciousness of characters closely resembling himself in their experience, circumstances and temperament: Cumberland in 'Meditation on a German Grave'; Ellerton in 'Victory'; Hanley in 'At All Costs'; Davison in 'Sacrifice Post'; Henson in 'The Lads of the Village'; and, most of all, Brandon in 'Farewell to Memories', the most autobiographical narrative of them all. The titular character in 'The Case of Lieutenant Hall' also endures many of the aftermath's disappointments and humiliations and much of the guilt and trauma undergone by his creator. (Much of the account of Hall's nightmare world would reappear in the portrait of Anthony Clarendon in *All Men Are Enemies*.) These are men coping with the strains of war, or with post-traumatic stress in 'the almost as merciless life of Peace, with its grim slogan: Money or starve'.[5]

One feature saves them (apart from the tragic Hall): 'Yes, one can be hungry, sore, unshaven, dirty, eyes and head aching, limbs shivering and yet love beauty.'[6] A decade on, Cumberland in 'Meditation on a German Grave' marvels at the landscape between Rome and Naples, the 'pageant of colours' in a Naples market, the moonlit islands in the Bay of Naples, the wildlife of a Mediterranean island. In contrast we are given vivid descriptions of the desolate Western Front in the war's final months. Davison, the protagonist in 'Sacrifice Post', is struck by the contrast between the battered landscape he leaves behind him, as he goes off (like his creator) on a signals course, and the lush, fertile countryside he enters: 'Which was the reality, which the dream? They couldn't both be true, they couldn't both exist in the same world.'[7] The world, he concludes, is divided into creative and destructive impulses, and nationalism is a destructive urge. The determination to carry this message to others is the other feature that gives some of these characters a reason to live: 'It was the duty of the survivors to the dead so to warn the world that this abomination never occurred again,' says Ellerton in 'Victory'.[8] Brandon in 'Farewell to Memories' feels that 'the danger is that we shall say too much' but he, too, understands the importance of giving voice to memory: better this than that the tale be told 'by one who did not endure it, for the sake of those who will not care about it'.[9]

The short-story format does not allow for character development, which is why the use of these alter egos is so effective; but there are also some judicious 'pen portraits', such as Isaacson, Cumberland's kindly and generous business partner in 'Meditation on a German Grave', and the company commander in 'Victory', a former clerk, whose 'kindliness and paper fever involved him in long, carefully docketed correspondence with the relatives of the dead'.[10] Some of them are minor characters, like the 'handsome, but hard-eyed, hard-mouthed captain of twenty-five' in 'Meditation on a German Grave' or the landlord and the farm labourer in 'The Lads of the Village'.[11] The verisimilitude of so many of the stories is reinforced by Aldington's sharp ear for dialogue.

Nevertheless, there are several crude stereotypes, characterisations which serve to press home social critique rather than to embody a human story, for example the cuckolded husband in 'Of Unsound Mind'. Perhaps the nastiest story in the book is 'Killed in Action' with its two (working-class) competitive, bullying and brutal NCOs, whose crude Cockney dialogue throughout makes it highly unconvincing that one of them achieves the rank of captain. The note of personal bitterness and the lack of creative distance that at times characterise *Death of a Hero* are apparent in several of the stories, often accompanied by a strain of intellectual or social snobbery. In 'Deserter' neither the young protagonist, the older man who converts him 'to his own very crude and rather vague materialism', nor the young man's grasping lover is an engaging character. Aldington may have saved most of his scorn for middle-class conventionality, vulgarity and hypocrisy (displayed forcefully in the story 'Of Unsound Mind') but he found the working classes no more sympathetic: we are told at the beginning of 'Deserter' that 'Harry Werner was a rather lonely sort of a chap' and that 'His mother, with the not-unfounded working-class prejudice against hospitals, insisted that the child should be born in their own squalid home; and died of puerperal fever in consequence'.[12] There is an astounding lack of sympathy for Harry ('He was a good-looking youth in a curly, vulgar way') throughout the story, up to and including his death by firing squad.

Women come in for considerable contempt, the self-serving mistresses in 'Deserter' and 'Love for Love' particularly. '[W]e're helpless victims of the cowardice, greed and gullibility of man and womankind, especially womankind,' laments Lieutenant Hall.[13] An exception is the pitiful Evelyn in 'Of Unsound Mind', a victim of middle-class hypocrisy, but over-idealised, as is her artist lover. The Church is another target; Davison in 'Sacrifice Post' concludes that 'we must grow out of religion'. 'How on earth,' he asks, 'did it come about that all the things denounced in the Gospels are violently defended by the Christian sects?'[14] Aldington's world is still divided into those who fought and those who did not, and it is the indifference with which the latter treat the former in the postwar world that provokes the most bitter condemnation. The coroner at Lieutenant Hall's inquest remarks that, 'young men returning to civilian life . . . must . . . realise that they had no right to expect that they should drop into easy jobs, or that they could all keep up the standard of extravagant living they had been accustomed to in the Army.'[15]

One of the structural features that gives several of the stories their compactness and punch is Aldington's employment of the dramatic and 'distancing' ending: the bathos of the last sentences of 'Victory'; the demise of Hanley in 'At All Costs' and Davison in 'Sacrifice Post'; the suicides in 'Love for Love' and 'The Case of Lieutenant Hall'; and the execution of Harry in 'Deserter'.

The strongest of the stories are those in which the anger of the narrator of *Death of a Hero* is replaced by pity for the dead, particularly the 'framing' stories, 'Meditation on a German Grave' and 'Farewell to Memories', but also the exquisitely realised 'The Lads of the Village', 'Victory' and 'At All Costs'. The last three named share several features: they are short and employ unity of place and time along with understated and realistic dialogue; and all five narratives are filtered through the perspective and consciousness of an Aldington alter ego. He wrote the prose poetry extracts that punctuate the storyline of 'Farewell to Memories' in the last weeks of the war and the period immediately after the Armistice, and it is with one of these that the collection concludes: 'Lost terrible comrades, we, who might have died, salute you.'[16]

MacGreevy wrote of 'The Lads of the Village':

> Atmospherically, it was perfect, and humanly it was as tender as any piece of English written in our time. It had nothing tendentious, there was no propaganda – which made it all the better as propaganda; there was not a word wrong, or a word misplaced, or a word too many.[17]

Other responses to the collection were mixed but several critics remarked on the authenticity of the stories. 'Soldiers will like these stories. They deal with recognisable men. The dialogue is authentic. They have the manner and technique of the trenches; they almost smell of the trenches,' the *News Chronicle* reviewer wrote;[18] while Edmund Blunden commented in the *TLS* that, while the detail might 'slip away' from those who weren't combatants, 'they must be moved by the constant sense of the man behind the book: by a mind that, at this considerable interval after the War, is racked still on the disaster and the devastation.'[19] This was recognition by a fellow veteran of the continuing cost of the war in the emotional lives of its survivors. In the *New Statesman* Horace Gregory noticed that: '[Aldington] does what almost no other writer dealing with the horror and futility of war has done – he follows up the implications of war in the years of peace which have followed it.'[20]

Aldington's third novel, *All Men Are Enemies* (subtitled *A Romance*), would continue this preoccupation, and its protagonist shares even more with his creator in terms of experience and outlook than do the characters in *Roads to Glory*. The other major themes are also familiar ones: 'Anthony Clarendon,' the 'Author's Note' tells us, 'holds to two instinctive beliefs which I willingly allow to be romantic: First that the complete human being is formed by a man and a woman; second that living implies much more than acquiescence in a set of formal beliefs, more than getting and spending money.' Like his creator, Anthony abandons 'the secular religions of Nationalism, Socialism and Communism' just as he abandons 'a false marriage and a false career'. The 'finer fuller life' for which he opts is 'the life of the here and now, the life of the senses, the life of the deep instinctive forces'.[21] When Louise Morgan of *Everyman* asked Aldington what he would like his reader to take from the book, his answer was: 'This: that they should live life WITH ALL THEIR SENSES. That they should put themselves in harmony with the world.' He added: 'The artist ... must say not only what life is, but also what it might be. He shows how better life can be lived.'[22] As for the novel's title, Anthony Clarendon instinctively understands from a young age that:

> what for him were the essential, all-important experiences could be revealed to others only at his peril. . . . [I]f you went to life with all your senses open, with your body as well as your mind, with your own fresh feelings instead of abstract laid-down ones, then indeed all men were your enemies.[23]

The novel ends with Anthony's warning his lover that their hardest task will be 'to guard [their] love from the world of men'.[24]

The greater part of the novel completed on Capri in the early summer of 1932, Aldington and Patmore met up with Frere and his new partner, Pat Wallace, at Toulon and travelled with them to Bormes-les-Mimosas, near Le Lavandou, where he managed to write a further 4,500 words; but this was also a busy spot, and after two weeks he and Patmore travelled on by train to Brantôme in the Dordogne. At the Hotel Chabrol on the banks of the River Dronne, with 'a view of the sparkling river and the old bridge' from his window as he wrote, he completed the novel.[25] Patmore preceded him to England on 14 September to leave him alone to write the last chapter. Three days later he wrote to her: 'Darling, the end is the best of all, but it's been such an imaginative agony, so much weeping, all mixed up with indigestion, that I have been in a kind of daze, another world so real that my own life becomes the dream.'[26] On his return to England on 22 September (in the chance company of Lewis), he had to be admitted for two weeks to a nursing home with a suspected (but never confirmed) duodenal ulcer, a symptom of the exhausted nervous state in which the writing of the novel had left him.

The novel's first part concerns Anthony Clarendon's upbringing in the years before the war. While he grows up in the Kent countryside and has a mentor much like Aldington's own Dudley Grey, with 'his deep enthusiasm for Italy', Anthony's parents bear little resemblance to the writer's: his father 'has a love of truth and contempt for humbug and stupidity', while his mother is characterised by her 'sensibility and faith in an ultimate human goodness'.[27] Nor is there any of the financial insecurity that blighted Aldington's own upbringing. However, one autobiographical element, which appears also in *Death of a Hero*, is the sexualisation of the young boy through erotic experiences with both young girls and older women. (In Aldington's correspondence with Eunice Gluckman [née Black], a lover of whom we shall hear more later, he refers on several occasions to the 'active sex life' he lived in his 'pre-puberty' years.)[28] Scrope, Anthony's mentor, sees him as 'over-developed in some ways, under-developed in others, admirably unfitted for the rough and tumble of life'. 'You've been made sensitive to all the attacks of life,' he tells the young man, 'with no shield to protect you.'[29] On a 1914 tour of Italy that is intended to prepare him for a career as an architect, Tony visits the island of Aeaea (modelled on Capri where Aldington and H.D. had spent those five idyllic weeks in 1913) where he meets and falls in love with Katha, a young Austrian woman. Planning to meet again in London in August to begin a permanent life together, they return to their respective homelands.

Part Two opens in 1919, thus emphasising the rupture of the war, the outbreak of which has prevented the couple's reunion and in which Anthony, like his creator, has served as an infantry officer. He is suffering from post-traumatic stress, plagued by nightmares and vainly attempting to make contact with Katha. Meanwhile another woman, Margaret, with whom he had a brief affair during the war, is pressing him into marriage. He makes a fruitless journey to Vienna and on to Aeaea to find Katha.

A further time-shift takes us in Part Three to 1926 – the year of the General Strike (in which Anthony uneasily – like his creator – helps, out of personal loyalty, to get *The Times* out in the face of picketing). Here we find that Anthony has become a businessman and is married to Margaret; but he has reached crisis point:

> I've come to the conclusion ... that business is ... the gradual death of all vital instincts and feelings. ... It substitutes possession of objects for the true possession of oneself and of life; it substitutes stimulants for sensation, parties for conversation, self-interest for friendship, competitive games for the fine arts. ... Working and trading are essentials, but business is a parasite, it is the art of exploiting trade and work. To me it is a betrayal of the fundamental things. It enriches a few and impoverishes many, and destroys the genuine life of everybody.[30]

Nevertheless, he does not believe in the class war (and the characters who do are drawn unsympathetically): 'I'm concerned with my own individual life, and I'll at least say this for Capitalism, it doesn't wholly prevent my having one.' He resigns from his job and goes abroad for a while 'to think matters over'.[31] In Part Four, set in 1927, Anthony separates from Margaret and goes abroad once more – where he is reunited with Katha on the island of Aeaea.

In view of the novel's title, it is noteworthy, as Elizabeth Vandiver points out, that Aldington chose to make his heroine an Austrian. The 'ideal' is represented by a foreign national from one of the nations that had been the 'enemy' of 1914-1918.[32] Speaking of the war to his old mentor, Anthony says: 'It didn't seem to matter who won – it was a victory for evil anyway.' In a state of helpless rage at his circumstances, he thinks: 'He was no Christian, no conscientious objector. He was ready to kill right enough. But no fake enemies in field grey – the real enemies at home.' Towards the end of the novel, however, he tells Katha: 'We must pluck murder from our hearts along with old sorrow and old regret. We must sow love and happiness where they planted destruction and misery.' That Katha is infertile, owing to her sufferings in the war, casts doubt, metaphorically, on this project, and all her lover can promise her in the concluding paragraph is: 'To-day and to-day, that must be enough.'[33]

Despite Aldington's ultimate dismissal of socialism and communism, the novel would be taken up with enthusiasm in the USSR; a note in the 1983 Russian edition of the novel makes clear why this occurred:

> The novel ... narrates the fate of a bourgeois intellectual, a representative of the 'lost generation'. By pointing out the contrasts and contradictions of the bourgeois world, by unmasking the evil generated by it – war, parasitism, spiritual degradation, the author shows how in the consciousness of people like Antony Clarendon a recognition of historical truth took root: capitalism had become obsolete, and its downfall inevitable.

Prentice's reactions, as the novel reached him section by section, were totally supportive:

> The last batch of Part Three is CORKING; STUNNING; THE BLOODY GOODS – it IS!! When you feel that a thing gets you amidships, as if it were personally meant for yourself; when you read it swoosh and can see that it runs like the finger of fate, the writing is as pointed & lithe & beautiful, & the touch & mood so true that you begin to muse on Troilus & As You Like It & Hamlet – then you know that your confidence is simply recognition of a big marvellous thing. . . . [H]ow precise & firm the development of Tony, how dramatic; & how lovely the Chartres passage; what a picture the Strike![34]

What Prentice does not appear to have recognised is the creative problem arising from Aldington's close identification with Anthony Clarendon and his beliefs. Aldington himself was aware of the difficulty; he wrote to MacGreevy as he was starting the novel: 'The puzzle is to present ideas as action, but without action and character there is only amateurishness.'[35]

The consequence is that the novel contains too much talk, both from Anthony and from those characters to whom he is ideologically opposed. While Aldington was able to invest the character 'types' of *The Colonel's Daughter* with individuality and vitality, the characters in his serious romantic novel are often too schematic. Unconsciously highlighting the problem, he told Prentice that the four female characters were supposed to show 'different types of women', with Katha representing 'the perfection'.[36] The contrast between Margaret and Katha is stark, and makes the reader wonder how the marriage could ever have taken place, although Anthony does offer an explanation to his young brother-in-law (one of the few sympathetic and subtle portrayals of a minor character): 'For some reason Margaret seemed to want me very much. Nobody else wanted me; I didn't want myself. . . . So there you are.'[37] Anthony himself, while a more rounded character and shown at times to be naive, is generally taken too seriously, is too much a mouthpiece for his creator, while the representation of the romantic relationship – a problem we encountered in 'A Dream in the Luxembourg', five years earlier – is often cloying.

The reviews were mixed. In the *Daily Mail* Compton Mackenzie argued that Aldington had made 'a profound appeal to the human heart without sacrificing a jot of his intellectual appeal'. In a comradely reference to shared war experience, he concluded that the book would demonstrate to the younger generation of writers that, 'if a man has known how to educate himself as an artist, he can survive even the obliteration of his mind by those years of war'.[38] In the *TLS*, Cyril Falls talked of the novel's 'crudity of ideas' but thought 'the workmanship so good that it disguises this', and remarked that '[t]he scenes of action, such as the strike and the hunt for Katha in Vienna, show Mr Aldington at his best, and that is good'.[39] Stephen Potter in the *New Statesman* similarly found that there were parts of the book 'which have the authenticity, the sense of uncontainable experience, the dignity even, of *Death of a Hero*'. (He identified Parts One and Two and 'the search for the girl' and commented further that while Aldington could write of falling in love, 'he describes the bleakness of falling out of love even better'.) However, he regretted 'the flat characters whose unhappy function it is to engage in arguments with the hero and come off worst'. Nevertheless, he concluded that Aldington's importance was that 'he has the power to speak for his generation'.[40]

Doubleday was as certain of the book's merits as Prentice, telling Aldington that it was 'a perfectly magnificent piece of writing', the best thing he had ever done.[41] Another reader who had always appreciated Aldington's romantic writing was Alec Waugh, who would write five years after Aldington's death:

> All Men Are Enemies is his most revealing [novel], because in it the two sides of his nature are most markedly contrasted. There is the poetic side of him, and the angry, aggressive side. They are not allowed to mix. They are kept separate. When he is writing of love he is tender, wistful, passionate: the same man who wrote A Dream in the Luxembourg and Crystal World; when he is concerned with social satire, he is the man who wrote Lawrence of Arabia.[42]

Like its predecessors, the novel was a censorship challenge for Chatto. Foreseeing the furore it would provoke, Aldington had suggested as early as July 1932, well before its completion, that the publisher's advance notice should be short and vague and the date of publication kept a secret. By the time it was at the proofing stage (Aldington and Patmore were in Portugal), there were disagreements between author and publisher. By late November Chatto had cut 28 passages, a total of 4,200 words.[43] Aldington wanted asterisks for these passages (mostly in Part Four); when Chatto refused, he withdrew permission for any cuts whatsoever. When Prentice remonstrated, 'It's a blow for us, for we don't see how we can publish AMAE as it originally stood before the cuts were made', Aldington came up with a proposal for a 1,000-copy unexpurgated edition to be published in Paris – at Chatto's expense – prior to British publication.[44] Although Prentice was with his parents in Scotland for Christmas, Aldington made an unplanned dash for the Channel and arrived in London on Christmas Eve. He met with Pinker on 28 December and Pinker met Raymond the next day. On New Year's Eve Aldington wrote to tell Prentice that he had agreed to drop the proposal for an unexpurgated text in favour of 'a bolder but still bowdlerised English version'. He, Patmore, Ralph and Vonnie Pinker were coming up with a proposed text; but, if this was unacceptable to Chatto, he would sell the novel elsewhere and offer the firm another novel.[45] Eventually, after the return to London of the conciliatory Prentice, a text was agreed. (Aldington told Schiff that Chatto had restored 3,000 words.)[46] However, Aldington determined to remain in London until the publication date in April. This time he would not be behind the lines when the strafing began.

He was ready to go into battle. Mustering his allies included enlisting the support of Morgan at *Everyman*; responding vigorously to perceived attacks was another. In the Chatto archives there is a copy of a letter Prentice wrote to him when Aldington reacted badly to the *TLS* review and sent him a copy of a letter of protest he intended to send to Bruce Richmond, the *TLS* editor; the ever-patient (and diplomatic) Prentice writes:

> It is a very good letter, but in general I think, and the others do too, that one is bound to lose something of one's dignity by coming down to newspaper level. . . . [T]hese people are not worth powder and shot. . . . However, your nature is a more combative one, & if you feel you must put the case to Richmond, we think that the letter would convey your protest excellently. I would, however, suggest some deletions.[47]

There is even a suggested alternative letter for Aldington to consider. The literary heartaches of the writer's later years might have been avoided had Prentice, with his affection for Aldington, his wisdom and reasonableness, remained in the driving seat at Chatto. That Aldington sought his approval before sending his letter indicates his awareness of how much he needed guidance from someone whose judgement he could trust.

Condemnation of the novel was much more muted, however, than he had feared (only Australia banned it) and it reached the bestseller lists, while Pinker soon negotiated an agreement with Twentieth Century Fox, who took out an option on the novel for $1,250. 'I cannot claim,' Aldington wrote to his friend from prewar days, the American philosopher, Henry Slonimsky 'that I have battered down the wall of Jericho of British Philistinism . . . but I achieved something. . . . It is not exactly a victory, but I have proved that I cannot be suppressed.'[48]

Richard Aldington, 1934

6. The Social Life Fragments
1932-1936

In the autumn of 1932, short of money and in poor health, having collapsed on his arrival in London from the strains of writing *All Men Are Enemies*, Aldington chose Portugal as a cheap winter destination. The one major purchase he had to make was another second-hand car. In early November he and Patmore arrived in Coimbra in central Portugal, where they started lessons in Portuguese and where Aldington made contact with a group of poets centred on the university. They moved on to Lisbon ('quite a dreary little place') and thence to Setubal.[1] They intended to stay in Portugal all winter, but once Chatto indicated that they were planning massive cuts in the text of *All Men Are Enemies*, they left for London after a stay of only six weeks.

They returned to the Iberian Peninsula the following autumn, after their summer on the Riviera, this time accompanied by the Glovers. Their tour covered 20 or more Spanish and Portuguese towns and villages and about 4,000 miles. It seems to have been on this trip that they drove along the southern coast of the peninsula and visited Gibraltar. The pattern was always the same: travelling by car, cheap hotels and restaurants and picnic lunches. In this manner they could – and did – cover a lot of ground inexpensively. The Twentieth Century Fox purchase of *All Men Are Enemies* had bought Aldington time but that money had to last until another novel was ready. It also appears, from cryptic allusions in several letters at this period, that his solicitor had embezzled his savings.

Prior to the 1933 visit, Aldington and Patmore took Glover on a week-long tour of the Bordeaux region, covering Saint-Emilion, Captieux, Mont de Marsan, Orthez, Oloron, Eaux-Bonnes, Argelès-sur-Mer, Luz-Saint-Sauveur, Gavarnie, Lombez, Auch, Condom and Pissos – some 500 miles. The trip was, Aldington told Prentice, 'a huge success':

Such lovely country, unspoiled old towns and villages, and everywhere good food and wine very cheap. Eight days for the three of us came to about £17, including all our expenses – everything. Glover has been in a kind of rapture. Of course, you do, and always will, come first, but since you couldn't come, I'm pleased I asked Glover. It is his first experience of our kind of motoring, and he lappitup like mad.[2]

The careful record-keeping is characteristic, but so is the joy that such travels are possible. The tour of Spain and Portugal is less well documented, but letters to Prentice and others came from Madrid, Aranjuez and, finally, Alicante. ('This is a rum place: England in southern Spain,' he told Pinker.)[3]

In May 1934, with his fourth novel, *Women Must Work*, completed and delivered to Chatto, he and Patmore returned to Portugal, covering some 750 miles, northwards from Lisbon to Óbidos, Santarém, Tomar, Leiria, Coimbra, Mafra, Alcobaça, Luso, São Pedro do Sul, Vila Real, Amarante and Arcos de Valdevez. 'Everything is like Italy before the war,' he told Orioli and in *Life for Life's Sake* he expresses a preference for Portugal over Spain, conceding that the former lacked 'the grandeur and the magnificent art', but claiming that its people were gentler and more friendly, and arguing (evidence of his increasing concern for the environment) that the countryside had been treated 'far more intelligently' and not 'rendered a treeless desert like so much of Spain'.[4] However, they crossed into Spain, where they covered a further 850 miles, travelling through Tui to Vigo and Santiago de Compostela and up to the coast at A Coruña, thence to Lugo, Guadalajara, Calatayud, Zaragoza, Tudela, Pamplona and Roncesvalles, before crossing over the French border and heading north for Bordeaux.

After this extensive tour they drove through France and Switzerland and on to Austria. They were bound for Vienna and, after that, for Budapest, Prague and Warsaw, where Aldington had 'blocked' royalty accounts to access – money that could not cross through the Iron Curtain. They got no further than Feldkirch in Austria; in *Life for Life's Sake* Aldington gives us a dramatic account of what happened:

On a level straight road between Feldkirch and Bludenz I saw a small car coming towards me at a furious speed. At about a hundred yards' distance from my car, it skidded, and rushed towards me swaying more and more violently from side to side. I stopped dead, hoping it would either upset or sweep past me in an outward swing. But no, it smashed sideways into the front of my car. I saw two people hurled out apparently dead from the wrecked car, and of course mine got a frightful jolt which hurled us first backwards and then forwards. As I recovered from the shock I heard a dripping sound, and instantly thought of fire from the gasoline tank. I shouted to my companion to jump, and scuttled out myself, only to fall helplessly on the ground. The jolt forward had broken my knee-cap against the ignition-key, and my companion's forehead was badly cut by the mirror.[5]

The accident occurred on 8 June and the couple were taken to the Feldkirch Spital. The support network sprang into action. A telegram to Prentice brought Derek Patmore out. He reported to Prentice that his mother was in good shape and would soon be discharged, and that Aldington had had a successful operation on his knee. Two weeks later Frere and Pat arrived, taking a detour on their way to the south of France. It was a month before Aldington was discharged, and progress thereafter was slow. After a fortnight in a hotel, the couple moved to a guest house at Fontanella: 'a tiny hamlet of Austrian chalets, at 6,000 feet [with] a magnificent view across a deep Alpine valley with a river at the bottom to the vast wooded slopes of high mountains opposite'.[6]

Now a more dramatic event occurred: on 25 July 1934 the Austrian Chancellor, Engelbert Dollfuss, was assassinated in Vienna. Frere immediately telegraphed Aldington to leave Austria. For a short time the peace of Europe hung in the balance as Mussolini threatened Hitler and swore to defend the integrity of Austria. The *putsch* failed, although there were uprisings in other regions of the country and, as Hitler distanced himself from the events and the heat went out of the international situation, Aldington decided to stay where he was. By early September, however, he and Patmore were restless and, although he had started work on the long poem *Life Quest* and was writing a series of articles for the *Sunday Referee*, the accident had affected his concentration. They set off, driving again, for Alsace and Lorraine and from there across France to Brantôme, where Aldington had completed *All Men Are Enemies* in the late summer of 1932.

Glover was in St Bartholomew's Hospital in London with tuberculosis and they now decided to drive south to Perpignan in search of a place to rent for his convalescence. There their plans became uncertain. They learned that Glover might not be well enough to travel; and Aldington himself had found that his mobility was poor and that he tired easily. Toying with the idea of returning to London, they drifted up to Saint-Emilion in the Bordeaux region ('where all the churches are empty and the cellars are full').[7] It was the assassinations in Marseilles on 9 October of King Alexander I of Yugoslavia and the French Foreign Minister, Louis Barthou, that decided matters for them: 'Continental Europe . . . seemed determined to get itself into violent muddles and disorders.'[8]

On their way to London, they called on the Glovers, who were staying with friends in Sussex after Hal's discharge from hospital – and here Aldington slipped on a path and fell, breaking his kneecap once more. He was operated on in the London Clinic in Devonshire Place; it would be nearly four months before he could travel again. To remain in London beyond that was out of the question he told MacGreevy: 'I feel once more as I felt so desperately in 1927-1928, that it's utterly impossible for me to fit into the life here. I suppose you feel much the same.'[9] The supposition is a little surprising, given that MacGreevy had returned to London from Ireland in November of 1933 and would remain there until 1941.

If he could not stomach Britain and was now disenchanted with Europe, then the Americas might be the answer. The Glovers were moving to Arizona, where the dry climate might help Hal recover. For Aldington North America in the winter was out for several reasons: he needed somewhere warm and cheap where he could remain for an indefinite period; and he craved solitariness – and certainly somewhere free of literary society. He chose Tobago.

This was a bold step: over the last five years he had needed the company of his close friends. Even at their most itinerant, he and Patmore had tended to take their friends with them; nor had Patmore been far from her sons. However, MacGreevy was now tied to a living from reviewing and translation and Aldington could no longer afford to subsidise his travel; Frere and Pat only left London (and Kent) in order to travel to the Riviera each summer; the Glovers had left for Arizona; and Prentice was retiring from Chatto in order to spend more time in Greece – and with Douglas and Orioli in Florence.

They left England on 9 February 1935. Tobago turned out to be 'a lucky dip in Fortune's bag'. For five pounds a month they rented an old plantation house, Terry Hill on Mount St George, 'six hundred feet up, with a tremendous vista over steeply sloping country to the Caribbean Sea', and '[e]xcept for the car of an occasional visitor and the infrequent mails, there was no sound or contact from the human world'.[10] In letters to Raymond at Chatto, to Lewis and to Orioli, amongst others, he extolled the delights of the island: the wonderful walks and bathes; the bougainvillea, the hibiscus, the bamboo and the coconut palms; the exotic fruits growing round the house. Ironically, however, so much reminded him of Europe. In the essay 'A Splinter of America' he writes:

> Oleanders always make me think of Sirmione, where a long line of them drops – or used to drop, for the world is being fast improved out of such sentimentalities – little flotillas of pink petals on the sulphurous water of Lake Garda. Bougainvillea brings back the south of France, only here they are not all that mauve purple. . . . The poinsettias are a disappointment, not to be compared with those of Portugal – but then Portugal is the land of flowers.[11]

What this essay also shows is how in this environment he was developing the ideas about humanity's relationship with the planet that he had begun to put forward in his articles for the *Sunday Referee* the previous year. He argues:

> It seems to me that there might be another attitude to life, based on an acceptance of life's mystery and on reverence for its many forms, a more modest conception of man's place in nature, and abhorrence of every kind of greed and destruction. One seems to get glimpses of it in the more ancient civilisations, in the lives of some men, in some poets and even in a few philosophers.[12]

It is not too far-fetched to see Lawrence's influence here. While in Tobago Aldington produced a 5,000-word pamphlet on Lawrence (to be issued free by Heinemann with their new edition of the writer's works) and edited the Lawrence anthology that would be entitled *The Spirit of Place*.[13] He had also edited a *Selected Poems* for Secker in 1934. In the pamphlet he speaks of 'the new vision of the world and of man's relation to it towards which [Lawrence] struggled, sometimes with brilliant clarity, occasionally with perplexed incoherence, but always with interest to the few who will patiently follow him'.

From Tobago he wrote to Richard Church, who had told him of his author's block: 'Don't worry – you'll do more poems and more novels. Nobody can be continually creative, not even a Balzac. There must be periods of tranquillity. . . . The great difficulty, as I know, is to make them periods of repose, not periods of anxiety.' He couldn't resist adding a warning to one whom he felt to be irretrievably immersed in the *Criterion* set: 'But if one keeps as free as possible from the sterilising influence of highbrowism and all the self-conscious city-bred "culture" then quietly but surely the creative mood returns.'[14]

However, while Tobago gave him the peace to write essays and to do the work on Lawrence, that very peace created a mental disturbance. As so often, it was Frere to whom he wrote about this: 'Curious how in this complete solitude one's past life comes up for review. I have been surprised to find how bitterly I still resent things I thought I had long ago dealt with and forgotten. But no, they are still there. . . . These things being so, I've practically decided to leave here at the end of May and make for N.Y.' He admitted that 'for reasons of economy' another month would be welcome, but it would be 'false economy' if the coming of the rainy season were to affect their health and if he were unable to work.[15]

Four months after their departure from England they were in New York. Derek Patmore was there to welcome them, as were Eric Pinker, Ralph's brother and manager of the American branch of the agency, and Aldington's American publisher, Doubleday. Aldington's letters to Raymond, now in control at Chatto, demonstrate his ambivalent reactions to America:

> Well, Harold, this is a great country. 120 million people, most of them morons. They talk more than any nation in the world, but they are the future. I find it all very exciting. . . . I've made more friends here in three weeks than I would in a year in England. . . . It has been a pleasure to me to meet cultivated people without malice, self-consciousness and conceit which are the unholy trinity of literary London.[16]

He told Douglas Goldring that he 'got on well' with the Americans: 'I like the old man-to-man attitude, the real decency and friendliness, something good in them (despite the obvious faults) which gives one back a little faith in the ultimate rightness of some form of democracy. . . . [V]astly more agreeable than English snobbery and that almost diseased malice of London.'[17] We might pick up here a patronising note, always a feature of his relationship with America.

Principally because of their mutual friendship with the Glovers and concern for their welfare, Aldington was in touch with Church. (They would not correspond again until after the Second World War.) Etta was writing from Arizona, and Aldington had to tell Church that the news was not good: Hal had had a relapse and they intended to return to England in early July. With Church (as with Read, and for the same reason) Aldington felt the need to impress:

> I asked Doubleday not to announce my arrival [in New York] so that I could avoid the usual interviewing farce. However, in a few days I was tracked down. . . . I have been surprised to find how much more my poetry is esteemed here than in England. They

have actually read it. And on the day I arrived a beautiful printed edition of the Luxembourg was issued by a private press here. They actually paid me a dollar a copy royalty![18]

His knee was still causing considerable discomfort. An X-ray showed that the bones had not knitted and he had to continue wearing the splint he had been given in Britain. In New York they had a lively social life, partly through the efforts of Derek Patmore, who was making a success of a career as an interior decorator and mounting a major exhibition in Altman's department store; but Aldington soon grew weary of the excitement. There were friendships he had been delighted to renew, particularly those with Slonimsky and with Bacon, but literary soirées and city life in the height of summer did not suit him. Fortunately, he and Patmore had formed a further friendship with Bertie Eskell, the New York doctor, himself an Englishman, whom he had consulted about his knee; and Bertie's wife, Greta, was a keen reader of Aldington's novels. The couple offered him a low-cost rental of their house, Brockway Manor on the Connecticut River at Old Lyme. He moved in on 8 July, his 43rd birthday.

Here he had time to reflect on his impressions of the New World. He wrote to MacGreevy:

There is much more simple goodwill and kindliness than one would ever imagine from the travelling American, and yet it is too often spoiled by an over-excited vanity. The ordinary American strikes me as naïf and very honest; indeed it is only because the average person is so honest that they can be preyed upon by those dreadful gangsters. Something of the old democratic simplicity still exists in New England, at least in the country round here – there are no ladies and gentlemen, but no proletariat or peasants. In N.Y. there is a certain amount of drawing room Communism among the intellectuals – far more than in England; but not much among the people.[19]

However, it was his love of nature that he was most able to indulge at Old Lyme: 'Except when the lightest breath of air comes up from the Connecticut River, the trees stand like some wonderful composition in green enamel. A few cicadas and the hum of bees.' He was struck by how New England was both like and unlike 'old' England, the forests and meadows resembling those of Kent, until one looked closely at the species:

And then except in the laboriously cleared parts, one sees the boulders from the moraines of the last glacial epochs. . . . And even the old farms have been abandoned, the forest is creeping back, deer come almost to the house, and in the evening one hears curious yelps and howls – foxes I think.[20]

Once more, however, he found his surroundings inimical to work. He told Raymond:

The odd thing here for me personally is that although the country is very beautiful and peaceful and I like it, I'm quite unable to work. That may be partly the effect of the two operations and partly the sense of uneasiness induced by our warlike friends in Italy. But everything I've started has been a failure and had to be scrapped. It is very tiresome.[21]

Whispers of war did indeed trouble him. He shared his anxieties with Slonimsky – as he would throughout the War when it came:

This beautiful American autumn is slowly burning up the green woods into lovely flames of brilliant colour. Every day winter is a little nearer, and each morning I think how the war flames are drawing a little closer to what is left of the old Europe. To me it has almost ceased to be a tragedy and has become a purposeless biological process. . . . I feel if anything can be saved, it will be saved here.[22]

He needed to return to England and take stock; and so, meeting up with Bacon and with Slonimsky in New York to say their farewells and spending a final week at the Doubledays' home on Long Island, he and Patmore set sail in the SS *Berengaria* on 11 October. They would spend the winter at the Cavendish Hotel on Jermyn Street.

By early April 1936 they were off again – to Portugal and Spain in the company of the Glovers. It was an act of friendship and proved a trial since age, sickness and failure had made Glover querulous and intolerant. Patmore told Derek that the Glovers were 'all right with Richard', but 'awfully disgruntled with other people'.[23] They landed at Lisbon and drove to Cadiz, Seville and Cordoba and thence up through Salamanca to Santiago. Because of Glover's poor health progress had to be slow, but they saw sufficient signs of military activity to make them cross over into France by late May, although Aldington had told Raymond from Cordoba:

'The papers tell us of "frightful disturbances" but nothing of the sort has come our way and everything seems exactly as usual.'[24] In *Life for Life's Sake* he expresses little sympathy for either side of the conflict, remarking that he was surprised that the Republic lasted as long as it did, for: 'while its intentions were of the worthiest, it was incompetent and lacked real authority.'[25] That this assessment was made in 1941 makes it even more surprising that, unlike many of his fellow writers, he did not see the Spanish Civil War as part of the wider struggle between communism and fascism, or the Nationalist forces in Spain as the kind of threat that he had seen Mussolini posing to his beloved Italy.

Crossing France and Switzerland, the party made for Feldkirch in the Tyrol, the site of Aldington's accident two years earlier, an area he and Patmore had come to love during his two months' convalescence. Here and at Fernpass, further east, they were 4,000 feet up in the mountains where the clear air was restorative for Glover and Aldington had peace to work on his fifth novel, *Very Heaven*. They spent two and a half months there, leaving Austria on 7 September for one of Aldington's marathon drives: through Switzerland and Alsace and up to Boulogne by way of Compiègne and Amiens. Leaving the Glovers at Boulogne (entrusted with the manuscript of Aldington's novel for Chatto), he and Patmore travelled down through France on a five-day journey to Le Lavandou. Aldington wrote to his young friend Eric Warman that he still thought France 'the most beautiful and varied country in Europe, and far superior to America'.[26] They arrived in Le Lavandou on 18 September.

Aldington had told Parsons at Chatto that their visit to the Riviera was necessary because 'Br feels she would like a dip in the Middle Sea after so much mountain air'.[27] In the light of later events it seems probable that she wanted them to have time alone together in surroundings they loved. They would not have long: a telegram from Malcolm Johnson at Doubleday informed Aldington that *Very Heaven* was, in the publisher's opinion, 'a major work of English letters' and that he and Doubleday would be in London on 1 October.[28]

On that day, Aldington and Patmore crossed the Channel, returning to the Cavendish Hotel in Jermyn Street, their most recent London base. In eight years they had covered three continents and ten countries, but never had a permanent home.

7. The Public Face
Reviewer, Philosopher and Essayist

'I am pleased to announce that, beginning from next week, Mr Richard Aldington, the distinguished poet, novelist and critic, will contribute a weekly critical causerie on contemporary literature to the *Sunday Referee*,' Hayter Preston wrote in the *Sunday Referee* on 17 November 1929. Aldington would be literary critic on the *Referee* for two periods in the early 1930s, initially at a salary of £400 a year, although Pinker would later negotiate this upwards.[1] In a term totalling less than three years he wrote a total of 140 articles, an astonishing feat given his mostly itinerant life during this period (although there were occasions when books for reviewing failed to reach him and he had to improvise). The paper, whose masthead declared it 'The National Newspaper for Thinking Men and Women' and which had a circulation approaching 400,000, gave him the opportunity to speak to a bigger and broader middle-class audience than he had reached through the *TLS*, *The Nation and Athenaeum* or *The Spectator*.

His reviews were invariably good-humoured, reflective and informative, revealing a consistency of outlook, both about writers – that good ones possess depth of feeling, intellectual rigour and a mastery of form – and about the purpose of reviewing:

> [T]he task of the Reviewer is . . . simply to give an honest opinion on new books, to recommend those one has read with pleasure or instruction, to ignore or warn against those which seem dull or pretentious or footling, and when necessary to prick the bladder of some inflated reputation or stunt publication.[2]

His enthusiasms and aversions are completely explicable within these frameworks. Lewis was admirable, but flawed by his distrust of all feelings and emotions, 'an amazing example of the power and limitations of pure intelligence'.[3] Eliot was a great poet but 'concerns himself with ideas about life, but never life itself'.[4] *Ulysses* was the most extraordinary masterpiece of creative literature since the turn of the century and Joyce had a greater 'power over words' than any other living writer, but his limitation was his despair.[5] Shaw was not a great creative artist because he was 'almost wholly cerebral'.[6] Huxley was praised for his 'positive belief in life', his sanity, shrewdness and tolerance, and his competent workmanship and 'expressive and personal' style.[7] Other respected writers included William Faulkner and Osbert Sitwell, and also Virginia Woolf and Colette, of whom he wrote: 'Whatever else you may say against them, their books are *written*.'[8]

Remy de Gourmont came in for the highest praise: 'His emancipation from every sort of educated or inherited prejudice was as nearly complete as we can expect from a fallible humanity. His exquisite sensibility was matched by an intellectual integrity just as exquisite.'[9] The master, however, was Lawrence, whose work formed 'one of the most important and vital contributions to the imaginative literature of our time'.[10] 'Have we anyone left,' Aldington asked, when reviewing *Apocalypse*, 'who can write with that effortless mastery, that passionate oneness of the thing felt with the thing said?'[11] He also acknowledged the influence on him in his youth of those fading stars, George Moore and Norman Douglas: 'I don't say that either Moore or Douglas seems perfect, but it was inspiring to watch Moore's almost anguished struggle towards a standard of perfection he had set himself and to enjoy Douglas's cool Atticism with its tang of Scotch brutality.'[12]

He started on the *Referee* at the height of the 'war-books boom' and brought to his reviews of those works all his own experience and empathy. In a column in which he is highly critical of all three of the texts under review, he suggests a 'rough working classification' of war books into six categories: 'Authentic and adequate personal records; ditto but inadequate; authentic personal experience used imaginatively and in the right tone; ditto mingled with bunk; war books by non-soldiers; complete bunk.'[13] A.M. Burrage's *War is War* (a memoir barely remembered today) was 'an admirably vivid, if slap-dash, record of the lives of hundreds of thousands of men between 1916 and 1918 . . . the bitterness, the grimness, the desolation of what our lives were.'[14] Helen Zenna Smith's *Not So Quiet: Stepdaughters of War* and C.E. Montague's short story 'Honour's Easy' were warmly recommended.[15] *A Farewell to Arms* was 'a masterpiece of our time', while Blunden's *Undertones of War* was 'one of the most genteel and urbane of War books', marked by 'deep feeling and sincerity'.[16] Amongst German texts, *Changed Men* by Paul Alverdes was:

> one of the saddest books I have ever read, sad with a kind of tender realism . . . a sense of the grandeur of common men overwhelmed by destruction . . . a lesson in humility for us all – that in all the

essential moments of life quality of feeling is what matters, and that so-called common men possess it, even when in other respects they seem stupid.[17]

The highest praise was awarded to Remarque's *The Road Back*: 'A dumb confused misery is here made articulate, the suffering and courage of men who fought two great wars – the War on the Western Front and the War back from death to life.'[18] In contrast, he wrote of Ernst Junger's *Copse 125*:

> It would be interesting to know … what frustration, what impotence, what pathology bring a man to praise murder, individual or collective, as the highest manifestation of human energy and vitality. … I see many death-worshippers in the world, but Herr Junger is certainly an almost unrivalled fanatic in the idolatry of destruction.[19]

There were plenty in the stream flowing off the presses for Aldington to condemn and he was horrified by what he deemed militarist texts, such as Alfred Pollard's *Fire-Eater* and Frank Crozier's *Five Years Hard*.[20] Perhaps the finest review he wrote of a 'war book' was that of Blunden's 1931 edition of the poems of Wilfred Owen. Reading the poems also moved him to write a poem of his own, 'In Memory of Wilfred Owen'.[21]

He reviewed very little poetry, his audience being in general the novel-reading public. With our own mythologised view of the output of the thirties, we might be surprised to find no references to what Samuel Hynes refers to as 'the Auden Generation', and, indeed, this may have been a deliberate omission. Where poetry is discussed, Yeats is 'the living poet *par excellence*'; while this evaluation was genuinely rooted in Aldington's admiration for the imaginative power of Yeats's writing, it was also the necessary corollary of his debunking of the other two giants of the age, Eliot and Pound. A variety of poets who were (or had been) personal friends were boosted: Barney, Cunard, Aragon, Lowenfels, MacGreevy and Beckett.

His aversion to university elitism, which had emerged in the early days of *The Criterion* and which stemmed both from his abhorrence of pretentiousness and from his sensitivity about his own education, remained strong. The appearance of *Cambridge University Studies* edited by Harold Wright, with its essay by F.L. Lucas on the teaching of English literature and in particular the critical theories of I.A. Richards, afforded him the opportunity to remark on 'the delusion that a University is the nursery of literary genius and that it has a duty to set a standard of taste in contemporary imaginative literature'. The 'New Criticism' left him cold; he dismissed Empson's *Seven Types of Ambiguity* as self-indulgent, and commented with reference to the Leavises: 'I have found vastly more self-criticism and genuine reverence in the despised "popular novelist" and playwright than I was ever able to discover among those whose self-conscious superiority chiefly rested on the fact that they could produce neither novels or plays.'[22] A review of William Rose's *Men, Myths and Movements in German Literature* allowed him both to pursue his programme and to pay a debt of gratitude:

> Dr Rose belongs to almost the only category of 'critic' that I can now read without boredom – *i.e.* the man who has information to bestow, the man who is absolutely *au courant* with 'what is known' about a given subject and who has the sense to tell it simply, without affectation or pedantry. He is neither the aesthetic teacher nor the polite essayist, but the man who has a job of work to do and does it.[23]

One of his sharpest attacks on a critic appeared in a review of Pound's *How to Read*:

> I cannot get it out of my head that literature is something to be loved and lived, a part of my life, a part of experience without which I should be very poor indeed; and for Mr Pound it is something to be *studied* and learned, like biology and book-keeping, something which can be taught.

He could not resist an additional attack on Pound as a poet: '[H]is use of words whether in prose or verse [is] so allusive and personal as to become a kind of crotchety shorthand.'[24]

In view of his later emergence as a biographer, Aldington's views on that genre are of interest.[25] He found Catherine Carswell's *The Life of Robert Burns* 'the most sensible, sympathetic and impartial view of Burns yet published'.[26] It possessed the qualities he looked for in a biography:

> a thorough knowledge of the subject without pedantry or hair-splitting; a sympathy with the poet, which is neither mawkish nor patronising; an understanding that a biography is the exposition of a human character, not a commentary on a set of books interspersed with anecdotes; a knowledge of human life beyond that afforded by reading books; and a lively style, which equally avoids dullness and facetiousness.

Edwin Muir's *John Knox* and Edward Hallett Carr's *Dostoevsky* were also admired. [27] Of the former he noted: 'He lets the man reveal himself and damns him with his own words [while] Mr Muir's careful understatements and cool ironies (the last perhaps a trifle overdone) complete the picture.' Another illuminating review (that compliments a friend of former days who would always retain her sympathy for Aldington) is that of Rebecca West's *St Augustine*: 'very well written and almost entirely free from the various brands of affectation which have nearly destroyed the art of biography, which does not consist of being facetious at the expense of one's subjects, but in presenting a human character.'[28]

Quitting the job in April 1932 in order to be free to concentrate on the writing of *All Men Are Enemies*, he tried to get back on the paper on his return to London that December, but his place had been taken by Huxley and it was April of 1933 before he was taken on again. That month he also began a series of fortnightly articles on the English poets for *Everyman*. By mid-July, partly because the sale of *All Men Are Enemies* to Fox had freed him from financial worry, he was itching to escape again from the demands of weekly reviewing, and the *Referee* agreed to cancel his six-month contract.

However, he did make a final appearance in 1934, writing a non-literary column for several weeks on issues of the day. These articles show an impressive, if idiosyncratic, grasp of the contemporary economic and political problems. In the first article he suggested that these could be grouped under the headings of: machines, population and religion, with the additions of nationalism and political liberty. He proceeded over the following weeks to deal with each of these. What comes across most of all is a passionate concern for the environment along with an awareness of its increasing destruction – from the threat posed by the burning of coal and petrol to the desertification of habitats across the Mediterranean region. Unlimited population growth was another of his concerns: it could not, he said, fail to lead to wars, and he pointed to the problems of heavily populated countries like Italy and Germany, which lacked colonial space, and Japan, with its lack of natural resources. As a libertarian, he acknowledged the dilemma that most of these modern ills could only be addressed by supranational regulation.[29]

That same year his fourth novel, *Women Must Work*, appeared.[30] Covering a similar period to his last, 1900 to 1928, it follows the attempts of a young woman to make a success of her life on her own terms. Unlike Georgie Smithers in *The Colonel's Daughter*, Etta Morrison is attractive, intelligent and ambitious. She tells her uncomprehending parents:

> I want to live for a time quite by myself, very simply, and think
> things out. I should like to shape my own life as far as a person can

in this world, without having it all moulded for me. I don't want to spend my days sitting back and saying 'Hurray!' to everything my men relatives think, say and do. I don't want to be just a dependent on Daddy and Teddy. If I marry a man, I want to marry him as an equal, not a parasite. I want to respect myself. And I want to find out other girls and women who think and feel as . . . I do.[31]

Rejecting the drab town of Dortborough (modelled on the Dover of Aldington's childhood), Etta heads for London, where she first experiences poverty and humiliation working as a clerk in a business that she leaves when she becomes a victim of sexual harassment. Over the next few years, most of which are the wartime years, we see Etta become increasingly hardened. The process begins early on when a kind and wealthy suffragist takes her under her wing:

Without perceiving it, [Etta] had become a little ruthless, more than a little calculating and wary. She thought her eagerness to please Ada Lawson came from gratitude and devotion; and so it did, but there was a grain of calculation – Etta wanted so much not to be sent away, and what better means of avoiding it than making herself indispensible? Long before, she had determined to meet people and be friendly with them; but now she selected, unconsciously trying to please those who might be useful to her.[32]

By the end of the novel, now a successful businesswoman and a mother, she realises: 'I had to use so much energy merely getting free and then merely keeping alive when I had broken away that I've never had time to develop.'[33]

As always, Aldington's twin targets are middle-class, conformist moral values and materialism. Etta's desire to challenge the first is frustrated, by men, by society, by chance and by her own naivety, and she takes refuge in the second. Anthony Clarendon in *All Men Are Enemies* succeeds in his bid for emotional fulfilment (at least at the point at which the novel ends); that Etta Morison does not is an outcome of her gender: her primary need for self-preservation drives her into adopting the very patriarchal values against which she has rebelled. It is a much more subtle and realistic narrative than *All Men Are Enemies*; furthermore, it avoids both the sentimentality of that novel and the savagery of the satire in *Death of a Hero* or *The Colonel's Daughter*. Aldington also, for the most part, resists the temptation to intervene in the narrative with passages of exposition. The result is a serious but low-key narrative, in which the reader engages sympathetically, but not uncritically, with the main character. Aldington clearly found it easier to maintain a degree of detachment from his female protagonist than he had in the case of Anthony Clarendon, his alter ego.

The *Sunday Referee* was enthusiastic, Crickmay calling Aldington 'the most powerful contemporary novelist in reaction against the folly, disorder and squalor of modern life'.[34] Other reviews were more measured. David Murray in the *TLS* was pleased to find 'a good deal less of the fierce indignation, and a good deal more of the pity and sympathy' than in previous books, and observed of the heroine that, 'Whether it was her own weakness or the strength of the forces she was fighting that beat her down, Mr Aldington leaves us to conclude; but he has made her too real and too brave a woman for us to despise her whatever our verdict.'[35] The *Times* reviewer also approved of the portrayal of Etta ('too vital and charming for the end to seem irreparably tragic') but in the Sunday press Straus and Gerald Gould were more critical, remarking that the novel lacked the qualities of some of Aldington's earlier work, although acknowledging its skill.[36]

Aldington's fourth long poem, *Life Quest*, was written in Austria and in London in 1934 when he was recuperating from his two knee operations, although the settings of the first few sections (El Escorial, Guadarrama, Santillana del Mar, Irun, Roncesvalles, Biarritz) suggest that they may have been composed in the latter stages of his tour of Spain and western France earlier that year. The 500-line poem consists of 20 free-verse lyrics, ranging in length from nine to 62 lines, the most effective of them around thirteen to 20 lines long, loosely organised into irregular four- or five-line stanzas. Most of them could stand alone but together they constitute the development of ideas on the characteristically Aldingtonian themes of *ubi sunt* and *carpe diem*. It is the philosophy, rather than a narrative (as in *A Dream in the Luxembourg* or *A Fool i' the Forest*) or a legend (as in *The Eaten Heart*) that gives the poem its structure and direction. Nevertheless, Aldington warned in an 'Author's Note' to the first edition that the poem was neither a narrative nor the exposition of a philosophy, but 'a loose string of moods and meditations, variations on the theme of the "Life Quest"'. He referred his readers to a section in *Human History* by the Egyptologist Sir Grafton Elliot Smith for 'the historical description of the life quest'.[37] A glance at those pages suggests that Smith's contribution to Aldington's thinking was little more than the concept of the 'life quest' – the search of human beings throughout history to safeguard – and prolong – their lives, a striving seen as the source of all religions and the impulse for all art forms.

The first thirteen sections develop the notions of the mortality of the soul and the vanity of human religion. Thereafter the poet turns his attention to the twin themes of the need to live for the moment:

> Kiss her now
> Kiss her now
> Kiss her now, Sweet Life.
>
> Says the wild thrush
> To the sleet
> From the hawthorn bush.
>   (Section 14)

and humanity's destruction of its culture and environment:

> But men and women
> Before it is too late
> Will you not draw back from greed and destruction
> Ere the earth becomes a cruel desert
> And the sea a sterile pollution
> And the sun black with anger against you.
>   (Section 20)

The voice is consistently authorial and the reader directly addressed. The passages of exposition are generally the least successful parts of the poem. Sometimes the voice is hectoring, as in the above example; occasionally, it employs a slightly heavy-handed satire:

> Let's hitch our wagon to a spiral nebula
> And live for ever backwards
> Faster than light –
> Oh to unsmoke that mathematical cigar!
>   (Section 8)

At other times, however, the idea is expressed with taut eloquence:

> The ship of the Dead has never come to port,
> It never started.
>   (Section 7)

In the finest of the lyrics, Aldington's passion for place and history work with his sensuousness and ear for rhythm to turn thought into poetry:

> Tonight it will be very lonely
> In the woods of Roncesvalles,

There will be a sighing in the damp branches
A cold smell from the leafy ground
In the blackness of pilgrim shadows.

Listen, listen until hearing dies
For the echo of the ivory horn,
Stare your eyes to stone
But you will not see . . .
                            (Section 1)

A few sections present us with almost surreal dream scenarios. In one, the poet envisages Tutankhamen's Ka awaking, 'blinking new baby eyes in the muffled tomb', to face 'thirty centuries of knowing death is death', eventually to find 'sweet relief' when the tomb is broken into, bringing 'the cool killing air' and 'he knew he could die at last'. In another, Aldington recalls a moment during his stay at Brantôme in 1932 when writing *All Men Are Enemies*, when he saw a dead snake lying in the river:

        . . . softly swaying in the water
    On its back with its dead white belly
    Turned under water to the sun
                            (Section 16)

The experience, he tells us, 'was both more and less than thought', the body of the snake becoming first the body of a dead English soldier on the fire-step of a trench, then the body of a young German officer. Finally:

    I saw the rag-clothed skeletons of Loos
    I saw my own body lying white and helpless
    Belly turned to the sun.

This is the manifestation in dream form of his experience on Hill 70 in 1918, fictionalised in *Death of a Hero*.[38] However, he tells us, 'I was not afraid, it was a great peace', as he saw 'that which was the snake/And myself and those others':

    Softly dissolve and drift with the stream
    Down to the Dordogne
    Down to the Gironde
    Down to the great rollers of the sea,
    And return as rain or cloud or air

But never again as a crisp-gliding snake
Rustling its way over dry grasses,
Never again as a human soul
Avid for much living . . .

This is immortality as Thomas Hardy understood it. In fact, the poem resonates with echoes of the poets Aldington loved, Browning especially, in particular, *A Toccata of Galuppi's*:

Tonight they will dance till dawn at Biarritz
And the *milors* will see their fun is clean
Dancing among the gold-topped bottles
Euro-African and clean
Between the futile mountains and the silly sea.

These are the Koh-i-noor
The diamond point of living light
Cresting the shadowy pyramid of the dead.

The third 'dream sequence' is the most grotesque. The poet is on the top of a mountain, when:

An enormous ghost comes creeping,
Lifting a flat head on a sinuous neck,
Peering above the highest peaks, and after
Slowly pulls its huge and misty bulk.

This 'mist ghost' 'swallows up the valleys, crushes out/The tiny forests' and eventually encompasses the poet, who sits 'like Jonah in his whale', wondering:

Whether the gods love evil and ugliness
Or have no power or no goodwill to us,
Or whether Herakleitos saw the truth –
That strife is harmony and everything
Lives through its opposite.

In the final section of the poem, however, the poet is once more on the top of 'the last mountains of Europe' and is transported into a dream-like experience in which he finds that his 'deathless body' is 'accepted by Earth Sun and Sea' and he knows that he is 'one of the remnant of life-seekers'.

The poem employs a style very like the one Eliot had begun to favour, alternating passages of exposition with lyrical passages. 'Burnt Norton' (which also references Heraclitus) would not appear for another year, but stylistic resemblances between the two poems are marked. The London section of Aldington's poem also recalls 'The Love Song of J. Alfred Prufrock' and 'Preludes':

> Sharp-lined and glinting
> The traffic clots go curdling
> Through the dark veins of the town
> In sharp mechanic spasms
> Like the fierce bleeding of a great machine.
> Breaking the rhythm of our blood
> Until the soft swirl and lapse of Thames
> Alone seem unreal
>
> . . .
>
> Even in winter
> There are lovely dawns
> Over the gutters and the chimney pots
> To break my heart.
>
> . . .
>
> Grim monstrous lotus of the dirty Thames . . .
>   (Section 15)

Even more precisely:

> In the south in winter
> When the sun hangs too low in the hard sky
> And the night wind remembers the frozen snow,
> The yellow soil crumbles and breaks
> As the thin bright iris petals push through
>   (Section 13)

evokes the opening of *The Waste Land*; but perhaps by the 1930s the Eliot landscape was inescapable.

The most important influence was Lawrence. Aldington had edited *Apocalypse* and *Last Poems* in Florence in the winter of 1931/32 and admired both.[39] A favourite passage from *Apocalypse* reads:

[T]he magnificent here and now of life in the flesh is ours, and ours only for a time. We ought to dance with rapture that we should be alive and in the flesh, and part of the living incarnate cosmos. I am part of the sun as my eye is part of me. That I am part of the earth my feet know perfectly, and my blood is part of the sea.[40]

Lawrence wrote in his 'New Mexico' essay that in the old native-American religion 'the whole life-effort of man was to get his life into direct contact with the elemental life of the cosmos, mountain-life, cloud-life, thunder-life, air-life, earth-life, sun-life. To come into the immediate felt contact, and so derive energy, power, and a dark sort of joy.' This 'effort into sheer naked contact, without an intermediary or mediator' was, he maintained, the root meaning of religion. Furthermore, he was convinced that humankind would eventually return to this concept of life.[41] This pagan notion is the message of Aldington's poem:

> In a touch beyond prayer I ask
> That my life quest go on till I die,
> Oh, let the Sun still be mine
> And the undying Sea
> And the Holy Earth!
>   (Section 20)

He had to defend his poem to his Catholic friend MacGreevy:

The answer to your '*Et Après?*' is that there is no *Après*. If we do not live here and now, we never live – that is the theme of the poem. It also postulates that all revealed religion, all abstract metaphysical gods, all religion based on the assumption of an after-life in which conscious personality persists – all these are false, and divert energy from the true human task of making the good life.

He acknowledged, however, that: 'If a poem, whatever its views or attitude, doesn't please as a poem, then it's a failure.'[42]

The poem was not exactly a publishing failure, but it caused few ripples, much to his disappointment. In *The Spectator* Michael Roberts grouped it with new works by W.H. Davies, Alan Pryce-Jones, G. Rostrevor Hamilton and Mark van Doren, and commented of all of them: 'It is not merely that they contain no striking metaphor that reaches beyond the immediate occasion and extends the bounds of language, nor is it that their feelings are commonplace. It is rather that their diction and their rhythms seem not adequate to the occasion.'[43]

Once he reached Tobago in the spring of 1935 Aldington turned his hand
to a collection of essays, modestly sub-titled 'Sketches and Ideas'. This was a
natural development from the *Referee* articles of the previous year, an outcome
of the reading and reflection that had led to *Life Quest* and a relaxed activity to
accompany the compilation of his anthology of Lawrence's prose (chiefly the
fiction), *The Spirit of Place*.[44] More significantly, it was a distraction from his
temporary inability to write another novel. He had begun one in London over
the winter but was dissatisfied and scrapped it. Of the eighteen essays that
make up *Artifex* (the title being that of the opening essay), many are indeed
'sketches', of varying length, mostly light-hearted in tone and anecdotal in
origin, while two more substantial essays display his aptitude for travel writing.
An essay on Lawrence was written for Heinemann to issue alongside their new
edition, Frere having recently acquired the publishing rights for Lawrence from
Martin Secker, as Aldington had always hoped he would. An essay on the early
nineteenth-century naturalist, explorer and conservationist Charles Waterton
had already appeared twice: in the *TLS* in December 1932 and as a Heinemann
pamphlet in 1934. Aldington was not done with either of these two subjects,
on whom he would attempt full-length biographies at the end of the 1940s.[45]
His admiration for Lawrence we already know; Waterton was an attraction for
his eccentricity and for his passionate concern for the environment.

In the title essay and a handful of others Aldington sets out his
ideas about contemporary society. Artifex is the artist, 'servant of the
life impulse, maker of myths, music and images' who '[h]as turned the
world of things and of human beings from a mere environment noticed
only for the immediate purposes of existence into a deeply significant
and glorious pageant to be enjoyed and revered'.[46] He is set against the
theologian, the scientist and the businessman who have exercised power
over human beings and allied themselves with the militarists and those
who exploit the earth. Aldington also finds an opportunity to attack
modernism, which he describes as 'the art of hyperaesthesia, the art of
exasperated neurasthenics ... [t]he music of atonality, the painting and
sculpture of super-realism, the literature of the stream of consciousness,
the aestheticism of concrete and cocktails': 'The sensationalism of the
art mob is the snobbish brother of the newspaper mob's sensationalism,'
he maintains. 'Over-production for a public of snobs results not only
in perversities to attract attention, but in the vices of intrigue, back-
scratching and malignant disparagement of rivals.'[47]

In 'A Splinter of America' he suggests a way forward for society, involving 'a
more modest conception of man's place in nature, and abhorrence of every kind
of greed and destruction.' However, he rejects the role of prophet and saviour:
'The most one can do is to follow one's own daimon as far as the swarming

masses and their perplexed officials will allow one.'[48] 'Purpose in Life' enables him to review some of the ideologies by which human beings have made sense of their lives (including nationalism and 'the dictatorship of the proletariat') and to conclude: 'There is no "purpose" in life. It is an end in itself.' In 'Freedom of the Press' he argues that society is based on 'the suppression of the vital impulse along with the sexual impulse and the natural (not revealed) religious impulse ... for the benefit of commerce, war and social organisation'.[49] In 'A Letter to a Young Man' he preaches the gospel against nationalism and militarism, although he absolves the fighting man of responsibility for war: the modern soldier may be misguided but he exhibits 'the virtues of abnegation, self-control, subordination to a purpose believed to warrant sacrifice, devotion to friends, even sometimes pity to enemies'. 'I sometimes think,' he reflects, 'that war is so willingly accepted because it asks so much of men; and that peace is despised because it seems to ask so little.' Ultimately, he argues, as he did (reluctantly) in his *Referee* articles, that the only way forward is the 'experiment of world government'. 'Love your country, if you will, but love the world more,' he urges the young man.[50] Similarly, in his discussion – in an essay entitled 'What Fools These Mortals Be' – of that other topic on which he had strong opinions, overpopulation, he opts for compulsory regulation.[51] We might note these inconsistencies in Aldington the individualist and libertarian.

As the international scene grew more troubled and the prospect of war more certain, he would cling to his philosophy of life, inconsistent as it was in many respects. A year after the completion of *Artifex* he would write a letter to another young man, his friend Warman:

> For us human beings Life is the supreme fact. Communism and Socialism are not facts, nor are they life; they are theories....
>
> Moreover, the supreme objection to both Communism and its inevitable counter-force, Fascism, is that they entirely overlook the human element. The 'rightness' or 'wrongness' of any particular political economic social theory is a matter of opinion. But its working depends upon the kind of people we all are. True progress consists in the substitution of co-operation for hostility, knowledge for ignorance, reason for prejudice, justice for tyranny, richness and variety of life for penury and power. And so long as they remain cruel, bigoted, vain, dishonest and intolerant, so long will they pursue power by any means and abuse power when they have it. The problem of right human organisation is an immense one. And it is merely confused by over-simplifying the issues, by imagining that it can be solved by such puerilities as Nordic blondism or collective ownership of property. The psychological problem still remains.[52]

8. The Private Life
Leading a Double Life
1930-1936

The life Aldington and Patmore shared in the 1930s seems from the outside to have been idyllic. MacGreevy and Prentice felt great affection for Patmore, an affection she returned. When she visited London from Florence in February 1931 Prentice told Aldington: 'Brigit brightened a gloomy yesterday. She was not only looking marvellously sweet and well, she brought lots of news of you and Tom and the two Florentine members.'[1] The following year, when the couple departed for Portugal, he wrote:

> Dearest Richard ... How glad I am you are out of this bumphy stupid place & living the life you want, provided, like a 40-mph testudo, with your own travelling house, and Brigit with you, Brigit without whom it would all else be just a journey! You are both very dear to me & I shout with lusty joy that you are both so happy.[2]

MacGreevy expressed his affection for Patmore by dedicating his monograph on Aldington to her.

In Florence in 1931 and 1932 the couple spent most of their time in the company of Orioli and Douglas, who seem to have appreciated Patmore's warmth and intelligence. They enjoyed a full social life in both Italy and France, which, nevertheless, accommodated Aldington's need to work. While attempting to turn her own hand to a novel and some travel writing (neither of which was completed), Patmore was a discerning critic of his work and the first person to whom he would turn for an opinion.

In the early stages of their itinerant life, she twice returned alone to London, to the apartment she and Derek still rented in Millman Street, in order to see her sons and to maintain her link with the social world she had occupied as a single woman since her separation from her husband in 1925. She made the first of these journeys on 11 March 1930, after their return to Paris from North Africa, for a separation of three weeks, with Aldington crossing to London on 3 April. The following year she left Florence in February for another three-week trip to London.

Those two periods of separation give us a glimpse into the relationship, since they corresponded daily and Patmore retained all Aldington's letters. The affair had not lost any of the intensity of its early days. From Paris in March 1930 he wrote to ask her to marry him: 'We are really married, Soukie dear. I mean that we love as lovers who want to spend the rest of their lives together. Don't you feel we ought to be married?' He told her that he would not divorce H.D. unless it was in order to marry Patmore; he did not want other women to pursue him. 'Soukie dear,' the letter continues:

> I have been sort of crazy without you. I didn't know that a woman could mean all life, as you mean to me . . . I often think that I really live <u>positively</u> only for you. You are my life and my happiness, my beauty and my desire. And that is happiness – to love more and more the person who loves you.[3]

Patmore's only reservation about marriage seems to have been the disparity in their ages, as he wrote back to her: 'As to age – first, the War blokes like me and Tom and Frere, are pretty "battered" to start with; then, a man gets old sexually much sooner than a woman.'[4] It seems, however, that Deighton Patmore refused to divorce his wife, so the plan came to nothing.

The letters from Florence the following February show the same degree of ardour: 'I feel about ¾ dead without you and wonder how I lived before there was the perfect life of Brigit. My own beauty and adored one!'[5] He also used this separation as an opportunity for a particular project: he asked Patmore to set about recording her sexual history for him:

> I see why you feel difficulty in putting down your erotic experiences. I did mine because it seems to free me more completely for you, but I dissociated them completely from emotion. . . . Maybe that is not possible for you but do it if you can, for it does free one to look back at everything as a sort of learning – not to love, though perhaps that too – but to fuck.'[6]

The request, two years into their relationship, suggests a need on his part to bring some novelty into their affair. His own account amounted to 12,000 words.

It seems that Patmore gradually came to feel more secure in the relationship and able to let go of her independent life in London. Their only other documented separation was for the week Aldington spent completing *All Men Are Enemies* in Brantôme in September 1932. Patmore preceded him to London and he corresponded with her daily, but only, for the most part, by way of brief postcards: 'Do please forgive the scrappy cold notes,' he wrote in one of the few letters he sent:

> but this is the most concentrated, the most intense piece of writing I've ever done. . . . [I]t was right for me to be alone at the end, because it needs the peculiar hallucinatory quality of solitude. . . . Dear dear love, don't, don't feel hurt that I'm somewhere else these few days. It won't be the begetter of Tony and Katha who arrives in London.[7]

That Patmore had no need of more frequent visits to see her sons was chiefly because both Derek and Michael spent quite long periods over the summers of 1930, 1931 and 1933 at the Riviera villas, while Derek also made a visit to Florence in the early summer of 1932. These visits do not appear to have gone entirely smoothly. A letter from Patmore to MacGreevy in November 1930 hints that there had been conflict between Derek and Frere:

> Derek says Frere asked him to lunch & was very charming. He says, and I agree, that it would be stupid to have complications. I have sometimes wanted to get up and murder Frere – but I am a fierce & wicked woman – I never say anything about it & it must just wear out of me. . . . Dear Provence, I do hope it won't have too sad memories for Derek. No, I know his temperament, it's very sweet & sound – he's all right.[8]

Something had clearly gone wrong in that otherwise beautiful summer of 1930.

We get hints of the discord again, when in the spring of 1931 Aldington writes to Derek about the coming summer: 'If you will forgive my saying so, I think it will be much nicer if you can arrange to come with Mickey and not when Frere is there. I think Frere is fond of you but also rather jealous.'[9] That Frere should be jealous of the attention accorded to Derek by Aldington and Patmore seems unlikely. That the problem was serious is clear from a letter Aldington wrote to MacGreevy at around the same time, in which he begs the latter to visit that summer, because if he and

Aldington and Patmore are all working, it will be an excuse for asking other visitors to stay elsewhere: 'Pino and Norman say they prefer to stay in a pub, and we can park Frere and Charles out likewise.'[10] He continues: 'I don't want a repeat of last year – I mean in way [sic] things got entangled through having the wrong people.'[11] That he was not entirely able to prevent 'a repeat' of the previous year is evident from a letter MacGreevy wrote to Prentice that July:

> Frere arrived to schedule on Saturday [25 July] and all is pretty well. Things looked bad on Monday night. Mickey was too obviously [illegible word] and I got enough abuse for us all as I took Frere home. But fortunately Mickey decided himself that it was intolerable so went off yesterday morning for a few days and as Richard is slightly off-colour – nothing that you need be alarmed about – the [illegible word] is being considerate all round. And Brigit has behaved beautifully. Frere leaves for Lady Russell's on Monday. He's so lovely when he *is* a good boy that one would do a lot to spare him botheration.[12]

It is a letter that raises more questions (not only because of the indecipherable words) than it answers but it seems that it was not just Derek, but also Michael, who was a provocation to Frere.

In 1933 the situation was still stressful. Aldington had rented Villa Devos jointly with Frere. 'Consequently,' he explained to Derek that June:

> I am not master of it as I was at Koechlin [in 1931]. However, Frere will certainly be in London in July, and we should be happy to see you. The only snag is that Pat may stay on (you won't mind that – she's very nice) and Frere and Charles may come for a few days in August, for Frere and Pat to be married here. (For God's sake don't mention this to anyone, since the divorce isn't through yet.) If the place were entirely mine I should naturally arrange for Frere not to be here when you are. But since it isn't, and since he obviously has a right to come to a place for which he has paid, I think the only way is for you and Mickey to go off for a few days if he should happen to come while you're here. I don't believe he will, but he might, and it's best to be prepared. In any case, it would only be for three or four days, since he is having his holiday now, and can't have another long one. Moreover, the Doubledays will be in London all July. So the earlier you can come in July the better.[13]

Whatever the reason for Frere's objections to the Patmore boys, and Derek in particular, those objections would become a permanent cause of distrust and hostility between Frere and Patmore, devoted as she was to her sons. Aldington's own devotion to Patmore and his genuine liking for Derek seem to have kept in check his accustomed antipathy towards homosexual men (an antipathy that Frere may well have shared), but he wrote to MacGreevy in February of 1931:

> Pino says 'Derek is getting a very bad name' in London, and that if he goes on something serious may happen. It is worrying. I can't talk to Brigit about it, because she simply will not hear of anything against Derek; and, in a way, she is to blame for having let him do exactly what he likes and always giving way to him. Pino wants me to warn Derek, but I've already dropped him the very broadest hints. I don't know what Brigit would do if it ever came to an open scandal. Be careful what you say to Brigit about it, and for God's sake don't mention Pino, or she'll take a scunner against him, as she did with Frere. I wish I could talk it over with you, and try to find if anything can be done. I feel in my bones that England is getting ripe for a thundering scandal, which will involve nearly all these silly young blighters. Why the hell can't they keep quiet?[14]

Derek seems to have been unaware of the extent of Aldington's anxieties. At the Villa Devos in the summer of 1933 the two of them worked companionably together on turning Aldington's Cunard story, 'Now Lies She There', into a play entitled *Life of a Lady*.[15] In his introduction to his mother's memoirs (and in his own), Derek spoke of Aldington with affection: 'I found in him the father figure which I had sought in vain in my own father.'[16]

Aldington and Patmore also spent increasing periods of time in London. Spending a fortnight there in April 1930 in order to have meetings with Pinker, Aldington made use of Garland's Hotel in Suffolk Street and for his month's visit in 1931 stayed in Frere's flat in St Martin's Lane, but thereafter he and Patmore rented apartments together. They had come to feel less socially vulnerable as a couple; and Patmore no longer had her flat in Millman Street. Derek's increased prosperity in his post as public relations director for an advertising firm enabled him in 1933 to purchase a lease on an apartment of his own in St James's Square. Patmore and Aldington found inexpensive rented flats, always in the Mayfair area, close to the London Library and to Derek's apartment: at 60 Brook Street for Aldington's month of recuperation after his post-*All Men Are Enemies* breakdown in 1932; at 4 Palace Chambers in St James's Street for their three-month stay over the winter of 1932/33; at Carlton Court in Pall Mall Place from December 1933 until April 1934; and at Georgian House, Bury Street, from October 1934 until they left for Tobago in early February 1935. When they returned from America in October 1935 they went into a hotel – the Cavendish at 81 Jermyn Street (run by the renowned Rosa Lewis); they left for their travels with the Glovers in early April 1936 but were back at the Cavendish at the beginning of October.

Often these were enforced stays: in December 1932, for example, Aldington made his precipitate journey from Portugal to battle with Chatto over the cuts to *All Men Are Enemies* and then felt that he must stay to see the novel through to publication. He told Church:

> I am only waiting until a few things are settled here, to start south [i.e. to the Riviera], find a cottage, and get down to it. I wish I could do serious work in London but I can't. I'm so used to country ways and quiet skies, that all these telephone and postal deliveries and people calling and newspaper placards distract me.[17]

He made much the same complaint to Raymond in December 1934 prior to his departure for Tobago.[18]

Patmore, who enjoyed seeing both her friends and her sons, felt rather differently. In July 1931 MacGreevy, confiding to Prentice that Aldington was contemplating going to London when he left the Villa Koechlin, warned, 'Only not a word. I think it would be splendid for him, only he mustn't feel we are pushing him', and added, 'Brigit would love it.'[19] In the event, Aldington spent only a month in London that year, staying with Frere and making trips to visit bookshops in Peterborough, Middlesbrough, Leeds and Sheffield to promote *The Colonel's Daughter*. A letter he wrote to MacGreevy at the end of his stay shows that, while he relished his friendships, he had found the political climate abhorrent:

> As always, Charles [Prentice] was perfect, & it was a great treat to be able to drop in on him nearly every day. . . . Frere was very nice this time and talked more intelligently about the state of England than anyone except Charles and possibly [Sydney] Schiff. The Labour people I saw were good-hearted boobies. The Tories are simply fat-heads and crooks. There is a wave of sentimental 'patriotism' in England. Coward's *Cavalcade* is most shrewdly on the mood of the moment, and the satirical intent is lost in the audience's sentimentalism.[20]

Another cause of tension between Aldington and Patmore was his renewed relationship with H.D. The two had not met since the two occasions in Paris in 1929 but Aldington had written to her at the time: 'I want to say, dear Dooley: "Let's make a pledge that whatever happens you & I will never get out of touch again." Do you agree? You're so rare & beautiful, and it's made me so happy to be friends again', and in a later letter: 'Please don't let anything separate us.'[21] On her part, she had told several correspondents how important to her their reconciliation was. 'I have the greatest feeling of joy and tenderness in Richard though any serious renewal of an "alliance" other than delightfully superficial and intellectually very poignant is out of the question,' she had written to Glenn Hughes; and she told George Plank that their meetings had all been in the company of others because, 'I was afraid of too much intimacy & he was altogether charming and dear.' In particular, she had been touched by the way he remembered their shared past, the memories 'perfectly fresh and untouched, the minutest details startlingly preserved, and fresh and fragrant with none of the intervening dust'. 'We are very, very close to one another, intellectually and spiritually,' she told John Cournos.[22]

A letter Aldington wrote at the beginning of 1930 reveals how intent he was on keeping those shared memories 'fresh and fragrant'; he told her that he had visited Capri (with Patmore – although he doesn't mention her) and called at the Pensione del Lauro, where he had 'thought very tenderly over old times'. A reference to Robert Browning in a letter the following year is not only made for the purposes of argument, but because Browning was a shared love and the Browning marriage a mutually understood icon of their own.[23] A year later, he shared with her his response to Lawrence's *Last Poems* when he was editing them: 'I was glad, and I think you will be, to know that at the end it was the beautiful side of Lorenzo which found utterance again.'[24] This was probably a less successful attempt at retrieving recollections of an idyllic past – he never grasped that H.D.'s memories of Lawrence were rather more problematic than his own.[25]

He was keen to restore their working relationship, constantly suggesting publishing projects, and encouraging her to make contact with Prentice ('He is a fine Greek scholar and admires you tremendously').[26] Chatto published her poetry collection *Red Roses for Bronze* in 1931. He wanted her to do a Dolphin – perhaps Greek women poets – or to put together enough translations to make a companion volume to his own *Medallions in Clay* which Chatto were publishing in the Phoenix imprint.[27] Perhaps she could do a complete Greek tragedy – Sophocles' *Antigone* or *Electra*?[28] He also encouraged her, with equal lack of success, to move from her current American publisher, Houghton Mifflin, to Covici, Friede.

The early letters are also flirtatious. From Algeria in 1930 he asked her:

> Darling, can't you come to Paris soon – in March or early April. I
> want to see you most awfully. Please do come, if you can. It would
> be so lovely to see you. I am being horribly successful, and will
> blow any amount to amuse you! There, isn't that a proposition?[29]

From Tunisia he sent her a postcard picture of 'a Tunisian beauty' and
commented: 'On second thoughts Tunis is no place for you! Those veils!'[30]
He was covertly sharing an understanding of her (and his) attraction to
beautiful women; Caroline Zilboorg suggests that, 'H.D.'s sensitivity to
women played a role in the erotic chemistry between her and Aldington
from the earliest days of their courtship in 1912.'[31]

Patmore felt threatened by this friendship (particularly since her own
relationship with H.D. and Bryher had been frosty since around 1925).
Aldington tried to reassure her: 'Our love delights me – I like the idea
of *us*. . . . You mustn't ever worry about my being unfaithful to you!'[32]
The relationship between the two women, however, became more, rather
than less, frigid, perhaps aggravated by Patmore's awareness of H.D.'s
closeness to Stephen Haden-Guest, Patmore's former lover. At first both
women made an effort at friendship. In May 1930, writing to thank H.D.
for flowers she had sent, Patmore asked: 'Aren't you coming to Paris
at all?'[33] By July, however, she had begun to suspect H.D. and Bryher
(probably not without cause) of spreading rumours about her, and she
told H.D. 'The seeming reconciliation you arranged was not a real one . . .
perhaps you have a certain undefined desire to persecute me – the things
you have told people about me seem to point to it – but I thought that
was over.'[34] At the end of the year Aldington wrote to H.D.: 'I didn't give
[Brigit] your messages, because I wasn't sure how she'd feel about it. . . .
Perhaps the best thing would be for you to write to her – some time. . . .
I feel so very sorry that things are not quite "right" between you two.'[35]

An incident in February 1931 must have forced him to recognise
that he could not sustain both relationships over the long term. On 6
February, two days after Patmore's departure from Florence to London,
he wrote to tell MacGreevy of a 'minor fly in the ointment' – H.D. was
coming to Florence: 'It would be awful if she came here before Brigit
returns, and I can't very well go away.' On the same day he told Patmore
that he had received a letter from H.D. indicating that there was 'no
chance in 1,000' of her coming to Italy – although he clearly decided
that this was too risky a strategy and told her six days later that he was
'menaced by a visit from H.D.', at the same time writing to tell H.D.

how glad he was that she was coming – and suggesting that it might be 'easiest all round' if, to account for their shared surname, she pretended to be his sister-in-law! Meanwhile a flurry of letters and telegrams between Aldington, MacGreevy and Prentice aimed to get MacGreevy to Florence in time to act as chaperone. Aldington was forced to apologise to Patmore on 19 February for having even mentioned H.D.'s name, but the next day informed her that there was 'no news of the saphs [H.D. and Bryher]' and that, 'Tom will be here in 48 hours and he will be my chaperone.' Four days later he made arrangements to meet H.D. that evening, informing her that Patmore would not be back until the end of the week, but that he had a friend with him (MacGreevy had arrived two days earlier), 'a gentle and charming creature, an H.D. fan', who would much like to meet her.[36]

Although the evening appears to have gone well, and H.D. was to be in Florence for a fortnight, to accompany Bryher in her meetings with Douglas and Orioli (Bryher would provide Douglas with financial support until his death in 1952), there were to be no further meetings. The chief reason for this was Patmore's return to Florence, only two days later; but Aldington explained to H.D. three weeks afterwards: 'I was sorry indeed not to see you again in Florence, but I did not want to embarrass you in any way; so I left it to you.'[37]

He and Patmore kept away from Douglas and Orioli for much of that fortnight, feeling increasingly resentful. He told Derek Patmore:

> Another smaller thing has made Brigit and me quite furious. Our little friends from Territet have been here nearly a fortnight with McFerson (as Orioli spells it) and have been seeing a lot of Norman, particularly McPherson. From something Norman let drop we now suspect that Norman is being cajoled into recommending our Charles to publish one of Mr McPh's unreadable masterpieces. I don't suppose Charles would be such a fool, but the promise of an introduction from Norman (which of course Bryher would pay for) might induce Charles to take it. I am going to warn Charles obliquely. . . . If they can get in touch with Charles, they'll do their best to down me there – not much hope for them![38]

His suspicions would prove quite unfounded, but they are a startling manifestation of a paranoia which would flare up again from time to time – and, no doubt, in this instance it was stoked by Patmore. Bryher, of course, was a *bête noire*, but Aldington may also have felt jealous of MacPherson's intimacy with H.D.

Zilboorg describes the H.D./Aldington correspondence between 1930 and 1932 as 'characterised by gaps and clusters of exchange'.[39] Aldington had written 32 letters to H.D. in 1929; there were only a further seventeen over the next two years. The gaps were probably attributable to H.D.'s preoccupations at the time: with the film work on which she, Bryher and MacPherson were engaged; with the move to the new Bauhaus home (named Kenwin) that Bryher and MacPherson had had built at Territet; and with her own deteriorating relationship with MacPherson. However, Aldington must have begun to recognise the limited possibilities for the growth of their friendship, and his letters, still expressing interest in her work and confiding about his own, become less intimate, the eager requests for meetings being replaced by wistful requests for her to write 'from time to time' or when she has 'a few minutes to spare'.[40] Her failure to keep in touch led to her having to write to Prentice in November 1931 for a forwarding address: 'I have been wanting to write to them, one or both, but heard they had pulled up stakes and did not know exactly where they were.'[41] It must still have taken her some time to get around to a letter, since it was 21 February 1932 when Aldington acknowledged it, telling her how glad he was to hear from her. He was discouraging about her suggestion of meeting in Venice in April, after her return from her forthcoming cruise to Greece with Perdita (a rare venture for H.D. out of her London-Switzerland cycle of the 1930s), explaining, rather unconvincingly, that he could not afford to drop the tenancy on his Florence apartment, which would run until May. He complimented her on *Red Roses for Bronze*, which had her 'own rare quality' and was glad to hear of its success in America adding, characteristically: 'In England at present they seem unable to see any poet but Eliot, and for my part they're welcome to him.' The only reference to their shared past is a suggestion that she try to meet up with Slonimsky (then travelling in Europe and the Middle East) in Athens: 'He is still a noble figure.' It was the last communication between them for five years.[42]

In the early 1930s Aldington also entered into at least two secretive sexual relationships with younger women, mostly, but not entirely, conducted via correspondence. There may have been others, but the only sets of letters to have survived reveal two relationships, in particular, and they only contain Aldington's side of the correspondence. Both women first wrote fan letters: Eunice Black in response to having read both *Death of a Hero* and *The Colonel's Daughter*, and Marjorie Pollard as she embarked on *All Men Are Enemies*. Black was an expatriate South African living in London and 22 years old when she started to write to Aldington in the spring of 1932. Their correspondence ran until August 1933, after

which time she returned to her family in South Africa, although there
were a few letters exchanged between them in 1935 and 1936.[43] Their
relationship was consummated on Aldington's visits to London in 1932
and 1933. Pollard was older – 29 in 1933 when Aldington's seven letters
to her were written; they never met.

Although we cannot access the women's side of the correspondence,
it is clear from Aldington's replies that his steady move from risqué
comments to explicitly erotic content was one they encouraged. Both
women would initially have been attracted by publicity photographs
of him, and their acquaintance with his novels would have led them
to expect openness about sexual matters. Pollard consulted him about
her love affairs and sent him some of the correspondence, as well as
photographs of herself, in some of which she was naked. By his second
letter, Aldington had begun to speak about love affairs and the need for
lovers to recognise that affairs have beginnings, middles and ends, an
indication of his own openness to sexual adventures. He also described
how he had been pottering about the rocks 'with only a pair of slips on',
clearly inviting voyeurism on her part. In response to her confidences
about her sexual experiences, he gave her a detailed account of his own
sexual history, although without mentioning the names of his partners:
the clumsiness with which he had taken the virginity of H.D. and her
ultimate choice of female sexual partners; and the fact that it was not
until his fourth sexual affair (with Yorke) at the age of twenty-six that
he 'achieved a really full physical satisfaction with a woman'.[44] He asked
her for more explicit details of her own experiences, including lesbian
ones, about which he displayed particular curiosity. After six letters from
the Villa Devos in the summer of 1933, his only remaining letter to her
was a hastily handwritten one from Alicante towards the end of the year,
suggesting a meeting in London. We must assume that this did not take
place; Pollard, as Aldington knew, was engaged to be married and may
well have thought a meeting with him a complication best avoided.[45]

The correspondence with Black has many of the same features. By the
second letter, the subject of naked bathing had surfaced – both his own
and that of Tony and Katha (he was writing *All Men Are Enemies*), which
he was sure would be censored. 'I believe people should live physically,
enjoy their bodies and enjoy the bodies of others,' he declared. Black must
have asked where love fitted into this philosophy of sensuality, because
Aldington told her:

> There are so many kinds of love . . . the difficulty lies in getting a
> just equilibrium between one's sensuality and feelings, and other

> passions . . . [T]here is a flowering of the senses which is useless
> and beautiful like poetry and should exist for its own sake. . . .
> What I am thinking of is a sort of tender sensuality.[46]

The sexual subject matter became gradually more explicit, although he
made sure that he was not leading his correspondent where she did not
want to go: 'I will write freely if you say to, but then you must do the
same,' he told her.[47]

That autumn of 1932, when Aldington was hospitalised for his
breakdown on arriving in London from Brantôme, he asked Black to visit
him in the nursing home. She was only there for half an hour but either
then or at a later meeting they became lovers. From Portugal in November
he was shocked to hear that she suspected she was pregnant, although
another letter followed to tell him that her fears had been unfounded.
Nevertheless, he gave her the name of a doctor whom she should see 'to
arrange things' should her sickness return. His letters in this period are
tender and affectionate, but there is an undercurrent of unease, a concern
that he has led her into expectations he cannot fulfil:

> All you write is perfect and unselfish, but, my sweet, I tremble a
> little. I don't want to hurt you and make you unhappy. But then I
> try to tell myself that one has to be hurt by loving, and think the
> sweetness of it is worth all the pain. You only know the best of
> me. If only I could be <u>sure</u> that you won't suffer. Do believe that I
> shall always want to [sic] gentle and tender with you. I don't want
> to hurt you or make you unhappy . . .

and even: 'It would be awful if you felt I'd not been fair to you.'[48]

Gradually, the letters settle into a more relaxed mood and more explicitly
erotic content, although he continues to check Black's willingness to have
these kinds of conversation: 'Shall I sometimes write you about sexual
things and will you write me what you think and feel about them?' These
discussions include the relaxed attitude of Portuguese peasants to infant
sexuality: 'Though it is a Catholic country & outwardly very decorous,
they haven't yet stopped the sexual play of the children which used to be
so pretty in Italy until the Fascists prevented it.' He tells her of having
once witnessed an Italian man fondling his two small daughters: 'And
didn't they enjoy it and ask for more!'

This leads him into a detailed account of his own childhood sexual
experiences, both with young girls and with older women. He told Black:
'Those young sensations are very keen & beautiful & should be allowed

within sensible bounds,' and added: 'I believe that that is why I adore the female and have absolutely no sexual feeling about males, as too many Englishmen have.' An account of how he learned to masturbate is followed by his asking her whether she first masturbated spontaneously or was 'shown by another girl or boy'. [49]

In late December (as a consequence of the battle with Chatto over the text of *All Men Are Enemies*) Aldington and Patmore were in London and he resumed the affair with Black, on one occasion making elaborate arrangements so that they could have a whole night in a hotel together (the Midland: 'large and anonymous').[50] A further opportunity for an assignation was the invitation to Aldington from the young Richard Rumbold to speak to the Oxford Literary Club on literature and censorship, with specific regard to Lawrence. Aldington drove to Oxford at the end of January, picked Black up from Oxford Railway Station after giving the lecture and drove to Stratford-upon-Avon for the rest of the weekend. A letter to Patmore to tell her that the lecture had gone well ends: 'All my love, darling one.'[51]

There is a gap in the correspondence after Aldington's departure for the Riviera in March that year, the next letter being written on 15 August – a day on which he also wrote to Pollard, with whom he had been corresponding since his arrival at the Villa Devos. In the letter to Black he apologises for his long silence and blames the pressures of work. The letter is affectionate but brief and concludes: 'You are a darling, Eunice, and I love you very much. I send you many kisses and wish I had your cool body in my arms.'[52] Black left England to join her parents in South Africa shortly afterwards, from where she resumed the correspondence two years later.

Black married the South African poet Vincent Swart in 1939, but they were divorced two years later and she subsequently remarried. Speaking of her affair with Aldington to David Wilkinson in 1982, she recalled:

> [W]hen he arrived, you know, for me it was like Apollo descending – as you can imagine, you know, this famous author and all the rest of it you see. And then – we were always apart from each other. There was a long gap when Richard had gone to America . . . and I'd gone to South Africa when we didn't write at all.[53]

In London in October 1932, Aldington gave her an introduction to Arlen (then staying at the Mayfair Hotel), thinking that he might have contacts which would help her find a job. (Gaumont Pictures had made her redundant.) In the interview with Wilkinson, Black recalled that

Arlen, noticing how infatuated with Aldington she was, 'tried very gently and swiftly to put [her] off', explaining that Aldington's relationship with Patmore was 'forever'.

Aldington's preoccupation with the technicalities of physical sex, and particularly with childhood sex and sexuality, is displayed not only in his correspondence with Black and Pollard, but also in his novels, where George Winterbourne in *Death of a Hero* and Anthony Clarendon in *All Men Are Enemies* are given childhood sexual encounters similar to Aldington's own but presented in a much more idealised fashion.[54] He told Black (now Gluckman) nearly 30 years later that it was only in adulthood that he began to retrieve memories of these encounters and to realise 'what an active sex-life [he] lived in those pre-puberty years'. He saw – or claimed to see – these experiences in a positive light, but his memories of his sexual initiation by a nurse and two older girl cousins over a period of several years, as related in detail in these later letters to Gluckman, strike the reader as accounts of child sexual abuse. 'From those experiences I am sure,' he told her, 'stem the lusts and satisfactions – and disappointments – of a lifetime.'[55] It is difficult not to see them, rather, as a root cause of the imbalance in adulthood between his sensual and emotional instincts and even the failure of each of his long-term relationships. To quote the letter to Patmore mentioned earlier, this was a childhood spent 'learning – not to love – but to fuck'. That it was only in adulthood that he began to retrieve these memories is also an indication of the confusion, and even guilt, that he had experienced over much of his childhood. In both *Death of a Hero* and *All Men Are Enemies*, as well as in his correspondence with Gluckman, he attempted to deal with those memories in such a way as to normalise the experiences and cast them in a positive light.

A broader survey of his childhood suggests his family life, and particularly his relationship with his mother, as a further cause of these long-term difficulties. In particular, as has already been noted in the earlier volume of this biography, Aldington's mother seems to have practised a dubious sexual code, on the one hand aspiring to middle-class respectability, on the other entering into extramarital relationships, which, if not full-blown affairs, were satisfyingly risqué and served to humiliate Aldington's father.[56] The portrait of George's mother in *Death of a Hero* conducting 'affairs with bounderish young men' seems to have been based on actuality, if we can trust Ursula Bloom's account of her visits to the family and if we take into account May Aldington's relationship with Vivian Watkins, who became her second husband.[57] It is also slightly disturbing to read in Aldington's account of his sexual initiation by his nursemaid that his first sight of her naked body had not 'startled' him because he had seen his mother's on several occasions.[58] The sensuality of his mother's nature, combined as it was with materialism, hypocrisy, and a sentimentality which is evident in her novels, was something Aldington grew up despising. However, as Dorothy Yorke discerned, when she told Walter and Lilian Lowenfels that 'Richard spent his life trying to get away from the mother in him and to attain the father in him', both the sensuality and the sentimentality were traits that he inherited.[59]

The affairs with Pollard and Black were not the first since the beginning of Aldington's relationship with Patmore. As early as 1930 he had begun a secret affair with the novelist Irene Rathbone. Like Pollard and Black, Rathbone initially contacted him to express her admiration for his work – in this instance *Death of a Hero* and *A Dream in the Luxembourg*. He read the manuscript of Rathbone's semi-autobiographical war novel, *We That Were Young,* and attempted to persuade Prentice to publish it. Prentice was not enthusiastic, although Chatto would eventually publish the novel in 1932, after another publisher had taken it on and then gone out of business.

As always, Aldington's support for a friend was wholehearted. At the time of the publishing collapse in 1931 which denied Rathbone's novel its audience, he wrote in the *Referee*:

> It seems to me extraordinary that such a novel should have been rejected by several publishers and even now remains without a publisher. It is written from an intense personal experience with a wonderful sympathy for the lives and sufferings of others. . . . [A] book which wrote itself, something which simply had to be expressed. The people are ordinary enough, but they are alive, and the genuine pathos of some of the scenes is heart-rending. It is a frank and honest book and expresses in its own way the strange and lamentable tragedy of modern England.[60]

On 18 September 1930 Aldington informed MacGreevy that, as he needed time to work on *The Colonel's Daughter*, he had suggested that Patmore and Derek go to Toulon or Marseilles until Derek's return to London. 'So I shall probably be alone for about a week,' he concluded, although extending an invitation to MacGreevy to join him – an invitation that he must have felt certain MacGreevy, only recently returned to Paris from the villa, would decline. That week was spent in the company of Rathbone, whom he had invited to visit him from London. It was their first meeting.

Irene Rathbone, 1933

What we know of that week we learn from an 800-line, free-verse narrative poem, *Was There a Summer?* (clearly modelled on *A Dream in the Luxembourg*) that Rathbone wrote in 1937.[61] Her description of their first meeting is reminiscent of Black's account:

> He stood in front of me, sunbeams about his head
> And smiled through the midst of them.
> I thought a god was there.

Rathbone's infatuation with Aldington, however, was the infatuation of a mature woman – she was the same age as him – and a fellow writer, and it would not fade with the years. She never married – partly because her fiancé died in 1920, but also because she spent her mature years as her parents' carer, dividing her time between the family home in Chipping Campden and an apartment in London. Her love for Aldington and her gratitude – and pain – for the short time they spent together never diminished, as is evident from her letters years later to Morgan and Cunard.[62]

The poem describes, in a very similar vein to *A Dream in the Luxembourg*, the routines of those days at the villa. Rathbone stayed in a nearby hotel (her bill paid by Aldington), walking over to the villa in the late morning, when Aldington had completed his work for the day. Their time was spent swimming, sunbathing, lunching, making love, talking about poetry and 'old loves, old losses, regrets, hopes', and sitting on the terrace in the warm Mediterranean night. According to the poem, as the idyll came to an end, Aldington gave Rathbone his reassurance that he would come to London when the summer was over. The poem tells us:

> He did not return
>
> . . .
>
> There was a letter from him – a dear letter – one
> Then no more ever.
> And I heard from someone who knew him
> That he had gone far off
> Farther south still than that coast
> To.. . . It does not matter.
> I was told, too, that he was not alone.

What it does not tell us is that there were two summers. In May 1931, she wrote c/o Chatto to congratulate him on *The Colonel's Daughter*. 'You must have had a heavenly time in Italy,' she comments, with only a hint of reproach for the broken promise. At the end of the letter she adds: 'If I said anything to you last summer that seemed annoying – or excessive – please believe that I am sorry. It was unintentional.'[63] On 5 September Aldington told Prentice that Rathbone had 'turned up' at La Cavalière and that Patmore and Derek had gone to Cannes for a few days. That the poem is an amalgam of the two visits is clear from an account of driving to a mountain village 'in his battered sort of a car' to spend a night together. (Aldington only learned to drive and purchased his own car early in 1931.)

The poem was written after the affair had ended and it is clear that the effect of its ending was devastating for Rathbone, although she would not blame Aldington:

I have been blind with pain
But then
Blind almost with bliss too;
And it is a thing to accept
That the men who are the joy-bringers
Are inevitably the grief-bringers.
It is not their fault. Why should I call him faithless
Because his wings are not pinioned?
Because others beside myself are sung to?
. . .
. . . and if that self in me – that other who bleeds – cries:
Songless your life now
Starless and fooled you go
I shall not say it's a falsehood;
Only
Only that its opposite is also true.

In her succeeding novels the male heroes resemble Aldington in some respect – whether it be appearance, calling as a writer, beliefs and opinions, or a combination of these features – and many of the narratives carry poignant echoes of her experience. In *October* Jenny avoids the Luxembourg Gardens because of Gilbert:

who would have sprung to life once more, imploring her to write, making her promise to, swearing that he would write himself, that there should be no real break, that letters would keep their love alive, and that they would meet – abroad or in London – at intervals, for always. . . . Gilbert . . . whose work she had fallen in love with before ever she had met him.[64]

In *They Call It Peace* (dedicated to Aldington) when Joan is abandoned by Paul, her married lover (and a writer), she reflects:

A man 'walked out on you'. Right! But not cleanly and for ever. How could he? – someone who had been part of you? – who *was* you? Nor could you let him. There was such a thing as wisdom, friends said, such a thing as pride. They didn't know. . . . Actually there was no wisdom, no pride. Only love.[65]

In fact, Aldington did not 'walk out' altogether on Rathbone. The poignancy of *Was There a Summer?* is as sharp as it is because he had only just left her life for good when she wrote it in 1937. Her diaries and his letters to her – which she kept throughout her life – were destroyed on her death in 1980 by her niece and literary executor, Patricia Utechin; but Utechin, in conversation with Lynn Knight, when the latter was preparing a new edition of *We That Were Young* in the late 1980s, told Knight that Aldington had continued the affair with Rathbone through furtive visits whenever he was in London until his hasty departure for America at the end of 1936.[66] Rathbone's poem was an outpouring of her grief at this abandonment.

She wrote to Cunard in 1953: '[Richard] was not (you have probably concluded) my only lover; he was the one, though, who made the sharpest, deepest impact on me, gave me the most delight & the worst suffering.'[67]

9. The Private Life
Meltdown
1936-1937

On 10 August 1935 the 24-year-old Michael Patmore was married to 23-year-old Netta McCulloch in St John the Baptist Church in Pinner, Middlesex. His mother and her partner were unable to attend as they were in Connecticut. His brother was also in the United States, preparing his autumn exhibition at Altman's department store in New York.

Aldington and Patmore must have met with Michael and his new bride on their return to London in mid-October. Another young couple of whom they saw a great deal were Eric and Violet Warman. Aldington also made one new acquaintance and picked up another from the past. The new friendship was with C.P. Snow, whom he visited in Cambridge on several occasions. In his memoir, *Stranger and Brother*, Philip Snow recalls Aldington's first visit: 'He was outstandingly handsome, the most impressive-looking writer I was ever to know. . . . During the weekend he stayed with Charles his stock grew with us. He was gentlemanly; this need not have followed from his rough war experiences starkly described in *Death of a Hero*.'[1] The problematic relationship between art and science, which Snow would publicly debate 23 years later, was already a concern to Aldington, and the two men had much to discuss.[2] Aldington would contribute an article, 'Science and Conscience', to the journal *Discovery*, of which Snow became editor in 1937;[3] and it was Snow to whom Frere would turn in 1938 for *Richard Aldington: An Appreciation*, the pamphlet issued by Heinemann to accompany new editions of Aldington's novels.

Alec Waugh was the friend with whom an acquaintance was renewed. He and Aldington had met sporadically over the years since their first encounter at the Poetry Bookshop in 1919, but their more recent friendship had been occasioned by a scoffing remark about *The Eaten Heart* by Beachcomber of the *Daily Express* in 1934.[4] Coming across this, Waugh had obtained a copy of the poem, then one of *A Dream in the*

Luxembourg, both of which confirmed the opinion he had expressed in 1919 that Aldington was a fine love poet.[5] He wrote to him and over the next three years they met whenever Aldington was in London.

By April 1936, when he and Patmore set off for Portugal, Spain, France and Austria in the company of the Glovers, Aldington had completed 60,000 words of what would become *Very Heaven* and had had the approval of both Prentice and Raymond. The title is drawn from the lines in *The Prelude* in which Wordsworth celebrates the early days of the French Revolution: 'Bliss was it in that dawn to be alive/ But to be young was very heaven!'[6] With reference to the life of Chris Heylin, Aldington's protagonist, these lines are tinged with irony. Aldington worked on the novel throughout his travels and completed it during his two-and-a-half-month stay in Austria.

Very Heaven is the story of a young man in the postwar world who is forced, as a result of his father's financial losses, to give up his undergraduate life and make his way in the world without qualifications for any kind of employment. In the final pages of the novel, overcome with a sense of guilt and unworthiness and in despair at the state of the world around him, Chris determines to throw himself off a Portuguese clifftop. However, the sight of a butterfly caught in the wind on the rocks below him but wafted up to safety triggers his reflections on the place of the individual in the chain of life, a passage that recalls the final section of *Life Quest* (and Lawrence's *Apocalypse*):

On the edge of barren land and barren sea under the same sun, life was born. For millions of centuries life has struggled and perished under these three great powers. Yet it has always been passed on. The salt of the sea is in my blood, the radiance of the sun and the chemicals of earth in my cells. In all that unimaginable stretch of time what an infinity of chances against my ever existing! One broken link in that tremendous chain of life, and I could never have been. And I exist.

The novel ends with Chris walking away from the clifftop towards the little town, trusting in the human capacity for progress. 'And if the whole adventure does fail,' he concludes, 'at least we shall have had the exultation of the attempt.'[7]

The novel is flawed by the weight of the ideas it has to carry. The protagonist is treated sympathetically and with some humorous critique of his youthful naivety and earnestness, but he also has to act as a mouthpiece for the author. In consequence, he engages in lengthy discourses, either with himself or delivered to other characters, and these are supported by further passages of exposition in the authorial voice. The targets are the usual ones: the older generation, materialism and greed, bourgeois codes of ethics (particularly sexual ethics), Christianity, militarism and the state of international politics; but no opportunity is missed to deliver the messages. This is particularly noticeable in the representation of the characters, many of whom are little more than caricatures. Even those with 'walk-on' parts are used in this way, for example a young university acquaintance of Chris who is 'an intelligent Catholic aesthete with a tendency to fascism' or a police sergeant who is 'one of those bluff hearty fellows who stand no nonsense from agitators – of the Left'.[8] The young female characters, like those in *Death of a Hero* and *All Men Are Enemies*, are either enchanting, insipid or controlling.

As in *Death of a Hero*, the portraits of the protagonist's parents are damning. Chris's father's incompetence has led to the family's financial downfall, for which he evades responsibility, retiring to his bed and leaving his son to sort out the mess. However, there is a moving scene towards the end of the novel where Chris has to identify his father's body, a duty Aldington himself had been forced into undertaking. At the time he had written to Frank Flint: 'For me the dead are yellow faces, pools of blood, muddy khaki, hurried burials under shell-fire. . . . I became addicted to wholesale death; so retail death, although it touches me closely, cannot move me greatly'; but the account in *Very Heaven* prompts us to think otherwise.[9]

Nell Heylin, Chris's mother, is an ignorant and grasping materialist, pushing her daughter into a loveless marriage to improve the family's financial prospects, preoccupied with her and her family's social standing and possessed of a love of drama and a sentimentality which includes her conviction that she 'can read [her] own son like a book': 'Nobody can understand a boy as his mother does.'[10] She is drawn with a savagery even greater than that employed in the portrait of Isabel Winterbourne, suggesting that the intervening seven years had done nothing to diminish Aldington's contempt for his mother.

During his travels he told several correspondents that he intended to be on the Continent until September and then to visit Japan, but this plan seems to have been abandoned by late August when he informed Bacon that, after all, he would be spending the winter in 'smoky London' in order, he said, to write another novel.[11] An undated entry in one of Patmore's personal notebooks gives us a clue as to the real reason for the change of plan. The entry tells us that she and Aldington had opened and read the mail that was awaiting them at a French village which they had given as a poste restante and that she had recognised her daughter-in-law's handwriting on one of the envelopes addressed to Aldington. It was their habit to exchange their letters after they had read them, but she did not find the one from her daughter-in-law amongst those he gave her. When she enquired about it, he silently passed it to her; reading it, she experienced 'a curious gasping pain' around her heart.[12]

It is hard to know exactly what happened after the return to London and the Cavendish Hotel on 1 October, but the events were dramatic – and agonising for those affected. First, Aldington seems to have had a major dispute with Chatto, such that he instructed Pinker to terminate his contract and arrange the transfer of all publishing rights to Heinemann – just as *Very Heaven* was going through the editing stage. The letters exchanged between Pinker, Raymond and Frere show the cordial relations between these three parties – and their utter puzzlement, embarrassment and consternation. Pinker informed the other two that Aldington was so enraged with Chatto that he could not bear to correspond with the company and wanted Pinker to conduct all the negotiations.[13] Frere wrote to Raymond: 'I had talks with Richard, who was emotionally upset and deranged, but was also both determined and adamant. . . . I want to thank you personally for being so damned decent about the whole thing.'[14]

Chatto were compliant, agreeing to release Aldington from his contracts if the company could come to 'a reasonable arrangement' with Heinemann regarding his already-published work.[15] '[W]e have worked hard over Richard's work for more than seven years and it goes without saying that he is a very considerable asset to our list,' Raymond wrote to Pinker, estimating a figure of £3,100, which included £1,000 for Chatto's loss of profits on the existing publications, particularly the eight titles in the Phoenix Library. He concluded: 'This is a very laconic letter, I fear. You know how we must be feeling about all this. But I don't think there is anything to be gained by protestation. One can only accept the situation.'[16]

Of course, Prentice's retirement from Chatto had been a disappointment to Aldington, but his relationship with Raymond had always been a good one, and Raymond and his wife Vera had visited Aldington and Patmore in France on at least one occasion, as well as socialising with them in London. Aldington's correspondence with Parsons, the other Chatto director, with whom he had dealings whenever Raymond was on holiday, had always been cordial.

There had been two slightly awkward exchanges between Raymond and Aldington when the latter returned from America in the autumn of 1935, fired up – as he had had no ideas for a new novel since *Women Must Work* in 1934 – with Doubleday's suggestion of a book on the Borgias and still keen to have *Life of a Lady* published. Raymond had 'declined' to publish the play: 'We don't feel it is worthy of you. . . . I can't seem to find a whiff of R.A. in it.'[17] About the Borgia book, he had been discouraging. 'The slump, combined with the general pursuit of the bestseller, has dealt a heavy blow to any serious work of non-fiction,' he had told Aldington, adding that the outline the latter had provided might make the book 'a trifle episodic', 'a fact which we think accounts more than anything else for the disappointing sales and reviews of *Artifex*'.[18]

By January 1936, however, the Borgias abandoned, Aldington was communicating excitedly with Raymond about the early stages of *Very Heaven*. He thanked Raymond for Chatto's forbearance during what he called his 'ghastly interregnum', which he blamed on his accident and the subsequent operations. He had, he said, only felt fully recovered in the last month, but was delighted to be able to inform Raymond that he had already written 5,000 words of a new novel and even had an idea for another. 'Only Charles and Brigit know that I've got off the mark again,' he wrote, 'but I feel you ought to know because of the subsidy, and because you are you!'[19]

Writing to his friend Alister Kershaw twelve years later, Aldington described Raymond as 'a chump' but called Parsons 'an excretum of purest ray serene, and my reason for leaving [Chatto]'.[20] Quite what had caused his objection to Parsons we do not know – but the fall-out was massive. Whatever the cause of the rupture, Aldington became a Heinemann author. It was an acquisition about which Frere would have cause to be ambivalent over the next two decades. Reconciling the conflicting demands of his professional and his personal relationships with Aldington would prove wearing. That this had never been the case where Prentice was concerned may be due to the fact that the latter had been Aldington's publisher before he was his friend. On the other hand, it may tell us more about the personalities involved: Prentice was a tolerant and gentle man; both Aldington and Frere were made of more explosive material.

* * *

Frere was called on to play a part in the even more dramatic and agonising events that were taking place in Aldington's personal life. Aldington had begun an affair with Netta Patmore, Michael's new wife. He told H.D. in January 1937 that the affair had been going on for over a year.[21] This means that it must have started not long after his return from America in the autumn of 1935 – and only a few months after Netta's marriage. H.D. encountered the pair on one occasion in a London teashop ('The Nell Gwynne' she noted ironically). She subsequently told Jessie Capper that Netta had seemed very young: 'a slight little thing with no hat, no vamp, little if any make-up, a nicely tailored little dark costume, rather on the tiny, petite side'.[22]

There seems to have come a moment when Aldington decided that this would not be yet another affair and that he must marry Netta. She, meanwhile, had to choose between the two men – or retain Aldington as an extramarital lover. He proposed that they run off to America. On 5 December 1936 he wrote a long letter to Pat and Frere, arranging for them to meet Netta and himself for lunch. He acknowledged difficulties: the 20-year age gap; his sense that she admired him as a writer rather than as a man; and her affection for Michael. Brigit's feelings are not mentioned. What he does say is that he feels 'utterly married' to Netta and that this is a feeling he has never experienced before. (We might recall his telling Brigit in 1930 that he felt 'married' to her.)[23] He concludes, melodramatically: 'I died in 1916, and came alive again in 1936. And it's damned painful, for I don't know whether I am coming or going.'[24] This statement implies that it had taken him 20 years to recover from his wartime experiences and that the relationships of the intervening years were somehow aberrant.

Netta, it appears, did not want to hurt either Brigit or Michael. Aldington had always believed that Michael, like Derek, was gay. He told Frere: 'If she's really in love with the pansy, it's a god-awful tragedy.'[25] He subsequently told H.D. that 'the marriage with Michael was not a real one – you know what I mean'.[26] It is possible that the physical aspect of the marriage had proved unfulfilling; Netta does not seem to have contradicted Aldington's views on this matter. We need to note here, however, that Michael Patmore would remarry in 1940 and have two children.

Aldington decided that, with or without Netta, he would go to America. There were what he referred to in a letter to H.D. as 'terrible scenes with Brigit and Michael'.[27] On 16 December Netta told him that she would not leave Michael and, in an undated, hand-delivered letter explaining her decision, wrote: 'I don't want to leave Micky more than I want to lose you. . . . If it weren't for the "tangled web" and loving Micky, your passion would be pure glory.'[28] From the SS *Normandie*, bound for New York, Aldington wrote Pat and Frere another long letter. He told them:

> I loved and, alas, still love that girl more than anyone in my life; for a time I was nearer to her than to any human being; and until Wednesday I trusted her utterly. But how can one go on trusting a woman who allows a dagger to be put into her hands, with careful instructions, and who uses it ruthlessly? She accused me of pride when I refused the position of spare-time lover and sugar-daddy. What the hell else has she left me? . . . I thought I had found, indeed I had found, someone with whom I was in complete harmony, with whom there was no necessity for defences. That made me so damnably and ridiculously vulnerable.[29]

The reference to 'instructions' and the implication of betrayal suggest that Michael and Brigit had had a hand in Netta's decision. Much of the letter is concerned with professional matters: he was correcting the proofs of *Very Heaven*; but he concludes: 'My first business is to learn to stand quite alone in life, and for that these five days of solitude at sea are useful.'

Arriving in New York, he was met by Malcolm Johnson and driven to the Doubledays' mansion in South Carolina. They were welcoming and hospitable, but Ellen Doubleday wrote to Patmore, expressing their regret that she was 'slipping out' of their lives. As Aldington's American publisher, Doubleday had little choice. 'Oh, Brigit, my dear, my heart does ache for you and Michael and my mind is nearly bewildered,' Ellen wrote. 'I can only send my love and tell you if some sorrow comes to me I pray to meet it as you do.'[30]

Writing to Slonimsky from the Doubleday home on 2 January, Aldington was less than frank. Arranging to meet his friend in New York, he told him that the Doubledays had issued a 'general invitation' and that he had 'suddenly decided' to come over for Christmas. 'Brigit is staying in London with the boys,' he ended.[31] The proposed meeting would not take place. A cable arrived at the Doubleday residence three days later: Netta had changed her mind. On 7 January Aldington set off from South Carolina to board SS *Lafayette*, bound for Plymouth, telling Slonimsky that he had been suddenly called back to England on 'urgent affairs'.[32]

On board the *Lafayette*, he was bombarded by telegrams from Netta, telling him how 'crazy with impatience and love' she was and that she would meet him in Plymouth.[33] To judge from a letter Patmore wrote to the Warmans, the Freres had had a hand in the matter. Telling the Warmans that Aldington had left her '& not just with "another woman"' but with her son's wife, Patmore continued:

> Michael has been terribly run-down with overwork & trying to steer her through all sorts of emotional strains. She said up to the last moment – i.e. Thursday [7 January] – that Michael was the one she loved & that she was taking him away to a cottage in Dorset where they'd both been so happy. Then on that morning, Frere-Reeves of Heinemann's rang her up & arranged for her to go somewhere the next day & R. was going to meet her – straight back from USA. Until Frere-Reeves came into the affair things might have settled into some order, but he's just pushed them into it – violently.[34]

Whether or not the Freres had taken the initiative, they had certainly picked Netta up from her home in Dorset Square once she had decided to leave Michael, and she was their guest until her departure for Plymouth. Aldington felt indebted. 'I can't ever thank you for what you've done and are doing. You have literally made this possible & thereby really saved my life. I'll never forget this,' he wrote to them as, reunited with Netta, he set off for France. 'I must have those divorces,' he added, 'It's a damn crime if we don't have a child.'[35]

This desire is echoed in a letter to H.D. (the first communication between them for five years), written five days earlier from on board the *Lafayette*: 'We want to marry and have a child. . . . If you will set me free to marry her, I shall bless you indeed.' He painted a picture of rescuing Netta from an 'angel in the house' existence: 'With me she can live the adventurer's life for which she was born.' He told H.D. that he was giving Brigit part of his income and added: 'It is horrible to have to hurt other people.' Echoing Anthony Clarendon in *All Men Are Enemies*, he wrote: 'Dooley, I trust you. I felt you ought to know about this.

Forgive me if anything in this letter gives you pain. Lovers are selfish. They have to be. The world is against them. Don't be against us. Let us have our life together.'[36]

Characteristically, H.D. was excited by the drama, writing immediately to tell Plank what had happened:

> I had a thunder-bolt by way of letter from RA. . . . I am perfectly willing to do this + am consulting experts to see if divorce is feasible, but psychically I fear a catch + think the state of Denmark pretty rotten. . . . [Brigit] is apparently on the war path + frankly, to me, the whole thing looks tricky + shady to a degree, not to mention incest. . . . My mind is cold like ice but my heart thumps when I even think of it – can't sleep . . . what 'doings'.[37]

Bryher, of course, was delighted: 'I do hope you manage to go through with it. Far better once and for all to be rid of dear Cuthbert.'[38]

'Cuthbert' meanwhile was in Brantôme with Netta, from where he wrote to Orioli, telling him that he hoped to bring Netta to meet him – and Douglas – in February. The letter ends: 'Dear Pino, I'm so happy, I hope you'll be happy with us.'[39] Like the letter to H.D., it is an appeal for support. Brigit and Michael were also travelling and she, too, was calling on the understanding of friends. In the letter to the Warmans she explained that she and Michael had felt they must get away. Surprisingly perhaps, given what must have been painful memories of the Riviera, they were at the Hotel Beau Rivage in Nice. She told the Warmans:

> It would be easier to bear if it had been anyone else & Michael too feels that but for his wife I'd still be happy – and you can understand all that. But in a way, it's good for me to be HERE to show him that there's a life even better than one had always ahead.

The rest of the letter concerns the divorce proceedings that might ensue and it is clear that there has already been an argument between themselves and Aldington in which the latter had indicated that Netta would sue on the grounds of non-consummation, while Michael would only proceed on the grounds of Netta's adultery. 'How can I possibly ask [Michael] to take the blame?' Patmore asked the Warmans. 'He's too young to spoil his life in that way. . . . It's strange to have to protect my son's name in connection with the fair name of someone I thought was my husband – I mean that in its deepest and most enduring sense.' 'I fear we've spoiled a sort of ideal for you,' she told the couple, continuing: 'I wonder what I did that was so very wrong. In a way, Mickie's burden is more than mine because he can't believe that R. would do this to him – he's got two deceptions.'

This sense of responsibility for the events surfaces again in the personal notebook mentioned previously:

> My own finding is that while not exactly regretting having loved, my remorse is for having loved without wisdom. It seems now to me that my failure was in greatness and strength. I loved in a fervour of worship and a fear of loss which took away all possibility of wise behaviour, for I was cold and hid my real feelings when they ought to have flared out, & then not become emotional & verbose when a smiling silence would have arranged things very nicely.[40]

One of the few photographs of the couple during their 'Riviera years' endorses this perspective on the relationship: Aldington faces the camera cheerfully and confidently, his arm around Patmore; she looks up at him with a gaze full of anxiety. She told H.G. Wells, one of the friends to whom she turned:

> Apart from the natural desire for youth & change & the rather pitiful desire for a child there are in Richard the almost universal ache to make others suffer what one has endured in one's own life & a complicated hidden anger with me for not being as beastly to my sons as his mother was to him.[41]

It is a harsh judgement but its location of the source of Aldington's behaviour in his childhood is perceptive.

The astounding feature of the events is not so much the end of Aldington's relationship with Patmore – although there are very few hints in the correspondence (despite the evidence of his other affairs) that all was not well between them – but Aldington's determination, first to conduct an affair with, and then to marry, her daughter-in-law.

Derek Patmore remarks in his introduction to his mother's memoirs that *All Men Are Enemies* (published in 1933) symbolised 'the apex' of Aldington's love for Patmore. 'Although it took several years before this love affair broke up, it foreshadowed the tragedy to come,' he wrote.[42] What led to the deterioration of the relationship can only be speculation, but the restlessness of their existence in its later years and

Richard Aldington and Brigit Patmore in the south of France in the mid-1930s

the consequent loosening of ties with their closest friends, leading to comparative isolation, may well have been a contributory factor. Not that they were without a social life on those travels: Derek Patmore recalls how charming and hospitable their neighbours in Connecticut had been and how, on his weekend visits from New York, they had enjoyed 'picnics with neighbours and small evening reunions'.[43] These, however, were no substitute for the close – and shared – friendships with Prentice and MacGreevy, and even – for a couple of years – with Douglas and Orioli. Only the friendship with the Warmans had seemed to offer a possible replacement. The Glovers, of course, had been their closest companions in the later years but towards the end, particularly in the period they spent together in Austria over the summer of 1936, that friendship had made heavy demands on them.

Alec Waugh's memoirs contain some penetrating observations about how this state of affairs had come about. He describes finding, when he met up with Aldington in 1934, that the latter was living with 'a widow rather older than himself'.[44] His description of Patmore is complimentary: 'She was red-haired and extremely handsome; it was obvious that she had been a very great beauty in her youth. She was still most attractive. . . . Hers and Aldington's had clearly been a high romance.' Then Waugh adds: 'One said to oneself, "The disparity of age. How long will it last?"'

He realised, in retrospect, he says, that, during the three years of their friendship in London (1934-1936), he had never seen Aldington 'against the background of his personal life': 'He was either my guest, or the guest of someone else, of Douglas Goldring, at least once.' 'It is my belief,' he continues, 'that he was one of those men who cannot be bothered to organise a social life, who socially live from hand to mouth, making the most of what happens to be around.' While this does not match our knowledge of the life the couple led in the south of France in the summers of 1930, 1931 and 1933, it does apply to the periods they spent in Italy and in London and, in particular, to the later years. They had no settled home – eventually living in a London hotel.

Waugh goes on to argue that it was because Aldington 'left things to chance' in this way, that he 'found confusion in his private life'. The following passage is worth quoting in full:

> I think the nature of that collapse [of the relationship with Patmore] was determined by Aldington's indifference to the organisation of a personal life. Most men, *l'homme moyen sensual*, manage to conduct their *passades* so that they do not impair irretrievably the fabric of their domesticity. They do not make love to their wife's best friend. They maintain appearances. I do not say that this is an admirable characteristic, but it is a social lubricant. Aldington, like Shelley, within the narrow limits of his domestic circle, stumbled,

Alec Waugh, October 1937

unknowingly, unwittingly into confusion. He fell in love with his consort's daughter-in-law. Could anything be more humiliating for a woman than to have a lover younger than herself desert her for her son's wife: and to become the father of that woman's daughter? Yet, let anyone who feels censorious read Aldington's *The Crystal*

World. It is a fine and noble poem. It is not an apologia. It says quite simply, 'When this happens, when this ultimate mystery is revealed, there is no alternative but to accept it.'[45]

Of course, Aldington himself would see 'maintaining appearances' as Victorian hypocrisy. Nevertheless, it was how he had managed his relationship with Patmore alongside his affairs with Black and Rathbone. *The Crystal World*, the poem he wrote for Netta over the next few months (just as he had written *Reverie* for H.D., *Images of Desire* for Yorke, *A Dream in the Luxembourg* for Dobrée and *The Eaten Heart* for Patmore) was not, as Waugh points out, 'an apologia'. He wrote:

> You see for them it is not enough
> To have a biological affair –
> Which would be quite easy –
> Or to meet as intimate friends,
> Which would be even easier.
> You have here two passionate natures
> Unable to compromise
> Under the smug winking of the hypocrite world.
> They must have everything,
> Must share each day and night,
> Must grow together closer, closer
> And build their crystal world.[46]

The poem provides a further clue to his conduct. The narrative follows his courtship of Netta and at the point where the poet thinks that he and his lover have parted for good, a section of the poem is addressed to the child they will never have. At the end of this section, he turns to the dead of the Great War:

> O comrades lying in the fields of France,
> Strange is our fate; childless like me you died;
> For us the coloured flame of love fades out,
> The million generations have an end,
> The ship of life sinks in a dusty sea.

The letters he wrote to Frere and to H.D. that are quoted above both indicate that having a child was an important element of his vision of a life with Netta; this passage from the poem shows that fatherhood was something he now craved. Patmore could not give him a child, as Derek explains in his introduction to her memoirs.[47] This would not have been a concern for her; she already had two much-loved sons. However, two of Aldington's closest friends were now fathers or would-be fathers: the Warmans' daughter, Jean, was now four years old; and Pat and Frere were about to become parents.[48]

Setting aside the desire for a child, we have seen a similar pattern of behaviour on several occasions in Aldington's past: in his determination to persist in the affair with Yorke; in his angry parting from H.D.; in his pursuit of Dobrée; and in his abandonment of Yorke. His childhood years and early relationships were complicated and troubled ones. In a settled relationship with H.D. in his twenties he might have been able to resolve the resultant emotional tensions. Two events made that impossible: one was the stillbirth of their child, for which he had never allowed himself to grieve and which destroyed the sexual side of their marriage; the other was the war. Both events served to complicate the tensions already within him. The remark he made to Frere in 1935 ('I have been surprised to find how bitterly I still resent things I thought I had long ago dealt with and forgotten') demonstrated his awareness of the problem. In several of his relationships – with Eliot, Read and the *Criterion* set for example – we see behaviour suggestive of low self-esteem and an inability to accept criticism, the inheritance of that troubled childhood. The writing of *Death of a Hero* and *Roads to Glory* had helped him to come to terms with the war bitterness and trauma – although they would never be entirely resolved – but even the savage representation of his parents and his family life in the former of these – and more recently in *Very Heaven* – had hardly begun to relieve him of this burden.

The travelling years were not so much a cause of the breakdown of his relationship with Patmore, although they may well have been a factor, as a symptom of his inability to resolve his inner chaos. Only excitement and constant change could distract him from that painful process; and by these means it was postponed. Travel acted as work had done in the 1920s, as a means of avoidance. However, once the genie had come out of the bottle in Tobago, it could not be put back. Writing *Very Heaven* only succeeded in making him reflect further and even more painfully and bitterly on the confusions and humiliations of his childhood and youth. The affair with Netta bolstered his self-esteem at this difficult time, given both her admiration for him and his own sense that he was a more worthy partner for her than Michael Patmore. It also displayed all the characteristics of his previous sexual behaviour during the war and its aftermath and at the end of the twenties when he was struggling to contain the chaos within: the infatuations, the obsessiveness, the ruthlessness. Between those two major eruptions, and in the more recent period of his life with Patmore, minor affairs – Capper, Black and Rathbone – had served to keep the demons at bay. This time, however, as in 1919 and 1929, only the complete destruction of his current life would serve.

Whatever the cause, he was now embarked on his fourth long-term relationship. As for Patmore, even in June 1938 she was writing to Morgan: 'I'm so glad you think I look all right. Half of me wants to die and the other half knows it's got to live decently – and therefore beautifully.'[49] In a letter to Gluckman 25 years later, Aldington would call Patmore 'a very sweet and good woman whom I still love in retrospect', but the intervening years were to see a bitter and relentless battle between them over the financial settlement made at their separation.[50]

Part Two

The Exile

1937-1950

10. Divorce
1937-1938

The new relationship, with its aims of marriage and parenthood, necessitated two divorces. Although the H.D.-Aldington divorce (on the grounds of his adultery) would go smoothly and without acrimony, it caused H.D. a great deal of anxiety. She had spent much of the 1930s in analysis, as she explained to Capper:

> [I]t is a strange fatality that I should get my inner life clear with such excruciating pain (the analytical work) only just as I am recovering from that, to have another sort of search light trained on me. . . . It is a terrible thing to go back twenty years, especially as it seems all that happened yesterday.[1]

Like Aldington, she saw the war as having had a devastating effect on her subsequent development: '[T]hat is what the war did to us, took away our youth and gave us eternal youth.' She added, with humour (and perceptiveness): 'Richard acts as if he had arrested development, though, I must say.' On Bryher's advice, she went back into analysis.

Her lengthy 'Petitioner's Statement' detailed the story of her marriage and separation and of events over the subsequent years. She knew she was treading a minefield but, no doubt with advice from the shrewd and practical Bryher, she negotiated it. She confessed to her affair with Gray (although making clear that this was fleeting, and subsequent to Aldington's affair with Yorke) and to his parentage of Perdita; she said that 'apart from two or three accidental meetings' she had not seen Aldington since their separation in 1919 nor (and this was true) received any financial support from him. She had, she said, gone to live with her mother in Switzerland until the latter's departure for the United States in 1926 and death a year later. (She thus skirted the issue of the relationship between herself and Bryher.) She explained why she had not filed a divorce claim sooner: 'I was afraid it might entail harmful publicity for my daughter and I was also afraid I might fail because of my own misconduct.' In an earlier – and even lengthier – account written for her solicitor she admitted that, although there was nothing in her conduct 'over the last five or six years' which could appear 'incorrect', there might have been occasions in the three years following her mother's departure for the United States 'that would possibly have been open to criticism'[2].

The Statement referred to her weak state of health after the stillbirth of 1915 and to Aldington's excessive sexual demands, to his conduct of his affair with Yorke and his rage over the registration of Perdita's birth. It also stressed that Yorke, Patmore, and now Netta Patmore had all 'passed off' as 'Mrs Aldington'. In notes she wrote at the time she remarked: 'Arabella was Mrs A. of course. Everybody is Mrs A. It is a sort of Greek chorus. I suppose I might be presumed to be leader of the chorus, who has been asked to step out (vide Richard's letter) to play before the fall of the curtain, the Deus ex machina.' She saw the latest development as another play: The Seagull, with Michael Patmore as Konstantin, Netta as Nina, Brigit as Irina Arkadina, Aldington as Trigorin – and herself as the seagull.[3]

To Capper, who had always felt sympathy for Yorke, she wrote: 'I am truly sorry about Arabella, she was let down badly'; but, adding a sting in the tail as she was wont to do, she remarked: 'But who of us has not been?'[4] Yorke would be cited as co-respondent, and Capper would be the witness. Barbara Guest tells us: 'What happened was that H.D. began simultaneously to suffer from and to enjoy the fancy drama of the forsaken wife who now controlled the fate of the negligent husband. H.D. may have made malicious remarks, but she did not behave maliciously. It was simply not her way.'[5]

Michael Patmore's plea for divorce from Netta on the grounds of adultery, with Aldington cited as co-respondent, was both more straightforward and more bitter, involving as it did Aldington's betrayal of Brigit. He had offered to give her a financial settlement, but the battles over the extent of damages he would pay both Michael and his mother were fierce. In November 1937 Michael was granted a decree nisi with costs and £1,500 in agreed damages.

The H.D. divorce took longer. The decree nisi was granted on 13 May 1938, only two months before Netta and Aldington were expecting a baby, but there were to be a further six months before the decree absolute. Aldington was desperate for his child to be legitimate, probably not recalling his insensitivity 20 years earlier to H.D.'s similar need. The couple returned to England in early June and Aldington contacted H.D.

to ask if he might visit her at her flat in Lowndes Square as a matter of urgency. He came on the afternoon of 9 June. It was the only occasion in those 20 years when they had been alone together, although H.D. had carefully arranged that her friend Silvia Dobson, who had come an hour earlier, would stay on for the first fifteen minutes of his visit. He stayed for two hours. He wanted her to intervene in the case to bring the decree absolute forward; he also had to tell her that he had no money and could not pay any of the costs of the divorce, for which they had agreed to share the expense. 'I never knew anyone make such a muddle of anything,' she wrote to Plank.[6]

The divorce was finalised on 22 June; the couple were married three days later; and Catherine Aldington was born on 6 July.

11. A Crystal World?
1937-1939

At the Cavendish Hotel Patmore was trying to adjust to life on her own. She told the Warmans:

> I don't want to stamp Richard out of my life – don't think it's right anyway, for I believe in our life together – it stands for something. But then it's harder than ever I imagined to get used to the blank. Nine years is a long time of habit, isn't it?

She continued:

> And I can't just keep quiet about everything as I would if it only concerned myself. Michael has got to be protected from all the false rumours and humiliations attached to such a situation. Going to France was hell for almost every road is associated with R. but it did Michael good.

She ended:

> I can't cook a dinner here because I've moved to other rooms but when you're free one night at least take beer & bread & cheese if you can stand that. We won't be sad either – this is just a bit of a lonely road for me, but it will be good for me, stiffen up my muscles & mind & if R. is happy it will be good for him too.[1]

The Warmans were kind and sympathetic; but it was Aldington with whom Warman would keep in touch in the long term.

From the moment Aldington was reunited with Netta in Plymouth, he chose to take her to all the places which had romantic associations for him. From Brantôme they drove through France to Italy – first to

Florence to visit Orioli and Douglas and then to Capri. By April, as *Very Heaven* was published, they were settled in a villa on the Riviera – but not just any villa: the Villa Koechlin at Rayol-Canadel, which he had last rented in 1931.

Reviews of the novel were mixed, *The Times* describing it as 'a slender achievement' and the *TLS* noting that the hero's 'moralisings take up a large proportion of Mr Aldington's 376 pages', but Strauss called the book 'sharply provocative, outspoken, uncomfortable, and whether you regard Christopher Heylin as typical of his generation or not, exceedingly interesting'.[2] The *Daily Telegraph* reviewer, while finding Chris Heylin 'little but a projection of Mr Aldington's sympathy and indignation' and the other characters 'cardboard caricatures set up for the author to pelt with verbal brickbats', nevertheless acknowledged the 'immense vitality' of the writing: 'If he flogs dead horses, he flogs them with gusto.'[3] Douglas West in the *Daily Mail* similarly felt that the 'walking ideas' remained 'real people' and that the invective was 'so wholehearted' that few readers would complain.[4]

The Crystal World, written throughout the early months of 1937 and published in the spring of 1938, was a return to the style of *Life Quest* – a 600-line poem organised into a series of lyrics recounting the story of Aldington's courtship of Netta, its setbacks and triumphs, and celebrating the life they had created together.

> Out of our love we have built a crystal refuge
> Unseen but very strong and ours,
> Only we can enter it and be safe.
> We dwell at the very heart of life . . .
>
> 'Give us our world.'
> It will not be given; you must make it.
> Only from the purity of extreme passion,
> And, alas, the purity of extreme pain,
> Can you build the crystal world.

The first half of the poem consists of 21 short and intensely personal lyrics, but the second half (section 22 – itself divided into eleven sub-sections) provides an epilogue which re-tells the whole story in more discursive and prosaic language, providing the writer with opportunities for reflection. In a critical review in *Poetry* Kerker Quinn thought the lyrics 'commonplace', 'giv[ing] us emotion unrefined, untransfused', and suggested that the 'dry expansive poetic essay' at the end would have been more effective if broken up and woven into the main body of the poem – the technique Aldington had employed in *Life Quest*. Quinn found a 'flowering beauty' reminiscent of Aldington's best work in several of the lyrics, but felt that this was insufficient to compensate for the rest. He concluded by remarking that *Very Heaven* and *Artifex* had displayed a similar lack of concentration and self-criticism, which subtracted a good deal from 'their potential excellence'.[5]

Aldington himself, advising Frere on promoting the poem, linked *The Crystal World* not to *Life Quest* but to *A Dream in the Luxembourg*, arguing that:

> both poems go counter to the current intellectualist trend in poetry – they are purely poems of *la sensibilité*, and depend, not on any abstract theory of how poetry should be written, but on the validity, depth and poignancy of the emotions. Instead of seeking the intellectually rare and striking, they accept the obvious, commonplace universal feelings. And they are not written from the attitude of the Bard condescending, but of the ordinary man in and out of a pickle.[6]

That both he and Quinn used the word 'commonplace' is of interest; for Aldington the word was a recommendation – and a rebuttal of the school of Pound and Eliot.

In July, Frere, Pat and their baby arrived for a month's stay at the villa. That month, Aldington wrote to Orioli: 'There is a rumour here that Uncle N. is in serious trouble. I do hope it isn't true. Will you let me know? And if it is true, tell me if there is anything I can do.'[7] Twenty years after his flight from England to escape charges of assaulting a teenage boy, Douglas had been banished from Italy over charges of raping a young girl. He settled in Vence, just inside the French border and 85 miles from Rayol-Canadel. He would be there until 1941.

Meanwhile, Aldington had started on a comic novel. If *Seven Against Reeves* reflects his state of mind at the time of writing, then his 'crystal world' was giving him much contentment. It is a relaxed and entertaining novel concerning an innocent and likeable 50-year-old, moderately-wealthy and recently-retired businessman. He is brought into contact, for the first time in his life, and by the insistence of his wife, with the world of the pretentious bourgeoisie and, through their patronage of the arts, with the world of minor artists determined to divest him of some of his money: he is, in turn, persuaded to subsidise a bad musician, to buy the work of an equally bad painter and to purchase the services of a shockingly bad interior decorator; only because he has become more shrewd and confident, does he turn down the opportunity to invest in an even worse literary magazine project. The latter incident gives Aldington the opportunity for witty portraits of Douglas and Orioli, while the character of the young social climber and interior decorator Anselm Hawksneetch is clearly inspired by Derek Patmore.

Reeves's observations about the art world remind us of Lewis's *The Apes of God* or of Aldington's own satirical account in Part Two of *Death of a Hero*:

> There were young men of means who dressed elegantly, collected many quaint and delightful *objets d'art* to furnish their houses and studios and painted at leisure. There were other young men who painted in haste because they had no money, who affected the garb and deportment of tramps, and lived in surroundings of revolting squalor. The females all had incomes or allowances of some kind, and seemed to be divided into those who wore arty clothes and did their hair in bangs and buns, and those whose hair and clothes were comparatively normal and pretty. In his own mind Mr Reeves further divided them – from their conversation – into painters who were Communists and Communists who painted, an over-subtle and arbitrary distinction. As a matter of fact, some of them were Fascists, but Mr Reeves had not yet learned to distinguish between the intellectual supporters of these rival revolutions.[8]

The novel, however, has none of the savagery of those two works. Labelled 'a comedy-farce', it is a successful venture into the *genre* – characterisation, dialogue and incident handled with poise and elegance. Aldington even manages, through Reeves's brief encounters with a young writer named Willoughby Houghton and with two academics, Underwood and Remington, to air some of his own ideas with lightness and humour.

Moderately successful though the novel was, when published in March 1938 (with a subscription sale of 6,000 and reviews commending its 'gusto', 'vitality', 'wit', 'liveliness' and 'fun'), it was not quite what Aldington's publishers wanted from their new author.[9] Charles Seddon Evans, chairman of Heinemann, wrote to him in August 1937: 'For better or for worse, I take the view that you are amusing yourself with Reeves – at least you should be; and there are plenty of people at this moment waiting to be confounded by a light-hearted novel from you', but he continued: 'It is good news that you have got the idea for a more solid novel; and that you will start on it as soon as you have polished off Reeves.'[10]

In November 1937 the couple returned to England; Netta was pregnant and the Villa Koechlin was in bad repair, it let in the rain and had no satisfactory heating system. He also needed to be in London to fight the Patmore lawyers: 'It is extraordinary,' he told Warman, 'how people with highly refined feeling and aristocratic pretensions are so damn keen on money. Not to mention revenge.'[11] They moved into Ashley Bank, South View Road in Pinner, Middlesex, near to Netta's brother, James, and other members of her family. Aldington was able to renew his friendship with Prentice, but the latter's health gave him cause for concern, as he confided regularly to Orioli.[12]

The Patmore divorce was settled that month and in February 1938 the couple returned to the Villa Koechlin, where Aldington made a start on the next novel. They were not without friends as the Glovers had been spending the winter on the Riviera. Glover was in better health and they had travelled extensively since their return from Arizona in July 1935. Another visitor that spring of 1938 was Aldington's (and Glover's) old friend George Gribble. In April, however, Aldington and Netta moved to Lausanne, having been told of the gynaecological expertise available in Switzerland.[13] They did not take to the country. 'This, my dear boy,' Aldington told Warman:

> is a perfection of civic organisation such as England has never dreamed of – no slums, handsome public buildings, fantastically neat clean streets, infinite garden suburbs, well-drilled vineyards, fruit trees in every garden, and real genuine beauty of lakes and mountains, even the picturesque past most carefully preserved. It's quite unbearable. Everything which is not obligatory is forbidden.[14]

This disenchantment and the pressing need to ensure that the decree absolute for his divorce would come through in time for them to marry before the baby was born, drove them to London (to the Astor Hotel in Princes Square) – and Aldington to that awkward meeting at H.D.'s flat at Lowndes Square at which she agreed not only to hasten the process but to pay all the costs.

Catherine Aldington was born on 6 July – eleven days after Aldington's marriage to Netta and two days before his 46th birthday. By the end of the month the family were living at Bramshott Cottage in Liphook, Hampshire. Meanwhile, Heinemann had issued a uniform edition of six Aldington works, accompanied by a pamphlet written by C.P. Snow.[15] Aldington was thrilled, telling Warman: 'Heinemanns have taken immense trouble and spared no expense, and I think they are the nicest pocket editions on the market. . . . As you can imagine, the appearance of "Works of" is rather an event for me, a sort of jubilee of 25 years of writing.'[16] To his satisfaction, both the *TLS* and *John O' London's Weekly* ran short reviews of the edition alongside articles contributed by Aldington himself. The Warmans visited Liphook, Eric showing enthusiasm for what he was shown of the next novel.

Parenthood was all Aldington had hoped it might be. He delighted in his daughter and she in him. Her name was shortened to Catha, a reference to the heroine of *All Men Are Enemies*. Orioli received regular reports on her growth and ailments. MacGreevy, who managed a brief visit, recalled 20 years later: 'I only remember your daughter's waking from sleep and smiling instantly at the sight of her father standing at the end of her cot.'[17] In September the family returned to the Villa Koechlin. At the end of that month Neville Chamberlain signed the Munich Agreement, an action Aldington approved. 'I hate the idea of another war,' he told Warman.[18] It would not be long before he perceived that war was inevitable. He wrote to Bacon – an awkward letter to write since it was his first for three years and he had a favour to ask: could Bacon help him obtain a post in an American university, teaching English Literature?[19] Bacon was at first hopeful of a post at Yale, but by December was writing to say that the university had no money to spare.[20]

The crystal world seemed fragile, and several of Aldington's friends were in similarly depressed circumstances: Prentice's health showed no improvement and, in Florence, Orioli was tending to the dying Reggie Turner. By the New Year, Aldington had decided to go to America even though there was no job for him and little prospect of increasing his revenue from writing. Netta was prepared to use money she had inherited when her father died in February 1938 to get them established on the other side of the Atlantic.[21] Returning to England at the end of January 1939, they embarked for New York on the SS *Aquitania* on 11 February. They checked in at Hyde Park Hotel, 25 East 77th Street six days later; they would stay in the city for six weeks.

Richard and Netta Aldington in the early 1940s

12. The New World, Again
1939-1942

The first task Aldington faced was having to write to Bacon – currently in Honolulu – to apologise for throwing himself and his family on his friend's good will. Meanwhile, he had other friends in New York to whom he could turn: the Slonimskys, Bertie and Milla Eskell (Bertie having recently remarried) and Johnson and his family. (Despite Aldington's departure from Doubleday, Doran, Johnson would still prove a useful friend and adviser.) Paul Willert, another friend from former times and now at Oxford University Press in New York, offered him work as a reader ($25 a commission) and took him to meet members of the English Faculty at Harvard. He also visited Princeton. Neither university, however, would offer him a post. His pursuit of academic employment was almost entirely fruitless, despite the support of Bacon and others. There were isolated invitations: he gave a lecture at Wellesley College in late September, another at Harvard in mid-October and a reading at the recently opened Queen's College, New York, in November; he had a week as 'visiting poet' at Wesleyan University in Connecticut in March 1940, delivered a series of five lectures at Columbia University over a week in July and August that year and another at the Library Company of Philadelphia in January 1941.[1]

By early April 1939 the family was installed at the Bacon home on Rhode Island, The Acorns, Peacedale. Aldington first met Bacon in Italy in 1930 and the friendship was revived during his 1935 visit to the United States. A member of a wealthy New England family, the Hazards, Bacon had met Martha his wife, known as Patty, when he was a young professor at the University of California at Berkeley and she the daughter of a Mathematics professor. They married in 1912 when she was 20 years old and he 25. He abandoned his academic career while still a young man in order to devote his time to writing poetry. He was also a translator of French and Spanish literature, and had translated one of Aldington's

The Acorns, Peacedale, Rhode Island, home of the Bacon family

favourite texts, *The Song of Roland*. Both he and Patty had been analysands of Carl Jung and remained his friends. They had lived in Florence with their three small daughters from 1928 until 1932, when, disenchanted with the Fascist regime, they had returned to America. Patty herself was a talented musician, painter and writer of children's stories, but she was shy and retiring and had never had any work published or paintings exhibited.

The Aldington family had landed in heaven. The kindness and generosity of their hosts overwhelmed them. Aldington told Slonimsky:

> About forty yards from the dwelling here is the library, one vast room with a lofty roof and big stone fire-place. Leonard Bacon works at one end and I at the other. There are several thousand books, and we have much pleasant literary talk. All this is a fine flower of civilisation, with that peculiar graciousness and sweetness of the New England character so striking to a European. There are three daughters, two at universities and one just graduated, and the happiness of the family is a delightful sight. . . . Catha has been the almost perfect baby here, and lives surrounded by admiring females. She scarcely ever cries and smiles benevolently on all.[2]

They had brought with them from New York a nanny for Catha: Zita Zimenstark, a Jewish refugee medical student from Austria whom Willert had referred to them. Now Aldington set about obtaining Slonimsky's

(top and bottom) Leonard Bacon
in his library at The Acorns, Peacedale, in the 1940s

Henry Slonimsky

help in getting her parents to England. The Aldingtons were assured of a home for the immediate future: they were to stay for a month at The Acorns, before borrowing, rent-free, two Hazard family homes, one in Saunderstown for eight weeks, and then The Scallop Shell at Peacedale for a further three months. At the end of June they would have a week's gap between the two homes, a week which Catha spent at The Acorns with her nanny and the adoring Bacon household, while Aldington and Netta toured New England.

The Saunderstown house was on a small private road in half-wild country looking over a slope to Narragansett Bay, with Connecticut Island opposite. The tangled woodland and its wildlife were a joy to Aldington. 'I have not felt so tranquil and happy for a long time. With all its faults and toughness this country seems like a paradise after Europe,' he wrote to Warman.[3] Their stay was also the opportunity for a reunion with James and Mildred Whitall, (close friends of Aldington and H.D. from before the war) whose young son, born in London, was now fifteen years old.[4] The playwright Basil Dean spent a weekend with Aldington at Saunderstown looking into the possibility of creating a stage version of *Seven Against Reeves*; ever since the failed attempt to have *Life of a Lady* produced, Aldington had hankered after staging one of his works. Meanwhile, periodical publication proved almost as fruitless an avenue as academic employment. *Atlantic Monthly* gave him the task of reviewing *Finnegan's Wake* and followed up by commissioning an article on Norman Douglas; he also wrote a piece on Lawrence for the *Saturday Review of Literature*, followed by one on Imagism and one on Shelley, and two articles for *Esquire*, but no regular reviewing offer was forthcoming.[5]

Shortly before leaving Europe, he had moved from Doubleday, Doran to Viking, where his old friend Pascal Covici, formerly of Covici, Friede, had moved in 1938. His final publications with Doubleday were *Seven*

Against Reeves and an appreciation of Somerset Maugham.[6] *Rejected Guest*, his new novel, was published by Viking (and by Heinemann in the UK) in the autumn of 1939. Bacon, who had recently completed his memoirs, suggested that Aldington write his own.[7] Harold Guinzberg, chairman of Viking, was open to the idea and by early October Aldington had negotiated with *Atlantic Monthly* to publish a series of articles under the title 'Farewell to Europe', which would form the basis of the memoirs. He would be paid $1,000 for each of the four instalments.[8] In January 1940 Viking approached him about a further project: an anthology of English poetry, comparable to the *Oxford Book of English Verse*, but with a larger selection of American poets. Compiling this would occupy a great deal of his time over the next two years. Viking gave him a three-year contract for two non-fiction works and a novel, advancing him $7,500 on the novel and the memoirs and committing $40,000 for the anthology project.

Bacon had suggested scriptwriting as another source of income and Aldington had a short correspondence with the Hollywood agent Alvin Manuel between April and July 1940. Hoping that he might obtain a commission which could be combined with his work on the anthology, the memoirs and the as-yet unplanned novel, Aldington enquired: 'Can you tell me what hours must be worked in a studio and if an energetic person who dislikes cocktail parties would be able to get other work done.'[9] Manuel had two proposals: the first was from Alexander Korda, an offer of $1,000 for a 12,000-word story; the second was from the actor-director Kenneth McKenna for a Cyrano de Bergerac script. Aldington had a short interview with McKenna, but neither offer came to anything.

While at Peacedale Aldington heard from H.D. Replying to her letter, he apologised for his failure to pay any of the divorce fees. '[L]awyers, doctors and Patmores between them' had used up all his savings and, with 'all the upsets and events', he had taken over a year to write *Seven Against Reeves*. With his most recent novel soon to be published, he was more hopeful of restoring his income – and of paying H.D. what he owed her. (In fact, *Rejected Guest* would sell only 6,000 copies in America and Aldington would never repay H.D.) He gave her news of Catha:

> a very healthy young woman, with blue eyes and dark hair, and singularly like the photographs of me at her age. She is just beginning to say words and to totter about holding onto her pen, and creeps with incredible energy. She is an amiable infant and very little trouble. I like her very much indeed.[10]

In a further letter, he enclosed a photograph of his daughter, telling H.D.: 'I am selfish enough to believe that she loves me more than anyone else in the world, because that is how I feel about her!'[11] There is no mention of Netta in this – or any – correspondence. He does, however, mention Slonimsky: '[He] is still fascinating and eloquent, but has unfortunately abandoned greek philosophy for rabbinical theology. A sense of loyalty to his people, I suppose, but quite ridiculous for a man of his gifts. . . . His life is dignified and uncorrupted by the prevalent yahooism. But what a waste!'

He was able to give her news of another mutual acquaintance:

> I didn't see Ezra. He arrived in New York, gave out (rather courageously, considering the anti-Fascist feeling here) a number of pro-Fascist interviews and then, as he would say, 'vanished into the hinterland' with his buddy, e e cummings. I haven't the faintest idea where he is – Idaho maybe. I believe he lectured at Harvard, and rather perplexed the students.[12]

Pound was in America from late April until July 1939, ostensibly to receive an honorary doctorate from his old university, Hamilton College, but principally to proclaim his economic doctrine as loudly and influentially as he could. To this end he visited Harvard and Yale and sought interviews with a variety of senators. A reporter on the New York *Sun*, one of the many who awaited his arrival in New York, wrote: 'Literature . . . is now a minor theme in the Poundish symphony. . . . Immediately the talk turns to economics, propaganda, and to what he calls "left-wing Fascists in Italy".'[13]

On 3 September Britain declared war on Germany. 'All that we have hoped and worked for has gone, perhaps never to return,' Aldington wrote to Slonimsky:

> There seems to be nothing worth living for. There can be no 'winning' in this war. There will simply be chaos. . . . If men could have learned wisdom and co-operation they would have learned it from 1914-18. They didn't, and perhaps the death warrant of the whole species is already signed. At the best we have entered another Dark Ages.[14]

His first thoughts, however, were for his friends in Europe, H.D. (in Switzerland, while Perdita was in England) and the recently divorced Eric Warman. He was also anxious about his own circumstances; more than half his earnings were from English and continental royalties. By late September he had moved to New York, writing to Bacon: 'Those six months in and near Peacedale have been amongst the happiest in my life. Nothing I can say or do can ever repay what I owe you.'[15] On the same day he told Slonimsky: 'Things base and petty wither away when you are near. The strange thing is that you seem quite unaware of your own grandeur.'[16] He knew that he was exceptionally fortunate in these two friendships and wanted the two men to meet.

He was relieved to hear from H.D. at the end of October. Basle, she told him, was like a garrison town and one could not switch on the radio without hearing Berlin propaganda; despite the beauty of the lakes and mountains at this time of year, she was desperate to get back to her flat in Lowndes Square.[17] Aldington wrote back:

How can this struggle result in anything but an all around collapse, financial, economic, political, cultural? The war against Hitlerism will probably result in Bolshevising Europe, including England. Suppose at the cost of enormous sacrifices they do clean up Hitler, what are they going to do about Stalin? And Mussolini? And the Japanese? And what earthly reason is there to suppose that people and governments will be any wiser, more tolerant and constructive after this war than they were after the last?[18]

His anxiety was affecting his work on the commissioned memoirs:

Abstractly I feel so crushed by the European debacle that I should like to evaporate quietly with a bottle of chloroform. ... [but] I realise that I must devote myself to Netta and Catherine. For myself, I have thrown away ambition, and it is a purification. ... I still have 2,000 dollars left of my depleted savings, and 850 dollars promised for occasional lectures in 1940. On this we can live for more than a year.[19]

By May 1940, he had found coping strategies, telling Slonimsky:

I think it a mistake for us, you and me especially, to take upon ourselves too heavily vicarious responsibility for the war and its conduct. Where there is no power there can be no responsibility beyond obedience to lawful authority. We must not delude ourselves into thinking that we are called upon to hold the train on the tracks. We have our own work to do and should do it as well and as long as we can, and when the time comes when we must abandon it to fight, *eh bien, mourrons*. . . . When I am called on, I will go, but until then I will do my own work, and in no event will I acquiesce mentally in war. Moreover, I shall endeavour to survive, to bear witness of this tragical and futile criminality.[20]

He would return to this position frequently in his dialogue with Slonimsky. 'I am responsible to the extent that everyone in a shipwreck is bound to lend a hand as cheerfully and energetically as possible,' he would write in August 1942, 'but I am not "responsible" for running the ship on the rocks, nor have I any responsibility for getting it off since I am not a ships officer nor entrusted with any power.'[21] We might wonder whether it was Slonimsky or himself he was trying to convince. Certainly, in postwar Britain there would be some resentment towards those – like Huxley, Auden, Isherwood and Aldington – who spent the war safely in the United States.[22]

Nevertheless, the fall of his beloved France was a terrible shock. Sometime afterwards he composed an undated (and unpublished) long essay entitled 'The Horn of Roland' which must have constituted for him a major therapeutic exercise:

[A]cross the centuries the sound of Roland's horn has come to have a symbolical meaning – the call for aid of civilised France when she is hard pressed by the barbarian hordes. The [*sic*] heard the horn of Roland sounding desperately in 1914, and again more and more insistently in 1918; and each time it was answered. But in 1940, when we heard it sounding with such bitter notes of appeal and warning, it was not answered; and the chivalry of France went down before the machine.

In the crash of that ruin, which stunned the civilised world, it seemed as if Roland's olifant were silenced for ever. But no! The vitality of France is inextinguishable. Very faintly at first, but in these last few days, more and more loudly, the horn of Roland sounds once more.

Shall it go unanswered, and be extinguished for ever?

The essay goes on to argue that 'with all its faults, the French republic was infinitely worth saving':

In the course of centuries France had evolved the most nearly perfect way of life known in Europe since Renaissance Italy; but unlike the Renaissance despots, France did not seek to bar the people from the good life; on the contrary, the Republic wished them to share in it. Yet this democracy never degenerated into the fatal error of cultivating the moron. '*Français, respectez vos élites.*' While all the essential rights of the common man were jealously guarded, the Republic never sought to destroy the instinctive respect of Frenchmen for the natural aristocracy of talent. ... Moreover, the prudent economy of France, with its balance of industry and agriculture, its avoidance of reckless over-population, averted the widespread destitution so unavoidable in over-industrialised countries.

The piece concludes with its author placing his hopes in the Royal Air Force, the Royal Navy and 'the determination of subject continental peoples to oppose the usurper by passive resistance and timely revolts': 'If they fail, we shall not see again in France or in Europe the kind of life which to us alone seems worth living.'[23] The essay represents the most explicit expression in Aldington's work of his passion for the European tradition and for the culture of France.

Meanwhile, New York once more proved too distracting – and expensive, and in mid-June 1940 he retreated to Connecticut, as he and Patmore had done in 1935, renting a cottage in Old Lyme, only five hundred yards from Brockway Manor and 'situated', he told Slonimsky, 'in country which has quiet beauty in spite of the neglect, and emigration of the old families'.[24] He was arranging to give a home to Warman's eight-year-old daughter Jean, although Warman would finally decide against evacuating the child.[25] Netta's widowed mother, now living in Jamaica, was a guest in Connecticut in the early autumn, as were the Slonimskys. 'I shall never forget what true and loyal friends you and Miriam have been during this last difficult year,' Aldington wrote to Slonimsky in July.[26] He missed their intellectual dialogue although much of it continued in their letters. The topic was often religion or the war but he also wanted to talk about the Connecticut landscape:

[This is] the America of powerful forests, rocks, rivers, beautiful but violent, a harsh land that was conquered by indomitable courage and energy. The men who civilised this land had dreadful limitations, but they were magnificent. All this land needs is to be loved. It has been conquered by the iron-willed pioneers and exploited by their successors, but now if it is to be loved and treated as men treat the soil they love, it will be of great beauty.[27]

However, after four months he moved to Washington, ostensibly so that he could make use of the Library of Congress to help him compile the remainder of the Viking anthology.[28] This seems not to have been the only, or even principal, reason for the move, since in Connecticut he had access to the resources of Yale. In April 1941 he told H.D.: 'We got into a rather stuffy upper-class set in New England (and you know what that means) which made [Netta] restive.'[29] He also remarked on how much cheaper rent and living expenses were in the south. He would tell Violet Schiff, resuming correspondence with her in 1949, that it was in the autumn of 1940 that 'our best time began'.[30] He may have been referring to the new sense of economic security that he felt at this time, with the memoirs completed (and appearing in serial form in *Atlantic Monthly*) and the anthology well underway; he may have been alluding to the scope of his travels during that year and, in particular, to his appreciation of Florida (where they would move in March 1941); but what is notable is that that autumn was the beginning of a period when the family was independent and self-sustaining. Looking back several years later, he clearly saw it as having been a magical time.

On 5 November 1940 he saw Franklin Roosevelt driving from the station to the White House, 'looking very well and cheerful', and expressed to Slonimsky his 'immense relief' at the president's election success: 'a demonstration that democracy is not wholly foolish and corrupt'. Nevertheless, he was anxious about the complacency and optimism of American opinion and afraid that France would make a deal with Hitler.[31] Work on the anthology accomplished by the end of February 1941, he moved once more – travelling via some of Netta's friends in Martinsburg, West Virginia, down the Shenandoah Valley and through North and South Carolina and Georgia to the west coast of Florida, where he took a cottage on Jamay Beach, Nokomis, 70 miles south of Tampa. He was shocked by the poverty he saw in the southern states, telling Slonimsky: 'I have seen nothing so bad in the worst parts of Europe. . . . The Carolinas and Georgia are riddled with malaria . . . the villages are without schools, churches or doctors, and the conditions of the negroes and poor whites is appalling. Rags and emaciation.'[32]

Florida was different, 'prosperous with tourists and residential rentiers'.[33] He described their new home in a letter to Warman:

> We are on a long narrow island, joined to the mainland by two bridges over a narrow creek which opens into a large lagoon. The cottage is about thirty yards from the Gulf of Mexico, and behind it is a sandy stretch of land with palmettos, palms, southern pines, and mangroves along the edge of the lagoon.[34]

D.H. Lawrence's ranch-house at Kiowa Ranch, Taos, New Mexico

He told H.D. that they had 'a nice little cottage with all the American gadgets' and a wooden hut, with shelves and a desk, for him to work in. Catherine, he told her, 'well and sunburned and beginning to say "cute" things', was enjoying life in Florida very much, 'running on the sands, bathing and picking up shells, and playing with another little girl'.[35]

In late May they set off for New Mexico, having arranged with Frieda Lawrence to rent Lawrence's three-roomed ranch-house on the lower slopes of the Lobo Mountains near San Cristobal, 20 miles north of Taos. It was a journey of over 2,000 miles, by way of Tallahassee, Mobile, New Orleans, San Antonio, Del Rio, El Paso and Santa Fe, a journey which Aldington described in a lengthy letter to Frere. His daughter would recall in later years that in their long journeys across the United States the luggage was stacked in the back of the old Buick to form an even surface on which she could play or go to sleep – or, looking through the back window, watch the road unroll.[36]

Lawrence had lived at Kiowa Ranch for six months in 1924 and a further five in 1925. 8,600 feet above sea level, the site was not habitable in winter. Frieda had returned to Kiowa with Angelo Ravagli in 1933 and they had built themselves a home alongside the ranch-house. In 1935 Ravagli had returned to Europe to have Lawrence's body exhumed and cremated so that his ashes could be interred in a specially built chapel at Kiowa.

The Lawrence chapel at Kiowa Ranch

Aldington told Frere that Frieda was 'still amazingly her old self, and though well over 60 as full of zest and energy as ever'. Ravagli was 'a little man, a bit like Pino, but without Pino's wit or vices – a bit dull, but very conscientious and industrious'. In Taos Aldington heard little talk of the war: 'They simply don't believe that anything that happens outside the U.S., and principally their own state, can have the slightest effect on them.' For Catherine, the whole experience, including Frieda's livestock collection of three horses, a cow and calf and a pig, was an exciting adventure, and Aldington expressed his sympathy with Frere, who was temporarily separated from his own wife and children, evacuated to America in the summer of 1940.[37]

In the tiny hut where two years earlier Huxley had written his pacifist treatise, *Ends and Means*, Aldington worked on the indexes for the Viking Anthology.[38] Fifty yards away, on the slope behind him, was the simple memorial chapel. In an unpublished essay written at the time, he recorded his vivid sense of his friend's presence:

Few remember better than I that mysterious gift Lawrence possessed of making life around him seem exciting and wonderful, as if in his world the very air were not common air but pure oxygen, where everything glowed and vibrated with more intense colour and vivacity. Up here I am constantly reminded of him – the bed I sleep in he made, on the rough stone seat by the hearth still lies the little rope mat he wove; the first thing I see from the porch in the morning is the great pine he loved so much, and from everywhere you catch glimpses of that intensely silent and peaceful little chaple [sic].

Strange resting place, if indeed it is the last resting place, for the ashes of the 'common' Derbyshire coal-miner's son, ashes which seem to share the restless wanderlust of the living man, having already journeyed so many thousand miles over sea and land. Strange but most fortunate among the many literary exiles of England who lie buried in other lands. I think of the graves of Landor and Elizabeth Browning in what is now a dullish Florentine suburb, of Keats and Shelly [sic] in the little Roman cemetery, of Fielding in Lisbon. They cannot compare with the serenity and majesty of Lawrence's burial place, where the extreme simplicity of the grave is so right. . . .

I come out of my New Mexican shack and look about me. There in the sunlight stands so quietly the grave of the English poet, with above it the white phoenix which he chose as his emblem. . . .

I turn and look, as I look nearly every hour of the changing day, over the vast New Mexican landscape, with its ring of majestic mountains and the desert cut by the vast winding canyon of the Rio Grande, which from here looks very much like the No Man's Land of the last war as seen from a distant height.[39]

Yet he did not feel inspired by the 'stupendous vistas' and reflected that Lawrence himself had not written much here apart from 'a few short stories and poems, one or two sketches of the Indians and the play "David"': 'Landscape on too tremendous a scale seems to check rather than stimulate the human urge to be doing and making with the mind and hands.' He was neglecting the fact that Lawrence's New Mexico output had included the novellas *St Mawr* and *The Woman Who Rode Away* (both of which he had included in his 1935 Lawrence selection, *The Spirit of Place*) and such essays as 'The Hopi Snake Dance' and 'Reflections on the Death of a Porcupine', all powerfully imbued with Lawrence's sense of the place. Lawrence himself would write towards the end of his life:

[F]or a greatness of beauty I have never experienced anything like New Mexico. All those mornings when I went with a hoe along the ditch to the Canon, at the ranch, and stood, in the fierce, proud

silence of the Rockies, on their foothills, to look far over the desert
to the blue mountains away in Arizona, blue as chalcedony, with the
sage-brush desert sweeping grey-blue in between, dotted with tiny
cube-crystals of houses, the vast amphitheatre of lofty, indomitable
desert, sweeping round to the ponderous Sangre de Cristo
mountains on the east, and coming up flush at the pine-dotted
foot-hills of the Rockies! What splendour! . . . Those that have spent
morning after morning alone there pitched among the pines above
the great proud world of desert will know, almost unbearably, how
beautiful it is, how clear and unquestioned is the might of the day.
. . . Ah, yes, in New Mexico the heart is sacrificed to the sun and the
human being is left stark, heartless, but undauntedly religious.[40]

An additional problem was that the altitude of Kiowa affected the
health of the whole family, particularly Netta, who was experiencing pains
in her lungs. ('Whoever persuaded a TB patient to try to live here must
have wanted to kill him,' Aldington remarked drily in his letter to Frere.)
By August 1941 they were back in Florida, although they had planned to
stay at the ranch until October. 'I think of you both very often and of the
famous ranch which I am glad to have seen,' Aldington wrote to Frieda:

It is a beautiful place, and I am so sorry that we got upset by
the altitude. You were both so good to us – and so sweet with
Catherine. . . . [She] is very well and enjoys her sea bathing and
running about the place, though she regrets Anita and the piggy.
'Where's Angie?' she asks about milking time. And in the morning:
'Shall we go and see Frieda?' To console her we say that you and
Angie will come and see her here one of these days.[41]

The anthology was published in September. It had been chosen as the
book of the month by the Literary Guild of America, which took 60,000
copies, yielding him $2,000. The total first impression was 100,000, but
he would receive only seven cents per copy for the first 30,000 straight
sales (and fourteen cents thereafter) as the book had been massively
expensive for Viking to produce. Now he had to find another project. He
had no inspiration for the novel he was committed to deliver. Instead he
contemplated writing an historical biography. The Duke of Wellington,
military saviour of Great Britain, seemed an appropriate choice at this
moment in history. The most recent work on the subject was Philip
Guedalla's 1931 biography, but Guedalla was not a soldier and Aldington
prided himself on having an infantryman's understanding of military

Frieda Lawrence (centre) with Mabel Dodge Luhan (left)
and Dorothy Brett (right) at Kiowa Ranch, 1938

strategy.[42] He had also, though less than Guedalla, some acquaintance with the battlefields of the Peninsular War. His attraction to Wellington as a subject was also rooted in his own childhood: Wellington, as Lord Warden of the Cinque Ports, had been the occupant of Walmer Castle between 1829 and his death in 1852, and therefore a respected figure in local folk memory when Aldington was growing up.

At first sight Wellington does not seem to be a character with whom we might expect Aldington to feel sympathy. He was, to quote the latter's introduction:

> a fox-hunting aristocrat of the Protestant Ascendancy in Ireland, a Dublin Castle man, an Anglo-Indian, a professional soldier with a laugh like a horse with whooping cough, a martinet who opposed the abolition of army flogging and unpardonably described his men as 'the scum of the earth', a Tory who fought the Reform Bill of 1832 to the death and opposed many of the long overdue changes in England, a prodigious collector of titles, orders and monetary rewards.[43]

However, Aldington argues:

> The curious thing is not that he was a Tory, but that on the whole
> he was sensible enough to hold staunchly to the belief that even the
> Tory party must yield to the constitutional will of the people [and]
> [a]s a soldier he considered himself a public servant independent
> of party politics and owing obedience to any lawful government.[44]

Furthermore: '[N]ever once in his long career did he use his power or
persuasion to advance his money interests.'[45] He believed Wellington
to have possessed the qualities he most admired (and the absence of
which had been the constant target of his fictional satires): 'strong
common sense, honesty, integrity, unceasing hard work'.[46] Perhaps most
importantly of all: '[H]e was a successful soldier who disliked war, a
conqueror who never acquired Napoleon's cynical disregard for human
life, and [who] earnestly worked for peace.'[47]

As soon as he began his research, he was fired up with enthusiasm,
writing to Bacon:

> It is amazing to find in 1808-14 many of the phenomena we
> deplore or rage against today – the unscrupulous enemy (and
> Boney was *very* unscrupulous, a real preview of Schicklgruber),
> the fifth columnist, the rash or silly journalist, the slick politician,
> the wild rushes of public opinion, delays in 'war production',
> inflation, sinkings of merchant marine &c. &c. . . . The heartening
> thing to remember is that Boney had 375,000 troops in Spain,
> Wellington never more than 40,000 English, 30,000 Portuguese
> and 20,000 Spaniards. Of course the resistance of the Spanish
> people & guerrillas was all important. In the earlier stages he was
> as short of cavalry as the boys this time have been short of planes.
> And he had to conduct his first (unsuccessful) sieges with too few
> Engineers, because the Duke of York disapproved of them![48]

The Bacons were spending 1942 in a New York hotel while Bacon worked
on a military dictionary for the US Army. The two men corresponded regularly
with support and advice for each other's projects. Aldington began to discover
how hard it was, first to establish exactly what happened in a battle, and
then to condense it into a few paragraphs. As with his *Voltaire* in 1925, his
research was exhaustive – and exhausting. Bacon would have to be particularly
supportive in July 1942 when he felt inclined to drop the project altogether,
having decided that the whole of his Peninsular War section – 150 pages and

three months' work – needed rewriting before he could even embark on the rest of Wellington's 37 years.[49] His problem, as he explained to Marshall Best, his editor at Viking Press, was that he had written the Peninsular War as military history; the section would not interest the general reader and needed to be recast in the personal tone of the rest of the book.[50]

He was also making a minor contribution to the war effort, as a volunteer Deputy Sheriff patrolling the coast at night to guard against the infiltration of enemy agents from Cuba. His Florida paradise continued to be a delight. In another unpublished essay, he wrote:

> [B]y a curious paradox, October here is much richer and more lively than April; for autumn follows hard on the warm summer rains and spring must struggle with the long winter drought. The golden-rod blooms in April, but most of the richer flowers in the autumn. . . . [Here] in south Florida the dawns are . . . a robust and vivid gold; you can feel the warmth of the huge dazzling sun the moment the horizon rolls beneath him. . . . To one born under the usually pallid skyscape of England, there is always a feeling of privilege and exultation in watching the tremendous surge of golden light from a cloudless sky.[51]

He was also aware of how healthy a life this was for his daughter, telling Bacon in March 1942 how 'amazingly well' she was, 'a rosy-cheeked little ragamuffin who seems to enjoy life'.[52]

Yet even here he could not forget the international conflict, and the Florida essay continues:

> While the days have passed here so peacefully, with such beauty of sea, sky and earth that the mere act of living seems an inestimable gift, those energetic northern States we are bidden to admire have done a lot of destructive work. If it were possible for us to realise as clearly as if we actually witnessed them all the violent deaths, torture and misery happening, we should be appalled. Mercifully, we are unable to do it, yet the little we can imagine is sufficient to poison the days, and to leave us restless, unhappy and inapt for concentration.

A shocking personal reminder of the war in Europe came in October 1941 when he read in the American journal, *The Nation*, that 'in his radio broadcast from Rome Ezra Pound has called on the negroes to revolt against "the white Jew Roosevelt"'. 'I find that really horrible in all its implications,' he told Slonimsky:

a sickening degradation of a human spirit who once meant a good deal to me and to you. I remember that young American when he was first in London, his apparent vitality, his amusing sayings, his intense enthusiasms, his real charm and generosity, his gifts. He seemed so much more alive than his English contemporaries, the Georgians. Was all this a sham? Or can it be that mere rancour, the disappointment of comparative failure, can lead a man to such Judas depths?[53]

Meanwhile his southern paradise turned out to have its drawbacks. He had told Frere in October 1941 that he would hang on in Florida as long as possible, but by July 1942 he had decided to move to California, partly because petrol-rationing was making life difficult but also because the only school Catherine could attend was closing down and because there was no company for Netta. 'I hate to leave here, a place I like as well as anywhere I've ever been,' he wrote to Bacon, 'but it's not the place for Catherine or Netta. Venice and Sarasota are practically deserted settlements, and I really believe Netta has seen nobody to talk to for several months.'[54] He told Warman that he 'groan[ed] in spirit at having to leave this beautiful lonely shore,' but had realised that it was wrong to keep Netta and Catherine there 'during their youth', a surprising bracketing together of his wife and daughter which demonstrates his consciousness of the age gap between them and himself, as well as his determination to give them the best life he could.[55]

13. A New Life
Hollywood
1942-1946

In late July and early August 1942 Aldington spent a fortnight in Boulder, Colorado, as 'General Adviser' to the thirteenth Rocky Mountains Writers' Conference, and from here he wrote to Manuel, his Hollywood agent, who was now hopeful of finding him studio work, asking for advice on where to live in California: 'somewhere more bohemian than bourgeois and without frills'.[1] He had, he told Manuel, sufficient funds to live modestly for two to three years. Now that younger writers were likely to be called up for the draft, he thought his prospects of studio employment quite high.

In late August, the rewriting of the Peninsular Wars completed, books and possessions packed up and sent ahead, he and his family set off from Nokomis, only eighteen months after their arrival there. They reached Los Angeles in mid-September, having driven from Florida by way of a stop-off in Boulder. During the 3,000-mile journey, Aldington had studied the sample scripts and treatments he had asked Manuel to send him; with him, he also carried his own playscripts, *Life of a Lady* and *My Wife Won't Let Me* (the dramatisation of *Seven Against Reeves*), less as possible film material than to demonstrate his scriptwriting skills to a potential employer. One surprise awaiting him in California was a reunion with the Glovers, who had been living in Berkeley since the beginning of the year. Having left France in 1938, they had continued their travels, first to Cuba, then to Mexico, South Carolina and New England. They had been passing through the Panama Canal in December 1941 when the Japanese struck at Pearl Harbour.

Aldington took to Hollywood at once. He told Eskell: 'It is much more civilised than New York and the climate is perfect.'[2] He rented an apartment at 8349 Sunset Boulevard in West Hollywood, within easy reach of the main studios, and in late October began work on an open-ended contract with Paramount Studios at $500 a week. This lasted only a month, as the studio cancelled their plans to make the film for which he was developing a treatment, an adaptation of Maugham's most recent novel, *The Hour*

Before the Dawn.[3] He was undaunted, telling Warman at the end of the year about the perfect climate, the wide tree-lined streets (with their excellent second-hand bookshops) and the wonderful views over Los Angeles. He hoped that his friend would move to Hollywood after the war: 'Believe me, this Pacific coast of America is not only beautiful and unbelievably rich, but many people think it will be one of the great creative centers [*sic*] after the war – and I am inclined to agree. . . . I wish I had come here twenty years ago. Whatever happens I shall never return to Europe.' Turning to the war, he told Warman how delighted he was to hear of the victory of the Eighth Army at El Agheila on 11 December, although he doubted his friend's optimistic forecast that the war would end in 1943.

Nonetheless, he went on to tell Warman: 'I can't claim to be a hell of a success myself, but I've been unwell until recently, and then I've been too sharp-tongued in defending England against all and sundry!'[4] His concerns about his state of health – emotional and physical – crop up in other correspondence in late 1942 and early 1943. He told Eskell that he had done a month's work at Paramount 'and spent the rest of the time being rather unwell and depressed'.[5] He apologised to Bacon at the start of 1943 for not having written for a long while: 'I have failed to write, not because I have not thought of you often and affectionately, but because I have been unwell, depressed and discontented; and it is an elementary duty of friendship not to inflict such moods and whims on others.'[6] To Slonimsky a fortnight later he confided: 'I have felt too harassed, too dismal to feel that I dared write. Why should I depress you with my pessimism, my feeling that the war is going to end in a vastly magnified version of the humbug and self-seeking and general collapse as the last war?'[7] In a subsequent letter he told Slonimsky: 'If I were not worried to death and on the verge of a nervous breakdown, I should be very happy here.'[8] This paradox of feeling both pleased with the move to Hollywood and yet anxious and depressed is a recurrent motif.

Fortunately, his wife and daughter were happy. Aldington told Slonimsky that Catha was 'very well and strong' and attending an excellent private nursery school which she liked so much that she complained about having to take holidays. She also belonged to a 'Girls' Club', which took her on picnics, to the ice- and roller-skating rinks, and on other expeditions, while riding on Shetland ponies seemed to her 'one of the most important aspects of her life'; he told Eskell that she was also being invited to 'extravagant parties' given by the children of movie executives.[9] Meanwhile, Netta was enrolled in an art school and enjoying the opportunity to develop her own talents.

The war was clearly a contributory factor to Aldington's state of mind, but, as so frequently in his career, much of his stress was caused by financial anxieties. He told Bacon in June 1943 that, despite having published *Rejected Guest*, *Life for Life's Sake* and the Viking anthology in his four years in the United States, the loss of European sales had left him struggling financially and he was now living off the money he had brought with him (Netta's inheritance) in 1939. 'I am delighted with California and my little family,' he told his friend, 'but here is this infernal difficulty of getting the right work done in a changing peculiar epoch. . . . I think I bet correctly with Wellington . . . but you can see how one might easily waste a year's work by doing something for which the cultivated public would feel no interest.'[10] He was searching for the subject for the next biography. His first choice was the American artist James Whistler. Manuel was now his literary, as well as his screenwriting, agent and the two of them considered that this was a biography that could be written with the screen in mind. 'Treating a biography as a comedy is something of an experiment, I admit,' Aldington wrote, 'but I see numerous possibilities.'[11] Nevertheless, the project was abandoned.

He had certainly 'bet correctly' with *The Duke*, which he had completed to his satisfaction by the end of February 1943: when it was published in October of that year, it sold 9,000 copies in the first three weeks, netting him $4,600 in royalties. He told Warman that Viking had offered him a large advance for another biography and that his success had attracted wider interest: Hollywood bookshops were displaying the book; the *Chicago Daily News* had asked for an article; and he had received an invitation to speak at the Los Angeles Book Fair.[12] By the end of November 21,000 copies had been printed.

Now more studio work started to come in. Manuel obtained him an assignment with Metro-Goldwyn-Mayer – this time at $1,000 a week – working on a screenplay of Robert Nathan's 1940 novel, *A Portrait of Jennie*.[13] The job lasted less than two weeks, but in early December Warner Brothers offered him a contract – at $750 a week – to work on Karl Vollmöller's play, *The Miracle*. The film was to be a Technicolor musical. 'The life of writing for the movies is a strange one,' he told Bacon:

> but I should be very glad if I could succeed. Far from being easy, it is a very difficult and specialised job, and most of those who have succeeded started young and gradually worked their way to the front. Unfortunately, the superstition of a reputation means that I have to start at the top and succeed at once, or not at all.[14]

He told Warman in February 1944 that English writers were not very successful (although he was pleased to report that Huxley had just been given a screen credit for *Jane Eyre* and that James Hilton 'makes pots and everyone likes him'), and he put this down to the fact that they too obviously despised Hollywood and, mistakenly, thought screenwriting easy. 'The only way to avoid disaster' was to have some other means of earning a living which could be taken up or dropped at a moment's notice. He estimated that he had been employed for thirteen weeks of the eighteen months he had so far spent in Hollywood. He would have been 'in the soup' if *The Duke* hadn't been a success. However, he still had no intention of returning to Europe: 'America isn't perfection, but I've always liked it from the first day I landed, and I like it more now.'[15]

His 75-page treatment for *The Miracle* met with approval and he was invited to write the screenplay. 'This means three or four months more of employment here, and if I can succeed in living up to the standard a new career, and not on fame and a shoe-string!' he wrote delightedly to Bacon.[16] He told Slonimsky: 'People complain much of their treatment by the Hollywood studios. All I can say is that they have been both civil and patient, given me every chance to show what I can do, and making no bones about payment.'[17]

Warner Brothers, however, was in turmoil; Aldington wrote to Bacon:

> Two producers have left shaking their contracts behind them and writers have been sacked nearly every day. From being congested the Writers' Building now resembles a cloister after the passage of the Black Death. Actually it was more like Alice in Wonderland. The 'Colonel' sat on his peak in darrien [*sic*] and as he read each script shouted 'Off with his head!' Actually this massacre is a great relief to me, most of those dismissed being about the most poisonous little communists you ever set eyes on.[18]

He would soon follow in their wake; he completed the screenplay by 27 April, but at this point the project was shelved.[19] It had given him 20 weeks' employment. Warner Brothers did ask him to collaborate with the Welsh screenwriter Tom Job on a murder story but this job lasted only a few weeks.

Although Aldington had entered the studio system at a time when many American males were serving in the forces, it was also a period when production had been cut. The war had brought a boom in cinema-going and the Federal government, which had grasped the role the movies could play in propaganda and the boosting of national morale, was supportive of the industry, but the studios had discovered that they could maximise profits by making fewer but more prestigious films. Warner Brothers, for example, released 48 films in 1941 but in 1943 their output was only 21. In 1944 they made the further step of moving to a unit-production system, whereby the making of each film became almost autonomous, with its own producer, director, screenwriters, cast and technicians, not a set-up which facilitated access for new writers.

It is surprising to find no evidence of any meetings between Huxley and Aldington during the latter's Hollywood years, particularly given Aldington's respect for Huxley as a man and a writer and their shared interest in maintaining the reputation of Lawrence. Perhaps his awe of Huxley – and of his success as a screenwriter – made him diffident. However, at Warner Brothers he made friends with William Faulkner, whom he drove to work each morning. '[V]ery Southern, very shy, but pleasant,' he told Warman.[20] The strongest friendship he established was with Frederick Faust, the highly successful pulp-fiction writer and Hollywood screenwriter, whose principal *nom de plume* was Max Brand.

Aldington contacted Faust as soon as he arrived in Hollywood, principally because Faust was a close friend – and former student – of Bacon. Indeed, Bacon and Faust had moved together to Florence in 1926, and Faust had only finally left his villa there in 1938. It is surprising to find no indication of Aldington's having met him during that period, despite his friendship with Bacon. The two men had a great deal in common. They were of the same age and both had experienced dysfunctional childhoods, although Faust's was unquestionably the more deprived. Both men had failed to graduate and felt that as a humiliation. Both had a passionate love of Italy, of beauty, of the classical and pagan worlds, but were prone to addictive behaviour, particularly with regard to sexual relationships, although Faust was also a drinker. His biographer (and son-in-law), Robert Easton, remarks that: 'Faust was quite capable of hurting other people, even those he loved. He was able to convince himself of the validity of almost any action he wanted to take. . . . His failure to understand the consequences of his actions . . . constituted one of his major shortcomings.'[21] We might recognise the applicability of this assessment to Aldington. Each man saw something to admire in the other: while Aldington must have found Faust's vitality and huge commercial success enviable, Faust's own ambition was to be a serious and well-regarded poet.

The two men took to each other immediately. Easton tells us that, whereas Warner Brothers expected their writers to work from 8.00 a.m. until 5.00 p.m., Faust would arrive at about nine o'clock, 'complete his fourteen pages by about eleven and spend the rest of the day in having lunch or in agreeable conversations with Aldington or some other friend, or in pushing coins at a crack in the floor, a recognised pastime in the Writers' Building'.[22]

There was one aspect of Aldington's life that Faust envied in particular: his war service. Faust had joined the Canadian Army's American Legion

Frederick Faust, early 1940s

in 1915, but the Legion's existence was such an embarrassment to the US government that its departure for France was constantly delayed. Desperate to get to the front, Faust had deserted, travelled to New York and made unsuccessful attempts to enrol in the Volunteer Ambulance Service and then the British Army. Once America entered the war he was rejected for military service because of his need for varicocele surgery. He was finally accepted, post-surgery, in September 1918 but assigned to the Army Corps of Engineers in Virginia, where he contracted the Spanish flu. By 11 November 1918 he had just secured a transfer to the Infantry Branch.

When the United States entered the Second World War, Faust, now 50 years old and suffering from a fibrillating heart, was desperate to be involved, and arranged to be sent to the Italian Front as correspondent for *Harper's Magazine* and for a service magazine entitled *The Infantry Journal*. He would live with a platoon of combat infantry, in action and out. En route to the front, he wrote to his wife, Dorothy: 'I wish you would ring up Aldington and tell him that I miss him regularly. He was the one really green oasis in my California desert, and over here, where he knows everything so well, my thoughts keep turning to him.'[23] On the night of 11 May 1944 he went into battle with E Company of the 2nd Battalion of 351st Infantry Regiment (88th Division), who were spearheading the attack on the village of Santa Maria Infante on the Gustave Line. In the early hours of 12 May he received a fatal wound in the chest from a shell fragment.

For Aldington, Faust's death was a great loss. He and Netta continued to keep in touch with Dorothy and her daughter, Jane Easton, and her two small daughters, who, along with Faust's younger daughter, Judy, were all living together in the Faust home in Burlingame Avenue, Los Angeles, while Jane's husband was fighting in France. In a letter to her husband written six months after Faust's death, Jane Easton mentioned that the Aldingtons had been to dinner at Burlingame Avenue. 'I do like him immensely,' she wrote, 'He is very well versed in all subjects, very sensitive, very aware. His only give-away is his immense despair with the world and humanity. He simply has no hope. I think that shows a weakness . . . [but] I do want you to meet him for his knowledge and his wit.'[24]

Aldington's despair was partly driven by his personal circumstances. He returned to MGM in late August 1944 to work for five weeks on a treatment of Alec Waugh's 1941 novel, *No Truce with Time*, and entertained high hopes of being given the screenplay, but the film was never made. His view of the studios had undergone a change. 'It is a strange and hideous world,' he told Slonimsky. He felt that his own world had narrowed:

> Apart from Netta and Catherine, my only interests are books (if they are not new), pictures (ditto) and Nature. I read biology and biography, poetry and essays. . . . I write trash here [at MGM] by day, go home and read Aeschylus. . . . I sometimes yearn for a little simple peace and silence. . . . I still keep my restive Pegasus hitched to the extraordinary and improbable movie wagon; but as I cannot write seriously in these disastrous times, it seemed sensible to try to earn and save a little money.[25]

Meanwhile, Netta had undergone a tooth extraction in the course of which a bone had splintered; she had required (expensive) nursing care and been in extreme pain.[26] Further bad news came with the revelation that Ralph Pinker (recently jailed for theft and fraud) had never paid tax on the money paid for the move rights of *All Men Are Enemies*. This had now to be paid, along with a weighty fine. May Aldington was also on the warpath. She had had a fall, breaking her arm, and therefore losing her job as a hotel receptionist. Aldington had to provide funds for his mother's care for a year (recorded on his tax return as $175) – funds which his sister Margery was careful to put in a bank account in her own name, to be paid out to her mother on a monthly basis for the twelve months. 'Perhaps I shall not hang on for all that time,' May wrote to her son, '& even if I do, I shall hope to be in some sort of work, & my dear, wonderful son, you will have the satisfaction of knowing that I shall not be cold or hungry again.' She reminded him that this had been his first communication for nearly two years.[27]

One better piece of news was that Aldington's friend Lawrence Clark Powell, Librarian at the University of California at Los Angeles, was planning an exhibition of Aldington's work for November 1944, and Aldington wrote to all his American friends to ask for loans of books which he had given them down the years.

In September 1944 he told Manuel that he would not take on any studio work for the rest of the year. He was suffering from recurrent bacterial infections and needed time to develop an idea for a writing project, having written nothing since *The Duke*.[28] In March 1945 the family had a short vacation trip to the Mojave Desert (a 500-mile round journey) where he was able to indulge his lifetime hobby of lepidoptery. It was, he told Bacon, his first venture outside the Los Angeles city limits in the whole two and a half years of their residence there.[29] Unless petrol rationing had been too restrictive, it is hard to understand why this naturally curious man with a love of landscape who had driven his family the length and breadth of America since 1939 and who had not been continuously employed since he came to California, either in the studios or on his own writing projects, had confined himself in this way.

A letter to Slonimsky in mid-April 1945 paints a bleak picture:

> I receive too many cold shoulders not to realise that what I have said is not wanted, nor anything I might say. Weeks, even months pass without my exchanging a word with anybody outside my family. ... Days pass without my even receiving a letter. ... People no longer like me either as a writer or as a person. I don't

Lawrence Clark Powell, 1950

blame anybody – even myself – it is just a fact. If only I had a little income this wouldn't trouble me in the least … but a writer's living depends on reputation, and mine has vanished. That is my fault – I never bothered about it, never cultivated or flattered anyone. That was a mistake – I was too indolent and conceited.[30]

It is a letter marked by self-pity but also by a reluctance to acknowledge what must have been his real fear: a decline in his creative powers.

As so often in his career, he compensated by throwing himself into a variety of projects demanding hard work and scholarship rather than originality. One was actually a novel, but a novel in which he had little belief, a fictional rendering of the life of Casanova, which he and Manuel conceived as a film project as well as a book. In March 1945 Marshall Best at Viking read the first part of the novel and rejected it. Columbia Pictures had bought the movie option for $10,000 and required the book to be published by a reputable New York publisher if they were going to proceed with it; Manuel placed it successfully with the young publishing company Duell, Sloan and Pearce. In addition to *The Romance of Casanova* ('this repulsive novel' he called it in a letter to Bacon), Aldington had taken on: a commission from *Encyclopaedia Britannica* to produce a poetry anthology of the Western world ('a long, arduous and underpaid job' he told Slonimsky); the preparation of an edition of Oscar Wilde for the Viking Press Portable

Library imprint; and the writing of introductions to four French romances to be published together in translation by the Pilot Press in London.[31] He also co-operated with Netta on a children's book, which never came to fruition, but she drew illustrations for his 1917 translation of Folgóre da San Gimignano's *The Garland of Months* and the book, entitled *A Wreath for San Gemignano*, was published by Duell, Sloan and Pearce. Aldington would tell his brother in April 1946 that it had been included in the US top 50 books of the year for production and illustration.[32]

A few days at Santa Barbara in May visiting Dorothy Strauss, who had moved there to be near her daughter, allowed the family to recapture some of their Florida existence, swimming, walking the sands and collecting shells, but Aldington had generally adopted a punishing routine: a ten-hour day, he told Warman in August. Even VE Day in May and VJ Day in August brought him little pleasure. 'It seems to me that America is in exactly the same position vis-à-vis Stalin that England and France were vis-à-vis Hitler in 1938,' he wrote to Bacon. 'You either keep giving in or you fight. Which will it be? I think I can guess.'[33] He reacted to the landslide Labour victory in Britain in July with a scepticism towards socialism which would become more deeply entrenched as the years went by, and which would cause a rift between himself and Frere. 'This "nationalisation" is a mere nostrum. Atlee's share the wealth is really a share the poverty,' he told Warman. 'I agree with your base of despair, especially in view of the cult of the envious, stupid, ignorant, unteachable average man.' His advice was not to get involved: 'Once let yourself be bull-dozed into thinking you are responsible for the world – and that way madness lies.'[34] He was certainly not contemplating a return to England, unlike the Glovers, who were planning to leave during the course of the coming year: 'I hate to lose them, but I shall stay here if I am not thrown out,' he told Bacon.[35]

He had begun to put his British financial affairs in some order after the Pinker fiasco, by asking his brother to take charge of his existing contracts and to try to call in any royalties due. News from Heinemann at the end of the year seemed promising too: despite the paper shortages Frere thought it probable that the firm could publish *The Duke* and the Wilde selection in the spring of 1946 and *The Romance of Casanova* in the autumn. However, he was discouraging about the publishing prospects of *Life for Life's Sake*, a view which would become a fracture point in their relationship.[36]

In early 1946, Herbert Read came on his first visit to America in order to give four lectures at Yale. He contacted Aldington, who was unable to travel east, busy as he was on the *Casanova* project at Columbia. As always with Read, and despite his disillusionment with Hollywood and his own career, Aldington could not resist the opportunity to boast:

> Hollywood is really very pleasant, about the nicest congeries of town
> to live in I know. . . . [F]or intellectual life there is Mount Wilson to the
> north, Cal Tech at Pasadena . . . and to the West U.C.L.A. with its library
> (rapidly growing) of 500,000 books of which I have the free run at all
> times, the Librarian being a crony of mine. I admit the Museum is no
> great shakes, but there are good art schools, more shows of modern
> stuff than I can afford time to visit, and the best music. We have far
> more opera and ballet here than you have in London.

We get a picture of a busy cultural and social existence belied by his
letters to his more intimate friends. As for his own career: 'I am not much
good at present – my salary is only $1,000 a week – but I have a kind
of obstinate hankering to master this infernal trade at which nearly all
English writers fail.' In fact, he told Read, 'Your suggestion that I should
return to Europe is rather like telling someone who, by dint of forethought
and at some expense, has got a Pullman seat in a train deluxe to come
frolic in an Hommes 40, Chevaux 8! Merci, mon prince!'[37]

Hearing from H.D. – their first exchange of letters for nearly a year – that
she was also coming to the United States shortly, to give a lecture at Bryn
Mawr, her former college, he made more modest claims: 'I do a little work
for the movies here from time to time, and like the climate very much.'[38]
The truth was that he had had enough of Hollywood: he thought it unlikely
that Columbia would proceed with the *Casanova* project; he was subject to
crippling taxes on past earnings; and future earnings looked precarious.
Part of his anxiety stemmed from a conviction that Frere had misled him
over Heinemann's commitment to publish his work. He heard from Arnold
Gyde, Frere's deputy at Heinemann, that *The Duke* would not be published
until June, despite Frere's earlier promise that it was scheduled for April.
Aldington liked Gyde (although he had not met him in person) – both for
the courteous tone of his letters and because he had been in military service
during the war, but he was furious with Frere. He told his brother: 'I've
been properly let down by a man who for years has professed the greatest
friendship etc. What his motives are I don't profess to know.' He told Tony
that he had given Gyde an ultimatum: publication of *The Duke* before May
or it would go to Constable.[39] A volatile phase in Aldington's relationship
with Frere, which would last for the rest of their lives, had been set in train.

By mid-March, after what he told Bacon had been a bad dose of flu but
described to Warman as a nervous collapse from overwork, he had decided
on a move to Jamaica. He told his brother: 'We can batten on Netta's Mam
during the coming famine. She has some land there, and very wealthy
friends. . . . Even if we have to pay income tax in Jamaica it will be cheaper

than here, believe me, and much pleasanter.'[40] On 15 April he started to keep a diary: perhaps he thought that their journey would provide material he could use later as travel writing; or perhaps he felt that this move – more than the others over the past seven years – was a momentous one that required a record. If Columbia decided to proceed with *Casanova*, he would have to return; he clearly thought this unlikely. His entry for 22 April 1946, the last day before their departure, reads: 'Hollywood (44 months of it) has been a crucial experience, salutary perhaps, damaging perhaps, certainly profitable & certainly a place to leave!'

He drove to New Orleans via Palm Springs, Uma, Gilabad, Tucson, El Paso and San Antonio, a 2,200-mile journey. A vivid account of the experience appears in a letter he wrote to H.D. six years later:

> On that Jeff Davis Highway between Orange and El Paso, there are stretches of 100 miles without even a shack. There is a motel at a little place called Marathon, just on the East side of the Great Divide, which is as remote as the moon. . . . From San Antonio to El Paso is close on 500 miles with nothing but a few motels and 'shack' towns. I remember Sierra Blanca, and the hugest sun I ever saw going down flaming crimson over the desert and the mountains turning blue. And Wyoming. I remember coming up from Boulder, Coloraydo [sic], to Laramie and Medicine Bow, and, stopping off at Rawlings, Wy., found a saloon with pictures of all the famous cattle brands of the West, and photos of all the famous hold-up men, including Calamity Jane. And they were very sweet to us, and gave us wonderful beef steaks, and whipped up ice-cream for Catha, and told us lots about cattle rustlers.[41]

The truth, as revealed in the diary, is rather different. There were rewarding moments, for instance 29 April when the entry reads: 'ONE OF THE BEST – IF NOT THE BEST – DAYs of the trip . . . into the mountainous uplands of western Texas. – a tremendous almost uninhabited world of desert, mountains & cattle range which is most exhilarating.' However, such entries are the exception. Tucson was 'unpleasant', El Paso 'a dull American town'; 3 May was 'a longish day's drive through Louisiana with the squalor of the South in evidence'. The chief problem was his poor emotional and physical state; at the end of the second day of travelling, he contemplated abandoning the car and making the rest of the journey by train. Instead he rested for a day before continuing, but he had frightened himself. He blamed: '(A) overwork in Hollywood, particularly the last four months on the anthology; (B) the strain of anxiety, personal & over the war; (C) too little sleep, particularly on the nights of the 22nd and 23rd; (D) the narrow embankment road across the Yuma sand dunes.' 'Feel better for the rest,' he concluded, 'but hope for an easy ride tomorrow. We should now go slowly & rest a day. I am certainly more exhausted nervously than at any time since the end of the last war, & in flabby physical condition.'

The journey became his final disillusionment with his American dream. On 27 April as he arrived in Deming, New Mexico, he wrote: '[O]ne's nerves grow raw with the continual vulgarity of America, the gross coarse food, the gum-chewing coarse-faced people, the vile trashy periodicals & "books".' He noticed, too, 'as far west as Uvalde', the many cafes with their 'Coloured patronage not solicited' notices. 'Sweet land of liberty,' he observed drily. By the time he reached New Orleans ('much more interesting and alive than any town to the west') he was writing: 'This journey has been a test of endurance,' but also: 'I shall be very glad to get out of this country after 7 years of it & hope to goodness I never see it again.' A few days earlier he had written: 'How thankful I am that I have resisted all pressure to naturalise!' It was a very different judgement from the one he had given Read only three months earlier.

On 10 May 1946 they flew from New Orleans via Tampa and Miami to Havana, where Netta's mother met them before the final leg of their journey to Jamaica. After two days of rest and sightseeing in Kingston, they took a 'long, dirty and tiring' train journey to Montego Bay, where they set up a temporary home in the Chatham Hotel. Rest, swimming, observing marine life through a glass-bottomed boat and relishing the peacefulness 'after that raucous America' became the order of the day, but the social attentions of the expatriate community soon became oppressive. The incompetent bureaucratic processes which had to be endured over the next few weeks, necessitating visits to Kingston in order for them to retrieve their car and luggage, including Aldington's library, also became frustrating. Stranded in Kingston, Aldington wrote in his diary on 27 May: 'This whole Jamaica trip has become a financial disaster, with the threat of malaria and typhoid and the impossibility of finding somewhere else to go.' The following day he had an acute attack of dysentery from 'over-exertion in the heat, coupled with the annoyance and indignity of the whole proceedings'. Back in Montego Bay a coastal drive produced the entry: 'Picturesque enough country, but somehow rather meaningless to me in my present mood.' A puncture and meeting yet more 'dull people' had not helped.

By 2 June he was writing: 'Netta and I have decided we not only can't live here but must leave as soon as possible.' He told Warman: 'It is a great relief to be out of the U.S. – both of us were about at the end of our power of endurance of the raucous bastards,' but continued:

Aldington publicity photograph, 1946

Jamaica is rather a disappointment – turns out to be very hot and
muggy, malarious, and politically a kind of negro republic flying
the Union Jack. The people are mostly lazy, and the big idea is
to wangle loans and grants from England. It has the depressing
quality of derelict countries – the old sugar estates gone to hell,
the coconuts dying of one disease and the bananas of another.
The scenery is very beautiful, so are the Mediterranean colours

of the sea, and the bathing A1. But we are constantly scared of
malaria for Catherine, and there are too few white people to make
any society. ... [T]he only tolerable company is that of the few
elderly descendants of the last remaining 'great' families.[42]

He wrote on 17 June: 'No wonder there is so little intellectual life in
Jamaica & that the people are so ordinary. There is something indescribably
depressing about the climate. It is not only de-energising, but positively
makes one gloomy & despondent. ... It is certainly a very undesirable
place of residence.' He was becoming aware, however, that his depression
was more fundamental – and that it was a burden to his family. He started
to work – on an idea he had proposed to Duell for a Nineties anthology
– but his library would not arrive until mid-July and he was restricted
without it. He tried to improve the state of his relationship with Netta,
and his diary entry for 4 July reads: 'Spent a wonderful morning with
Netta. Bathed three times.' Four days later came his 54th birthday.

He recorded on 7 July: 'Very depressed and unwell feeling today as I am
so often in Jamaica. ... I wish I could be in some peaceful place, among
my books, with a few friends; but that modest wish is like hoping for
immortality in these bitter days.' Netta, who, according to a letter Aldington
wrote to Warman, now hated the United States and refused to return,
wanted to go to England.[43] It might have appeared a tempting solution,
with his affairs now being put in order by his brother and the arrival of long
friendly letters from old acquaintances like Prentice, Glover, Gribble, Snow,
Carl Fallas, Osbert Sitwell and, of course, Warman. John Arlott, the Literary
Programmes Producer for the BBC Overseas Service, also wrote, regarding a
radio programme on Imagism that he was going to broadcast in July.

However, the bureaucracy he had encountered in Jamaica served as a
warning. He told Powell:

> I am not a Socialist I discover, and this 'government control' of
> everything and everybody in British territory gives me the willies.
> Don't be taken in – Socialism isn't justice, it's a dismal tyranny of
> bureaucrats. We are hopping it, and I'll be damned if I ever get
> back into British dominion again, if I can help it.[44]

He and Netta had agreed on Paris, Gribble's offer of his studio
apartment for as long as he remained with the Reparations Committee in
Belgium clinching the decision. Once that decision was made, Aldington's
spirits lightened. On 26 July he wrote in his diary: 'After a regrettable
outburst on my part Netta has promised to do all she can to help with

these multitudinous difficulties and arrangements,' and the next day's entry reads: 'A quieter day. I am beginning to get control of myself, although in the morning I totally failed to start work on the anthology introductions.'

One item he received in the post from Britain would come to have considerable significance in his later life. The small parcel contained two books of poetry by a young Australian, Alister Kershaw. 'In his Preface,' Aldington's diary records, 'he attacks much of what I dislike in modern verse (and citing RA, DHL and RC as poets "who have opposed this horror with ferocious genius"). His poems good and his prose direct and vigorous.'

Now more bureaucracy had to be faced: a flight to New York to meet with the French Consul-General and procure the documents needed for the family to gain residency visas for France. (Fortunately, the Consul-General turned out to be a fan of *Death of a Hero* and *The Colonel's Daughter*.) By 3 August they were at 440 Park Avenue. Aldington squeezed in a visit to the Metropolitan Museum of Art: 'The pleasure of being back once more with the art of the world is indescribable,' he wrote in the diary. On 11 August they spent a day on Long Island with Johnson and his family. Aldington met with Duell the next day and agreed a four-book contract: the Nineties anthology, a Walter Pater selection, a biography of Louis XV and a novel. He wrote to tell Frere of the agreement.

On the night of 13 August he wrote in the diary: 'I write this in bed on my last night in America. The Slonimskys dined with us and were delightful.' The following morning he wrote to Bacon to thank him 'for all the good and kind things of the past eight years'. There was also a final note to Slonimsky: 'On Friday we shall be in the Luxembourg Gardens.'[45]

On Thursday 15 August 1946 he and Catha flew to Paris. (Netta was to follow.) The Glovers were there to meet them at the airport.

14. The Public Face
Novelist, Biographer, Memoirist and Anthologist

While the scope of Aldington's output during the American years illustrates his versatility, it also suggests desperation. His seven-and-a-half year sojourn in the United States, with its combination of extensive travel and residence in a variety of communities, produced no material for poetry or prose. Several years later he would tell Martin Secker that he had 'a half-formed subject' for a short novel in a south-west Florida setting, but the idea came to nothing.[1]

We might have expected his marriage, fatherhood and the strong, if few, friendships of this period, as well as his exposure to a new environment, to have enabled him to throw off the emotional burdens of the past and to seek imaginative inspiration in the world around him. Instead, the familiar pattern reasserted itself – in New York, in New England, in Washington, D.C., Florida, Taos and Los Angeles – of initial excitement and hopefulness followed by disenchantment and recurring bouts of anxiety and depression. It is important to recognise, however, that he carried with him to America the problem he had lived with all his adult life, compounded now by the war and by his responsibility for his young family: his need to earn a living from his writing. The war itself – and perhaps his isolation from it – was a further cause of anxiety.

Rejected Guest, mostly written at the Villa Koechlin before the move to America, came out of the stable that had produced *All Men Are Enemies* and *Very Heaven*. Its close resemblance to those earlier novels not only demonstrates the narrow, and very autobiographical, range of Aldington's preoccupations, but suggests a loss of inventiveness. Once again, he took a phrase from a Romantic poet as his title, this time Shelley.[2] The 'rejected guest' in question is David Norris, the illegitimate child of a young British officer killed in the First World War. Brought up by his maternal grandparents in impoverished and isolated circumstances, he tries on their deaths to use his small inheritance to gain himself some higher education. He makes himself known to his wealthy paternal grandfather, a baronet, with the intention of asking for a loan to complete his studies. Instead, his grandfather lavishes money on him but requires him to abandon his studies and to live on the Riviera with a guardian in order for his identity not to become public. Here David falls in love but this apparently idyllic relationship is brutally terminated by the outbreak of the Second World War and the intestate death of his grandfather. At the end of the novel – like Chris Heylin in *Very Heaven* – David returns to England, penniless, alone and with no prospects.

One of the most successful aspects of the novel is its evocation of place: the interwar utilitarian town of 'Ruxton' and David's sordid London lodgings give way, in the second half of the narrative, to the brilliant and sensuous beauty of the Mediterranean:

> April, we know, is the cruellest month; but at Saint-Australe it was beautiful. Snow-bearing east winds from the Alps had gone, and the mistral itself grew rarer. Long ago the swallows and swifts had come darting and sweeping from across the sea, a small black arrow-storm in the vanguard of spring. In the sheltered valleys of mimosa and holm-oak the first nightingales startled the air with brief fragments of unpractised song. Like a golden wave slowly flooding the mountains, the broom and thorn broke into yellow flower, with a foam of white cistus. As in the Spring poems of the Anthology, the wine-dark sea calmed itself into smiles, and navigation became safe even for the intrepid Hellenes of old and the modern Mediterranean fishers.[3]

The hills, sea and weather of the Riviera both influence and reflect David's circumstances and moods in a lightly applied pathetic fallacy. A felicitous touch is that David's guardian's Mediterranean home is – transplanted to the mainland – the vigie on Port-Cros where Aldington had stayed with Lawrence, Frieda, Yorke and Patmore in 1928 – and where *Death of a Hero* was begun.

Character types re-emerge from the earlier novels: David's guardian, Mr Martindale, is a variation on Mr Chepston in *Very Heaven* or Purfleet in *The Colonel's Daughter*, intelligent and even at times a mouthpiece for the author, but ultimately cynical, self-serving and thoughtless; Margy Stuart of *The Colonel's Daughter* becomes Diana Rockingham, the woman with whom David falls in love and who carelessly abandons him at the end of the novel; O'Hara and Cowley, the friends David makes in his home town, are shadows of Stephen Crang and Robin Fletcher in *All*

Men Are Enemies; Prince Alleoti, the wise and cultured aristocrat who befriends David is a variation on Henry Scrope of *All Men Are Enemies* or Dudley Pollack in *Death of a Hero,* older male characters whose presence allows the protagonist to air his ideas and concerns in lengthy passages of dialogue, and who offer him guidance and advice which is sound but ultimately inadequate. In keeping with the general tone of *Rejected Guest*, Prince Alleoti turns out to be a fraud – at least in David's view, an 'absentee Calabrian landlord' entertaining the young man with his 'urbane intellectual parlour tricks' and 'fake Hellenism': 'The old man wasn't a fool; he had both feet firmly planted on a 20th-century income in order to live in a cloud-cuckoo-land utopia of the 5th BC.'[4]

In addition to this cast of main characters we have vignettes of literary society very like those in *Death of a Hero* in their accuracy, acuteness – and malice. Here the two writers satirised are H.G. Wells and Michael Arlen. Wells had never expressed much interest in Aldington and had taken Patmore's side when he left her; but Arlen had always been an amiable acquaintance. Another malicious portrait is of David's London landlady, 'built on a flabby Rubens scale', who 'mythologised herself and everything about her with impudence and self-deception'. In case the reader misses the allusion, her name is Watkins.[5]

The novel's major weaknesses are ones we have encountered before: an intrusive and urbane authorial voice which disengages the reader from the world of the narrative; and a naive and passive central character. Aldington explicitly calls our attention to David's weakness, describing him as one of 'the silver change of humanity, the people who cannot find repose in the commonplace, who are aware of the great struggle of minds but are not quite good enough to take any real part in it'.[6] Like George Winterbourne (another *naïf*), Chris Heylin and Georgie Smithers, David is presented to us as a victim of his social and family circumstances, although the reader may feel that the protagonist carries some responsibility for the tragic outcome.

The extensive passages of authorial comment that weaken *Very Heaven* are gone, replaced by David's long conversations with Martindale, Alleoti and Diana. However, rhetorical flourishes abound: 'Rosamund Norris had two or three nice dresses and no brains to mar her prettiness or interfere with romance'; 'Having lost her man through a stray shell, Rosamund went off to make shells to destroy other women's men'; 'It is the misfortune of the self-educated that they invariably associate with their mental inferiors, and hence rate themselves too high'; '[Martindale] went in for the maximum of good living with the minimum of responsibility'; 'There can be little doubt that his first real love affair has a very stimulating effect on the human male. He becomes fully aware of what a remarkable chap he is.'[7] Here reader engagement with the narrative is sacrificed to short-term entertainment.

The *TLS* review was critical:

> The distaste or disgust or 'disillusionment' that is so pronounced in Mr Aldington's novels is not abated here. Once more he disapproves of a great many things – of snobbery, prudery, industry, Christianity, numerous forms of art and literature. The motive of his criticism is often plain enough, springing as it does from an acute and deeply fretted sensitiveness; between an antiquated ideal and the commercialism of our day, he suggests, lies a morass of the spirit in which normal humanity founders. With all the good will in the world, however, it cannot be said that this all-inclusive condemnation of his is delivered here with sufficient imaginative force or weight. David, no doubt, is the type and symbol of a frustrated generation, the rejected guest at the feast of life. But you cannot make a good novel out of frustration alone or out of the indictment of an entire civilization.[8]

The *Times* reviewer focused on the authorial intrusions:

> Mr Aldington is one of the most personal of authors. To read one of his novels is like having the next-door flat and seeing him several times a day. He is always dropping in to see how his characters and the reader are getting on together, and this habit, which is at first amusing, becomes wearisome.[9]

Life for Life's Sake has a very different tone. The memoirs, subtitled *A Book of Reminiscences*, were written for a middle-class American audience typified by the readers of *Atlantic Monthly* where it was serialised. It is chiefly about Aldington's place in the literary world and is reticent about his private life, which barely intrudes on the narrative. The first five chapters focus on his upbringing in rural England, and here his ability to evoke the spirit of place is strongly in evidence. There is little hint of disharmony or disadvantage; only his schooling is criticised: 'My days at school were . . . a perpetual struggle against a conditioning which was repulsive to me.'[10] There follow four chapters about his life in the literary world of pre-war London. The portraits of Lawrence, Pound, Ford and Eliot have none of the vitriol of those in *Death of a Hero*. Of Pound he concedes, 'It seems to me hard to deny his flair or that he has at least a streak of genius', and of Ford, 'I have known many men in my time, but few so fundamentally innocent of real harm', and he speaks of the generosity of both men towards other artists.[11] The portraits of Lawrence and Eliot come in the wartime and postwar chapters. The profile of Eliot is restrained and focuses on the way in which he 'succeeded . . . by merit, tact, prudence and pertinacity . . . in imposing his personality, taste, and even many of his opinions on literary England'.[12] As for Lawrence: 'Of all human beings I have known he was by far the most continuously and vividly alive and receptive.'[13]

Three chapters deal with the war and its aftermath and a further eight are devoted to the 1920s, Aldington's retirement to the rural home counties society of Berkshire and his visits to Italy and France, ending with (a version of) the events at Port-Cros and the writing of *Death of a Hero*. The 1930s and his travels throughout that period are covered swiftly in the final two chapters. Along the way there are many other portraits: of H.D. ('I have never known anybody, not even Lawrence, with so vivid an aesthetic apprehension') and of Yeats, Monro, Hulme and Gaudier-Brzeska, Orioli and Douglas, Joyce, Wells (a far more charitable portrait than in *Rejected Guest*), de Gourmont, the Sitwells, Storer, Read and Barney; and of less prominent friends and acquaintances such as MacGreevy, Prentice and Frere, Gribble, Slonimsky, Henry Church, Fallas and Whitham. One of the most sharply critical evaluations is of Read:

> [H]is poems seem to me to lack the passion which gives life to even the worst splurgings of D.H. Lawrence, and the intellectual concentration which so effectively conceals Eliot's emotional sterility. . . . [M]uch of Read's work suffers from a kind of metropolitan provincialism, addressing itself to a small group of super-aesthetes whose mental fashions change as quickly as those of *couturiers*.

Not only what he wrote of Douglas himself but also his account of the 'Maurice Magnus affair' were badly received by Douglas, a refugee in Portugal when the memoirs appeared in *Atlantic Monthly*. Aldington would return to the Magnus story in biographies of both Lawrence and Douglas in the 1950s and consistently took Lawrence's side in the matter. Magnus, an American, had been one of Douglas's acquaintances and it was through Douglas that Lawrence had come to know him. Magnus was a spendthrift and constantly in debt. He received a small loan from Lawrence and subsequently followed him to Sicily to ask for more money, with which he travelled to Malta where he was pursued by the

Italian police for his debts and committed suicide to avoid imprisonment. Douglas was his literary executor and agreed that Lawrence should write an introduction to Magnus's memoirs of his wartime experiences in the Foreign Legion. Taking exception to the account of events that appeared in this introduction, Douglas published a pamphlet entitled *D.H. Lawrence and Maurice Magnus: A Plea for Better Manners* in which he blamed Lawrence for Magnus's death, asserting that Lawrence had been too mean to give Magnus enough money to escape imprisonment. In *Life for Life's Sake* Aldington demands:

> Why on earth should Lorenzo have given more than half the small sum he had in the world to a comparative stranger who, he had every reason to think, was a waster and perhaps a crook? Norman had much more money than Lawrence, and Magnus was *his* friend, not Lawrence's.[14]

However, the tone of the book is generally cool and urbane. One of the few departures from this is the impassioned account of the 'indifference verging on hostility' with which the civilian world treated 'the men of the returning army' in 1919. Furthermore:

> It was not enough that the returning soldiers were snubbed and left to get on as best they could. Our dead were insulted; our battlefields were made a show for money. ... Every night as I read or lay sleepless I heard the raucous shouts and whoops of drunken revellers, a strange disorderliness in the decorous West End. I am no enemy to rejoicings, but this debauchery over ten million graves seemed to me indecent. I saw nothing to rejoice about, having too many vivid recollections of endless desolation and rows upon rows of wooden crosses.[15]

On his experience of the war itself he is more detached – deliberately: '[W]hat I have set down here has been the trifling, not the tragical. To have re-lived it all once in the making of another book was strain enough.' He admits, however, that: 'Unexpectedly, in a flash, it may break through that laboriously built wall of forgetfulness. Certain smells, sounds and sights are the battering rams which suddenly demolish the wall and let the memories escape.'

On his personal life he is brief – and in some cases disingenuous. He is candid about the break-up of his marriage in 1919: '[T]hrough my own folly or worse, I had got my personal life into a tragical mess, which added to my difficulties, and resulted in separation from H.D.'[16] However, the equally dramatic events of 1928 are accounted for with no sense of personal responsibility: 'I missed most of my twenties, when most people have a lot of fun ... there was a repressed young man under my sedate exterior clamouring to be heard. I let him be heard. And why not?'[17] The break-up of his relationship with Patmore (who, along with Yorke, is never mentioned) and his elopement with Netta are lost in an invented narrative that has him deciding in 1935 to spend 'the rest of [his] life' in the United States. In Connecticut that year, he maintains, 'I made up my mind that henceforth I would make my headquarters in America.' Subsequent events are subsumed into this construction: 'Twice the complications of life took me back to Europe for rather long periods, one of them being my second marriage and the birth of my daughter, about eighteen months later; but at the third attempt I succeeded in getting permanently free from European entanglements.'[18]

The New York Times focused on the 'fine and meticulous reticence' that seemed 'determined to keep *Life for Life's Sake* on an even and detached keel': '[T]here are moments when the private memoirs, the unwritten confessions as it were, peer through the more objective pages, but these moments are fleeting, swift shadows glancing across the more solid aspects of things ...' The reviewer called the work 'a book of pictures, of personalities, of places, of literary urges and movements', and commented on the skill with which the author brought people and places to life. He concluded: 'He has brought us the sense and spirit of vanished times and he has done it without hurting any feelings or baring any wounds or betraying any confidences, and that is something indeed in a period when a civilised reticence is considered either Victorian or cowardly.'[19]

Whether there was a market for the book in Europe Aldington would never discover. Frere consistently refused his requests for Heinemann to publish it, partly because he felt that it would have little appeal for a British audience that, unlike Aldington himself, had endured the deprivations of the Second World War and its aftermath and felt some resentment towards wartime expatriate writers, but also, surprisingly in the light of the book's genial tone, because he feared that several of the portraits would at best make Heinemann unpopular in literary circles and at worst attract libel charges.[20]

The Viking Book of Poetry of the English-Speaking World, published in September 1941, was the product of extensive reading and research, drawing on all Aldington's expertise on poetry from *Beowulf* onwards, and necessitating meticulous selection. Personal inclinations are occasionally discernible, as in the provision of six poems by Lawrence and five by H.D.

when most contemporary poets are represented by one or two. Yeats and Hardy both have six, but Robert Frost a surprising five. Swinburne has ten and William Scawen Blunt a remarkable twelve, while Browning's fifteen contrasts with Tennyson's seven.

Predictably perhaps, although the anthology consisted of over 1,200 poems by about 300 known poets (and a number of anonymous ones), and the selections were generally well-judged and even-handed, many of the reviews consisted of adverse criticism of the contemporary choices. When the book appeared in Britain in December 1947, the *Manchester Evening News* reviewer called the last hundred pages 'a serious blemish on a selection which, for some two thirds of its length, is very good indeed'.[21] However, the book fortuitously appearing in Britain in the run-up to Christmas, Edward Shanks commented in the *TLS* that he could think of nothing finer to put in the hands of a young person beginning to take an interest in poetry.[22]

It is an indication of Aldington's financial concerns, but also perhaps of an awareness that he had run dry of creative ideas, that he took on towards the end of his residence in Hollywood the even more laborious task of compiling an anthology of poetry of the Western world for the *Encyclopaedia Britannica*. In fact, the work, though completed, was never published. Anthologies were becoming his means of earning a living – and gaining in the process some sense of scholarly achievement: in 1946 there were the *Great French Romances* and the Viking *Portable Oscar Wilde*; and over the following two years he would work on a Walter Pater selection and an anthology of the writings of the Aesthetes.[23]

His foray into biography – the first since his *Voltaire* in 1925 – was extremely successful. As he had done in the earlier book, he expertly synthesised vast quantities of information into a balanced and well-proportioned narrative – from which Wellington emerges, as Selwyn Kittredge observed, 'as a living, breathing human being'.[24] Aldington's command of his material is most evident in the chapters that deal with the Peninsular War and the Waterloo campaign. The military historian Cyril Falls, reviewing the book on its publication in Britain in 1946, called it 'firmly and decisively written' and commended its good military detail, particularly with regard to the Waterloo campaign.[25] Graeme Cooper, a contemporary authority on the two campaigns and an experienced guide on those battlefields, comments on the insights the book furnishes into Wellington's decision-making and strategic thinking, demonstrating his ability and effectiveness as a commander.[26]

Although the reader is aware of the author's presence, shaping, analysing and reflecting, that presence is never intrusive, the voice always informed and authoritative but also good-humoured and measured.

This is a particularly impressive achievement in the closing chapters, which deal with Wellington's disastrous political career after 1819. With respect to the Duke's misjudgements, Aldington points out that he had spent few of his adult years in the country and consequently had little understanding of either the English people or the Industrial Revolution, against which two powers he:

> fought blindly and disastrously for his reputation . . . an interesting example of a man brilliantly successful in a war where (unknown to himself) he was backed by the will of his own people, the spirit of the times, and the good wishes of mankind, turning to failure when that support was withdrawn because he failed to recognise the signs and trends of the newer age, a fresh generation, another world.[27]

Never excusing, but always explaining his subject's attitudes, behaviour and actions, he reminds the reader that the Duke had been conditioned 'by his birth and upbringing, by his profession and career and interests, to complete identification with the aristocratic party and a firm (if naive) faith that they, and they alone, made the strength, safety, happiness and glory of the realm'. He continues, in a passage that reminds us of his penchant for satire: 'He could scarcely have mistrusted the people more if he had been one of the people's friends, those Whig peers who jogged along on £40,000 a year and jeered at Tories and *jacquerie* alike over 10 p.m. rere-suppers of oysters and hot pheasants wheeled round on trolleys by obsequious flunkeys.'[28] 'Common sense,' he concludes:

> is valuable; but it doesn't cover everything as charity is said to do. In those days there was a need for faith, almost a mystic faith, to believe that these ignorant violent people could in their children become decent civilised people if only they were freed and decently treated. But you had to take the risk of freeing them. Arthur Wellesley, Duke of Wellington, had too much common sense to believe in freeing them, too great a feeling of responsibility to the throne (Prinny and his brandy bottle) to take the risk.[29]

When the book was published in Britain the historian Charles Webster noted Aldington's success in communicating his own pleasure to the reader and remarked how much he had enjoyed 'those spirited pages in which every now and again a modern idiom links up the campaigns with our own experience'.[30] The *Daily Telegraph* reviewer thought the book 'sensible and just': 'Under [Aldington's] brush . . . we see the firm features of a man great in character, foresight, courage, quickness of apprehension and mastery of the science of war.'[31] That year, the book was awarded the James Tait Black Memorial Prize for Biography.

The final production of Aldington's years in America was the novel *The Romance of Casanova*, completed on New Year's Day 1946 and published later that year. A spin-off from his involvement in the editing of *Great French Romances* for the Pilot Press, it is a derivative *genre* piece, although an accomplished one, in which the political intrigues of eighteenth-century Venice are darkly evoked and set pieces such as Casanova's escape from the Leads vividly realised. The intention for the tale to become a screenplay for a period adventure film is transparent, and Anthony Powell, reviewing it in the *Daily Telegraph* when it appeared in Britain in January 1947, found it to be 'rather in the manner of Baroness Orczy'. He might, with equal validity, have compared it to a Dumas novel. However, the *TLS* reviewer identified one interesting feature of the narrative: the way in which it casts the protagonist as 'the tool of women, not their master'; certainly the female characters are represented as more intelligent, determined and active individuals than Casanova himself.[32] The most enthusiastic review was in *The Manchester Guardian*, where Charles Marriott commended the way in which Aldington's 'firm, light hand . . . moves confidently about eighteenth-century Venice' and found the writing 'straightforward, smooth, flexible, and . . . sinewy'.[33]

Creatively, the years in America were disappointing. Just as he had earlier come to accept the end of his career as a poet, Aldington had discovered that he could no longer write novels. He had realised, however, that his erudition and passion for literature could earn him a basic living, if publishers could be persuaded that there was a market for his proposals. More importantly, his one success had been in the field of biography, which drew on both his meticulous scholarship and his skills as a writer.

Part Three

THE RECLUSE

1951-1962

15. Back to the Old World
1946-1947

On 16 August 1946 Aldington and Catha arrived in Paris and were met by the faithful Glovers. They checked in at the Hotel Aiglon in the Boulevard Raspail and met up daily with the Glovers and the Churches, visiting galleries and dining in restaurants, both before and after Netta's arrival on 26 August. A new acquaintance was Edward Gordon Craig, whose youngest daughter, Daphne, only three years older than Catha, became a new friend for her.

Paris was a disappointment: 'still a city of the dead', he wrote in his diary for 19 August. He told Gyde (in charge at Heinemann while Frere was on holiday):

> After the grimness and lack of gaiety of the people, the dirtiness of everything, I am chiefly struck by the apathetic resignation, the lack of that spirit of damn-the-government-let's-get-things-started-again which has already brought the U.S. pretty well back to pre-war in everything except housing and some items of men's clothes. . . . The way the gaiety has gone out of Paris is most striking. I haven't heard a laugh, seen a smiling or pretty face or a well-dressed woman since I arrived.[1]

Rathbone, who met up with him, was distressed by this 'thick-hided lack of realisation of all that has taken place since 1939 and of the epic of the Resistance' in a man for whom she still had enormous regard. She warned Cunard:

> If by chance you meet Richard Aldington in Paris be prepared for his taking a very queer line. He contradicts everything one says about France's sufferings and resistance. Says the Resistance was no help to anybody & has been exaggerated out of all sense of

proportion. .... His indifference to the English war effort & to anything else his old friends have been through is perhaps natural (part feigned, part real). But the indifference to, and denigration of, France's experiences really is a bewilderment ... but I have a theory ... that he nurses a guilt complex because of not having been in the War, & been so very far away & well-fed, therefore has to disparage the sufferings of others.

She added: 'What the French writers (Casson etc. etc. etc.) will think and say when he gets amongst them I daren't imagine.'[2] Aldington's comments do seem at the least to have displayed extraordinary insensitivity, but if Rathbone had seen his 1940 'The Horn of Roland' essay she might have been more forgiving.

Aldington was not Ezra Pound: he had no intention of 'getting amongst' French writers; he hankered after the Anglo-American community of the late 1920s and wrote to Cunard a fortnight after his arrival:

Dear Nancy
    I have just got an address which I'm told will reach you.
    We – that is myself, my wife and my 8 year old daughter – came in by air from U.S.
    If you are staying in Paris it would be very nice to see you and to show you *ma famille*, if it wouldn't bore you.
    Yours
    Richard[3]

Cunard did not reply; she had not forgiven him for the Hours Press row in 1930. Her response to Rathbone was simply: 'that bloody Aldington'.[4]

Only a fortnight after the letter to Gyde, perhaps invigorated by the prospect of seeing at least one of his pre-war friends, Aldington was writing to Frere:

It is an immense satisfaction to be free from the 'American way'. In spite of the large communist and socialist representation in the National Assembly, France is probably less pedantically socialist than England, less like a demonstration of the spectacular errors of the Fabian Society. .... Paris is still Paris, and you can see the people, the nation, struggling through the insanities and blunders of the politicians. .... France of course is fundamentally a richer country than England in everything that matters to human life.[5]

Alexander Frere, Cape Wrath, Scotland, 1943

While it offers a more positive view of his adopted country, there is also a sub-text here: he was well aware of Frere's connections with, and support for, Britain's Labour Government.

Frere's first letter had assured Aldington: 'You needn't worry about the immediate financial future . . . I shall be making a lot for you over here from now on.'[6] His promise was fulfilled: the 10,000 first print-run of *Wellington* sold out on publication; by the end of the year 10,000 copies of the Wilde anthology were sold, and it would be reprinted the following May; *The Romance of Casanova* would have a pre-publication subscription of 18,000. Yet Aldington's diary entry for 10 September reads: 'Odious letter from Frere. He is really intolerable and I hope he doesn't come to Paris', but he told his brother only a week later that he had had a 'very gracious letter' from Frere, due, he felt, to the fact that the first impression of *Wellington* had sold out.[7] Their relationship from now on would always be affected by such professional matters; Aldington was much less of an asset to Heinemann than he had been to Chatto & Windus in the 1930s and most of his proposals were not profitable ones. By April 1947 Frere would be writing: 'The reports are that [*Casanova*] is hanging fire in the shops. I think it is feeling the effect of some hostile reviews . . . everything has been sticking in the shops since what is known as the crisis burst upon us.' *Wellington*, he told Aldington, was also going slowly and *Wilde* halted waiting for paper. He told Aldington to send him the *Pater* but, 'in common with all other things it will have to be pegged back in the schedule for we are still comparatively in the dark as to what the future is going to be'. He assured Aldington that he still wanted the 'Nineties omnibus' and 'the various other things'. . . 'but there again a lot depends on the next 6 months'.[8] How far there was a general publishing crisis – and a paper shortage – and how far Frere was using these as an excuse for his reluctance to press ahead with Aldington's projects is not clear; but Aldington saw such letters as prevarication.

Gradually the old life came back and Aldington wrote to Bacon: 'We feel as if we have come home and are more and more happy to be here.'[9] 'Coming home' is the phrase he used in a letter to Slonimsky too.[10] Prentice, who had spent the war back at Chatto & Windus, came to visit with his new wife; so did the Gribbles; Frere eventually made it over the Channel, as did Warman. The diary entry for 22 September reads: 'Gave Eric Warman dinner at the Dôme. He looks well and prosperous, & his light-hearted attitude was in pleasant contrast to the dreary patriotism of Irene [Rathbone]. We enjoyed him very much. Met Irene for a drink. Joined by Eric who gave us lunch.' Warman might well have looked well and prosperous. Having worked at the Ministry of Information during the War, he had left to found World Film Publications, providing novelisations of feature films and annual guides to popular cinema. His first success was his adaptation of the 1946 Powell and Pressburger film, *A Matter of Life and Death*.

As for Frere, Aldington told him after their meeting on 3 October: 'That was a wonderful evening which I shan't forget, nor the possibility – which for so long seemed impossible – of the South together again.'[11] He told his brother (now managing all his legal affairs) that things with Frere were 'satisfactory', all was 'going through', a reprint of *A Dream in the Luxembourg*, his proposed Pater selection and Nineties anthology, plus proposals for a French anthology, a life of Louis XV and a novel.[12] Sales to Norway of *All Men Are Enemies* and *Seven Against Reeves* were further good news, as was the sale of French rights for all the novels since *All Men Are Enemies*; and by the spring of 1947 rights for *Casanova* had been sold to Spain, South America, Sweden, Norway, Denmark, Czechoslovakia, Holland, Italy and Switzerland.

John Arlott in the late 1940s

Another visitor (registered in the diary as 'our most interesting new acquaintance') was Arlott. Aldington told Church:

> We had John Arlott with us for a week, and found him a most delightful and charming companion, full of zest for the different life of Paris and appreciative of everything. We only differed in politics and about the UNESCO show of painting which he thought good and I thought wretched.[13]

It was from Aldington that Arlott acquired his appreciation of French wines.

The visits were all one-way: Aldington told Goldring: 'I have decided definitely against coming to England – it is too much like a prison.'[14] The Glovers departed for North Wales, the Churches for London and the Gribbles for Brussels, but other friends were living in Paris, including Willert, who had left New York to serve with the RAF during the war.[15] There were letters from old friends too, Fallas amongst them. In late October Aldington sought help from Gyde for Fallas, who had lost his post on the *Manchester Evening News*. Another welcome correspondent was MacGreevy, to whose letter Aldington responded enthusiastically (in his first letter for a decade), giving his friend news of his old haunts:

Yes, Paris, strangely enough, is still here, still very much ashamed of itself for bolting and ratting in '40, rather out-of-touch with the greater world beyond Europe but persisting in the old ways with an obstinacy which would be pathetic if it were not so engaging. Like my own countrymen they fail to realise that their greatness is past, that henceforth they are a second-rate power at best and so on. But the town and people are, as ever, so much more sympathetic and amusing than the British who have reverted to a kind of political Puritanism. ... The Closerie, Dôme, Rotonde and Coupole are bleak deserts of empty chairs. After Hollywood and New York the women look like servant girls. ... Western Europe is 'out' for half a century and there is nothing to do but live among the ruins and make the best of it.[16]

This exchange between the two old friends seems to have been an isolated one; there are no further letters extant until 1958.

Perhaps the most important correspondence of these months was with H.D. The last Aldington had heard from her was in January, when he was still in Hollywood and she was planning a visit to the United States to give a lecture at Bryn Mawr. He wrote as soon as he reached Paris to enquire what had happened and why he had not heard from her in the intervening period – and to ask her to visit: 'Paris is still in a mess, but still wonderful, and a million times better than America with all its money and morality and monkeys and morons.'[17] He told her that Netta had a great admiration for her and would like to meet her again.

No sooner had he written than he received a letter from Bryher to inform him that H.D. had had meningitis in February and that Bryher and Walter Schmiderberg, H.D.'s analyst and friend, had found her a clinic in Switzerland – the Klinik Brunner at Seehof near Küsnacht – and had her flown out there. The meningitis story was being told to all their acquaintances; in fact, after the strain of the war years, during which she had been confined for the most part to her London flat (which she shared with Bryher) and had developed an obsessive interest in spiritualism, H.D. had had a mental breakdown. Bryher wrote to her in September – by which time she had begun to recover – to tell her what had happened; H.D. had no recall of the circumstances which had led to her committal to the clinic. Bryher told her:

I beg of you only to listen to the wise counsel of Dr Brunner, eat well and sleep well, then we shall be re-united sooner. It is no question of sanity or otherwise, it is just that you, like hundreds of other English people, have suffered a terrible strain through the war and lost temporarily your memory.[18]

Aldington wrote to H.D. immediately:

> It was a great shock to hear from Bryher that you have been so ill,
> and this made poignant the very charming little note from you
> she sent on to me this morning. I hope you will take very great
> care of yourself, rest and eat the good Swiss 'essen', and keep out
> of the cold and foggy north as long as possible.[19]

There began a regular correspondence, in which he told her about his
family:

> My mother is still alive and still very nearly as belligerent and
> capricious as of old. Poor Tony has a terrible time trying to keep
> her quiet. He has authority from me to pay her anything she
> needs out of royalties of mine in his keeping but she complains
> bitterly it is too little. Between ourselves he keeps her short on
> account of the whiskey bottle, but of course it is widely reported
> that we starve our poor mother. . . . Margery is married to the ex-
> manager of an Indian railway, has a nice house in Rye, and helps
> Patty – poor Patty – who has never got far in life. They are both
> rather bigoted Catholics.[20]

(H.D. suggested, tactfully and charitably, that May Aldington's alcoholism
might be due to 'war strain'.)[21] A photograph of Catha accompanied news
of her: 'a nice little girl, a little given to fussing over trifles, a bit of a
perfectionist, but intelligent, warm-hearted and responsive to ethical
training'.[22]

He showed constant concern for H.D.'s well-being: 'I have just had a
letter from Bryher in which she tells me that you are mistaken about your
finances, which is good news; and that you must not work too hard for a
bit, which is not such good news'; 'I do hope you're getting on all right,
Dooley. And please do seriously let me know what I can do'; and 'Dear
Dooley, Your letter sounds ever so much stronger than the others, and I
feel you are getting better rapidly. However, you must not hurry away, but
see that you are properly established in health before leaving. Unless one
is well, people can be so destructive.'[23]

In some ways he saw her as more resilient than Bryher did. The latter
had protected her from news of Pound's circumstances, but Aldington told
her: 'The story of Ezra is very painful, but I think it absurd for you not to be
told.'[24] Pound had given himself up to the American military authorities in
Italy in May 1945 and been transferred to the United States in November

H.D., passport photograph, 1946

of that year, arraigned on charges of treason; but in February 1946 he had
been found unfit for trial on the grounds of insanity and committed to St
Elizabeth's Psychiatric Hospital in Washington, D.C. It seemed to be a life
sentence: as long as he was considered insane he would be incarcerated;
should he 'recover' his sanity, he would face the original charges. Aldington
had no news of Dorothy, Olga or Mary, but told H.D.: 'You shouldn't worry
too much about old Ez, who is quite safe, humanely treated, with his
economic problems solved pro tem. at any rate.' By February he was able
to reassure her further: the Glovers had heard from Olga's brother that
she was safe and at present in Vienna on musical affairs, although she had
been teaching English for 'a bare living', and Mary was recently married.

The correspondence between them was becoming a central fact of their lives. Barbara Guest comments: 'He was just near enough now for H.D. to be aware of his unobtrusive presence; this need became increasingly important to her. Again, he was her critic, her friend; the letters began to pass back and forth as if no time or lovers had intervened.'[25] As for Aldington, the very fact that the gaunt 60-year-old H.D. was not physically attractive to him made the relationship easier. He had never ceased to feel great affection and admiration for her and wanted, as always, to place his own practical grasp (as he saw it) of the world of publishers and readers at her service.

By the beginning of December, H.D. was well enough to leave the clinic; but she did not move to Kenwin. Her relationship with Bryher was as affectionate and loyal as ever and the latter continued for the rest of H.D.'s life to look after her welfare, to give her financial support and to make all the major decisions in her life – or at least to be consulted before decisions were made. They would always celebrate together the anniversary – 17 July – of their first meeting in 1918. However, after their shared residence of the war years in the small Lowndes Square flat, the longest period in their relationship that they had lived under the same roof, both women knew that the time had come for them to live apart. That Bryher could not merely tolerate, but actively encourage H.D.'s correspondence with Aldington is an indication of the more relaxed relationship between the two women. H.D. moved into the Hotel Alexandre in Lausanne, just a 20-minute journey from Kenwin. She remained there until the following summer when she moved to a hotel in Lugano. This would be the pattern of the coming years: Lausanne in the winter, Lugano in the summer. Like Aldington, she never returned to London.

By December, Aldington was also moving: to a studio apartment at 162 Boulevard Montparnasse, 'near the atelier of Othan Friesz where Netta goes to paint'.[26] Catha was at school nearby at the Collège Sévigné in the Rue Pierre Nicole. As the New Year opened, he reviewed his situation and that of the world around him in what would be his last diary entry for four years:

> Europe still welters helplessly like a great ship in the trough of the waves. . . . I have been too much disordered to do any writing, but have read & have made a little progress towards my edition of Pater. I must try to hope that conditions for work will improve, but the whole state of society is such that one is constantly being worried by petty officials. Any genuine creative work is almost out of the question in contemporary Europe.

As he had done in Paris in 1930 – and New York in 1939 – he would soon decide that the distractions of citylife were inimical to creative work. In the meantime, an old pattern was reasserting itself: physical illness leading to mental depression. He told H.D in mid-January:

> It has troubled me that I have been unable to write, but twice in the past six weeks I have gone down with particularly vicious attacks of influenza. Apart from the fact that I have to take care this doesn't reach my lungs, one is left so depressed by it, that the arrears of things to be done appear quite mountainous. At such times the ignoble self-slaughter of Europe during the past decade becomes an intolerable thought, the more so since they pride themselves on their heroism while trying to jump in any available political bandwagon. The collapse of Greece after Chaeronea seems less awful – though indeed 'from what a height of bliss' they fell![27]

The classical reference is a deliberate evocation of their shared world.

He continued to express concern for her, writing in March: 'I wish I knew how you are in health, and I wish you would regain your American citizenship and get your money back into dollars before there is some frightful crash in England.' He also wished he could visit her but said that he was tied by Catha's schooling. In this letter he allowed himself a rare reference to his domestic circumstances: 'In my opinion the present Mrs Aldington, who has opposed the purchase of a car on grounds of Scotch economy, will change her mind as soon as the warm weather comes!'[28]

The references to their shared past continued. In May he told her: 'I was in Capri as late as 1937, and alas, all our walk along to the Migliara had been dug up (destroying the wild flowers) in Musso's *battaglia del grano*.' He continued: 'Do you read newspapers? I am cutting down as much as possible, and wondering whether one should not stop. It seems to me my happiest days with you were when we never read a newspaper and thought of Greek and Italian and art.' He told her that he sometimes went to the Louvre 'to see our Lady of Melos and the Greek and Roman things, especially those bronze copies of the Greek'.[29] In reply, H.D. told him that she had not been to Capri for many years:

> But the second time I went, I felt the whole had grown a bit dim and the flowers and trees not as I remembered them. . . . I was so sorry you lost your watch that time at Ana-Capri when you chased a boy for laughing at us. It was a wonderful spring and I remember

the pear-tree in the garden and the occasional quince trees in blossom and that odd German painter with his butterflies, and the coral wash on the houses – we have that here. I have not seen the familiar cytisus but there is gorse in blossom such as I first met on the Amalfi drive and they are beginning to plant the jars and boxes with those huge marguerites.[30]

She was encouraging, even prompting, his recall of their history. In April a reminder of that history came with the news that May Sinclair had left them each (along with Pound) £50, one or two specified books and a choice from her library.[31] They both regretted that they had lost touch with Sinclair. 'I wish we could have assured her of our continuing affection,' Aldington wrote.[32]

He also shared his feelings about America. Sometimes, he told her in May, he got homesick for Florida: 'with its sheets upon sheets of lovely water hyacinths and great butterflies and live oaks with Spanish moss'. He reflected:

[I]f only the bulk of Americans were not such impossible people, what a wonderful place America could be. . . . What a pity America didn't stay anywhere near what it set out to be. It has become the biggest humbug in history, which is disquieting to me, as I don't like those Russians one bit.[33]

He would tell her months later that Florida was 'the only place in God's Own' for which he got really homesick.[34]

Meanwhile he was labouring on his self-appointed writing tasks: the Walter Pater selection ('an ever toiling up a toiling wave job' he told H.D.) and the broader Nineties anthology.[35] He was also preparing a reprint of his *Complete Poems* for publication by Allan Wingate under licence from Heinemann, since Frere claimed to have insufficient paper stocks. It is a measure of his inability to grasp publishing realities that he was now contemplating an anthology of the work of the Nineties writer John Addington Symonds. He told H.D. that neither Heinemann, Viking nor Duell, Sloan and Pearce appeared interested: '[T]hey do hate beauty – though they know they can sell at least 10,000 of anything I sponsor they hesitate, demur – am I wise to risk my reputation?'[36]

He was also increasingly vexed by his financial obligations to the Patmores. He arranged for his brother to take over the legal management of the case from Hilbery, who had already taken it over from the original lawyers. However, Tony could offer him little comfort and Aldington wrote to him in May: 'I feared you would not be able to find a loop-hole in that Patmore document as it was drawn by shrewd lawyers while the people acting for me were jackasses. But I didn't want to go to Hilbery and got recommended to that fool (by Frere).' He asked if the payment could be extended over a longer period, telling his brother: 'There is no chance of the dame croaking – tough as buffalo meat.'[37]

Now H.D. asked him to look at the draft of her *The Sword Went Out to Sea* (sub-titled *Synthesis of a Dream*), the autobiographical novel which she had been writing in London before her breakdown. Guest describes the work as 'a kedgeree of spiritualism', combining as it does, the ideas of Air Chief Marshall Lord Dowding, based on his writings and the lectures he gave in wartime London and which H.D. attended, accounts of seances at Lowndes Square, characters representing important figures in her life, such as Bryher, Aldington and Dowding, and historical contexts of mediaeval France and the England of William Morris and his circle. H.D. described it to Aldington as 'fantasy cum reality'.[38] It would not be published in her lifetime.[39]

Aldington's first response was that it was 'a remarkable piece of work', but he saw the publishing problems, particularly in view of the 'mixed genres'. While it might be publishable in its present form it wouldn't 'sell'. In another coded reference to their shared past, he quoted to her Browning's comment on his *Men and Women*: 'I have written not what the few must but what the many may like.' He added: 'If you prefer to leave the material as it is I shall try to think of some way of getting by with it.'[40] Soon he had to tell her that Frere was not interested. In the current climate, none of the big publishers were likely to be interested and the smaller ones would not have the paper stocks. H.D. told him:

> I feel I struck a sort of oil well or gold mine – my own. I have not plumbed the depth or yet veined the ore. . . . I feel that the book is so very precious to me, that having satisfied myself, I am satisfied to have two or three readers – until/if the time comes, when it could be set up by someone who really wanted it and believed in it, and would do the business part altogether.[41]

He responded tactfully but firmly. Perhaps she could find an American publisher? If it were 're-shaped into a novel of an objective kind, expressing all its sensations and ideas, its emotions and beliefs through action and character', then he thought it would have 'the chance of a very big success'. 'You wilfully put obstacles between yourself and the common reader,' he told her. 'Why do you? Is it so much harder to be lucid, to put things in such a way that any educated reader of good will can, indeed must, follow you? You are a lord of language and can so easily make speech obey you.'[42] He was taking very seriously the role of literary advisor and mentor.

Now two life-changing events occurred. The first was the entry into his life of the young Australian poet, Kershaw, of whose two volumes of poetry he had already approved.[43] Kershaw had now arrived in England, 'the first step,' he told Aldington, 'in a journey to see how much of the Europe you evoked in *All Men Are Enemies* and *Life for Life's Sake* is left'. He asked: 'I wonder if you would allow me to meet you if I came to France? ... [I]t would be a great honour.'[44] Almost immediately – and increasingly as time went on – he would become one of the most important people in Aldington's life.

That his visit to Paris at the end of May was a success is demonstrated by a letter from Netta to Warman:

> Dearest Eric, I wonder if you would meet a very young friend of ours and tell us what you think of him. His name is Alister Kershaw, he is twenty-six, writes poetry, comes from Australia and has apparently brought himself up on Richard's books. ... He is most frightfully nervous, and you may get nothing out of him, or you may even get unpleasant defensive things, but I ask you please to be patient. It took us four days to dig him out of his shyness, and then he became as vivid, charming, and amusing a campanion [*sic*] as we have ever seen, which is saying something, when you consider Richard's roster. We became extremely fond of him. I'm not asking you, God forbid, to be patient for four days, but just to see him once or twice and let us know what your opinion is. You may find it extremely rewarding. I very much hope so.[45]

Kershaw's first impression of Aldington is recorded in his 1989 memoir: 'Broad-shouldered, broad-chested, with (until he felt able to let down his guard) somewhat stern features, he was physically imposing and might have been intimidating, had it not been for his smile, which was of singular sweetness, and his manner, which was a touching blend of friendliness and shyness.' Kershaw also gives us one of the few descriptions of Netta we have:

> She was enchanting ... gay and beautiful and welcoming, with a marvellous capacity for enjoyment: she drank a glass of wine as though it were the best wine in the world and the first she had

ever drunk, she laughed as though laughter was her natural mode of expression. The spring of that year was particularly wonderful, and Netta was spring-like in her warmth and eagerness.[46]

By mid-July Kershaw was already making himself useful. 'Ever so many thanks for seeing Deutsche [of the publishers Allan Wingate],' Aldington wrote. 'If you can find out what prospects are for an early 10,000 of All Men, I'll be most grateful. That book and Complete Poems are what I want to keep in print.'[47] Thereafter, he handed over to Kershaw all his negotiations with Allan Wingate, although the *Complete Poems* and a new edition of *Fifty Romance Lyric Poems*, along with an Aldington introduction to a new (Chawton) edition of Jane Austen's novels, were to be the only outcomes. By the end of the month Kershaw was also negotiating on his behalf with Allen & Unwin (the original publishers of Aldington's poetry, including the *Collected Poems* of 1929), Heinemann (Frere having taken two months' sick leave) and the BBC Third Programme (who wished to broadcast Aldington's translation of François Villon). Whether or not he was receiving any monetary reward for these services is unclear. He had, however, made the acquaintance of the poet Roy Campbell, who, as Talks Producer at the BBC, had hired him for a talk and would give him further occasional work.

It comes as a surprise to find that it was only now, through Kershaw, that Aldington came to know Campbell. Kershaw told Aldington that, on the publication of Campbell's latest collection, *Talking Bronco*, Stephen Spender had written to accuse him of slander against the group of poets whom Campbell had labelled MacSpaunday (Spender, Auden, MacNeice and Day Lewis), and of being a Fascist. Aldington told Kershaw: 'Tell Roy from me – and no kidding – that I know I've no business to give him advice but he can't take that from Stephen Spender lying down. Either he must knock his block off or take a libel action.' He even gave Kershaw Tony Aldington's address and added: 'I can arrange that Roy isn't asked for costs.'[48] Out of this exchange grew what would become, when Campbell came to visit the Riviera in 1950, a very close friendship. Kershaw, although only 26 years old, had conservative political views that were aligned much more closely with those of Aldington, Campbell and another writer whom he would also introduce to Aldington – Henry Williamson – than with those of the 'MacSpaundays'. In this respect (and only in this respect) Kershaw perhaps did Aldington a disservice, reinforcing rather than challenging the latter's conservative – though never fascist – views of the world.

The second life-changing event at this time was Aldington's move to the Riviera. He was beginning to feel swamped by Paris life. On one day, he told H.D, he had had Frere visiting, the Albatross representative to see for lunch, business letters to write and a visit from 'an old sweetheart of Netta's who became a hero in Burma and is bringing his new bride to Paris'. 'Casual visitors eat up one's days,' he complained. [49] Visitors from England and America were generally on holiday and tended to forget that Aldington required an uninterrupted working day. There were other drawbacks to Paris: '[I]t is an absolutely dead city in August/ September, and then the winter chill gives me one bad cold after another.' 'It is a shame,' he told H.D., 'to move the child from school where she is happy, but it won't help her to have a bed-ridden or deceased father. I lost four months' work last winter, and haven't nearly made up.'[50] He told Slonimsky (thanking the couple for Catha's birthday present):

> Paris has been very lovely this spring, the people still crushed and withered by the evil days so recently gone, but recovering a little. A little of the harshness has gone, I think, but there is a growing sense of helplessness, of being ground between the alien ideologies and imperialisms of Russia and America. Today I am 55, and resolved not to worry about humanity, not to intervene between herds of Gadarene swine and steep places, but to escape for all I'm worth – and may social-minded uplifters get everything they deserve![51]

Finding a villa on the Riviera was not easy: their 'old stamping ground' had been 'knocked so heavily by the Allied landing' and rents for the undamaged villas were high.[52] By late July, however, he had found the Villa Aucassin at Saint-Clair, two miles east of Le Lavandou, property of Hildebrand Harmsworth of the newspaper family. Frere would share the cost for August and part of September so that he could bring his family there for a holiday. At the end of July 1947 Aldington moved out of Paris for the last time in his life.

16. The Sociable Life
Paradise Regained – and Lost
1947-1949

'It is as if one had never been away,' Aldington told H.D, '– blue sky, blue sea, gold-furnace sun, baked mica-spangled hills, the endless cri-cri of the cicadas.' In mid-October he would write: 'The weather is warm still and we are able to bathe . . . today it is lovely and sunny, and it is such bliss to look at the cypresses and olives. There is really no life away from the Mediterranean basin and the adjoining lands.'[1]

A vivid account of life at the Villa Aucassin is provided by the Australian writer and teacher William Denison Deasey:

> St Clair was a dream of the South. A small bay between two rocky points, a scatter of small houses, mimosas and eucalyptus, vines and olive trees, half-circled by low hills. There was a daily bus service along the narrow road but no traffic of any importance. The nearest shops, post office or police station were kilometres away.
>
> The Villa Aucassin stood back from the road, half-hidden by trees and reached by a dirt track between fields. There Aldington worked from early morning until lunchtime, tapping away in his upstairs room. Netta, his wife, was dark and attractive, quite a bit younger than Richard; their daughter, Catha, was saxon fair and blue-eyed, about nine, at that wonderful age before secondary schools and 'normal development' spread their blight.
>
> . . . At the villa, the dining room table was just inside

Alister Kershaw and Richard
Aldington at the Villa Aucassin,
Le Lavandou

The Villa Aucassin

the windows, opening on the verandah. Conversation would be riveted on some weighty problem in nineteenth-century poetry when Catha would burst in, carrying some new marvel, a flower or insect in the palm of her hand for Richard to identify.

I lodged at the inn and came up the track when Alister, Richard, Netta and any visitors were reaching the cheese course and conversation was allegretto over the Muscadet or Blanc de Blancs. . . . Lunch at the villa was a sort of quest, a gateway to finding out what was left undestroyed in our world – Europe and Australia.[2]

Kershaw would tell Norman Gates in 1980:

The best moments . . . were when there were just the four of us . . . and then best of all were the evenings. We would go for a swim just as the sun began to sink . . . stroll back to the villa, drink our aperitifs on the terrace as we listened to the nightingales' enchanting and tireless rippling away in the garden, dine on bouillabaisse or an aioli or (when the season came round) snipe or wild boar. Netta would read poems to us, or Richard would reminisce about D.H. Lawrence or Ezra Pound, Eliot or H.D., or we would put a record on the gramophone ... or discuss what Richard was writing or what he would write next.[3]

* * *

The first visitors, however, were the Freres and their three children.[4] Aldington told Kershaw: 'It has been rather sticky with the Freres. She has been angelic, but he was on the verge of a nervous breakdown which took the form of a chauvinism so relentless . . . that even in an invalid one could scarcely let it pass unsatirised.'[5] When the visit was over, he told H.D.:

> We are beginning to recover from the visit of the Freres. I used to be fond of them both, but they have changed so much that friendship is out of the question and even a visit from them a penance. This new mixture of violent chauvinism and imperialism, plus the quite untrue British legend that England saved the world (it was in fact saved by the US and Russia), combined with social climbing and Socialist politics is disgusting. It is National Socialism of a British brand, capable of being just as nasty as the German variety. . . . [H]ow Lorenzo would have loathed it.[6]

The letter continues: 'By way of a change we have a happy-go-lucky and gifted young Australian poet, who belongs to one of the "good" families there, but who is wholly without snobbery and affectation. And intelligent.' The nod to H.D.'s own snobbery and the inference that, unless a pedigree were offered, an Australian visitor might be assumed to be uncouth should not divert us from the fact that Aldington was looking forward with pleasure to Kershaw's visit, as was Kershaw himself: 'You don't know – how could you? – how hugely I look forward to being with you again for a while. I feel such a deprivation away from you. That sounds phoney, I know. But it is so.'[7] It was now that Kershaw started to deal with Aldington's incoming correspondence as well as taking on much of the liaison with publishers. For Kershaw this was 'a golden time': '[Aldington] had no financial worries at that period, he was pleased with the work he was doing, the cellar never ran dry and, as a matter of principle, the local peasants saw to it that the food rationing regulations imposed by Paris were systematically circumvented.'[8]

Richard Church, May 1939

Kershaw was not the only guest that autumn. Glover, recently widowed and in a distressed state, stayed through the autumn and winter, and Richard Church, with his wife Rina, came for several weeks to convalesce from a recent operation.[9] 'Trying to make them comfortable and to write a book at the same time is a full-time job,' Aldington told H.D.[10] However, 'make them comfortable' he did. Church recalls in the third volume of his memoirs: '[F]or some six weeks Aldington's villa, standing up a valley in a thicket of winter-blooming mimosa, was more a nursing-home than a literary household. There, Aldington, approaching his own professional autumn, showed an aspect of his personality that, alas, rarely appeared in his books. He was benign, considerate, restrained.'[11] Aldington frequently

Alister Kershaw, Geoffrey Dutton and Denison Deasey, 1948

showed generosity towards Church; only the previous autumn he had
written to tell him how much he admired his latest poetry collection, *The
Lamp*, and to say that he had recommended it to Duell, Sloan and Pearce
for American publication.[12] This generosity was rarely reciprocated,
and publicly Church often expressed that disapproval and wariness of
Aldington that was common amongst the *Criterion* group.[13]

Aldington would comment to Frere in April 1948: 'He tries to be all
things to all men, and never realises that the only thing in literature as
in life is to stick to your guns. But then he probably hasn't got any guns,
not even a muzzle-loading Brown Bess.'[14] Kershaw was of much the same
opinion, referring in his memoirs to 'wishy-washy Richard Church' as
'[a] visitor I could have done without . . . a harmless enough creature, but
intolerably provincial . . . preoccupied with the doings of literary London.'[15]

Kershaw brought new friends into Aldington's life, visitors who made
the Villa Aucassin a joyful place and who would never forget the welcome
they received. Foremost amongst them was Deasey, commonly referred
to as 'Dease'. He and Kershaw had met in bohemian literary circles in
Melbourne in 1940, and he had followed Kershaw to London in the
summer of 1947, abandoning a year-old marriage; but he had been unable
to join his friend in Saint-Clair that autumn because he had contracted
tuberculosis on the voyage from Australia and was hospitalised, first
in Dublin, where he was visiting relatives, and then in a TB clinic in
Switzerland. It was March 1948 before he made his first visit. He was
housed, as were most of Aldington's visitors except Kershaw, at Les Sables

Geoffrey Dutton, Alister Kershaw and Denison Deasey, 1948

d'Or Hotel in Saint-Clair, owned and run by the eccentric Russian emigré Serge Berkaloff. Deasey stayed for three months, was back again in July and August, and again from March to June 1949, with further visits in July and September that year. He subsequently married a Parisian girl, Gisèle Satoor de Rootas, and lived in Paris until his return to Australia at the end of 1954. A talented pianist, he brought music into Aucassin and Aldington had the villa's piano specially tuned for him.

The friendship between Kershaw and Deasey was a close one and for periods they lived together, both in London and in Paris, but there was rivalry between them, in part for the affection of Aldington. Kershaw had become Aldington's indispensable adviser and closest friend – a replacement for Frere – but the impulsive, engaging, accident-prone and physically delicate Deasey became a surrogate son towards whom Aldington felt protective. (For both Netta, only ten years their senior, and Catha, their junior by fifteen years, Kershaw and Deasey were fraternal figures.) Deasey shared Aldington's historical and aesthetic interests and, perhaps more importantly, had also been scarred by his wartime experiences.[16] Kershaw at times resented the happy-go-lucky lifestyle of Deasey, who had independent means, having been left an annuity by an uncle. Deasey, on the other hand, was generously supportive of Kershaw – and had paid for his voyage from Australia, another factor that complicated their relationship.

The other members of this friendship group were Geoffrey Dutton and his wife Ninette, also people with whom Aldington's relationship would be lifelong. Like Deasey, Dutton and his wife came from privileged backgrounds and the two young men had been friends since boarding-school days. Dutton had served in the Australian Air Force during the war and had come to Magdalen College, Oxford, in 1946 as a mature undergraduate student. Kershaw had landed on the doorstep of the Duttons' two-roomed flat in Banbury Road a year later and spent his first months in England sleeping on a sheepskin rug on their living-room floor. The couple first arrived at the villa in the spring of 1948, but the following summer, when Dutton had graduated, they rented a flat in Sanary, west of Toulon, where he wrote his first novel.[17] A year later, at Aldington's suggestion, they rented a tiny cottage high on the hill above Villa Aucassin, where Dutton settled in to write another – never published – novel. Dutton had his own theory about the attraction of the young

Denison Deasey, Catherine Aldington and Ninette Dutton, 1949

Australians for Aldington: '[W]e came from a less overbuilt land and, however sophisticated we thought we were, retained a certain freshness, if not naïveté.'[18]

In January 1948 Kershaw's girlfriend, Patsy Wright, arrived from Melbourne to join him at the Villa Aucassin. She would need work, however, and soon moved to London, followed in June – to Aldington's distress – by Kershaw. He was back by the end of July and remained at the villa until mid-September, returning again for a few weeks in December. In early March 1949 he wrote from London that he felt as though he had been away from Saint-Clair for three years rather than three months, but he was only able to make a short spring visit.[19] He and Patsy needed to earn a living and spent those years moving from one loaned flat or bedsit to another, relying on the good will of friends like Warman, Deasey and the Arlotts. They married in January 1950, Kershaw telling Aldington that '[t]he operation was performed before a wildly enthusiastic multitude of one – i.e. Eric [Warman]'.[20]

Deasey and Dutton threw a celebratory party for the newly married couple, the guest list for which is revealing about the London world into which Kershaw – both on Aldington's behalf and because of his own inclinations – had entered. The evening was dominated by the presence of two writers whom both Aldington and Kershaw revered, Rachel Annand Taylor and Roy Campbell, each of whom, according to Kershaw, 'held separate court at opposite ends of the room and never exchanged a word'.[21]

Taylor, a Scot, was formerly a poet of the Celtic Revival but better known for her critical writing about the Renaissance in the 1920s. Patmore had introduced Aldington and H.D. to her during their early years in London: she had moved there from her native Scotland in 1910 after separating from her husband because of his mental illness.[22] She was now in her 70s and Aldington, determining that she would be the final artist in his Aesthetes anthology, both for her poetry and for her 'eloquent, coloured, sensitive prose', had been making enquiries as to whether she was still alive.[23] It was another of Kershaw's acquaintances, the middle-aged civil servant and amateur book-dealer William Dibben (who was fast becoming indispensable to Aldington for his ability to track down and acquire the rare books he needed for his research), who 'found' Taylor in May 1948. Thereafter, she and Aldington were in regular correspondence, while in London Dibben and Kershaw (sometimes with Patsy, who was a discerning lover of poetry) visited her regularly. Kershaw told Aldington: 'She's vastly envenomed and I love it.'[24] Eager as always to help his friends, Aldington enlisted H.D. for financial support for the impoverished writer, although Taylor rebuffed his offer to help her to leave London for France or Italy; she was too old and unwell to risk her security after forty years in the capital. What she really wanted was recognition for her writing and Kershaw arranged for her to meet Frere, but the publisher, although delighted to make her acquaintance, knew that her work was not a realistic financial proposition.

Campbell had been Kershaw's idol since the age of seventeen when he had discovered *Adamastor* in a Melbourne bookshop and Campbell's 'lion-roaring poetry struck [him] full in the solar plexus'.[25] Shortly after he arrived in Britain in 1947 Kershaw had received through Dutton an invitation to meet up with Campbell in London, at the George in Mortimer Street, the public house frequented by personnel from the BBC, where Campbell worked as Talks Producer. The poet did not disappoint the young Australian:

> Massive and powerful-looking, dominating the whole place with his sheer physical vitality and shedding around himself a joyous meridional radiance . . . [h]e was wearing a Spanish sombrero . . . and carried under his arm what looked like, and may have been, a huge Zulu knobkerry. . . . Dressed in a rumpled grey suit, balding, fleshy, he nonetheless had what can only be called glamour.[26]

Iconoclastic and anti-socialist as they both were, the Australian and the South African hit it off immediately.

It is surprising that Campbell and Aldington had never met. In the 1930s they had shared a strong distaste for the literary establishment – upon which both had made sharply satirical attacks – and had weighed in with support for Lewis's *The Apes of God*.[27] Campbell had spent the years from 1928 to 1933 at Martigues in the South of France, not too far from Aldington's summer homes near Le Lavandou; Huxley, living in Sanary, half-way between the two places, was a frequent visitor at the Campbells' home and also – though less frequently – called on Aldington. Even though it was to be some time before the two men would meet, Kershaw ensured that each was aware of the other's esteem. Aldington was made particularly conscious of Campbell's regard for him when the latter wrote to the *TLS* in February 1949 remonstrating with Alan Ross for his disparaging review of Aldington's *Complete Poems* and followed his letter up with a full-length appreciation in the *Poetry Review* in May entitled 'The Happy Pagan'.[28]

Another guest at that party was John Browning, chairman of Evans Brothers, with whom Kershaw had struck up an amiable relationship two years earlier, when Browning had expressed an interest in coming to an arrangement with Heinemann to publish new Aldington work and even reprints. Aldington was still unable to produce a novel but he was working on biographical pieces, and Evans published his *Four English Portraits* in 1948, followed in 1949 by a biography of Charles Waterton.

Kershaw's work with Aldington's publishers smoothed the latter's path, not only in freeing him to concentrate on his writing but in ensuring that relationships with those publishers were more cordial than he himself could have achieved. Kershaw, though always loyal, recognised how self-defeating Aldington's behaviour could be, and was possibly the one person in his life able to persuade him into rational responses – or at least into allowing Kershaw to behave rationally on his behalf. In particular, Kershaw worked tirelessly to improve Aldington's relationship with Frere. Aldington conceded in a letter to H.D. in June 1948: 'I must not be unjust to Frere. No other publisher in England or America would at this time do the Pater and the Aesthetes. He is doing them only out of friendship and will lose money on both!'[29] Generally, however, he was both at odds with his former friend's politics and suspicious of his motivation. He appreciated Kershaw's patient negotiations on his behalf, telling him that same month: 'I'm very glad the meeting with Frere went off so well. He is so damned capricious nowadays I never know what line he'll take. You evidently worked marvels.'[30] Kershaw kept up the good work, writing to Aldington the following month that he had had lunch with Pat: 'Wallace and I got along well enough I think. Be assured we shall soothe the Freres and all will be well thereafter.'[31] In August when the Frere family arrived for their second annual visit to Villa Aucassin, Aldington told Dibben:

> It has been a bit sticky at times, for though he is a very old friend of mine, he went all political and patriotic in the war and is only slowly recovering. And then it is hard to mix poets and businessmen. But it is going, and Al has been wonderful.[32]

By October, his correspondence with Kershaw reveals an attitude verging on paranoia:

> Keep clear of the Freres all you can. Frere sails on the 12th, and you can be called to Oxford or something. Don't be taken in by a social manner which can be turned on at will. They are not real friends. Remember. Don't tell them anything which can be used against either of us. We must indeed dissemble but not be taken in any more.[33]

These feelings have to be contextualised: whether correctly or not, he thought that the whole literary establishment was against him. He told Kershaw that October:

> There is no doubt that the Eliot and MacSpaunday interests – who thought my long war silence meant I was wiped out – are growing seriously alarmed. I am to be attacked and silenced. I fight without an ally, with a treacherous public who is ready to betray me against a formidable coalition.[34]

At the end of the year, reporting on Browning's satisfaction with the reviews of *Four English Portraits*, he warned Kershaw: '[B]ut the opposition have not yet had time to consult and decide on their line of attack – as they clearly did with Pater. I know the bastards. They are most ingenious in thinking up specious lines of attack and quite unscrupulous.'[35] He felt this particularly in relation to the BBC, telling Kershaw, who had, at his own instigation, been having discussions with the Corporation on how it could use Aldington's work, that it was futile to attempt to gain access there. He had received a letter from Church telling him that Roy Fuller had expressed on the Third Programme his regret, in relation to the work of both Aldington and Church, that 'two men of no small talent should have been born too early to be influenced by the poetic technique of Eliot and Auden, who had rescued English poetry from its utter decay'.[36]

Aldington was convinced that Frere's current postponement of a publication date for his Aesthetes anthology, now entitled *The Religion of Beauty*, was 'tied up with this general counter-attack'. We might remark this re-emergence of the terminology of war in his correspondence (although we should also note that it would be 1950 before *The Religion of Beauty* appeared). Malcolm Muggeridge had become a reader for Heinemann and Aldington saw him as 'a spy from the Eliot camp in Heinemann's office'.[37] A further irritant was Frere's continuing refusal to consider publishing *Life for Life's Sake*. Kershaw continued to act as mediator, insisting that Frere's remarks about Aldington were 'invariably warmly affectionate' and that it would be 'wrong to throw him away', but Aldington's tendency to fire off angry letters when the whim overtook him made the young Australian's task a difficult one, causing him to plead: '[P]lease don't write him a savage letter, the thing is to cosset him for your own ends. After all, if he is attacked he'll presumably be WORSE.' He even suggested what shape a 'tactful and amiable letter' might take.[38]

Kershaw's most successful coup was the plan for Heinemann to license Penguin Books to publish ten of Lawrence's works simultaneously with the reprinting of twelve by Heinemann, all to be provided with introductions by Aldington.[39] This major re-launch of Lawrence's work would mark the 20th anniversary of his death. Aldington was not only to produce a monograph for Penguin to issue with the slipcase of the Lawrence editions but also a full biography of Lawrence for Heinemann. The plan was conceived in early 1948 and involved visits to the villa by Allen Lane, founder-director of Penguin, along with Frere, in June and August of that year. Fortunately, these visits went well. Kershaw would tell Gates in an undated letter circa 1980:

> There was no evidence that [Lane] had ever read a word of anything published by himself or anyone else, and he was supposed to be a monster in his business activities; but in the insouciant atmosphere of the Villa Aucassin, he proved to be an engagingly ribald and carefree character, and he took us to some memorable meals.[40]

One of Kershaw's biggest challenges was clearing up the problems Aldington had created in respect of his American market. He now had four different British publishers but this had been accomplished with Heinemann's full agreement.[41] In the United States he had spent two years playing off Duell, Sloan and Pearce, to whom he was still contracted, against Viking and E.P. Dutton in a way that not only lost him Charles Duell's goodwill and caused Manuel, still his American agent, considerable embarrassment, but which delayed – and in some cases, prevented – American publication of his work. His concerns were understandable: if an American publisher was only willing to import sheets from a British publisher, the author's copyright was not protected and his income would be lower. However, he did not appreciate what unattractive commercial propositions such works as *Walter Pater, The Religion of Beauty*, *Fifty Romance Lyric Poems* and *Four English Portraits* – and even his *Complete Poems* – were for American publishers. Duell was attracted by the prospect of the D.H. Lawrence biography and was also hoping for a new novel, but Aldington accused the company of 'wanting to pick out the juiciest plum and leave the others' and, as far as his writing a novel was concerned, insisted that in Britain there was currently a bigger demand for biographies than for fiction.[42] At the end of 1948, Kershaw, on the grounds that he was returning to London and that Aldington needed to be freed from administrative demands in order to be able to concentrate on the Lawrence biography, took over the correspondence with Manuel and made the best of the situation: Duell, Sloan and Pearce imported

sheets for the Pater, set up the Waterton biography and took on the
D.H. Lawrence but *Four English Portraits, Fifty Romance Lyric Poems*, the
Complete Poems and *The Religion of Beauty* were never published in the
United States.

Throughout 1949, while Aldington was wrestling with the Lawrence
biography and the Penguin and Heinemann introductions, there was a
stream of visitors to Villa Aucassin, friends and publishers, some welcome,
some not. One was another introduction from Kershaw: the writer Henry
Williamson, whom the Australian had contacted on his arrival in Britain.
Kershaw had read *The Story of a Norfolk Farm* and was hoping to work on
the land with Williamson.[43] The farm, however, folded at the end of the
war and the writer had left his wife and six children and moved back to
Devon alone.

In *The Pleasure of Their Company* Kershaw gives an account of his first
meeting with Williamson in early 1947. In response to Kershaw's letter,
the writer had called on him at the Duttons' Oxford flat. Afterwards:

> He took abrupt leave of us. From the window we watched him
> jump into the Aston-Martin and screech off down Banbury Road.
> 'Bit of a ratbag, isn't he?' said Dutton without animosity as he
> poured us a drink.
>
> There was no getting around that: he was a bit of a ratbag. But
> in his books he had depicted himself as just that – tormented,
> feverish, slightly cracked. Meeting him, then, one didn't feel one
> had been tricked. One had had fair warning, so to speak. The
> man and his books were identical twins. And he was in any case,
> an interesting ratbag, vulnerable, unsure of himself, yet with a
> queer strength of his own. . . . Plenty of people considered him an
> intolerable egomaniac. Personally, I admired his unabashed belief
> in himself as an artist and his fervent attachment to his art.[44]

Kershaw knew that Williamson and Aldington had a lot in common.
Both had served as infantrymen in the First World War; and both had
written novels constituting bitter attacks on the war and its causes; both
had distrusted socialism in interwar Britain, although only Williamson –
along with Lewis and Pound – had seen fascism as the desired alternative.[45]
In the postwar world the two men continued to distrust left-wing politics.
Although there had been a single exchange of letters between them in
1929, when Aldington had written to congratulate Williamson on the
publication of *The Wet Flanders Plain*, their relationship was initiated
when Williamson took over the editorship of *The Adelphi* in 1948.[46] He

edited the journal for only three issues but through Kershaw – whose own poetry was featured – elicited a chapter from Aldington's forthcoming Waterton biography for publication in the October-December 1948 issue.

On 27 April 1949 Williamson and his new wife, Christine, arrived to spend their honeymoon at Le Lavandou. They stayed for a month. Meanwhile, John Holroyd-Reece of Albatross had called on Kershaw in Paris and was on his way to Saint-Clair to see Aldington. Deasey, currently engrossed in the vain courtship of a young American woman, was staying at Les Sables d'Or. Aldington told H.D.: 'We are rather over-run with people at the moment, several at St Clair and Henry Williamson and his newest wife in Lavandou. ... Hope you are not swamped with people. One is so tremendously vulnerable to unintentional intrusions when putting out nervous energy and perception continuously in a long book.'[47] How chaotic such situations could become is evidenced in his letter to Kershaw on 15 May:

Enter the Bird.[48] HW bursts in upon us demanding to know whose Rolls was preventing him from taking out his car. I introduced them and a brief colloquy occurred on the terrace. ... The Bird went about 6, Netta went out and returned about 7 just as I was giving Catha her supper, accompanied by Dease ... Jean appeared – Punch and Judy – as Dease vanished, caterwauling like a gibcat in excitement at the absurd over-estimate of her tenuous charms owing to D's temporary insanity. Netta went with them to dinner at the Auberge du Dome, Deasey – ever more insane – paying a taxi to bring along Louie and his Commie friend. The Commie – a perfect Christian – waxed ever more indignant over the luxury of omelette and stewed

Henry and Christine Williamson at Le Lavandou, spring 1949

rabbit and when Dease bought champagne and Netta asked him
to sing Giovanezza the Commie flung out into the Fôret du Dome
and has not been seen since, the others driving home by way of
St Tropez (most rightly) without bothering to ask about him. . . .
They turned up at the 'apolaustic' hour of dawn.

Despite the distracting circumstances of Williamson's visit, the two
men got along well, Aldington telling Kershaw: 'I see what you mean
about Henry being nuts, but he is really very sweet and affectionate.'[49] As
for Williamson, his 1965 memoir of the occasion displays some striking
insights into Aldington's make-up. He remarked that 'the barbed wire
was still encircling his heart, the iron fragments of shells in the bone of
his skull'. 'But of course,' he continues:

> one knew that was only part of the story; for a division of the spirit
> occurs in childhood, and the war was but a visible extension of that
> split between a child's parents. The lonely, rebellious soldier was the
> lonely unhappy child . . . Richard, one divined, was still a lonely man,
> bound by invisible fetters forged in the shadows of childhood.[50]

Perhaps these observations seem less remarkable when we reflect that
these men had more in common in their lives than their war experience:
their problematic lower-middle-class childhoods and their difficult
relationships with their parents; and, in adulthood, their constant search
for sexual fulfilment and the ideal partner.

To return to Aldington's 15 May letter to Kershaw, what we can read
between the lines of that account is that Netta enjoyed the opportunity
for livelier entertainment than was on offer at home. Another letter,
written to Kershaw at the beginning of the year, gives us some indication
of the relaxation that Aldington himself preferred:

> We are just back from a lovely Thursday picnic with Catha at the
> Favière – walked it along the plage of Lavandou, crossed dos arroyos,
> went over that cape where the campeurs infest the landscape in
> summer, and sat among the dunes. No one passed except an old
> couple, artists, taking provisions out to whatever cottage they have
> out there. There was brilliant sun, a very light north wind, there
> were tracks of wild birds on the sand, stunted pines and coarse
> grass and sea plants, we ate bread and ham and pâté and cold veal,
> bananas and oranges. It was so peaceful, so outside the vile world
> of too many people. As calm as 1880, if you know what I mean.[51]

He often shared such moments with H.D., in what had become a regular correspondence:

> It is full summer here now, and as we are not really far distant in a straight line, I suspect you will have much the same weather at Lugano. . . . Beautiful, beautiful wild flowers – so many I didn't know or have forgotten grew here. In one place I found many wild gladiolus, tall, slim, with blood-like blossoms, so incomparably more graceful and lovely than the garden ones. All the wild lavender in flower, with long stick-up petals like blue rabbit's ears. Wild mignonette, delicate, and many poppies, the white cistus flowers as abundant on the hills as a storm of snow.[52]

Only days after the Williamsons' visit, Netta departed for London for her first UK visit since embarking for the United States ten years earlier. Aldington told Kershaw: 'Catha and I are getting on pretty middling, She is enormously enjoying her role of lady of the house, discussing house-keeping with Mme Giraud and even – but this will not last – cleaning her shoes and putting away her washing.'[53] Netta was back a few weeks later and, in September, the Lawrence biography completed, Aldington took his first holiday of the year, spending time with his family walking and relaxing on the beach. A letter to Bacon shows us, however, that his world view remained gloomy:

> For nearly a year I have been over-working. . . . At the moment I am taking a vacation at home. . . . Europe totters on from week to week, only too conscious that it is raised above the starvation line more by the bounty of America than any genuine recovery. Poor old England has taken the place of Turkey as the sick man of Europe and retains only enough energy to cling to its musty social errors and to oppose and often thwart all efforts at the re-establishment of freedom, which alone can bring some prosperity. By having a real showdown with the communists and defeating them France has really done wonders.[54]

Nor was the vacation trouble-free: an angry letter came from his brother-in-law regarding his inadequate financial support for his mother, threatening to make public his neglect of her; at the same time, he received a writ from the Patmore lawyers, his brother not having kept up the payments due to them. He was soon back at his desk working on the Lawrence introductions for Heinemann. A visit from the Duttons prompted the remark to Kershaw: 'Both look extremely well, with that amiable and placid optimism which is one of the many rewards of virtuously inherited and unearned income.' He had the grace to add: 'How spiteful I am.'[55]

Perhaps because he saw him less frequently than either Kershaw or Deasey, Dutton, despite his enormous affection and respect for Aldington, tended to observe him with an element of detachment, and in the summer of 1949 found some despair that had not been there the previous year. He explained in his 1994 autobiography:

> Richard, when expansive and relaxed, was as wonderful company as ever. But the world, that deception of magnitude, wounded him too easily. Even in the South of France there was plenty of evidence of man's folly and cruelty, from the wreckage of the war, which could be found in a peaceful corner of the coast, to the growing frenzy of the Cold War. He took it all personally, and seethed with a Swiftian loathing, not of individuals, but of man and his works.

He added:

> However, Richard's worst wounds came not from the jagged world but from himself. The bearings of the love-hate seesaw screeched in his soul. For all his profound personal culture, he lacked the nurturing of nature, the fertile simplicity of water and manure on a garden. For him the manure remained shit, the compost did not meld with the soil.

How much Dutton knew of Aldington's upbringing we do not know, but this observation shows remarkable perceptiveness.[56]

Browning also arrived in Saint-Clair in September, with his wife and his mother-in-law, Lady Evans, for a visit arranged by Kershaw, who told Aldington beforehand: 'I hope you'll consider carefully any suggestions he makes. I've told him that the Heinemann set-up is complicated in the extreme. Privately, I believe that it could be tactfully arranged for Browning to reprint you and to have new work – without Frere being too upset.'[57] Fortunately, Aldington took to Browning, who stayed at Les Sables d'Or with his wife and mother-in-law, and he told Kershaw: 'He would have signed me away from Frere at once.'[58] Kershaw's big idea was for Evans to commission Aldington to write a biography of one of his own personal heroes, T.E. Lawrence. Aldington was receptive, telling

Kershaw in November that he thought it 'a brilliant idea' and authorising him to talk it over with Browning. He suggested terms, which included a sum of £100 a year, to be matched by himself, in order to pay Kershaw to become his researcher on the project, and Browning's permission for him to approach Duell, Sloan and Pearce about American publication.[59] Kershaw argued that Doubleday – as T.E. Lawrence's own publishers – would be a better proposition, but was delighted by Aldington's interest in the proposal: 'I would anticipate a greater success for this than for the DHL – and an even greater book.' Kershaw himself possessed copies of 'all the books on TEL that exist[ed] only in frantically limited editions' and was having them sent over from Australia.[60] Browning arranged for a copy of *The Mint*, Lawrence's as yet unpublished memoirs of his life in the Royal Air Force after the First World War, to be made available for Aldington to read.[61]

Kershaw's proposal – ironically, in the light of subsequent events – was an attempt to rescue his friend from a state of despair. In November 1948 Aldington had told Dibben that he was postponing the writing of a novel 'for the sad reason that I haven't the energy to create one at the moment'.[62] Nevertheless, corresponding with Martin Secker in the spring of 1949 over matters relating to the D.H. Lawrence biography, Aldington had told the publisher:

> It would satisfy an old ambition of mine if I could publish something with you, for you introduced and supported so many of the writers I admire. . . . The thing would be to do something really creative – through a chapter of accidents I have got involved in work which is too literary, and I'd like to break free.

When Secker suggested he might like to submit a short novel, he responded with enthusiasm: 'This is a form which can be very effective, and I have a half-formed subject (which only needs developing) in a setting of S.W. Florida, which might interest people.'[63] Now, however, he told Kershaw that he had never before had such a feeling of 'complete blankness and sterility' and did not know how to set about another book. As in the past, the anxiety triggered illness and insomnia – and regrets: 'Of course, it was a mistake to leave America – we should have gone quietly back to Florida.'[64] At the beginning of November he told Dibben:

> Since I last wrote there seems to have been nothing but evil news and unprofitable if necessary labours. My old mother, who is 77, has had to have financial help again. Packet of queries from Duells

re Lawrence. Then the Penguin proofs. Browning says Albatross has gone out of business – taken over by Stanley Unwin. . . . And there has been a Witter Bynner book on Lawrence![65]

By December he was laid up with severe bronchitis, but still dealing with proofs for the D.H. Lawrence biography and for the Penguin introductions, and answering the queries from Duell, Sloan and Pearce. By the middle of the month he was out of bed although still feeling 'wretchedly unwell', but he had promised Catha a Christmas trip of a few days to Monaco, where the principal attraction was the Oceanographic Museum and its aquarium, a reminder of the glass-bottomed boats of Jamaica which she had loved.[66] They were back in Saint-Clair on 30 December and three days later Netta left for a flight to Jamaica – via Paris, London and New York – to see her mother for the first time since their departure in 1946. In poor health and confronting financial hardship, Aldington was at a low ebb. The year 1950 would bring troubles with which he no longer had the resilience to cope.

17. The Public Face
The Old Loyalties

Aldington approached the Lawrence project in a heightened state of anxiety, torn not only between his keenness to do his friend justice and his fears that whatever he wrote would be misunderstood, but also between his own conflicting feelings about the man. As early as April 1948 he was seeking encouragement from H.D. and attempting to use her as a sounding board. This could only ever be a partially successful exercise, given both her agonising memories of her relationship with Lawrence and Aldington's own continued ignorance of those memories.[1] He told her: 'I still feel he was the greatest writer of our epoch, though a bit of a blackguard in some ways and horribly treacherous and gossipy. But he was – and still is – something, and what is the use of being a great writer if you can't be a blackguard too?'[2] He was also wary of becoming involved with the Lawrence 'circle'.[3] 'Trouble is,' he wrote, 'that most of them are nothing in themselves and never had anything in their life but their association with DHL and so cling on most fiercely to their little property and resent anyone else touching it'.

H.D. gave some hint of her feelings in a letter written in June:

> I feel sort of sick when I see him – only once – on a book-stall here; the first Mrs – no, Lady C. with an introduction by Frieda giving portrait of the artist as a great man, sitting in a bower, past the cyclamen slope – but – but –Yes; Norman D[ouglas] said, 'he opened up a little window to people in the suburbs'. Somehow, how dreary that preaching of L., 'marriage is thus and so, but I myself, *EGO SUM*, think it should be, it must be thus and so. I will never ask you who was the father of your children, should we have any after we are married.' It is, isn't it, suburban?[4]

Both the incoherence (a sign of the difficulty she has in speaking of Lawrence at all, particularly to Aldington) and the malice of these comments betray the continuing painfulness of the 1917 and 1918 memories that she had attempted, and still was attempting, to exorcise, both in her sessions with Freud in 1933 and – at the very time she was writing this letter to Aldington – in her redrafting of *Bid Me to Live*.[5] Aldington may have been surprised by the vehemence of the response, but replied:

> I understand your revulsion against DHL. I had a similar feeling recently, as I think I told you, on re-reading St Mawr. I disliked intensely the acrid underdog hatred, not a generous hatred of indignation and scorn, but a hatred of envy and grudging – the very things his better self inveighs against. And then those ridiculous primitives – who are to save the world (from what, *mon Dieu*?) by going to bed with upper-class women.

Then his ambivalence resurfaces: 'But then there was greatness in him, more than anyone else in our time, I think.'[6]

Ultimately, it was the rejection of Lawrence by the literary establishment that put Aldington on his side. He told Secker:

> I suppose you and I know as well as anyone living how disagreeable and offensive DHL could be, but by God when I go over the evidence and see how those people tried to crush him by any foul trick I do feel on his side. And after all on the great (?) side we shall never know anyone like him, shall we? I do admire you for sticking by him.[7]

The ambivalence remained as the work got underway and is charted in his letters to Kershaw. In October 1948 he wrote: 'Lorenzo progresses but slowly, and yet progresses. I find I dislike him more every day. Alas, I shall never find another Duke, who gets better all the time.'[8] Two weeks later he tells his friend: '[T]he moment I read his enemies I rally round him – it's his friends who depress.'[9] Kershaw was reassuring: 'It will be among your best and a piece of magic and will delight everyone.'[10]

As the publication date drew near, his anxieties increased, especially as he and Frere had a disagreement about the photographs to be included, ending in Frere's proposal that they use no photographs at all! Aldington responded irritably:

> You must remember that this book will be scrutinised by L's enemies, by my enemies, by your enemies, and by those who think they know more about L than I do. Among the last we

have the possibility of Cynthia Asquith, J M Murry, Stephen Potter, Douglas Goldring, Herbert Read, Rebecca West, Edward Shanks, Desmond McCarthy, Peter Quennell, E M Forster *et al*.[11]

He demanded that Frere be in London for publication date as he anticipated 'violent attacks', particularly from the *TLS*, which he claimed had 'blackguarded' his work ever since Alan Pryce-Jones had taken over the editorship the previous year.[12]

Frere, however, had understood perfectly that Aldington was the right person to write the definitive study: a close friend and unswerving admirer but with a clear-eyed awareness of the complexities and drawbacks of Lawrence's remarkable personality; a discerning literary critic with a thorough familiarity with the totality of Lawrence's output. The result is a measured, searching but also profoundly touching portrait. There are few references to the two men's personal acquaintance (one being a delightful account of Lawrence in the company of small children at the Villa Mirenda in 1926) but the analysis is rooted throughout in a thorough understanding of the man and his work. Aldington's own battles over the censorship of *Death of a Hero* and *All Men Are Enemies* and the refusal of the libraries to stock *The Colonel's Daughter* made him deeply sympathetic to his friend's sufferings over the banning of *The Rainbow* in 1915 and the reception of both *Lady Chatterley's Lover* and the paintings in 1928 and 1929; and his own resentment of the literary establishment was intensified by his consciousness of its failure to acknowledge Lawrence's genius or to come to his support during these crises. It also took a writer who had himself grown up in a dysfunctional family to recognise how profoundly Lawrence's irascible nature was formed by his early training and environment. It is more remarkable that, despite his accustomed resentment of fellow writers who had not served in the Great War, he produced a moving account of Lawrence's persecution at the hands of the authorities in Cornwall in 1917. He also understood the source of Lawrence's revulsion from the war: it was neither pacifism nor a lack of patriotism, but 'that all his instinctive horror and fear of the industrial machine, so acute as to be almost insane, was transferred to the military machine'.[13]

This leads us to the most important reason why he was the right biographer for Lawrence: he shared so many of the latter's values, not only his horror of the military-industrial complex but also his love of the natural world and his belief in the relationship between a man and a woman as the centre of human experience. Of course, Lawrence, as he had insisted on Port-Cros in 1928, believed utterly in fidelity, whereas Aldington was driven by his desires of the moment. Revealingly, he writes of the start of the relationship between Lawrence and Frieda:

> Many people would have recoiled, but it is the mean, calculating, cold-blooded, under-sexed types who hesitate in such a dilemma and are cautious and draw back. When real people like these two fall in love they brush aside all the funny little legal rules, and even such genuine human difficulties as the children in his case were.[14]

Given Aldington's own history of infidelity, it is remarkable that he was able to recognise the power of the Lawrence marriage; the book is a moving tribute to Frieda. Her affair with Angelo Ravagli, which began in the last three or four years of Lawrence's life, is not mentioned, but Aldington would have recognised that it never affected the centrality of Lawrence in her life.

Nevertheless, he could treat his subject with detachment. He says of Lawrence's Croydon years: 'At this stage he had not yet elected himself Saviour of Society.'[15] This aspect of Lawrence's personality, 'his habit of unblushing and impudent dogmatism' is generally treated with humour: 'He was terribly at ease upon Sion. He also had to know everything and have the right answer to everything.'[16] Of Lawrence's four-year 'savage pilgrimage', he observes that it was wholly voluntary and consisted:

> in having headquarters for a couple of years at Taormina, the most fashionable resort in Italy, with pleasant excursions to Malta, Capri, Amalfi, Rome, Florence, Venice, Bavaria and Austria; in crossing oceans on luxury liners, staying with friends in Ceylon and Perth, living in a large Australian bungalow on the edge of the Pacific and a 'smart new house' in Taos.

The Lawrences, he remarks tartly, spent 'ten days at icy, mountainous Picinisco and ten weeks on the Lobo'.[17]

He makes no attempt to excuse Lawrence's 'peculiar personality':[18] 'His power to evoke warm responses of friendship and love in others was exceeded only by the perverse demon in him which seemed to compel him to outrage and repel the feelings he had himself created, perhaps because he dreaded the possessive claims of those who cared for him.'[19] Recognition of the faults is underpinned, however, by an understanding of their origins, as when he refers to Lawrence's 'attitude of overbearing self-confidence which he assumed to hide his own unsureness and vacillation'.[20] He also notes 'how remarkable it is that he tries to tell the truth – however unflattering – about himself as well as others, he makes no attempt to guild his perversities and very rarely defends himself'. The 'self-portraits' in *Sons and Lovers* and *Kangaroo* are cited to demonstrate this characteristic. 'It is truly remarkable,' he concludes, 'that a man should see through his most cherished pretences so accurately and record them against himself so ruthlessly.'[21]

Above all, he was able to appreciate Lawrence's gifts as a writer. Lawrence cared very little, we are told, about 'the art and craft of fiction', using loose poetic forms 'to hold together his life experiences and his preachings'. He did not set out 'to tell a plotted story with carefully worked out "characters", approved "construction" and much painful attention to his "prose"'. For Lawrence, 'the writing of a novel was an adventure of the mind, an exploration of his unconscious self, with his strange chaos of emotions and almost uniquely retentive memory'.[22] Alongside the novels stood the travel writings with their remarkable sense of 'the spirit of place', expressed in language 'not altogether faultless . . . but of peculiar intensity'.[23]

As Aldington had anticipated, the criticism that met the book on its publication in March 1950 came from one of the former Lawrence coterie, in the person of David Garnett, whose review in *The Observer* 'corrected' Aldington on several points of fact, although concluding he had written 'a true and just book, worthy of his tragic subject'.[24] Aldington protested, but despite Frere's claim that Garnett's review had 'reflected on the author's integrity', the editor refused to publish Aldington's letter until Frere threatened legal action.[25] Aldington turned to conducting a personal correspondence with Garnett instead and, for once, was able to settle the matter quite amicably.[26] Frere had more success with *The Spectator*, whose editor agreed that Hesketh Pearson, who had called the biography 'ably and sympathetically written' but had used the opportunity to mount an attack on Lawrence himself ('semi-demented and rather repellent') had acted entirely inappropriately.

In general, however, reviews were favourable. Malcolm Muggeridge, writing in the *TLS*, thought the circumstances of Lawrence's birth, upbringing and subsequent career and his numerous and turbulent friendships 'admirably conveyed' and his writings 'sympathetically, but acutely, considered'. Nevertheless, he remarked on 'a certain illogicality' of attitude: 'On the one hand [Aldington] wants to present Lawrence as a victim of collective, and particularly English, prejudice; on the other, his own innate good sense makes him draw attention to how maddening Lawrence could be.' However, this was 'a small and perhaps unavoidable blemish, in an admirable biography, honest in intentions, affectionate in spirit and generous in appreciation'.[27] V.S. Pritchett in the *New Statesman* noted that, while clearly aware of the 'exasperating contradictions' in Lawrence's life and work, Aldington had been sympathetic, exposing, without disparaging, 'some of Lawrence's vices of character'; but Peter Quennell in the *Daily Mail* felt the book was spoiled by 'the flippant and knowing manner in which Aldington jab[bed] his points home'. '[R]eal talent, let alone genius,' he observed, 'demands a certain regard and respect from those who presume to write about it.'[28] Aldington must have smiled rather wryly on reading this pronouncement from the *Daily Mail*. For the rest, he expressed his relief in his characteristic metaphors of war: 'I have a feeling we've driven in the outpost lines, and if Frere and Lane attack hard enough with the Pockets and Penguins the enemy's main defences will collapse.'[29]

He was concerned at having heard nothing from Frieda. In April he wrote, only to hear that she had not received the proofs from Duell. A copy of the book reached her shortly afterwards and she wrote enthusiastically:

> Many things, as our wills clashing, I had not really grasped, but it's true – I am glad you were nice about Aldous, but you did not say enough, how patient and kind you were and when Hilda took us in at that bad moment you had something to do with it too – you know how scared everybody was of us![30]

It probably did not surprise Aldington that the most unfavourable review he received was a lengthy essay by Read in *World Review* in July. Clifford Dyment's *Sunday Times* review, although commending the book's 'remarkable . . . vigour and level-headedness', had pointed out that it left out all discussion of Lawrence's politics and philosophy.[31] This neglect was the central plank of Read's thesis. He called the book a 'denial and a betrayal' of this vital aspect of the work. Lawrence had believed 'that the essential function of art is moral', and his greatest works sprang from 'a mind in revolt against the civilisation it had inherited'. Aldington, Read maintained, had tried 'to save a decorative, an aesthetic Lawrence from the glorious confusion of his work'. What was now needed was 'a more fundamental consideration of the art and philosophy of this irregular genius'.[32] Aldington had already suggested that such an exercise was futile:

> Those who go to Lawrence for a coherent philosophical system, or require him to state reasons and draw maps for everything he said or wrote, waste their time. What matters is not his opinions or prejudices, but himself, the life and beauty he can transmit more than anyone else of his age.[33]

Read also commented that the book 'might have been more scrupulously documented' but noted that Aldington was no longer one of the 'critical clerisy'. This is one of those occasions when we cannot help being persuaded by Aldington's view that the 'critical clerisy', and the *Criterion* set in particular, welcomed any opportunity to patronise and disparage him.

An insight into how reviewing was used for self-promotion is offered us in the shape of Harry T. Moore's review, which appeared in New York's *Saturday Review of Literature*.[34] Moore's own first attempt on a life of Lawrence was due to appear shortly and, although he began with some complimentary comments, he was quick to assert that Aldington's book had 'two serious faults': that it had 'no new information of any value', constituting merely 'a rehash of material long in the public domain'; and that it 'fail[ed] to develop adequately some of the secondary figures' in Lawrence's life.[35] Moore ('a somewhat brash academic go-getter', Aldington told Bacon) had even had the review published two weeks before the book's US publication date, thus impacting badly on its sales.[36]

The introductions to the Penguin and Heinemann editions (nine Penguins and twelve Heinemann, of which five were also in the Penguin series) are short by modern standards, consisting of only around 1,200 to 1,500 words each, but beautifully crafted to inform the reader of the personal context out of which each text emerged (so important because of Lawrence's 'unique power of crowding an immense series of emotional experiences into a very few days, of remembering them with precise and detailed variety, and of evoking them with a skill that makes the poet's experience the reader's'), to convey an understanding of the writing process behind the work and to provide an insight into the uniqueness of Lawrence's vision, particularly 'his perception of natural beauty'.[37] Nevertheless, weaknesses are identified, for example the descent of satire into 'almost the level of spiteful gossip' in *Aaron's Rod* and the 'too naturalistic dialogue Lawrence would not learn to prune', but in general the emphasis is on the originality, freshness and vitality of Lawrence's writing.

While these editions would have a long life, Aldington was disappointed with the sales of the biography, telling Bacon in October that Heinemann had sold only 9,000 copies and Duell 3,500.[38]

* * *

Prior to the Lawrence biography, between 1946 and 1950, Aldington edited selections of Wilde, Pater and the Aesthetes, as well as providing Allan Wingate with an introduction to their new edition of the novels of Jane Austen. We can include amongst the introductions he provided to these works the long essay on Dickens in *Four English Portraits*, published by Evans in 1948. Ranging in length from 4,000 (Jane Austen) to 18,000 words, Selwyn Kittredge accurately describes these introductions as 'lucid, informed and gracefully written yet full of balanced critical insights such as only a lifetime of reading for pleasure can unfold'.[39]

Indeed, Aldington's love of the Aesthetic writers stemmed from his youth. He tells us in *Life for Life's Sake* how one day he had come upon 'a dozen or more handsomely bound white books' (the new [1908] Methuen edition of Wilde's collected works) on the table in his father's library. He read eagerly, for, he tells us, '[w]ith all his faults and affectations, Oscar Wilde's attitude was one of yea-saying to life and art'.[40] Editing Wilde for Viking's Portable Series in 1945, he found himself being drawn again to the writers of the 1890s.

The introduction to *The Religion of Beauty* offers no theoretical discussion of Aestheticism. Reviewing the book in *The Sunday Times*, Raymond Mortimer commented that there was 'little attempt to estimate the value of the "religion of beauty" itself, apart from individual missionaries'.[41] In fact, Aldington actively refuses even to define the Aesthetic Movement, arguing that 'the whole point of this desultory little campaign is that art is to be enjoyed, not dissected', and adding later: 'If we cannot take Art and Literature with a certain lightness, among the many pleasures of life, let us take to grave-digging as a relaxation.' What we do get is a thoughtful discussion of the four 'Oxonians': John Ruskin and his 'prophetic energy'; Walter Pater with his 'delicate word mosaics'; John Addington Symonds and his 'delicacy of taste and sensibility'; and Oscar Wilde with his 'wit and light touch'.[42] Although there are some 70 poets and prose writers included in the selection (which begins with Ruskin and ends with Taylor), the only other writers mentioned in the introduction – apart from the 'predecessors' of the movement, Shelley, Keats, Tennyson and Arnold – are Whistler, George Meredith, George Moore – and Taylor. Neville Braybrooke in the *TLS* approved the 'generous selections' and praised the book for being 'no mere piece of compilation but a piece of editorship [with] a design and character of its own'.[43]

The Wilde and Pater selections preceded *The Religion of Beauty*. Reviewing the Wilde selection in *The Sunday Times* after its UK publication by Heinemann, Leonard Russell praised the way it brought together the best of Wilde and called the introduction 'strongly sensible and perceptive'.[44] This introduction follows Wilde's career from its early stages, commending the 'wit and charm' of the early poetry, noting how he developed into 'a prose writer of workmanlike quality', and praising the 'brilliant results' as he turned to the fairytale, the short story, the Platonic dialogue and the novel. Aldington commends the dialogues in particular: no other writer had produced dialogues 'so readable, so witty, so coloured, so eloquent and . . . so solidly constructed and full of thought and good sense'. He notes that Wilde had two distinct styles of writing, 'though he sometimes mixed them . . . with the happiest results': 'the aesthetic or symbolist, gorgeous and poetic, full of allusion and reminiscence and jewelled words . . . and the other, light, worldly, cynical, paradoxical, full of laughter'. He concludes his review with a consideration of *Salome* and the four comedy dramas, pronouncing *The Importance of Being Earnest* 'a masterpiece'. [45]

In view of Aldington's prejudice against homosexuality – as expressed in *Death of a Hero* and much of his correspondence, and as witnessed by Derek Patmore – it is of interest to note his comments on Wilde's sexual nature and conduct. He clearly retained his prejudices:

> It is a fact (which I suppose we can only deplore) that the male homosexual type often unconsciously annoys and irritates the average heterosexual male. . . . It was just this which made Wilde unpopular in spite of his wit and charm. The traits in Wilde's character which were stressed to his detriment by his sexual make-up might not be unfairly described as affectation, vanity, folly, and a curious lack of judgement almost approximating a failure to correlate the actual world with his own private world of wish and fantasy.

That he is on thin ground here he concedes with the observation: 'I am not going to venture on so hazardous a piece of psychology as "the homosexual character" (for what then is the "heterosexual character"?)', but he goes on to assert that 'these traits are often exaggerated in men of this type'. [46]

Nevertheless, he displays considerable compassion: 'If we say of Wilde that he brought his fate on himself by inconceivable insolence and lack of judgement, what on earth are we to say of a society which behaved in the savage and unpardonable manner it did in 1895 and after?' We are back with another, and more important, theme from *Death of a Hero* at the conclusion of the essay when Aldington returns to the 'savagery' of Wilde's sentence and punishment and the 'horrible public persecution to which he was subjected'. He concludes: 'For the victim one can only feel indignation and pity. Nobody was made a whit the happier or the more "moral" by this brutality; there was simply a great increase in hypocrisy and cant, and posterity was deprived of the mature work of a very distinguished writer.' [47]

With Pater, he was on less controversial ground, remarking that the writer 'was never in any danger of connecting himself with a life drama', being 'far too fastidious and timid':

> On the whole he is a mystery man without a mystery. . . . The rulers of Oxford seem to have decided that he was undesirable but comparatively harmless, and the most he had to endure was the negative persecution of frustration and such nagging caricature as is likely to befall anyone who specialises in a subject so unpopular as aesthetics.[48]

Aldington is clearly enjoying himself in this essay. We are first given an account of Pater's early life and career up to the publication of *Studies in the History of the Renaissance* in 1873, a book which 'repudiated the abstract metaphysical approach to art of the Hegelians and the ethical views of Ruskin' and offered in its conclusion 'an eloquent . . . statement of the author's "Cyrenaicism"'.[49] We begin to see why this reclusive character was so attractive to Aldington, particularly when he goes on to show the extent to which Pater was ostracised by the Oxford establishment. 'He could never have been a popular author,' Aldington concludes, 'for he makes considerable demands of his readers, but he was prevented by the opposition from reaching the limited audience possible for him and from enjoying the reputation to which he was entitled.'[50]

Aldington conceded that to the 'war-weary generation, scrambling on somehow from day to day', Pater's work might seem remote: 'How will a generation so sorely harassed look upon the writings of one whose chief problem was how to enjoy life with intelligence and sensibility and knowledge?'[51] The last third of the essay is devoted to answering that question through a thorough survey of the work. Pater is commended for 'his serenity, his cheerfulness, his fastidious good taste, his eagerness to put before us the best he has discovered', and Aldington argues that part of his achievement was 'to take subjects which the vulgar consider "dry" and the highbrows vote "academic" and to invest them with new glamour, a wistful attractiveness'.[52]

As might be expected, the book received few reviews, but these were approving, the *New Statesman* remarking that 'we ought to be grateful to Mr Aldington for reviving Pater without ridiculing him'.[53] Aldington himself was incensed by Church's review on the front page of *John O' London's Weekly*, but it is hard to understand why. Church made a passing allusion to Aldington's expressed hatred of philistinism, remarking that such 'hates and labellings', while giving drama 'to our relations with each other', had been shown by recent history to be dangerous; but the general thrust of his review was positive, referring to Aldington's 'wide but vigorous scholarship' and to his being a critic 'who refuse[d] to sit on the fence', and commenting that the selection had been made 'with great taste and skill'.[54]

We might wonder why Wingate gave Aldington the Jane Austen commission. For Aldington, Austen was 'a child of the sedate English eighteenth century ... out of sympathy with Romanticism', and his criticism of the society represented in the novels ('dominated by two passions, the snobbery of rank and the snobbery of money') does not entirely exclude Austen herself:

> [E]very one of Jane Austen's novels has a Cinderella in it, a Cinderella who marries the more or less rich and handsome young man while other girls with more money and less rectory culture either have to take the wrong man or commit the enormity of elopement or (at least on one occasion) the crime of adultery. Strict attention to conventional morality, good manners, and accomplishments will (the novels imply) achieve matrimonial success, while all deviations from the code will be appropriately punished.[55]

We might feel that the qualities Austen values in her characters run deeper than 'conventional morality, good manners and accomplishments', but the argument is persuasive. As in the Pater introduction, the final third of the essay is an enquiry into the writer's (in this case very patent) appeal for a contemporary audience. A successful novelist, Aldington argues, must know how 'to live vicariously the lives of characters and to communicate that vitality by words'. Dickens had that gift, but he also had 'faults of taste: predilection for melodrama, sentimentality, caricature'. While the gift was 'less vigorous, more sedate' in Austen, 'her taste was excellent, and she hardly ever betrayed it except under the pressure of absurd conventions'. So far, we are finding moderate praise, but it is in the conclusion that we feel him warming to her: 'There is scarcely a chapter which lacks some quiet deadly comment on human nature ... [but] [s]he never strives for wit, she never abuses her gift of irony.'[56] It is a restraint he clearly envies. He has come a long way from the 23-year-old who remarked (in relation to the work of the French poet Laurent Tailhade) that '[t]he three qualities of bitterness, disdain and obscenity are essential to satiric writing'.[57]

Despite reservations about Dickens, given expression in the comment that 'Like the Prince Regent, whom he despised, Dickens had a great deal of taste. Much of it bad', Aldington reveals in his portrait of the writer a greater warmth of appreciation than displayed in the Austen essay.[58] 'He concludes: 'He was a Philistine all right, but he was a Philistine of genius.'[59] The essay constitutes a compassionate exploration of Dickens's early life and an assessment of the way his early experiences shaped his writing: 'For Dickens was reserved the task of interpreting a world of human beings which his predecessors and contemporaries had neglected, and interpreting it with a knowledge and sympathy very rare in a literary man, owing largely to the peculiar conditions of his early life and later training.'[60] Dickens's limitations are acknowledged but, in Aldington's words, 'with the intention of doing so simply to arrive at a clearer idea of what in him is truly excellent and praiseworthy'.[61] Extracts from the novels are judiciously selected to demonstrate those gifts. The portrait is penetrating and balanced, yet informed throughout by Aldington's admiration. Two preoccupations of his own must have contributed to its success, one acknowledged, the other not. The first is his contempt for highbrow literary criticism, apparent immediately in an opening anecdote about two 'Eminent Critics' and their contempt for Dickens. He points out to such 'aesthetes and pedants' that 'Dickens wished to amuse and touch, to enthral and entertain ordinary men and women, and he has succeeded in doing so for over a century on a scale unsurpassed by any other English writer', and warns, in relation to Dickens's tendency to sentimentality: '[W]e must remember that in these matters of taste no judgment is final, that our attitude . . . is partly personal but also largely the attitude of our epoch and surroundings.'[62]

The other preoccupation exists only as a sub-text. Of Dickens's boyhood experiences Aldington writes:

> He could . . . not forget the wrong done him as a sensitive, ignorant little boy, nor forgive it, not cease to be haunted by the thought that other children were still suffering, as he had suffered. This intense feeling was basically self-pity, but, then, all genuine compassion arises from having suffered ourselves and from directing the natural self-pity away from ourselves to others.[63]

Aldington, of course, had not been subjected to anything like the blacking factory, but he had endured the humiliation of having a debtor as a father and the consequent educational deprivation. The observation about Dickens's capacity to redirect his sense of self-pity is remarkable in a man who had only imperfectly managed this transition himself.

The success of *The Duke* and his continuing lack of inspiration for a novel prompted him into, first, the *Four English Portraits*, published in 1948, and then, the following year and at Browning's instigation, a full-length biography of one of the four, the naturalist, explorer and conservationist Charles Waterton. The *Portraits* make for enjoyable reading. The preface announces the modest aims of 'sketching a personality and indicating an environment', but, though handled with an ease and informality of manner, the portraits reveal a depth of reading, research and analysis. All are of characters to whom Aldington was attracted, but they are also chosen for what they reveal about the first half of the nineteenth century – an age with whose culture, and specifically its political culture, Aldington was familiar from his work on Wellington.[64] The subjects were also selected for the different strata of that world they each represent, and so we are presented with 'the grand world of "Prinny"' [George IV], 'the lustrous world of Young Disraeli', 'the strange world of Squire Waterton' and 'the underworld of Young Dickens', Aldington's shrewd understanding of the norms of those societies informing his estimation of the personalities and behaviour of his individual subjects. His favourite character is undoubtedly Waterton, about whom he had written an essay in 1932, and 'for whose life and memory [he felt] a personal affection it would be vain to try to conceal', but his portraits of the other three, while more nuanced in their judgements, still display considerable sympathy.[65] He justifies his attention to the Prince Regent's 'quarrels with his parents, his unhappy matrimonial entanglements, his debts and extravagance, his political imprudences' on the grounds that these are what biographers have chosen to record, but he argues that, as regent and as king, George was cynically used by others 'in the game of domestic power politics' and he furnishes us with a much more positive character, distinguished by his culture and taste, his love of literature and the fine arts and his enjoyment of intellectual conversation 'in which he was fully competent to take part'.[66] Most of all, he brings his character to life by making connections with the contemporary world and with his own world view and experiences, as in the observations that 'Prinny had a talent for spending other people's money which would have done credit to a Socialist government', or (more personally) in relation to George's marriage to Maria Fitzherbert, that 'really it is hopeless to apologise for either of two people who commit imprudences because they are violently in love with each other'.[67]

His account of the life – and novels – of the young Disraeli is detailed, and his assessment of his character and actions balanced and dispassionate. He sees his subject as exhibiting extremes of self-confidence, ambition, abilities and failure, but concludes that: 'With all his faults and in spite of illness and debts, Disraeli was one of those who say "Yes" to life, responded warm-heartedly to the good things that came his way.'[68] This account of his subject prompts one of those not-infrequent criticisms of the contemporary world:

In an epoch of intellectual grumpiness and almost insane belittlement, as ours is, Disraeli's sunny enjoyment of life despite infinite worries and set-backs, above all his exuberant enthusiasms and admirations and grandiose dreams, are sneered at as absurd, vulgar, grotesque. The judgment is all wrong. Disraeli was perfectly ready to be serious when compelled, but he held that life is essentially to be enjoyed.[69]

However, it was Waterton for whom Aldington felt the most affection, and he was delighted to be asked by Evans to write a full-length biography. With Dibben's help to locate the rarer publications, he reviewed all the available material before writing his own account. His bibliography provides an assessment of each work he read, and he is keen to point out the errors in Norman Douglas's and Edith Sitwell's contributions to Waterton scholarship, as well as the extent to which Philip Gosse's book plagiarised Aldington's own 1932 essay.[70] We might expect Waterton's membership of the landed gentry, his asceticism, his devout Catholicism and his obstinacy and occasional bigotry to have repelled Aldington, but, while rejecting the hagiographical approach of several writers (including Sitwell), he clearly admired the Squire's love of Nature and desire to protect it in all its forms, his pursuit of knowledge, his kindliness and generosity – but, most of all, his eccentricity: 'A character so artless, a career so grotesque, an eccentric so unique form an irresistible combination.'[71] When he tells us that Waterton 'grew up to be one of the most uncompromising individualists in the most individualist epoch of once individualist England', we anticipate more of that critique of Aldington's own era which characterises the *Portraits*, and, sure enough, a few lines later we are told that 'in an age when the average, the general, the commonplace in human character and personality are earnestly put forward as the ideal, the *summum bonum* of humanity, it is difficult to agree with the Squire in his resentment against the title of "eccentric".'[72] In the *Four English Portraits* Aldington defines the eccentric as:

the man who knows what he wants to do, and simply and openly does it ... [who] never thinks of gain or applause, but of the satisfaction of doing, the supreme peace which comes from the object attained – whether it be riding a live alligator on the banks of the Essequibo or standing on one foot on the topmost pinnacle of the Castello di Sant'Angelo at Rome.[73]

For the first time, but not the last, Aldington had written a biography that provoked some sharp criticism – to which he, in turn, objected strongly. Roger Fulford's review in the *TLS* called *The Strange Life* 'an entertaining [but] altogether inadequate biography of a curious and distinguished personality' and accused Aldington of having relied too heavily on the account of Waterton written by his close friend, the doctor, Richard Hobson.[74] A further letter to the *TLS* from Sir Alan Moore, son of the editor of Waterton's *Essays on Natural History*, took issue with Aldington's criticisms of his father.[75] When Dibben sent him a cutting of the *TLS* review. Aldington replied: 'Believe me, the *TLS* is a dirty rag and stooping to dirty tricks to discredit me, who stand simply for the truth and not the Jesuits.'[76] He was convinced – particularly after the appearance of Alan Moore's letter – that Norman Moore had been part of 'a nasty little Roman Catholic conspiracy' in which he had been 'part dupe, part accomplice'. His claim was based on the facts that: Richard Hobson was a Protestant, while the younger Norman Moore, who had known Waterton towards the end of his life, was, like Waterton himself, a Roman Catholic; that Moore had edited out of Waterton's autobiography (included in Moore's edition of Waterton's essays) all tributes to Hobson; and that Stonyhurst College, where Waterton had been a pupil and to whom he had bequeathed his collection, had refused Evans Brothers permission to take photographs of the collection for Aldington's book.

As usual, Aldington's publishers (both Evans and Heinemann on this occasion) had to restrain him from writing to the *TLS*, aware that the chief damage Aldington did with angry letters claiming conspiracy theories was to his own reputation. He wrote to Dibben: 'I very much hope that someone with a knowledge of the facts may reply for me.'[77] Since Dibben had supplied him with all the books for the Waterton biography and Aldington had been feeding him 'the facts', there is little doubt who the 'someone' was intended to be. If Dibben did write to the *TLS*, the letter was certainly not printed. Meanwhile, Aldington was amassing all the evidence on 'the case of Dr Hobson and Mr Moore' for a preface to be issued to further impressions of his book. Since no further impressions would be made, it was never published. The whole affair was a small foretaste of things to come.

18. The Private Life
Crisis
1950

In January 1950, Aldington received two stunning blows, the first of which may have precipitated the second. The Patmore solicitors informed Tony Aldington that he had neglected to pay income tax amounting to £160 a year on Aldington's annual payments to Brigit. Aldington reported to Powell that the sum he owed now totalled £6,000.[1] Frere sympathised and suggested possible strategies, but the problem rumbled on until April when Tony was able to sell a property in Kent that had been left to Aldington by his father. The Patmore debt, however, would pursue Aldington for the rest of his impecunious life.

Meanwhile, Netta had left for London on 2 January. Aldington had no address for her and had to ask Kershaw to pass on the grim news. He was not reassured to hear that Kershaw had not seen her for a week. 'She seemed merry when we did see her, didn't much like me and has not replied to Patsy's messages suggesting that we meet again,' Kershaw told him.[2] Aldington replied: 'Netta seems to have given us all the brush-off. I had two laconic letters, and after a long pause there came a PC to Catha saying she expected to leave London by air on the night of Sunday, the 15th. Since then, niente.'[3]

Despite the reassurances of Kershaw and Frere, he was becoming dejected and anxious. He feared that Kershaw's marriage would keep him in London for good; the tax issue and the lack of communication from Netta were worrying him; and, as so often happened when he was suffering from stress, he was physically unwell. He told Kershaw on 13 January: 'I feel too ill (I have done for weeks, months) and disheartened, to undertake another book, particularly one so strenuous as the TEL. We ought never to have left America.' This nostalgia for the United States resurfaced in a letter to Bacon a few days later, in which he said that Netta had only bitter memories of their time in the States, whereas he had 'never felt anything but at home in America' and had wanted to go back to Florida when they left Jamaica in 1946.[4]

The dejection, as on previous occasions, fuelled his resentment towards the political and literary establishments. He told Kershaw:

> You will certainly cast me to Gehenna as a false traitor, but I hate the majority of the British professional and 'upper' class so much I hope the Socialists get in and sock them forever. They know if they fail at this election they are done, and so good luck to Cripps and Bevan. You understand that it's not that I don't hate the vile left but I hate the British more. I wish them Bevan because I think he'll squeeze them till their pips squeak.[5]

Meanwhile, Bacon was subjected to Aldington's views on Eliot: 'It is ten to one that the Archbishop got him his O.M., and persuaded the Foreign Office to recommend him for the Nobel Prize when it was England's turn for the cash.'[6]

Dibben was a further sympathetic listener. Aldington told him that he had had 'a bad go of bronchitis' in December and had had to work in bed for a time and dictate to Netta the index for his D.H. Lawrence book:

> I think there must have been an attack of flu in with it, for ever since I have felt run down, languid and depressed – though that is partly overwork. ... Then Netta had to fly to see her mother in Jamaica who is elderly [five years older than Aldington!] and not well. I had a cable to say she had reached Montego Bay but it is too soon for a letter. I fear she had a bad flight and got held up en route.[7]

The only correspondent who received a more positive letter was H.D. He was checking the proofs of the D.H. Lawrence essays and told her: 'They make a wonderful and living book, such a complete wipe-out of sterile highbrowism of the self-conscious straining-for-effect type. ... There is an almost unknown essay on Flowery Tuscany which is so beautiful and sensitive in its appreciation of wild flowers that you'll love it.' He was excited that the Lawrence biography was about to go onto the presses and there was no word of his financial worries or Netta's absence. He continued:

> All very quiet here, no tourists and no visitors. I have come to like it best in the winter when one is really peaceful. ... The wild jonquils are out, and the sweet alyssum seems to flower perpetually. The English daisy seems to flower all the year round

too, except in the August heats. Those pretty little Arum lilies are out, and the wild lavender. When I was up in the hills, the wild thyme was flowering and very fragrant.[8]

It was the first week of February when the second blow struck. A letter finally came from Jamaica. He acquainted Kershaw with its contents on 8 February:

> Even more amazing is the brush off from Netta, who writes to say she is setting up as an artist in London, on the usual Ibsen lines. It is done because my prospects are hopeless. The DHL will have only 'a REASONABLE sale', and apart from that there isn't 'a scrap more help or money to come from Frere'. (Not so far wrong.) Various articles are to be sent from here, including drawings and artists' materials, which I believe may not be imported into paradise. . . . Among other compliments I learn that it would be 'utmost folly' to borrow money to pay off Brigit as the debt 'would last forever' and nobody would lend me money anyhow. Also it would be similar folly for me 'to try to squeeze out another book' until I have 'rested a long time'.
>
> It is useless to argue with Netta over this. You know how blankly obstinate she is, and her vanity was wounded to the core when I told her some months back that she had no talent as a painter. Now I am to be shown what a genius I have insulted. I can't any longer support my family by writing, so SHE will blaze in the Chelsea firmament – a new Augustus Jane.
>
> Do you and Patsy please keep this to yourselves for the time being. I don't want Frere to know about it yet. Netta will be back about the 15th March, too late to do any particular mischief to the DHL.[9]

Quite what 'mischief' Netta could, or would wish to, do to the Lawrence biography is hard to imagine; but this was a devastating blow and came when he was at a particularly low ebb. He lamented to Kershaw:

> You see EVERYTHING has gone wrong. Loss of Czechoslovakia, loss of Albatross, failure of my books in France, Scandinavia etc., refusal of Alberto to transfer even the amounts I earn in Italy and to issue fresh books, failure of Four Portraits and Waterton, cabal of Times, Listener, BBC, Eliot and Sitwell gangs etc., loss of Viking, idiocy of Al Manuel and Duells. . . . Netta is quite

right – my career as an earning writer is finished, owing partly
to my own imprudence, partly to political events, partly to the
malice of enemies. . . . as Netta so sweetly says, even if I could
'squeeze out' another book it would probably not be worthwhile
economically.[10]

On 1 March he forwarded Netta's letter to Frere, telling him:

She went away cheerfully, leaving many clothes and all her
drawings etc.; wrote one very affectionate letter from London,
then after hearing of this income tax demand a brief and flurried
letter saying she thought she would get a job. I wrote her at once
to Jamaica suggesting she think again, and got this one in the eye
just a little while back. You see she says nasty things about Alister
as well – the only two real friends I have are cows according to her.
(How women hate a man to have friends!) . . . Something happened
in London, but what? . . . [Y]ou may wonder why you have to come
into it at all. Because, in trying to cheer her up in London over this
situation [the income-tax issue] I had quoted from you.
    The whole situation is a bewilderment to me. . . . [Y]ou'll see
that any chance of settling down to work is out of the question
until these things are settled. I was hoping the income tax thing
was over, and indeed wrote Netta twice to Jamaica saying it was,
but she never answered. Evidently didn't believe it.[11]

The situation may have been a 'bewilderment' to him and the incentive
for Netta's decision may have been his dire financial circumstances, but
other observers had seen the separation coming. Dutton tells us that:
'Catha could always take him out of himself; Netta was too languid, and
there were ominous signs of terminal exasperation between them.'[12] He
gives us a penetrating portrait of Netta at the villa:

[She] obviously welcomed some company; you felt that she was
too isolated at the Villa Aucassin. It was all very well for Richard,
who worked every day, but she had too much spare time. She was
a mixture of self-control and no control. You couldn't shock her or
surprise her, she was far too sophisticated, but she undermined
her own poise. There would be sudden changes, demoniacal
laughter, intense big-eyed stares that made you feel you must
quickly say something profound. Then there would be flashes of
genuine insight and intelligence. She was drinking too much. Her

idleness gave her a need for jabs of self-assurance, when she would tell you (and herself) that she was really rather good at painting and drawing, or that she was reading Proust for the third time.[13]

John Arlott, who, with his wife Dawn, had been a regular visitor at the villa, offers a more sympathetic portrait of Netta, but one which suggests further underlying causes for the breakdown of the marriage:

> Netta proved a very sensitive artist. Richard, though, was in many ways too big a character for her. . . . [She], unfortunately, never grew out of her awe of her husband. It was no surprise when finally she fled to England, took temporary shelter in the Arlott household and then settled down with a man of literary bent but much less of a heavyweight in mind and character than Richard. It was not that affection had died but simply that understanding had become impossible.[14]

It certainly appears that life at the villa had only been bearable for Netta when they had company and that (unlike Patmore before her) she viewed secretarial assistance to Aldington as a chore. His physical illnesses and, more importantly, his anxiety – about his career and his health – throughout the latter part of 1949, must have made him a difficult companion, making the 20-year disparity in their ages more marked. There are even hints of earlier disharmony: Netta seems not to have enjoyed the Hollywood years and, once Jamaica proved unsuitable for them all, to have wanted to return to Britain.

Whether either of them had taken other lovers during their residence in America – or after their return to France – is not clear. Aldington makes several references in the correspondence that he resumed with Gluckman in 1955 to having had 'mistresses' during his marriage (an American, a Scot and an Italian, in particular!), but it was important to him to come across to Gluckman as an experienced and knowledgeable lover, and it is hard to know when he is telling the truth. Furthermore, these stories seem to be at variance with the extent to which his family responsibilities and especially his relationship with his daughter had been at the centre of his personal life since 1938. He told H.D. in 1946: 'We lived too much to ourselves in Florida and Hollywood.'[15] However, he told Gluckman that Netta had taken a lover, 'with [his] permission', when they returned to Paris in 1946: 'I saw she was eager for it, so opposition was useless.' 'Later, in the south of France,' he continued, 'she got more and more restless, because she likes big towns, and I like the remote country.'[16]

It may be that Netta had begun an affair during her May 1949 visit to London and was planning by the end of the year to resume it. Arlott indicates in the passage quoted above that she entered into a long-term relationship once she settled in London. A letter written by one of her friends to Aldington's first biographer, Charles Doyle, shortly after his book was published in 1989, refers to 'the ghastly man [Netta] lived with for years' after she left Aldington.[17] In April 1951 Netta took on the lease of a flat in Knightsbridge with her mother and aunt, who were returning from Jamaica, although by December 1952 she had moved to a Chelsea address.[18] The only other hint about her London lifestyle is Aldington's agitated correspondence with Kershaw in the summer of 1954 when Netta appears to have been intending to visit with a male partner. By this time, Aldington and Catha were living in Montpellier and he told Kershaw: 'If you do see Netta please make clear that her coming to Montpellier with a man and staying with him in a hotel is the most damnable unkindness to Catha.' He explained in a further letter: 'Catha has made friends with the local bourgeois and this "social life" is the breath of her nostrils, as you realise. It would be imperilled if Netta turns up with a lousy Scotchman.' [19] It is hard to associate these comments with the author of *Death of a Hero* and *The Colonel's Daughter*. Parenthood – and perhaps jealousy? – had certainly changed his moral outlook. From the absence of further reference to the visit, we must assume that it did not take place. In 1960, he would tell Gluckman: '[Netta] doesn't want to live with another man but doesn't hesitate to have an affair when she wants.'[20] Clearly, if there was a long-term relationship, it had ended by this time.

In the Morris Library archives at the University of Southern Illinois there is a letter from the eleven-year-old Catha to her mother. It is dated 21 May 1950 and its contents make clear that, over four months after Netta's departure, Catha was still not aware that she would not be returning:

> How are you, I was so happy to have a letter from you. It does feel a little funny to be by myself with Daddy. I am sorry I made him mad by staying out late. I am happy that you find Paris nice; I would like to be with you.
>
> Deasey is staying with us so we are not completely by are [sic] selfs. My garden is allright even though the little cat is always making holes in it. . . .
>
> Send me some postcards of England and tell me how Patsy and Alister are going, and the whether [sic] in London. Desey [sic] is kindly doing the shopping he says that you should come back and relive [sic] him. Come back soon. With much love, Cathy P.S. Have a nice time.

Catha was not the only one kept in the dark. Frieda wrote on 27 May: 'I am glad that you have your friend Alister & Netta & the child! Now take it easy and relax!'[21] However, Bacon may have worked the story out from the letter Aldington wrote to him on 5 May (the first since the end of January), which declared:

> I have had one disaster on top of another until I know not where to turn. The whole culminated in an almost complete breakdown complicated with bronchitis, during all of which I was quite alone and had to steel myself to try to look after Catha. These troubles are far from settled, and the situation has not so much improved as I have begun to grow accustomed to it. An attempt to ruin me financially – on top of it all – has been temporarily staved off, but the future is uncertain in spite of my concentrated hard work, frugal living and general success as a writer. But a concurrence of legal trickery plus the atrocious modern tax laws of England cripples me. . . . We have had the worst, coldest and gloomiest spring I ever remember on this usually sunny coast.
>
> I must apologise for not writing, but indeed for many weeks I was forbidden to write except through my secretary who has been in London for months labouring to put things right for me.[22]

It was another five months before Aldington could bring himself to tell Bacon: 'Probably you know that Netta, unable to stand the strain, has left me and gone to London.'[23] As for the Slonimskys, it was December 1951 before they were told that: 'Some time back Netta decided that she wanted to live in London and have a job there.'[24] It was his first letter to them since December 1949.

H.D. may have guessed at the truth when his response to the news of Perdita's forthcoming marriage in June 1950 was: 'I do hope Perdita will be happy, but who is? We go through life looking forward to a future happiness which after a certain age we look back upon wistfully in the past.'[25] However, it was only after she expressed concern at a three-month silence – a rarity since the resumption of their correspondence in 1946 – that he told her in October: 'Netta is in London to get a rest from me', and explained that he had had a breakdown from over-work and 'infinite worries'.[26]

* * *

The T.E. Lawrence biography, on which he was starting to work, was by this stage causing him intermittent concerns. When Frere offered his personal support for the project in late March, Aldington told Kershaw: 'TEL was a murderer, a warmonger, and Frere hopes to push me into accepting and praising the war attitude, by writing a book on TEL. . . . I MUST stand up for the reality of life against all these official murderers and propagandists, these British Councillors.'[27] He told Bacon in June 1950: 'To keep going I've had to sell my name to a newish English publisher [Evans] and have bound myself to write a book I don't want to write and which is daily misery to work.'[28]

His mood fluctuated, however. His access to *The Mint* made him warm to Lawrence and he wrote to Kershaw in July: 'I am converted to him by The Mint, with the strong feeling that while he was a great guerrilla general I was a better private soldier', while he told Dibben that *The Mint* was 'the most human thing [Lawrence] wrote' and that there was 'nothing in it you and I haven't seen and endured in the ranks'.[29] Deasey was told in mid-November: 'I think I can be a great success if I do the job honestly and objectively', but, ominously, Aldington added: '[H]ard for me, since I dislike his pride that apes humility, his arrogance and Oxford posing and bloody lies.'[30]As late as December he was telling Dibben: 'In spite of my numerous literary enemies, I believe I can make a good and readable biography with a new slant, if ONLY I have health, quiet, and enough time and cash.'[31]

Nevertheless, by the end of the year he felt uneasily that there was something he was missing. He told Kershaw:

> I know it sounds foolish to say so but the real biographical material is so scanty though the stuff to be got through is wearisome and voluminous. TE does at times reveal himself, but mostly he is hiding behind his words. I think he is harder to know than any other character in history.[32]

* * *

Fortunately for Aldington, he had a tight network of friends to whom he could turn for support. Of his three closest pre-war friends, he had lost touch with MacGreevy, while his relationship with Frere blew hot and cold (although Frere would always offer him comfort in the bad times), but the saddest loss was that of Prentice. He and Aldington had been briefly reunited in Paris in 1946, but Prentice was married by then, in very poor health and seeking a warm climate. In 1947 he and his wife were in South Africa, planning to settle in Cape Province, but they changed their minds and decided on Cornwall.[33] There they purchased a 'tumbledown cottage' with 'a wilderness' of a garden. 'We'd love to come and see you and Netta and Catha,' he wrote wistfully, 'But how? How I'd love, too, lots of long talks.'[34] In July 1948 he told Aldington that they had had a worse time getting settled than in any other place they had attempted, and in November he was recovering from four weeks of flu in 'this hellish climate'.[35] By January 1949 he and Lyn were in Nairobi and he had been 'rather ill for several months' but told Aldington that 'this wondrous country and a Rhodesian doctor are leading me to new high levels of confidence and hope.'[36] In March they flew back to Cornwall to sell their house in order to settle in Kenya.[37] 'I nearly went west last winter in Cornwall, it was only Lyn that pulled me out,' he confided in May, when they had returned to Kenya.[38] By the end of the year he had died of heart failure. Sympathising with Bacon for the loss of a friend, Aldington wrote: 'Only a few months ago I lost my dear Charles Prentice, who was quite literally harried to his doom by the selfishness and neurotic restlessness of his wife.'[39] His affectionate tribute to Prentice in *Life for Life's Sake* would be echoed in *Pinorman*.

His American friends would continue to be supportive in the solitary years ahead, although Bacon died in January 1954 and Slonimsky ceased to write letters, leaving the task to Miriam (who, Aldington told H.D., was 'bigotedly Zionist') as he became increasingly depressed by his difficult circumstances at the New York Jewish Institute of Religion.[40] According to Aldington, he was under attack for being 'too humanistic' and in 1952 was forced to retire, after 26 years as Dean of Faculty.[41] Aldington felt great sympathy for him, telling Miriam:

> It is hard to abandon the eloquent teaching in which he excels, and sad to think that the noble tradition he had tried to create may be altered by successors. But by the formation of so many fine minds he has influenced his epoch more than most intellectuals are able to do.[42]

In 1954 he would ask the Slonimskys to welcome his oldest friend, Randall, now Sir Alec Randall, to New York as the latter arrived as a British delegate to the United Nations. 'He is,' he told them, 'the kindest and sweetest of men wrapped up in his children and in his intellectual interests.'[43] Randall's close friendship with Read may have made Aldington slightly wary of him in this period, but there was a long-standing affection between the two men, which is vouched for in the moving piece Randall contributed to the *Intimate Portrait* of Aldington that Kershaw compiled after the latter's death.

The breakdown of the marriage ended some friendships. Powell spent a sabbatical year in Europe from 1950 to 1951, bringing his wife with him. The fact that the couple met up with Netta in London and were also forced by bad weather to cancel a Christmas reunion with Aldington and Catha in France brought about an eight-year gap in the correspondence; and, in welcoming Netta to London, the Arlotts lost Aldington's friendship altogether, as Arlott ruefully acknowledges in his memoirs.[44] Warman, however, continued to be a loyal friend and the tables began to be turned in this relationship, Warman providing understanding and practical support – for Catha as well as her father – throughout the rest of Aldington's life.

Another, increasingly valued, friendship was with William Dibben, the amateur book-dealer on whom Aldington came to rely hugely for his T.E. Lawrence research. Aldington's letters to Dibben mainly concern the books the latter obtained for him, but they broaden out to cover their shared interest in (often obscure) works of literature and also in stamp collecting, an activity which Aldington and Catha had taken up. Dibben had visited the Villa Aucassin in the spring of 1949 but, despite Aldington's frequent invitations, the relationship became purely an epistolary one subsequently, although Kershaw, before moving to Paris in 1951, regularly met up with Dibben in London. Aldington would write to Dibben in March 1955: 'It's my idea of a pleasant evening to sit down at the typewriter after a day's work for a gossip to you.'[45] Sadly, the last letter referring to Dibben is one Aldington wrote to Kershaw in February 1957, expressing his concern that he had not heard from Dibben for over a year: 'He has been a very good friend and I hate to lose him.'[46] Dibben had mentioned health problems – including an operation – in his letters, so perhaps we should conclude that he had died.

Another important – and supportive – friend in the 1950s was the elderly Gustave Cohen, retired professor of mediaeval literature at the Sorbonne. Aldington had translated the fifteenth-century Liégois mystery play *Le Mystère de l'Incarnation et Nativité de Notre Saveur et Redempteur Jésus-Christ*, which Cohen had unearthed, as far back as 1924, and the two men had met in the south of France in the 1930s, but the friendship developed during these later years through regular correspondence and twice-yearly meetings.[47] Apart from their literary interests, the two men had their war service in common. ('You should see a real hero,' Aldington told Warman. 'He has been a cripple since 1915 when he was wounded on the Argonne.')[48] In 1956 Cohen translated *A Dream in the Luxembourg* and was completing a translation of *A Fool i' the Forest* at the time of his death in June 1958.[49] 'Travelling further,' wrote Cohen after one of their meetings, 'I felt wrapped in your warm friendship. In fact wine, excellent food, sensitive feelings played in my soul like a trio of exquisite human harmony. . . . I must add that Catherine's dear presence transformed that trio often in a quartet.'[50]

In early May 1950, Aldington at last became personally acquainted with Campbell, who rented a cottage that summer at Bormes up in the hills, only six miles from Saint-Clair.[51] He came with his 28-year-old daughter Tess, who had suffered a nervous breakdown in 1946 and had since made only a slow recovery, and they were joined in July by his wife Mary and their younger daughter, Anna, who had been on a pilgrimage to Rome. They stayed until late September and Campbell was almost a daily visitor at the villa. Aldington told H.D.: 'A great fellow, Roy, physically a colossus, though crippled with the war wounds and malaria, which did not somehow reach the heroic defenders of the BBC. A good poet, but above all a man – rather a rarity in modern England. True, he comes from S. Africa.'[52] However, he would tell Williamson a few years later:

> You must read Roy but with the same kind of approach one must have to DHL – i.e. he is a good poet and a life-lover with a special understanding of wild life, but his violence and militant Fascism-Catholicism are rather a bore (like DHL's solar plexus). . . . Roy has a Rabelaisian exuberance, and is a born jester, but is incapable of representing anything accurately.[53]

'Roy's preposterous tales, his love of life and people set the place glowing whether the wind blew or not. . . . I think [he] was the most vital man to go through this oasis and staging camp for writers at St Clair,' Deasey would tell Gates in 1980.[54]

Despite some important differences, Aldington and Campbell had a great deal in common. Aldington would tell Alan Bird (another new acquaintance): 'I no more accept his Catholicism than his bull-killing, but I can tell you that he is one of the most warm-hearted and generous men I ever met, keeps the table in a roar. And he is a very great poet, certainly our greatest satirist since Byron.'[55] Grouping together Aldington, Campbell and Lawrence Durrell (who would become another close friend in 1957), all of whom chose to live outside the United Kingdom, Richard Emeny argues that their individualism and their aversion to the welfare state, which 'put them at loggerheads with conventional mainstream social and political thought of the time', affected the reception of their work.[56] Certainly, the literary left could not forgive Campbell for his support of Franco in the Spanish Civil War. For these three men, however – unlike Lewis and Pound, or even Eliot – their right-wing politics were never

Roy Campbell, 1951

theoretically developed, nor, individualists as they were, did they ever subscribe to a political party. Campbell's biographer Peter Alexander comments that Campbell 'had no theoretical political views, he had only personal likes and dislikes. He was in no sense a deep political thinker. His attempts to weld his political likes and dislikes into a coherent system invariably failed.'[57] Aldington's own 'politics' are best summed up in an observation he would make about the Provençal poet, Frédéric Mistral: '[His] attitude was rather the reaction of the Conservative who sees all that he values in life menaced by forces beyond his control.'[58] His reaction in 1955 when Oswald Mosley made overtures towards him, was: 'Mosley's crowd are making great efforts to recruit me, thinking that the treatment I have received from the Brits will have disposed me to their brand of disloyalty. I prefer my own; and shan't answer them.'[59]

Campbell had, nevertheless, been at the heart of the literary establishment – albeit as a maverick: a producer at the BBC, a friend of the Sitwells and published by Eliot at Faber & Faber. He told Aldington in February 1951: 'If you come back here [London] you will find that everything wakes up.'[60] Aldington had neither the means nor the inclination for such a move, and Campbell himself moved permanently to Portugal a year later. For Aldington, their rejection by the literary establishment was a conspiracy. He would tell Campbell's young friend Rob Lyle in 1955:

> There is a complex of vested literary interests. First, hereditary – as Stracheys, Stephens, even Huxleys – though Aldous is now conspué for not playing the game. Second, there are the Civil Servants, especially the F.O. and Museum gangs. Third, the nominees of publishers, particularly wealthy firms like Macmillan, Unwin, Collins and even Heinemann. Fourth, this infiltration of Panzies which began with Frankie Birrell and [Raymond] Mortimer in the early twenties. In league with the sexologist quacks and the bloody Freudians, they seem to have persuaded our block-headed countrymen that buggery is next to godliness. Ridicule and contempt are the weapons, those are denied to us as libellous. Look at the things they've printed about me and Roy, and they did much the same to Lewis and to Pound, and in very early days to Eliot.[61]

One footnote to that summer in Provence was Campbell's discovery – fortunately (given his customary belligerence) months afterwards – that Kershaw had conducted a flirtation with Campbell's 24-year-old daughter Anna, a fact that the furious Patsy had communicated to Campbell's wife, Mary. Back in London, Campbell would write to tell Aldington that their stay in France had been 'perhaps the most enjoyable time in our whole lives' and that it had 'worked a sheer miracle' on Tess's health.[62]

Shortly after Campbell's departure, Williamson arrived for a fortnight's visit. The two men would continue to correspond, Aldington managing, despite his own difficult circumstances, to offer Williamson sympathy and understanding: 'I break off work on the TEL book,' he wrote in February 1951:

> to write to you, having a persistent intuition that you are unhappy and even a bit desperate about yourself and your situation. Forgive me if I am intrusive! I only want to hold out a hand on

the end of a 1,000-mile arm to yours in Devonshire and to assure you of goodwill and sympathy. I wish I could do more, something practical, something which would perhaps help you to change tyres, clean the carburettor, tighten the brakes and be off again. . . . I feel sure you need a rest and a change even more than I do.[63]

Pound was still incarcerated in St Elizabeth's Hospital in Washington, D.C., and Aldington was opposed to the efforts of many of his friends to have him released, arguing that this would constitute recognition of his sanity and that he would consequently have to stand trial for treason. Nor did he support the award of the 1949 Bollingen Prize to Pound for his *Pisan Cantos*. He told Bacon: 'I thought the engineering of that prize for Ezra by Tom [Eliot] was an insult to Congress, for after all, damn it, even if Ezra was cracked, he wasn't cracked on our side, but on the side of Musso and Hitler.'[64] He also refused the invitation to contribute to Peter Russell's collection of tributes to Pound in an issue of his magazine, *Nine*. Telling H.D. that he had not got on very well with Russell ('Ezra-booster Number One in London') when he had called to see him, Aldington commented:

They have taken up Ezra for motives mainly political and self-interested. . . . Of course there are good things, flashes in E's later work, but to me the Cantos seemed the product of a diseased mind long before the Yank doctors said he was paranoiac. I came to that conclusion when Brigit and I spent the winter of 1928-29 with him at Rapallo. He was still very sweet at times, but certainly suffering from delusions of persecution and of grandeur. . . . If I ever get round to writing anything on Ezra, I want to try to revive the memories of those magical early years in London.[65]

By June 1951 his feelings had softened and he began ('unwillingly' he told H.D.) to correspond with Pound.[66] 'Except that he persists in writing like one of the Katzenjammer Kids, Ezra sounds no more insane now than in 1912,' he told H.D. in July: '[H]e sounds well and fairly cheerful and good-natured.'[67] Three weeks later he reported that Pound seemed cheerful 'except that he says his "mainspring is busted"'. He had begun to feel more sympathetic, particularly because of his growing awareness of the poverty of Pound and Dorothy, although he insisted: 'Still, he did behave like a chump.'[68] The correspondence was becoming a regular one and Pound, as in the past, had plenty of advice for him, including a suggestion that he write a biography of Ford. Aldington's only comment

to H.D. – clearly in connection with his ongoing work on T.E. Lawrence –
was that 'biography is such hard work, such day-in, day-out drudgery of
verification and "fact-searching"'.[69]

An unwelcome reminder of their shared past came in Pound's letter of
January 1952: 'Pleasant enquiry from Brigit as to whether I heard from
you /as nacherly [sic] brot [sic] no address bks from woptalia, only located
Br / a few months ago.'[70] Aldington sent Pound some of his own recent
publications; Pound's response to *The Religion of Beauty* was: 'VERY good
thing to have it printed/ time to git [sic] relief from goat and garbage
can movement. Yu pult [sic] in a few s.o.b. that might be forgot BUT it is
clean of Georgian dead fish.'[71] Pound was, Aldington told H.D., beginning
to write incessantly and Aldington had started to think, after all, that
he was 'a bit cracked'. 'I hear frequently from the interned State captive
at St Elizabeth's Washington D.C.,' he told Bacon in March 1952, 'and I
still cannot make up my mind whether he really is nuts or not.'[72] He also
began to feel in an awkward position when Pound asked him if he could
get his work reprinted. He was clearly not aware, Aldington told H.D., 'of
prejudice; of how highbrow his stuff is; of the resentment TSE would feel,'
if Aldington 'butted in'.[73] At times he was the old irritating Pound: 'still
so coterie-minded, so full of blind prejudices based solely on personal
motives'. 'Am I too cantankerous about him?' Aldington asked.[74]

The regular correspondence with H.D. continued to be vital to them
both. There are moments when a note of defensiveness reminds us of his
continuing wariness of the Bryher set. In response to the receipt from
H.D. of cuttings of reviews of his D.H. Lawrence biography, he wrote:

> Perhaps I am wrong, but I think perhaps you are inclined to
> give more importance to newspaper comment and highbrow
> periodicals than I do. I don't subscribe for clippings, barely
> glance at those which people are good enough to send me. But
> I do care very much about the response of the public, and that is
> satisfactory, especially since there is a fierce slump in the book
> market.[75]

In the autumn of 1952 he heard from H.D. that Pat Aldington had
managed to obtain Perdita's New York address and had written to ask
her to correspond with May Aldington, who was now in a residential
care home and lonely. Aldington was mortified. Of course, his family
believed that Perdita was his daughter, but he knew that this approach
by his sister was the prelude to the 'begging letters' at which his mother
was so 'accomplished'. He apologised and insisted that Perdita should not

respond to any letters; if necessary, they should be sent on to him so that he could give his mother one of his 'broadsides'.[76] In fact, he had ceased to write to his mother altogether, although he was giving her financial support. He told Tony in November 1950: 'In the various experiments I have made to get on terms with her, she has never sent me a letter which was not either nauseous and repulsively sentimental and/or a whine for money or abusive.'[77] A year later he was shocked when Ursula Bloom, his childhood friend, not only wrote to him about his mother's situation c/o Heinemann, but sent the publishers a covering letter telling them how badly Aldington and his brother were treating their mother.[78]

The letters that passed between Aldington and H.D. are long, affectionate and filled with their news and common interests. As Zilboorg notes, 'Aldington's intimate connection with H.D. depended on ties established in the past and on the exchange of daily and parallel experiences rather than physical presence or a new phase of relationship.'[79] The coded references to their shared past are a constant motif. In December 1950 he sent her a copy of Browning's The Ring and the Book: 'I thought you might like it for the sake of old memories.'[80] He continued, too, to send her from time to time erotic postcard photographs of women or of women in art. Their reading and their writing, news of their daughters, their renewed interest in Pound and, above all, their enjoyment of their natural surroundings filled their letters.

His lifeline, however, was the young Australians, chiefly, of course, Kershaw, whose patience with him and diligence in his literary affairs were unflagging. As soon as it was apparent that Netta was not returning, Deasey arrived to help keep house for several weeks. That summer the Duttons were living in their cottage above the villa and took Aldington and Catha to Nice to celebrate his birthday with a fine meal, while Kershaw spent a month helping him sort out his affairs – before going on, with Patsy, to join Warman for a holiday in Frere's villa at Cap Ferrat. They were back in the autumn, Patsy to run the household and Kershaw to resume secretarial duties, but Aldington's income could not support them all and the couple had to return to London and seek work. By 1951 both Kershaw and Deasey had moved to Paris, visiting whenever they could, but tied to jobs in the city. Kershaw, nevertheless, continued to give Aldington all the support he could.

Within a couple of years Aldington would lose both the Duttons and Deasey. The Duttons returned to Australia in 1951; Deasey lived and worked in Paris much longer but by late 1954 he and Gisèle were finding themselves unable to survive there financially and moved, reluctantly, to Australia. The Duttons would return to Europe twice, once from 1954 to 1955 and again in 1960, but Aldington would never see Deasey again. 'Australia sounds wonderful, and I do wish I were with you both,' he would write to him in January 1955.[81]

* * *

Despite the convivial interludes supplied by the visits of the Australians and Campbell, 1950 had been a harrowing and life-changing year. In October Aldington told Bacon:

> After a lifetime of hard work and many fair words from those supposed to know, I find myself at 60 [actually 58] with most of my books out of print, none of them selling and forced to go on writing what I don't want to write when I am tired and ill and discouraged.[82]

He told H.D. in November, after visiting the doctor:

> At last I have found out what is the real trouble with me – overwork for too many years. For so long I've worked 12-14 hours a day for weeks on end without a single day off. Well, I can't do it no more [sic]. I've got to cut down to 5 days a week, and not more than 5-6 hours a day at that. This of course means a rather serious cut-down in output and reduction of income, since it is the new book which really earns. So I've had to construct (reluctantly) my own austerity plan, for I've made up my mind that Catha shall not suffer. I had cut out most things, so that practically all that remains is guests, books and wine. I gave up smoking nearly ten years ago.[83]

Frere was understanding: 'I know something about that kind of a breakdown and how baffled and helpless one feels. (I had a succession of them after 1918 and conquered them by concentration.)' With unconscious irony, he added: 'At least with that TEL book, you can take your time as well as feeling you are doing something worthwhile by putting that legend into its proper perspective.'[84]

19. The Public Face
Disaster

If the First World War had a devastating long-term effect on Aldington, the 'Lawrence saga' of 1950-1955 had an even more shattering impact on his life, his personal reputation and his career; and the reverberations carry on to the present day. The term 'Lawrence saga' is used here to refer to the events of the five years that followed Kershaw's proposal in 1949 that Aldington write a biography of Kershaw's own personal hero, T.E. Lawrence: the research and the writing of the biography from early 1950 through to April 1952; the legal and other challenges and delays that followed his submission of the manuscript to William Collins, lasting until the autumn of 1954; the publication of the book at the end of January 1955; and the furore which lasted for months afterwards.

A full account of these events is presented in Fred Crawford's 1998 book *Richard Aldington and Lawrence of Arabia: A Cautionary Tale.*[1] This chapter will attempt only to summarise the events of those five years, to estimate their impact on Aldington himself, his literary career and reputation and to ask, ultimately, whether things could have been otherwise.

* * *

We left Aldington speculating about what the enormous amount of material he had amassed on Lawrence was concealing. He told Kershaw on 2 January 1951:

> I feel that the job is too big for me. The biographer needs to know so many subjects and, above all, to be a trained psychologist. There is some unresolved mystery about him, which has many aspects, one of which I am sure is homosexuality. You will be staggered when you see my collections of his anti-heterosexual

T.E. Lawrence

and pro-homosexual statements. . . . It is a colossal subject to
treat with competence, and most difficult to treat frankly without
being or seeming hostile.[2]

Two days later he told Williamson: 'There is some mystery about his
family, a skeleton somewhere.'[3]

When, towards the end of that month, he began to unravel the
mystery, he was at first reluctant to believe it. It was the well-hidden fact
(although Lawrence himself had been made aware of it when still a child)
that Lawrence and his brothers were illegitimate. Aldington would be

publicly condemned for his lack of decency in revealing this fact while Lawrence's mother was still alive.[4] However, for him: '[T]o attempt to tell the story of Lawrence while ignoring this situation is like putting on Hamlet without the king and queen and, above all, without the haunting ghost.'[5] He theorised:

> [M]ight not the main clue, though perhaps not the only one, to Lawrence's peculiar psychology lie in his relation to his parents, in his discovery of what they thought their sin and its irreparable wrong to him, as well as to the dissonances set up in him by the influence of two powerful and opposite human personalities?[6]

To support his argument, he paraphrases a letter from Lawrence to Charlotte Shaw, one of over three hundred available for public inspection in the British Museum but from which he was refused permission to quote. (Fortunately for him, Deasey spent hours in the British Museum copying them out.) However, he acknowledges that: 'the fact must not be abused and dragged in to explain everything – he had his own remarkable gifts, and was as powerfully influenced by his environment in some respects as he violently reacted from it in others.'[7] Furthermore, he expresses characteristic sympathy for 'yet another highly-gifted man, sacrificed to nineteenth-century snobbery, hypocrisy, philistinism and "respectability" in a generation which was supposed to be in violent revolt against them, he above all!'[8]

What concerned him much more was his discovery, as he delved further into his sources, that much of Lawrence's own account of his actions in Arabia between 1916 and 1918 was exaggerated or even false.[9] Furthermore, he realised that those who had formed and perpetuated the 'Lawrence legend' had been almost entirely reliant on information furnished by Lawrence himself. These were: Lowell Thomas, whose 1919 lecture-film show, *With Allenby in Palestine and Lawrence in Arabia*, played to massive audiences around the world and was followed by a book, *With Lawrence in Arabia*, in 1924; Robert Graves, whose *Lawrence and the Arabs* appeared in 1927; Basil Liddell Hart, whose 1934 book, *T.E. Lawrence in Arabia and After*, made a case for Lawrence having been one of the greatest military strategists of all time; and Vyvyan Richards, a pre-war friend of Lawrence, whose *Portrait of T.E. Lawrence* was published in 1936.[10] Studying the correspondence between Lawrence and both Graves and Liddell Hart, Aldington discovered the extent to which Lawrence had influenced the content of these writers' books while requiring them both to publicly deny his involvement.[11]

He told Kershaw in the summer of 1951 what his own alternative sources were:

> Though I have used 7 Pills occasionally I have avoided repeating Graves's mere paraphrase of L's narrative and above all Hart's incredibly pretentious 'military history', using as authorities the Secret Despatches, the Official War History, Wavell, Barrow, Brémond, Bray, Young, and any outside authority who is not merely parroting TEL.[12]

To this list he added, in a further letter, George Antonius, King Abdullah, Sir Ronald Storrs, Colonel Robert Buxton, General Allenby, Captain Rosario Pisani and Colonel Walter Stirling.[13] With the help of Cohen, he also managed to gain access to official French documents of the period. Another source was a book that had questioned aspects of the Lawrence legend as far back as 1929, Sir Andrew MacPhail's *Three Persons*.[14] Aldington's own book became, as he states in its 'Introductory Letter', 'a criticism of those writings which have fostered the Lawrence legend . . . an analysis of the career of Lawrence the man of action and of the establishment and growth of . . . the Lawrence legend.'[15] Hence its title, *Lawrence of Arabia: A Biographical Enquiry*.

Testing and disproving several of Lawrence's tales about his early life accepted unquestioningly by his earlier biographers, Aldington concludes:

> Of course it can and will be said that hitherto these exaggerations and untruths I am pinning on Lawrence are trifles, and so they are, though truth itself is not a trifle. But it so happens that they can be convincingly shown to be untrue, while in other cases one may be perfectly certain the tales are false without having complete evidence to prove it. But what are we to think of a man so self-centred, so – there is no other word for it – conceited, so avid of *réclame* at any price, that he would stoop to such trifling deceits? And if he would deceive in trifles, for the sake of a worthless astonishment and admiration, what guarantee is there that he did not do likewise in more important matters where he cannot be so convincingly checked? And further, what is the value of a reputation which is based on a multitude of just such disprovable or suspect stories?'[16]

Ultimately, one issue became a 'test case'. Lawrence had told several correspondents, including his mother, Charlotte Shaw and Liddell Hart, that Churchill had offered him the post of High Commissioner for Egypt, both when Lord Allenby had threatened resignation in 1922 and when he actually left the post in 1925. Churchill wrote in *T.E. Lawrence by His Friends* (1937) that in 1921, when Lawrence left the Colonial Service, 'governorships and great commands were then at my disposal. Nothing availed.' He had, he claimed, told Lawrence: 'The greatest employments are open to you if you care to pursue your new career in the Colonial Service.'[17] As Aldington points out, this was several months before Allenby stated his intention to resign his post; furthermore, Egypt came under the auspices of the Foreign Office, not the Colonial Office.

To test Lawrence's veracity, Aldington had, through Browning and Colin Mann (then Public Relations Officer of the Conservative Party), queried the likelihood of the offer of this post to Lawrence with Leo Amery, who had been Colonial Secretary in the Conservative Government of 1924-1929, with Lord Lloyd, whose father had been appointed to succeed Allenby in 1925 and with Lawrence's friend Storrs (the author of the entry on Lawrence in the *Dictionary of National Biography*). The first two said that they had never heard of the offer and thought it extremely unlikely, while Storrs called it 'grotesquely improbable'. Frere (coming in useful, after all) had also arranged for Lord John Hope, the Conservative politician, to put the question to Churchill, who had answered (in writing) that Lawrence's claim was 'unfounded'.[18]

While gathering his evidence and writing the book, Aldington was in touch with Williamson, who had been a friend and admirer of Lawrence. Williamson and Lawrence had met only twice – and briefly – but their correspondence had spanned the seven years from Lawrence's writing to praise *Tarka the Otter* in 1929 until his death in 1935. Williamson's behaviour towards Aldington during the Lawrence saga was duplicitous – and he would acknowledge this and apologise for it in 1956.[19] Initially, he was of great help, undertaking the task of writing to the publishers of *Who's Who* to ascertain whether Lawrence himself was responsible for his 1920 entry and sending Aldington copies of his own Lawrence correspondence.[20] When he sensed that Aldington was sceptical about Lawrence's career, he told him: 'Write your book as though you were writing of Cathy [Catha]. We love TEL as you love Cathy and he is like a son to me. . . . You have a noble subject. He won't let you down.'[21] By 1954, when it was clear that the book was to be an exposure of Lawrence, Williamson contributed a two-part essay to *The European*, in which he wrote: 'Even if the much publicised (by others) and mortifying (to T.E.) Arabian Adventure turns out to be moonshine or mirage it will make no difference to my feelings about T.E. himself, as I knew him and perceived what he truly was, a wonderful man.'[22] In a review of *The Home Letters of*

T.E. Lawrence and His Brothers in the November issue of the same journal Williamson wrote: 'Since I wrote my *Threnos* I have been shown papers and letters which dispel all doubt. . . . He was entirely truthful; and the records will eventually prove it.'[23]

After the publication of Aldington's book, Williamson wrote to David Garnett, whose review of the book in the *New Statesman* had been damning, and told him: 'I read your review . . . with gladness and admiration. . . . I wrote to R.A. again and again (knowing how amateurish, "twenty-ish" mood was his writing in novels and character-drawing in sarcasm, jeers etc.) and begged him not to write like that about TEL.' Realising that he had better reveal his own personal acquaintance with Aldington, he told Garnett that their relationship was one of 'mutually guarded amity'.[24] Anne Williamson comments:

> Sadly . . . in his anxiety to appease David Garnett (for HW couldn't afford to make open enemies amongst publishers) and show his loyalty to TEL, HW betrays what should have been his equal debt of loyalty to Aldington. For this letter is not at all fair to Aldington; HW does not exactly do justice to their total friendship, nor to the intricacies of their total correspondence nor to Aldington's reputation as an established and respected writer.[25]

Aldington would never know of this letter but he did warn Williamson only a week later: 'The poison gas cloud of lies, malice, rage, put out by the little phoney's "friends" baffles description. Keep out of it, Henry, never mid [*sic*] which side. It is a very dirty business and I wish I had never got mixed up in it.'[26]

Even Kershaw had expressed anxieties about the direction Aldington was taking. On the one hand he tried to reassure him, telling him in March 1951: 'As always, you are more conscientious than your peers . . . and this, inevitably, is a vast strain on you; but the book will be a masterpiece, I suspect the best thing you have ever done . . . and may well solve your financial problems.'[27] On the other hand, he was anxious about Aldington's growing hostility towards Lawrence and constantly tried to counsel caution. By July he was writing: 'I shiver when you mention TE. Do not hoe him in too hard, I conjure you – not because he should be treated as sentimentally sancrosanct at all, but because surely the value of your biography will be the objectivity (and surely he WAS a remarkable man?)'[28] On receiving the completed manuscript in April 1952, he wrote:

> Dearest Richard At page 200, reading very carefully, and I think
> it's really magnificent. ... There's no question – and I hate to
> admit it – that you've served up an unassailable exposure of L. ...
> I've made one or two small cuts. ... I think ... you might make
> some more – of various envenomed allusions. My feeling is that
> it's deadliest when most urbane and dispassionate.[29]

The note of approval is (tactfully) qualified.

Meanwhile, now living with Patsy in Paris and working for UNESCO,
Kershaw had been busy on Aldington's behalf. John Holroyd-Reece,
formerly director of Albatross (and a yeomanry officer on Barrow's
staff in Egypt during the First World War), had offered to assist with
the project and had persuaded Collins to offer a £4,500 advance and to
agree to a contract with a trust which would hold Aldington's profits
for his daughter and thus exempt him from tax (and the demands of
the Patmore solicitors). Browning generously released Aldington from
his Evans Brothers contract. The transfer to Collins in October 1951
and the well-intentioned, but often bungling, efforts of Holroyd-Reece
would cause innumerable problems for both Aldington and Kershaw;
but Aldington's tendency to interfere with arrangements which he had
entrusted to Kershaw and thus to complicate matters and alienate Collins
was an even greater problem. The loyal Kershaw was tested almost to the
limit. He would tell Crawford in 1983: 'He was a strange man, Aldington
– genuinely an écorché vif. His sensitivity was unbelievably intense and
he reacted with a degree of violence which seemed incomprehensible
on occasion.'[30] Holroyd-Reece, Kershaw would tell Crawford, was 'an
excellent fellow and genuinely anxious to help Richard; but he adored
navigating among appalling difficulties to such a degree that when no
such difficulties existed he deployed all his considerable intelligence in
creating them'.[31]

* * *

On completion of his manuscript in April 1952, Aldington told Kershaw:
'I trust you and the Bird [Holroyd-Reece] are prepared for a really dirty
battle with the Lawrence Bureau, for they'll invoke libel and copyright
infringement for all they're worth. What I fear is that Collins will rat,
and turn round on me.'[32] One cannot libel the dead, but the first draft
of the manuscript would have given Lawrence's previous biographers,
still very much alive, plenty of scope for litigation on both libel and
copyright grounds. Aldington had good reason to fear both the Seven

Pillars of Wisdom Trust, administered by Lawrence's brother, Professor A.W. Lawrence, and what he began to term (in a parody of the 'Arab Bureau') the 'Lawrence Bureau', Lawrence's biographers, friends and supporters. These included Graves and Liddell Hart, but also the artist Eric Kennington and his wife, Storrs, Garnett, the historian Sir Lewis Namier, the Conservative politician Lord Winterton, E.M. Forster, Lady Astor and Lord Trenchard.

Because of Holroyd-Reece's well-intentioned attempt to keep the manuscript confidential and therefore to have his secretary type its 456 pages after business hours, William (Billy) Collins did not see it until late July. He was horrified: the illegitimacy issue, the extent to which it was claimed that Lawrence had fabricated exploits and the attack on all his previous biographers were a publisher's nightmare. Aldington was indignant when Collins's editor, F.T. Smith, demanded a virtual rewrite. Collins now consulted lawyers to ensure that the book would not invite litigation. Aldington decided that he too needed 'experts' to evaluate the manuscript and approached the young Oxford academic Alan Bird, with whom he had been in correspondence since early 1949, to act as a reader and 'scholarly adviser', a task which Bird took on enthusiastically, also checking on Lawrence's parentage when Collins's lawyers pronounced that his illegitimacy had not been satisfactorily demonstrated.[33] At Aldington's suggestion, Major Bray was taken on by Collins as 'military expert'.

The to-ing and fro-ing (in the course of which the Daily Mail pulled out of an agreement to serialise the book and the Daily Telegraph turned it down) between Collins, Smith, Ronald Politzer (Collins's Head of Publicity), Mark Bonham Carter (another member of the Collins staff, created a director in 1955), Collins's lawyers, Holroyd-Reece, Kershaw and Aldington to negotiate cuts and emendations to the text lasted over two years. Anxious about censorship, publication date (with no Aldington title having appeared since Portrait of a Genius in 1950), opportunities for serialisation arrangements and foreign rights and a formal contract between Collins and the Aldington Trust, Aldington, despite repeated promises to leave matters in the hands of Kershaw and Holroyd-Reece, constantly interfered and antagonised Collins.

American publication became a particularly fraught issue. Duell, Sloan and Pearce were uneasy about the book and withdrew. There was an ongoing misunderstanding between Aldington and Collins as to whether he or Collins was to obtain an American publisher, the problem aggravated by his hopes for both simultaneous publication and for an American publisher to agree to the uncensored text, neither outcome being desirable for Collins. Knopf, in turn, pulled out of an agreement with Collins, concerned about the criticism of Lowell Thomas in the book.

In the autumn of 1953 Politzer arrived in the south of France to negotiate with Aldington in person. Aldington told Netta (with whom he was now in an occasional and generally amicable correspondence focused on Catha's needs and educational progress) that Catha had 'played hostess to Mr and Mrs Politzer very gracefully'.[34] The personal contact certainly cooled the temperature of his feelings. 'He is a nice fellow but his news is a little depressing,' was his comment to Kershaw.[35] Bonham Carter visited in August 1954 to ask, at this very late stage (and after numerous changes made in compliance with the demands of Collins's lawyers) for 'a less biased version which would still make substantially the same argument'.[36] He returned in September and Aldington finally and reluctantly agreed to the majority of the changes requested. Again, personal contact had paid off; he told Dibben in November that the book was now 'in the hands of Bonham Carter who is a real gentleman, on whose word I rely'.[37]

Along the way, however, Kershaw's relationship with him was severely tested. In May 1954 he wrote to Aldington:

> You have repeatedly asked me to take all business worries off your shoulders; I have done my best to do so, asking only that you should not act independently of me with the inevitably consequent embarrassment. I am perfectly willing to withdraw absolutely and finally from the whole business if that be your wish; if you do not wish this, I once again ask that you should not write to anyone but myself or the solicitor.[38]

Aldington humbly replied: 'I have never been anything but intensely grateful for the utterly generous and noble aid you have given me; and if you withdraw it I am indeed alone and desolate.'[39] A month later, however, they had to have the same battle and, at the end of September, Aldington was threatening to withdraw the book from Collins, a move Kershaw had to prevent him from carrying out. Collins's securing of agreements for Spanish-American, German, Italian and US rights (the last of these with the young Chicago firm, Henry Regnery, publishers of Roy Campbell) helped to pacify him.

What Aldington did not know – although he suspected it – was the extent to which the Lawrence Bureau influenced the actions of Collins and caused the constant delays in getting the book onto the presses. In January 1954 – a whole year before the eventual publication of the book – the 'Londoner's Diary' of the *Evening Standard* announced:

Basil Liddell Hart in the 1930s

The reputation and integrity of Lawrence of Arabia are about to come under the most devastating attack ever launched upon them. A book is due for publication in May or June which the publishers claim will 'erase Lawrence from the pages of history, except as the creator of a myth that was all too readily believed by a credulous world'.[40]

Aldington was horrified: not only did he see all his efforts to maintain secrecy wasted, but he thought the quotation from Collins over-stated and inflammatory. He suspected that Fallas had been the leak, but it was Kershaw, who had alerted a young journalist friend to the story rather prematurely.

The Lawrence Bureau – under the direction of Liddell Hart – went to work immediately to have the book delayed or, if possible, suppressed. If at times Aldington appears to us to have been intransigent, Liddell Hart was his peer – with the added ingredient of excessive arrogance. In the T.E. Lawrence archives at the University of Texas three of the fourteen boxes – 20 folders – are entirely devoted to Liddell Hart's correspondence with other members of the Lawrence Bureau, with Collins and with reviewers over Aldington's book. He would complain to Walter Stirling in June 1955: 'That bloody man has wasted an appalling amount of my working time, and thus cost me a lot of money during the last eighteen months.'[41] We must hope that Stirling pointed out that the devotion of this excessive amount of time and effort had been entirely self-willed.

Liddell Hart was, like Aldington, approaching 60. He had served as a junior officer in 7th Battalion of the King's Own Yorkshire Light Infantry on the Western Front in the First World War, but had been invalided out in mid-July 1916, thereafter being involved in infantry training and producing training manuals until his retirement from the Army in 1927. He had gone on to become a full-time military historian and theorist, acting as military correspondent to the *Daily Telegraph* and *The Times* in the interwar period. In response to his experience of the attrition of the Western Front, he developed the doctrine of the 'indirect approach', the notion that it was better to open a second front or to make a strategic flanking movement than to risk the huge losses incurred in the First World War by attacking the enemy at his strongest point. He was therefore an advocate of strategic bombing and of mechanised warfare – and of Britain's relying on the Royal Navy rather than committing large armies to Continental warfare. Lawrence's involvement in irregular warfare in Arabia had been a gift to Liddell Hart who found 'nowhere . . . in the records of war such subtly conceived and skilfully gauged distraction as that developed by Lawrence in aid of the Arabs and Allenby'.[42]

This concentration on Lawrence the legendary leader (which included comparing him to Napoleon and Marlborough) ignored such considerations as whether Lawrence was the originator of the idea of provoking and exploiting the Hashemite rebellion, or of the strategy of sabotaging the Turkish rail network, or whether he was even the principal saboteur; Liddell Hart also failed to acknowledge that the factual basis on which he formed his judgements stemmed almost entirely from Lawrence himself. The military historian Brian Bond, who knew Liddell Hart well, believes that: '[h]e idealised Lawrence as the heroic figure he himself might have become: the intellectual and man of action . . . who could outwit the enemy by his learning, psychology and imagination . . . and depicted him as a messianic leader sent to save the world from future bloodbaths like the First World War'.[43] Peter Simkins, the other contemporary military historian who knew Liddell Hart well, points out the peripheral nature of Lawrence's activities: '[T]he real damage to the Ottoman cause was done by all-arms Western Front methods (including artillery and air power) under Allenby and Shea . . . at 3ʳᵈ Gaza and Megiddo.'[44] Aldington's book would be a challenge to Liddell Hart's integrity, doctrines and reputation.

The *Evening Standard* diary entry had referred to Aldington's success in gaining evidence that Lawrence's claims to have been offered the post of High Commissioner for Egypt were false. This is where Liddell Hart started work. He persuaded Collins to hold the book up if he could find proof that the 'offer of Egypt' had ever been made to Lawrence. However, despite the pressure he put upon them, he could not persuade Amery, Lloyd or Storrs to retract their original statements. In the case of Storrs, he resorted to blackmail, threatening to publish adverse comments about him that Lawrence had written in the original version of *Seven Pillars of Wisdom*; Storrs eventually buckled under the pressure, but since Collins only received Liddell Hart's word for this, they did not hold up publication. The most difficult task was to persuade Churchill to withdraw his original statement. Reading the correspondence between the two men, one is struck by Liddell Hart's brazenness and persistence to the point of bullying at a time when the Prime Minister was a sick man. Eventually he extracted a written concession: '[K]nowing Lawrence as I did, I have no reason to believe he was mistaken in his saying there was a question of his having Egypt if Allenby came away.'[45] Lord Hankey, Cabinet Secretary from 1916 to 1938, was similarly mealy-mouthed, his final attempt reading: 'I see no reason why Lawrence should not have been sounded out about the possibility of his succeeding Allenby.'[46] It was not enough. Churchill was badgered further and finally tried: 'I am sure the post of High Commissioner in Egypt was never offered officially to Colonel Lawrence, but I think it very likely that I talked over the possibility of his being offered it. . . . However, I cannot pretend to remember all these details.' He pleaded with Liddell Hart: 'I cannot however undertake even now to embark upon a prolonged study and research as I have a lot of other things to think about.' [47] It was, in any case, too late to hold up publication any further.

What neither Collins nor Aldington knew was that Kennington and Liddell Hart had gained illicit access to a set of proofs which Collins, as a courtesy to a major bookseller, had lent to John Gideon Wilson, the proprietor of J. & E. Bumpus Ltd. Kennington borrowed them from Wilson over the weekend of 12 and 13 February 1954, while Liddell Hart and his wife entered the Bumpus premises after the shop had closed on the Monday and stayed for five hours. Fortunately for Liddell Hart, on 8 March Collins invited him to go through the page proofs and indicate what corrections and cuts were required. (Aldington was not informed of this development.) Unfortunately for him, he could find few errors of fact and the criticisms he offered were too general to be useful to Collins. This did not prevent him from sending out an 'Analysis' of the proofs to all members of the Lawrence Bureau, stating that Aldington's case against Lawrence was 'built up by half-truths, omissions and twisted evidence', all 'clever enough to be plausible to a casual reader without background knowledge'. 'The rest of the book,' he maintained, 'is merely a catalogue of carping comment, and interjected sneers, which become extremely tedious.'[48] During the coming months he would entertain at his home, Wolverton Park in Buckinghamshire, Politzer, Bonham Carter and also Namier, whom A.W. Lawrence, perhaps wearying of Liddell Hart's methods, had asked to look at the book on behalf of the Seven Pillars of Wisdom Trust. Politzer and Bonham Carter were, we must assume, working in the interests of both Collins and Aldington, but the latter would have been disturbed to know that the 'real gentleman' whom he had welcomed to his home in August and September had on both occasions spent the succeeding weekend as the guest of Liddell Hart.

Nevertheless, in mid-January 1955, only a fortnight away from publication, Bonham Carter would point out to Liddell Hart that neither he nor any of Lawrence's other friends who had seen the proofs – and by now there were several of them – had been able or willing to point out an error in the argument which would have justified Collins in breaking its agreement with Aldington.[49] Billy Collins himself, bombarded with letters from Liddell Hart throughout the 'campaign', had told him in June 1954: 'Whatever the faults of the book, it represents a very decided point of view and the author is entitled to his point of view whether one agrees with it or not.'[50]

What the Lawrence Bureau were slow to realise was that they had shot themselves in the foot. A.W. Lawrence had warned Liddell Hart in March 1954: 'Any statement of yours as to errors in the proofs is likely to be construed into acceptance of the rest of the text.'[51] He was too late. In October, after Bonham Carter's reassurances that the book had been 'cleaned up', Liddell Hart expressed his concern to Kennington that this would have the drawback of making it 'less open to shattering counter-attacks'.[52] The Bureau's activities had also given the book a high public profile. A.W. Lawrence realised early on in the campaign that the majority of the Bureau members were more of a liability than a help. Celandine Kennington proposed the most bizarre strategies devised by the Bureau, suggesting that Aldington's book was 'Communist-inspired' and that they should have him followed by a private detective 'to see what company he keeps'. She admitted that it might be difficult to prove this case, 'but it could certainly be made to smell very strong'.[53] She also enlisted the support of Lady Hardinge of Penshurst, whose son had become a junior partner in Collins, and proposed that this 'very dynamic personality' could 'make mincemeat' of Billy Collins if she met him for lunch.[54] In August she would tell Liddell Hart that there were two or three 'avowed Communists' in Collins's office.[55] (The grounds for this charge seems to have been the fact that Donald Maclean's brother, who had been sacked by the Foreign Office on his brother's defection in May 1951, was now working for Collins.) The Bureau put pressure on Billy Collins, Liddell Hart telling him: 'I am much more concerned in this matter with your reputation than with Lawrence's.'[56] Through Celandine Kennington Lady Hardinge asked Liddell Hart for a letter expressing his view that the Aldington book would 'do harm to Anglo-American relations & to British prestige', a letter that she could show to 'people of influence' in order 'to strengthen her hand'.[57]

Having established that they would not succeed with charges of copyright infringement or libel, the Bureau conceived the idea of a 'Gladstone Defence'.[58] As the Gladstone family had done with the author Peter Wright in 1925, the group would attack Aldington in such a defamatory public letter that he would be forced to sue them for libel, thus giving them the opportunity in court to disprove his allegations against Lawrence.[59] Liddell Hart drummed up a great deal of support among Bureau members for this tactic, which they decided should target Collins too, only to be told by A.W. Lawrence not to go ahead. Unlike the Bureau, he was aware of Lawrence's as yet unpublicised predilection for masochistic beatings, and fearful that Aldington had found this out. The 'Gladstone' case would be too much of a risk.[60] Celandine's next ploy was to travel to Ireland to speak to the surviving Lawrence daughters (T.E.'s half-sisters), but her report (seven typed pages of foolscap) was of little use.[61]

Thwarted in their attempts to suppress the book, the Bureau, and Liddell Hart in particular, now set up their order of battle for the next phase of the campaign: the publication date, 31 January 1955. Church wrote to Aldington shortly before publication:

> The foreshadow of your Lawrence has been looming ominously over the literary (and indeed social and political) skies for the past two years, and everyone has been whispering in corners about it, some with glee, others with shocked horror. ... [Y]ou will have to seek a refuge in the South Seas as the fanatics come after your blood. What about all the deeply entrenched vested interests in the great legend? How are you going to cope with them? However, you are not lacking in courage and punch and I imagine that you have your jet planes and atom bombs fully lined up.[62]

He was over-optimistic; in the event the onslaught by the Bureau was overwhelming. Two years earlier Aldington had given Kershaw his 'main list of bars' for the reviews: 'Prof. Lawrence, David Garnett, Liddell Hart, Robert Graves, Vyvyan Richards, Storrs, Henry [Williamson], Sitwells, Raymond Mortimer'.[63] His fears were largely realised: Liddell Hart got the *Sunday Chronicle*, Mortimer, *The Sunday Times*, Graves, the *News Chronicle* (and *The New Republic* in the United States), Storrs, *The Listener*, Kennington, the conservative journal *Truth*, and Garnett the *New Statesman*.[64] Storrs was also interviewed on BBC Television's *Panorama* by Malcolm Muggeridge on 27 January; Celandine Kennington's comment ('Malcolm Muggeridge looks a nasty piece of work [and] I thought Storrs was fluffy') suggests that the Bureau could not altogether call this a tactical victory.[65] Other hostile reviewers included Harold Nicolson in *The Observer*, John Rosselli in *The Manchester Guardian* and A.L. Rowse in the *Daily Mail*; as Aldington would have expected, the *TLS* review (by Christopher Montague Woodhouse) was also unfavourable.

The charges made by almost all the reviewers were identical: the tastelessness of revealing Lawrence's illegitimacy and the unrelenting pursuit of what read like a 'personal vendetta' against a heroic figure.[66] Where all else failed them, they asserted, in the words of the *Times* reviewer, that Aldington had produced 'an uncommonly dull book'.[67] The strong similarities between the reviews were not only due to the fact that the majority had been written by the Bureau and its supporters. Liddell Hart had sent everyone on his extensive mailing list, including journalists on every national and regional newspaper, a seven-page document entitled 'Aldington's "Lawrence": His Charges – and Treatment of the Evidence'. Unfortunately, he had not seen the final proofs of the book and Crawford notes that it is easy to see which reviewers had not actually read the book (which had gone out for review a month before publication) but relied totally on Liddell Hart, as they referred to passages which were not in the final text; these included Graves and Garnett.

The next stage in Liddell Hart's campaign was following up all published reviews with a letter to the authors (enclosing yet again his 'Analysis') which opened: 'I read with interest and appreciation your review of Aldington's book.' He then congratulated those who had attacked Aldington; but those whose reviews had been less vitriolic or who had even given the writer some credit were told (sympathetically) that they had been taken in. Charles Carrington was told in the aftermath of his *Time and Tide* review: 'While most of the reviews of the book have reacted against Aldington's palpably prejudiced attitude, they have, very naturally, tended to assume that the book is at least careful and honest in its presentation of the events. But closer examination dispels that idea.' (Carrington had commented that 'in his search for mud to throw' Aldington had uncovered 'some damning evidence'.) A copy of the 'Analysis' was enclosed.[68] Lord Vansittart's response when similarly approached after his surprisingly sympathetic review in the *Daily Telegraph*, was to return the document – and to tell Liddell Hart firmly that 'no offer of the High Commissionership in Egypt was ever made to Lawrence in 1922'.[69]

The correspondence in the *Telegraph* that followed Vansittart's review included several Bureau letters, but also ones from senior military officers from the Palestine Campaign, like General Barrow and General Lord Burnham, supportive of many of Aldington's charges against Lawrence.[70] When *Illustrated*, which had featured an interview with Aldington, eventually printed a response from Liddell Hart, it placed alongside it 'anti-Lawrence' letters from two more senior officers, Squadron Commander G.F. Breese and Major General R. Dening.[71] A few other newspapers and journals had either given favourable reviews or had obtained interviews with Aldington; these included the *Daily Express*, the *Evening Standard*, the *Daily Mirror,* the *Daily Herald, The Spectator* and *Punch*, while the *Daily Mail* gave him the opportunity to reply to A.L. Rowse's damning review.[72] However, Liddell Hart stoked the fire with 'T.E. Lawrence, Aldington and the Truth' in John Lehmann's recently founded *London Magazine*; Lehmann was a family friend of the Liddell Harts and wrote in his editorial: 'Very little is left … of the laboriously constructed case for the prosecution, after it has been riddled with Captain Liddell Hart's well-aimed bursts of machine-gun fire.'[73] Meanwhile, Campbell's young friend, Rob Lyle, with the urging of Campbell, had stepped in to take on the press on Aldington's behalf (and with his assistance). Lehmann sent Lyle's long letter refuting Liddell Hart to the latter, so that he could have a right of reply in the same (June) issue of the magazine.[74] A letter from Aldington himself (unable to hold back) was once more accompanied, in the August issue, by a Liddell Hart rebuttal; Lehmann refused to accept any further correspondence.

The book's appearance in the United States in the autumn produced a smattering of unfavourable reviews but, as Aldington had predicted, publicity was low-key and sales poor as the Collins edition had been available in the US since the beginning of the year. Fortunately for Aldington, the French translation had appeared before the British one. Entitled, to his unease, *Lawrence l'Imposteur*, it included several passages that had been cut from the Collins edition and attracted considerable interest among the French, never fans of T.E. Lawrence.

* * *

It may have been the thoroughness with which Aldington set out his case, refuting *Seven Pillars of Wisdom* and the Lowell Thomas, Graves and Liddell Hart accounts of the man and his achievements, that caused the majority of reviewers, frustrated by the unanswerable and fired up by the Bureau, to resort to personal attacks on Aldington himself. It must be admitted, however, that he had laid himself open through his frequent resort to irony; his tone is often contemptuous or mocking. Just a few passages will illustrate this point:

> We may claim that Lawrence was the most adventurous and wide-ranging of these demolition raiders, but in frankness must admit that what the others lacked was literary skill to write up their achievements.[75]

> [On Lawrence's story of losing the manuscript of *Seven Pillars of Wisdom* at Reading Station in 1919 and having to rewrite it in two months without the help of all his notes, which he had destroyed] These statistics of re-writing solely from memory ... are prodigious, and calculated to raise envious admiration in all professional authors, journalists and even shorthand typists.[76]

> There is one achievement which nobody can deny Lawrence, and that was his capacity to convince others that he was a remarkable man. Of course he was, but what was chiefly 'remarkable' was his capacity for self-advertisement.[77]

> Lawrence appears to have agreed with Disraeli that everyone likes flattery, but that with some people you should lay it on with a trowel.[78]

His problem was that the case he built up against Lawrence was so strong that his 'enquiry' became a case for the prosecution. Had he been scrupulous in his choice of tone perhaps the book would have been less provocative, but the case itself was what most frustrated the Bureau and the reviewers; it was almost impossible for them to counter. Furthermore, as he worked on the material – and subsequently, when he saw the book savaged – his discoveries confirmed his convictions about British society. Celandine Kennington had been right in imputing a political motive to Aldington; but it was not the one she had hoped to uncover. He told Bird in 1953:

> I believe this Lawrence book is much more than a mere biography – it is the showing up and repudiation of a whole phase of our national life with Winston at the head. True, *he* is a hero, but . . . [o]ur life as a nation must not be based upon lies and liars, on *slick* 'policies'.[79]

A passage towards the end of the book reveals, finally, the source of his anger:

> I have tried, but perhaps not always with success, to give the evidence in this book fairly and in such a way that it can be instantly verified, though not without some indignation that such a man should have been given the fame and glory of the real heroes of 1914-1918.[80]

It outraged him that: 'the whole trend and assertiveness of *Seven Pillars* (and extracts in *Revolt*) are designed to insinuate that the Eastern war was the really important one and that the important contribution to that war came from Lawrence and "the Arabs".'[81]

Graves wrote in *The New Republic*: 'Instead of a carefully considered portrait of Lawrence I find the self-portrait of a bitter, bed-ridden, leering, asthmatic, elderly hangman of letters. . . .'[82] The work of the Lawrence Bureau and the reviewers in their circle ensured that this was the representation of Aldington put before the public in the years following. Nor did the book enhance his financial security: it had ensured that he had no income for four years, other than the Collins advance (less the repayment of the Evans Brothers advance); and, although the book was a bestseller, with over 30,000 copies sold, Collins withdrew it once they had recouped their investment. Two and a half years later, Four Square Books, by arrangement with Collins, published a paperback edition and sold over

40,000 copies, but the income for Aldington from this edition was small. Furthermore, now that he had become a pariah, publishers were reluctant to be associated with him. As Crawford points out, the three books he published subsequently were all under pre-T.E. Lawrence agreements and with his publisher friends, Browning and Frere.[83] Booksellers, too, had an enormous impact; in response to his unpopularity, they generally ceased to stock his earlier works.

The following tribute by Fred Crawford seems a fitting conclusion to this account of the 'T.E. Lawrence saga':

> Aldington's most striking achievement was to challenge the TEL legend despite encountering practically every obstacle that a biographer might face. With a minimum of resources and in virtual isolation, he overcame organised and dedicated opposition from powerful and influential friends of TEL, an uncooperative literary estate, a reluctant publisher, limitations on access to significant material and severe restrictions from libel and copyright laws, all of which hampered his ability to tell the truth as he saw it. That he succeeded was the result of incredible courage, intellectual rigor, and determination even as he coped with crises of confidence, domestic troubles, financial woes and failing health. His passion for truth gave him little choice. Had he foreseen the high personal cost of his TEL book, he would have written it anyway.[84]

20. Private and Public Lives
Trials of Endurance
1951-1957

The quality of Aldington's daily existence at the Villa Aucassin as writer and single parent is conveyed in his laconic diary entries for early 1951:

> *16 January 1951* YESTERDAY I WORKED AT T E Lawrence . . . flat battery . . . getting signatures on will . . . supper for Catha – boiled beef, vegetables, new potatoes, boiled & fried, riz au lait with sultanas. Read Byron's 'Childe Harold' instead of the Elizabethans.

> *17 January 1951* WROTE LETTERS. WORKED at TEL. Walk into Lavandou. Worked from 4.30 on at washing up and housework. Cooked dinner as usual, curry of beef and rice.[1]

He had not kept a diary for four years and, in the light of such entries, it is unsurprising that he soon gave up again. Nevertheless, it came as a terrible shock at the end of the month to receive from the Harmsworth family three months' notice to quit the villa, which had been his – and Catha's – home for three and a half years.

His straitened circumstances and the need to provide schooling for Catha made finding a new home difficult. Possibilities were researched, one of them being to find somewhere near the Gribbles' home in Sainte-Gemme-en-Sancerrois in the Cher, a much cheaper region than the Riviera. Aldington did not really want to leave the coast, telling H.D: 'What I like and want is a place a little back from the sea, with a piece of wild maquis around it, and a little car to be free to shop where one wants.'[2]

He purchased the car, a Simca 5 ('a sort of tub with a motor-bike engine,' he told Williamson) but no affordable accommodation had been found by the time he and Catha took to the road on 26 April, the boot of the little car filled with the books for the Lawrence biography while the remaining 3,000 volumes went into storage.[3] Taking Cohen's advice on the best

Richard Aldington at Les Rosiers, Montpellier, 1955

place for Catha's schooling, he had more or less settled on Montpellier. Meanwhile, however, a holiday was intended. 'I must have a bit of a change and bathe my hands in the calm twilight of Romanesque things,' he told Kershaw. 'We shall go to small rustic hotels and go as cheaply as possible. It will be wonderful if we can have the illusion of freedom again.'[4] He resumed the diary entries for the duration of the tour and they show that he was often too anxious about cost and too depressed by

Richard and Catherine Aldington in a village near Montpellier in 1954

poor weather to achieve that 'illusion of freedom'. He kept a record of all expenses, adding to the entry for 30 April: 'THE COST OF EVERYTHING really frightening.' It cannot have helped that in its entirety the month-long expedition covered some 1,400 miles. In the 1930s with Patmore and in the 1940s with his family he had covered greater distances, but as a younger, healthier and more hopeful man.

Nevertheless, there were highlights. On the sandy beach that runs the length of the Etang de Thau they found the best shells they had seen since their Florida days and were exhilarated by the 'brisk cool wind off the Mediterranean & a brilliant sun'. Having driven on to Capestang and Carcassonne, they set off north for Saint-Gemme, perhaps simply to assure themselves that it was not for them; but the Gribbles were away and after a few days in their house, depressed by a 'cold and sunless' Whit weekend, they returned south. Back near the coast their spirits revived and entries record a 'strenuous but very interesting day full of experiences' and a 'good lunch' in Albi, though they travelled back through Béziers to Montpellier in 'pouring rain and cold wind'. Having arranged for Catha's entry to school and visited estate agents, they set off again for day trips from Montpellier to Aigues-Mortes, the Roman ruins at Glanum and Saint-Guilhem-le-Désert, soon to become a favourite spot to take visitors. The weather was improving and he told H.D. that they had found the ancient village of Saint-Guilhem and its semi-ruinous basilica 'overwhelming', while at Glanum he thought he had sensed the 'lingering faint aroma of Hellenic days' – one of those subtextual messages he tended to send H.D.[5]

On 28 May, Catha, now nearing her thirteenth birthday, started at her new school while Aldington moved into their new home: three rooms with full board at Les Rosiers, a large, shabby pension about ten minutes' walk from the town centre. His own room opened onto the large neglected garden. He made remarkably light of this downturn in his fortunes, although a parallel downturn in his physical health is indicated in his correspondence, with recurring and increasingly severe bouts of bronchitis, the continuing legacy of the Western Front. Kershaw recalled in 1986:

> The pension was as dismal as any other pension, its occupants were a dreary lot, Montpellier itself has never been the most cheerful city in the world. The Villa Aucassin, the bouillabaisse on Port-Cros, Roy's marvellous stories, the golden girls seemed incredibly remote. In the circumstances, our meetings should have been gloomy occasions. They weren't. This was Richard's first experience of real poverty, but his stoicism was admirable. . . . He laughed as readily as ever, he retained all his capacity for enjoyment, he made new friends. . . . The only times I ever heard him complain were when he was lamenting his inability to offer me a good meal or to help out some acquaintance or other.[6]

In his memoirs Dutton recalled visiting the 'poky pension' when he and Ninette returned to Europe in 1954, by which time Aldington had been living at Les Rosiers for three years:

> When we arrived he was sitting under the pines in the garden of the pension, reading Provençal poetry. He was quiet, almost reserved. He knew all too well that last time we had met he had been the genial host of the Villa Aucassin. But he soon cheered up and when Catha came back from the University [sic], gay, grown-up and very French, he began to laugh.[7]

The Duttons moved on to Florence, taking a villa for four months, and inviting Aldington and Catha to visit over Christmas and the New Year. The opportunity to return to Florence after seventeen years – and to show it to Catha – was a joy to Aldington, although he told Williamson afterwards: 'I had twinges of melancholy – to be in Florence, and no Lorenzo, no Frieda, no Norman, no Pino, no Reggie, even no Frere and no Brigit – alas.'[8] The inclusion of Patmore in the list is telling.

For Dutton, the pleasure of their company was spoiled by the fact that his mother, also visiting, did not take to Aldington and had constant disagreements with him, culminating in a ferocious argument about Kershaw and Deasey, whom she had always thought to be bad influences on her son. On returning to Montpellier, Aldington wrote to Deasey:

> For dear old Geoff's sake, I put up with Emily who struck me as exactly like the English female of the moneyed class – ignorant, snobbish, vain, purse-proud, domineering, fatuous and disagreeable. I'm sorry to say that about Geoff's Ma, but you know I am right. I nearly had a sanguinary row with her in Firenze over you and Alister – I had to remind her you are my friends.[9]

Since the Duttons stayed in Montpellier on their way from Florence to Paris and London the following month (accompanied by Dutton's mother) and took Aldington and Catha out for some enjoyable meals, the events do not seem to have damaged their relationship.

Deasey was a regular visitor to Montpellier until his return to Australia, and he and Aldington, with their shared love of history, enjoyed exploring Provence and Languedoc together whenever Aldington could drag himself away from writing. Kershaw was more limited by work constraints but visited when he could. Although the T.E. Lawrence saga created tensions between them in this period, their relationship weathered them, founded as it was on strong affection. Kershaw himself went through a very difficult time over the next few years. His health and financial circumstances were in poor shape and all of this affected what had always been a volatile marriage. His employment with UNESCO was intermittent and he was reliant on freelance journalism and translation. The baby girl to whom Patsy gave birth on Christmas Day 1954 turned out to be frail – and not his child. The couple would separate in 1956, Patsy marrying her child's father and Kershaw remarrying – an English girl – the following year. A private man, like Aldington, Kershaw only revealed his domestic circumstances reluctantly, even to his closest friends.

The most important friend Aldington made in Montpellier (in May 1954) was Frédéric-Jacques Temple, a young poet, critic, translator and broadcaster, who had fought in the Italian Campaign in 1943-45. (Temple had, coincidentally, been born in the very room in Les Rosiers which Aldington now occupied.) He became an almost daily visitor, sharing,

Frédéric-Jacques Temple and Lawrence Durrell

in particular, Aldington's admiration for D.H. Lawrence; he had already translated *D.H. Lawrence: An Indiscretion* into French. He would write in 1965: 'Richard Aldington lived in Montpellier in almost total solitude. This man who loved France so deeply, who spoke our language faultlessly, who delighted in our finest wines, lived here like an outcast, or, rather, like a retired Indian Army colonel in exile.' 'I was,' observed Temple, 'a helpless witness of his difficulties, which he bore with a truly lordly stoicism and dignity.'[10] Temple's friendship became vital to Aldington and it is a measure of his trust in him that he agreed to Temple conducting a series of fourteen monthly radio interviews with him on Radio Montpellier between October 1955 and December 1956.

* * *

By April 1952 Aldington had completed his T.E. Lawrence manuscript. On 7 February that year Douglas had died on Capri and on 3 June Aldington told Dibben: 'I have begun a shortish memorial of Norman – to mingle personal reminiscences with informal notes on Norman's books.'[11] He told Kershaw that the book would be 'a panegyric of his way of living', but, once again, what emerged was very different from the intention.[12] Frere agreed to publish the book, which eventually became a memoir of Douglas, Orioli and Prentice, the title, *Pinorman*, being a portmanteau word for the former two figures, used, Aldington claimed (although others subsequently disputed), amongst their personal circle of friends. Gaining permission for quotations proved problematic: MacPherson, Bryher's former husband (and former lover of H.D.) was Douglas's literary executor and Aldington knew that he would be reluctant to assist with a book that denigrated its subject. Perhaps oblivious to the ambivalent attitude of Aldington towards Douglas, of whom she and Bryher had been close friends and admirers, H.D. mediated between MacPherson and Aldington, who thus gained all the permissions he needed.[13]

While the book's circulation was much smaller than that of the T.E. Lawrence nine months later (around 5,000), it was greeted with a storm of disapproval on its publication in April 1954. (That it preceded the Lawrence was the result of the constant publication delays of the latter.) In some ways, it is a very different book, only 50,000 words, informal and conversational in style and consisting chiefly of personal recollections and anecdotes of three men he knew well. In both cases, however, Aldington rejected the term 'biography', calling *Pinorman* 'nothing but notes and personal recollections of [Douglas] and two of his friends' and *Lawrence of Arabia* the work of 'an under-labourer clearing the ground a little and removing some of the rubbish that lies in the way of knowledge'.[14] Furthermore, in his profile of Douglas, he was once again mounting an attack on an admired figure, if one unfamiliar to the general public. Douglas's writing was criticised but, more provocatively, Aldington was scathing – as he had not been in *Life for Life's Sake* – about Douglas's personality and conduct ('[I]n all the time I was with him I seldom saw him put himself out in the least or do anything much for another person') and, in particular, about his paedophilia.[15]

The book contains affectionate portraits of both Orioli and Prentice, but it was the personal animus against Douglas which attracted attention – and outrage. Some of the animosity stemmed from Aldington's loyalty towards D.H. Lawrence and his anger at the way Douglas had attacked Lawrence – unjustly – in the 'Magnus affair'. He had dealt with this in *Portrait of a Genius, But . . .* and in *Life for Life's Sake* but he returned to it again, asserting that: 'That Magnus pamphlet was by far the cleverest and most damaging attack made on Lawrence and did him more damage than he realised.'[16] He told Lyle that: 'DHL was the real reason for *Pinorman*, though of course love for Charles and Pino came in too.'[17] As for Douglas's paedophilia, this was not – unlike T.E. Lawrence's illegitimacy – a secret, and a contemporary readership may be surprised to find Aldington attacked for condemning Douglas's behaviour. Indeed, one of the most vicious reviews of the book was written by Constantine Fitzgibbon who, during Douglas's lifetime, had abandoned an attempted biography 'partly because', according to Anne Chisholm (Cunard's biographer), 'of the awkwardness involved in writing truthfully about Douglas's relations with preadolescent boys'.[18]

The chief antagonist was Cunard, whose own memoirs of Douglas, *Grand Man*, appeared that August.[19] Not content with her savage review of *Pinorman* in *Time and Tide*, she wrote to Heinemann: 'It is astonishing that a reputable publishing firm such as yourselves should be able to bring out the gross travesty of Norman Douglas and Orioli by Richard Aldington entitled *Pinorman*.'[20] She threatened: 'All the friends of Norman Douglas will, I am sure, be as ready as I am to cooperate in whatever form of collective protest may be judged the most suitable.'[21] Frere would appear in court later that year on charges under the Obscene Publications Act (in relation to the firm's publication of Walter Baxter's controversial novel, *The Image and the Search*) but he was on safe ground here. The friends of Douglas, who included Fitzgibbon, Graham Greene, Compton Mackenzie, the cartoonist David Low and William King, as well as those friends from Florence, wartime London and Capri whose tributes to Douglas were included in Cunard's book (her cousin Victor Cunard, MacPherson, Acton, Charles Duff and Arthur Johnson) did not have quite the influence of the Lawrence Bureau, and one or two of them had personal reasons for being alarmed by Aldington's condemnation of Douglas's sexual preferences.[22] (In this regard, it is interesting to note that Bryher, Douglas's chief patron, did not contribute to Cunard's book.) Greene (presumably familiar with the concept of the 'Gladstone Defence') sent Aldington a copy of a defamatory review he intended to publish in the *London Magazine*, daring him to sue for libel. Aldington ignored the letter and the *London Magazine* found the review too risky to publish.

Aldington's own supporters included, somewhat surprisingly, Somerset Maugham, who arrived in Montpellier to take him out for a congratulatory dinner that September but did not commit himself to print. Frieda Lawrence, however, sent a letter to *Time and Tide* rebutting Cunard.[23] She wrote to Aldington: 'Of course I swallowed your "Pinorman" like a raw oyster. You made it all alive again. You give this wonderful bit of living, unique, never to be repeated,' and in a subsequent letter she told him of an occasion when Douglas had asked her if she would like to 'take over' from him a fourteen-year-old boy, because he 'preferred them younger'.[24] More moderately, Warman wrote: 'Your criticisms of Douglas as a man (which ring absolutely true to me) are entirely balanced by your treatment of him as a writer; of Orioli and Prentice as people; and of yourself as a mere observer in the group – which you certainly cannot have been.'[25] Campbell told Aldington that it was the 'finest portrait of a DOM' he had read for a long time, adding: 'I chuckled throughout. It reminded me of reading Tartuffe for the first time. It will infuriate the critics. ... At the same time it's a very noble and necessary vindication of DHL.'[26] Since none of them, Frieda apart, could get letters printed in response to the hostile reviews, Campbell came up with the

Catherine Aldington as a young woman

idea of a pamphlet to challenge the Douglas supporters; Lyle agreed to edit it and publish it at his own expense. Aldington was touched, telling him: 'I never had unselfish friends before, except Frere and Alister.'[27] Unfortunately for them all, when the Forty-Five Press, who had agreed to publish the pamphlet (entitled *What Next? Or, Black Douglas & White Ladyship, Being an Herpetology of Literary London*), sent it to print, the printers refused to proceed, on the grounds that it was libellous.

* * *

Aldington would publish only three more books. First came *Introduction to Mistral*, published by Heinemann in October 1956. Frédéric Mistral was a poet and lexicographer of the Occitan language of Provence, who had been awarded the Nobel Prize for Literature in 1904, 'in recognition of the fresh originality and true inspiration of his poetic production, which faithfully reflects the natural scenery and native spirit of his people, and, in addition, his significant work as a Provençal philologist'. Aldington had visited Mistral's house in Maillane, near Saint-Rémy-de-Provence, in April 1953 and told Bacon (himself an admirer of Mistral) that he had never been so pleased 'with the aspect and "atmosphere" of a great writer's home'. As for the Museon Arlaten, the *musée de vie* founded by Mistral in Arles with his Nobel Prize money, Aldington told Read that he loved it so much he had visited it 22 times.[28]

It is easy to see why he admired Mistral. He would tell H.D: 'It is the curse of "modern poetry" that it cuts itself off from the people in sterile intellectual pride. I love Mistral and my dear Roy because they fought against that.'[29] A list of some of the headings in the index entry for 'Mistral, Frédéric' in Aldington's book gives us further clues:

> his 'harmonious' life and character
> his serenity
> his moderation and simplicity
> his tact
> his sympathy
> his *bonhomie*
> his learning
> his relations with his country folk
> 'representative man of Provence'

One aspect of Mistral's thinking, in particular, chimed completely with Aldington's: 'There was a genuine "poetry" of the people which Mistral was not alone in thinking brought them more genuine happiness than the commercialised substitutes of the town. . . . [H]is life-task . . . was to be a defence of living values against mechanical, bureaucratic, statistical values.'[30]

Dibben found Aldington the obscure books he needed, but there were frustrations: Mistral's wife, who died in 1943, had placed an embargo on his correspondence, while the background literature was 'appalling both in bulk and detail', a challenge to his knowledge and language skills. Nevertheless, he found the task 'such a refreshment after the fetid Colonel!'[31] Once it was finished he had agonising doubts, about both his expertise and the book's saleability. The latter concern proved justified: he would tell Warman the following year that only 625 copies had been sold.[32] It seems likely that Frere had taken the book on as a favour to his old friend. One small piece of good fortune was that Pryce-Jones at the *TLS* asked Campbell, as an authority on Provence, to review the book. Frere told Aldington: 'He had it on his conscience obviously what Hayley MADE him print about Pinorman and Lawrence.'[33] Campbell's review was, predictably, enthusiastic: 'Mr Aldington makes the whole

Camargue come to life, with its auroras of phoenicopters, wild fighting
bulls, and wild (but alas! vanishing) white horses. . . . [His] scholarly but
unobtrusive erudition was required to do justice to that of Mistral.'[34]
Another favourable review – in the *New Statesman* – was also by a (new)
friend, Lawrence Durrell.[35] Aldington's own view was explained in a
letter to Read: 'The book is not as good as the TLS says, but it struggles
to express (a) my love of the earth, (b) my hatred of machines and
machine-worship, (c) my feeling that there should be a "reciprocity"
between the poet and the people, the real people.'[36] The book is dedicated
to Campbell ('who made me ashamed of my ignorance of Provence') and
also to Frank Flint ('who taught me to love France'). It is touching to
see Flint and his infectious enthusiasm for French poetry remembered,
and saddening to be aware that all Aldington's efforts to re-establish
contact with him in recent years had failed. In 1960, after Pound, too,
had expressed a desire to communicate with Flint, Aldington told H.D.:
'Pity about Frankie, but what can be done? I tried very hard to get in
touch with him, directly and through friends, and he let all advances go
without response. I even dedicated one of my best books to him, with
no answer.'[37]

* * *

Written almost in tandem with the Mistral book and published in
February 1957 was a commission from Frere entitled *Frauds*. Again,
Aldington was worried that it would fail to find an audience. He told
Bird: 'The educated will know it all beforehand, and the others will
not have the least idea what it is about.' 'How does this gap exist?'
he asked.[38] His 'frauds', which he enjoyed researching, included two
eighteenth-century figures, George Psalmanazar (a Frenchman who
claimed to be the first native of Formosa to reach Europe) and James
Graham (a fraudulent 'doctor' who devised many popular remedies),
two from the nineteenth century, Thomas Griffiths Wainewright
(forger and probable serial killer) and Arthur Orton (the son of
a London butcher who claimed to be the lost heir to the Tichborne
fortune), and a twentieth-century figure, Maundy Gregory (who acted
as a broker in the sale of honours from 1910 for a period of some 20
years). The final chapter is devoted to four literary forgeries of the
eighteenth and nineteenth centuries, those of Thomas Chatterton,
James Macpherson, William Ireland and Thomas Wise. Aldington
described the book to Bird as 'journalism in book form' and, while it
displays exhaustive research and those skills in interrogating myths

and hearsay that had landed him in such difficulties in the case of T.E. Lawrence, it reads like the work of a tired man. His fears of its not finding its audience proved well founded.[39]

* * *

The last book, commissioned by Evans Brothers, was a biography of Robert Louis Stevenson. Aldington was initially unenthusiastic. He told Kershaw in March 1956 that the task was 'a frightful chore' and a month later that '[t]here are heaps of books about him and no need whatsoever for another one'.[40] However, as his research progressed and as he read Stevenson's writings more closely, he warmed to the man and came to appreciate the work. He told Dibben: 'RLS was almost the same age as DHL when he died. What I love in both is the courage and sense of enjoyment, the refusal to be beaten.'[41] What is only implied here is the 'gnawing demon at [their] lungs' from which both men suffered and which made them the restless 'world's wanderers' that they became.[42] There were other demons too, against which Aldington was used to railing: 'the dour religion forced upon his frightened childhood and . . . the smug, purse-proud, conventional, repressive society that religion had created'.[43]

Like Aldington himself, 'Stevenson's vocation for letters was too strong for him to concentrate on other work.' He was an example of 'the writer, painter or "artist" who shrugged off the advantages and rewards as well as the responsibilities and duties of money-making man in exchange for freedom and art'. 'Until 1940 and socialism put an end to it,' Aldington asks, 'how many British artists of all sorts tried to follow his precepts?'[44] One of the consequences of such a lifestyle plagued both men: '[H]e was from time to time worried about money until the day he died.' Yet – and again we recognise the Aldington of earlier days – 'Stevenson's open-handed generosity with money was only equalled by the delicacy with which he gave or "lent" it.'[45] Aldington also admired Stevenson's qualities as a traveller: 'He was very seldom in a hurry, he prepared himself beforehand by learning something of the language and history of the country visited, he had an eye for the unexpected and a knack of getting into touch with persons he met.'[46] We might be reminded here of both D.H. Lawrence and Aldington himself. Another revealing observation – made in relation to *The Amateur Immigrant*, Stevenson's account of his voyage to America in 1879 – is that Stevenson 'has no particular axe to grind though, as a Tory, he likes people and is suspicious of humanity'.[47] Stevenson's later *The Day*

After Tomorrow also won Aldington's approval for its 'statesman-like ability to foresee the inevitable results of Socialist legislation', namely 'the golden age of officials' who will 'meddle' in all the concerns of the people.[48]

Aldington quotes from Stevenson's essay on Burns:

> To write with authority about another man we must have fellow-feeling and some common ground of experience with our subject. We may praise or blame according as we find him related to us by the best or worst in ourselves; but it is only in virtue of some relationship that we can be his judges, even to condemn. Feelings which we share and understand enter for us into the tissue of the man's character; those to which we are strangers in our own experience we are inclined to regard as blots, exceptions, inconsistencies, and excursions of the diabolic; we conceive them with repugnance, explain them with difficulty, and raise our hands to heaven in wonder when we find them in conjunction with talents that we respect or virtues that we admire.[49]

This passage makes an excellent starting point for the criticism of Aldington's own biographical incursions – into the lives of Voltaire, Wellington, the two Lawrences, Douglas and Stevenson. His study of the latter represents two fine achievements. The first is his refusal of irony and caricature. He offers a measured, tolerant and sympathetic assessment of the characters in Stevenson's life so often given short shrift: his father and his wife. He gives due regard to the 'genuine affection existing between father and son underneath all the quarrels and differences'.[50] In the case of Fanny Stevenson and the question of how far she was qualified to bring out the very best of Stevenson's literary gifts, he acknowledges that her conception of literary merit was probably what would achieve popular success, but sees this as no bad thing: 'She won, and on the whole she was right.'[51] As for Stevenson himself: 'We have to admit that [he] was rather egocentric, that he did frequently dramatise himself, and that he did consciously seek experiences in order to use them in his writings.' 'However,' Aldington adds, 'I should say that is characteristic of many writers, particularly of the "subjective-romantic" kind. What is far less characteristic is Stevenson's compassion and generosity, his pity for helpless suffering and instant impulse to give help.'[52]

The other achievement of the book is its comprehensive and sensitive evaluation of the full range of Stevenson's writing. Speaking of *The Amateur Immigrant*, Aldington again refers to D.H. Lawrence, remarking that Stevenson's capacity to present experiences and feelings so that the reader 'shares and relives' them makes him 'the predecessor or "herald" of the later writer'.[53] While appreciating fully the essays and travel writing, Aldington also treats the works of popular fiction with respect. Exercised so much at this time by the issue of audience and the gap between popular and highbrow taste, he recognised – as he had always done in the case of Dickens – Stevenson's ability to take and hold the reader's attention. He also understood his place in the literary tradition, noting, for example, the influence of Scott and Defoe on *Kidnapped* but suggesting that Stevenson, 'assimilating both ancestors, made the book wholly his'. In turn, he points to Stevenson's influence on later writers, citing the debt of Wilde's *The Picture of Dorian Gray* and Conan Doyle's Sherlock Holmes stories to *The Strange Case of Dr Jekyll and Mr Hyde*.

John Carswell, writing in the *TLS*, recognised the presence of these qualities in Aldington's book:

> The familiar astringency is still there, and so is Mr Aldington on the sidelines as commentator, offering opinions on the world and its foibles in season and out of it. But the astringency reinforces rather than distorts, and the occasional obtrusiveness of the asides is redeemed by much acute, unhackneyed criticism.

Carswell noted that Aldington had clearly come to like Stevenson and 'to extend sympathetic understanding to the odd and not in all respects attractive group in which he stands'.[54] The *Times* reviewer also noted the 'basic admiration, critical detachment, measured sympathy, and an author's wise understanding of a writer's problems' that made the book 'an absorbing narrative'.[55] Even Bonamy Dobrée, writing in the *Daily Telegraph*, praised Aldington's 'sensitive perception', his scrupulous fairness to all the persons involved and the way in which he had brought out Stevenson's 'indomitable spirit'.[56] Such reviews from the literary establishment might have shaken Aldington's view that after *Pinorman* and *Lawrence of Arabia* he could not expect a fair trial. However, in *The Sunday Times*, John Raymond displayed all the hostility towards him that he had come to expect, remarking that:

> A pagan expatriate, Lawrencian devotee and connoisseur of Provence and the blushing south, who keeps his sunny side for Mistral and a generous allowance of cantankerousness for his fellow countrymen (especially if they happen to be Eminent Georgians)... is the last man in the world to relish the chill, smoky wind-and-wynd background from which Stevenson sprung.

He found 'impatience, a dearth of light and shade, the failure to provide us with any genuine assessment of Stevenson's art'.[57]

* * *

In January 1957 Aldington's cause was taken up by a critic at the heart of the literary establishment but a long-time admirer of his work: the editor of *The Times*, William Haley. Writing under the pen-name of Oliver Edwards, Haley published in the paper an extensive article on Aldington's work, expressing his sadness at the bitterness and anger aroused by *Pinorman* and *Lawrence of Arabia* and confirming Aldington's own view that the consequence of these events had been a general desire to 'write [him] off' as someone 'whose opinions did not matter [and] whose work had never amounted to much anyway'. On the contrary, Haley felt that *Portrait of a Genius, But . . .* was 'first class' and *Death of a Hero* an important work. Haley went on to ask how it was possible to dismiss the writer of novels like *All Men Are Enemies* and *Women Must Work* and poems like *A Fool i' the Forest* and *A Dream in the Luxembourg* as well as 'one of the best single volumes on Voltaire', criticism like *French Studies and Reviews* and translations like *Alcestis* and *Fifty Romance Poems*. He argued that *A Fool i' the Forest* was a turning point in Aldington's development as a writer, proposing, as it did, the notion, further articulated in *Artifex* and *Life Quest*, that 'an art impulse exists in all men, has been recognised in preceding generations, but denied in our industrial civilisation with grave results'. Aldington seemed in *Life Quest*, continued Haley, to be 'reaching towards a new world, or at least an old world reborn'. However, he argued, 'something happened': from *Very Heaven* onwards Aldington had produced no major creative work. Nevertheless, Hayley concluded, his best work had a healthier, if less striking and dynamic, message than D.H. Lawrence's and gave him 'a firm place among the writers of the interwar years'. *Death of a Hero, All Men Are Enemies, A Dream in the Luxembourg, Life Quest, Voltaire* and *Portrait of a Genius, But . . .* were, in Hayley's judgement, works that would 'stand'.

Aldington was delighted at this defence of his work, but it did not change the views of the literary establishment, as some of his obituaries would later show. Had he followed Campbell's advice in 1951 that he should go to London, and the urgings of many of his friends that he appear on British television and radio, it might have made a difference; but he was too tired, unwell and disillusioned. The T.E. Lawrence affair had wounded him deeply. More importantly, he had no further creative work to offer.

Sir William Haley in 1967

He was ready, nevertheless, to applaud the successes of his friends. In 1954 Fallas's novel, *St Mary's Village: Through the Eyes of an Unknown Soldier Who Lived On*, was awarded the Prime Minister's Literary Prize and Aldington was delighted, telling his brother that the book was 'a vividly accurate report on that war'.[58] In January 1956 he responded warmly to Williamson's *A Fox Under My Cloak*. The book brought back his own experiences in the Loos sector in 1917 and 1918, but his criticisms were candid:

> I thought Madison on the whole an engaging character ... very self-centred, but then so are a great many people. I think what he lacks is moral indignation plus some philosophy of life to give meaning to his experiences; but doubtless that will come later. But all said and done, it is a great achievement.[59]

He told Williamson that *How Dear Is Life* and *A Fox Under My Cloak* 'together make about the best English war novel there is'.[60]

A writer whose success that year he was more reluctant to celebrate was Richard Church, whose autobiography, *Over the Bridge*, won the *Sunday Times* Award. 'Do you see,' he asked Kershaw:

> that Frere's Great Author now, after Willie [Maugham] and Graham Greene, is our old friend Dick Church, whose charming autobiography 'Over the Bridge' received the Sunday Times prize of 1,000 quid and is now in its fourth printing. What next? This is the reward of lick-spittle time-serving and of what Banabhard [Taylor] called 'his insincere and unnecessary opinions'.[61]

1956 brought events in the wider world to his attention, the Suez Crisis confirming his contempt for the governing classes. At first, he thought that Britain would do nothing about the Egyptian nationalisation of the canal, writing to his brother:

> Their Master's Voice in Washington (D.C.) won't allow any scrapping with an election coming on. The French are tied up in Algeria. Which means Mr E would have had to fight alone, and the more cowardly the Brits become the more they praise their heroes – and do nothing. He daren't fight and he'd get licked if he did.[62]

Once the events of November unfolded, however, his contempt was even greater: 'The heroic grandeur of Sir A E in attacking a little man is only exceeded by the superb dignity and courage with which he runs away from two big men.'[63] His scorn for Eden's government did not make him more sympathetic to the Socialist cause:

> There might be some slight consolation if this kick in the backside had dispelled some of the illusions which infest GB. But seemingly the Tories go on believing in their great and powerful empire, beloved by all, and the Socialists in a vast 'wealth' which can be indefinitely pillaged without weakening the economy of the whole concern. It is hard to say which is the sillier, the party which go ass-ing about with stars and garters and Lillibet and busbies and Oxford and Ascot, or the other lot always whinging about the downtrodden proletariat – at least 12 pounds a week and all found – and demanding another three or four hundred millions for social services and wages, for the laziest pack of bastards in Europe.[64]

His philosophy was still 'a plague on both their houses'.

He did, however, have a prescription for the future:

> The enemy of GB is not the USA or the USSR but GB itself and
> its silly conceit. The policy of the last fifteen years has been that
> of keeping up with the Joneses and keeping up appearances and
> keeping the old ostrich nut in the ancient sand. England is not a
> great power any longer, and in an atomic war is a death trap. It
> has lost its empire and is losing its trade and it can only survive
> by facing realities – drastic reduction of military and of 'social
> service' expenditure, abandonment of ridiculous attempts to
> rival USA and USSR which merely bring humiliation and derision,
> adherence to the EU, development of Africa not by pukka sahibs
> and polo players but by people who understand business, and
> above all a policy of peace. This constant scattering of ultimatums
> must stop. Let us get out of the garden of Eden and cultivate our
> own little patch. There is a decent future for England if it will, as
> far as possible, 'neutralise' (a pretence of fighting for the Yanks
> must be kept up), cut military bases and expenditure overseas,
> cut subsidies such as the 12 million a year to Jordan bequeathed
> by the Colonel and stop swarming itself into indigence with too
> many children.[65]

There were worries closer to home. Catha's success at school was erratic
and Aldington was conscious that she would have to be able to earn her
own living. He lamented to Netta in 1955: 'As a matter of fact, she is quite
good at schoolwork, but she is lazy. . . . Her main interests are her friends,
hopes of a Vesta, plenty of clothes, holiday and pocket money.'[66] In July
1956, after Catha had failed her *baccalauréat*, she went – reluctantly –
to stay with her mother in London for the summer vacation. Aldington
told Kershaw: 'What a cow is Netta. Her idea of entertaining that most
intelligent girl is to take her to see the Guards on parade, to number
10 and the Cenotaph, and to patriotic films. The rest of the time she is
dragged round pubs.'[67] The chief cause of anxiety, however, was money.
He told Kershaw in November 1956: 'We are in such a desperate state
financially that I simply don't know what to do.'[68] Kershaw's response was
to send him 2,000 francs. Others made generous contributions: Warman
– and also Randall, who came to Montpellier in the summer of 1956 for a
visit both men enjoyed immensely. These were friends who remembered
his kindness towards them in earlier years and were happy to repay it.

His own generosity towards others continued despite his financial
difficulties. The first recipient was the American novelist Edward Dahlberg,

Edward Dahlberg

whom Aldington had met when in the United States but who was now living in Denmark. Read wrote to tell Aldington that Dahlberg was writing him long letters 'full of the most magnificent invective but also bemoaning his fate' and pressing him to accept his latest work, *The Sorrows of Priapus*, for Routledge: 'I am almost at the end of my patience, and yet if I abandon him, I have a fear it would be the end.' Read confessed to having become involved in co-writing with Dahlberg a study of several major contemporary writers, a project which was proving stressful.[69] Aldington offered: 'I'll try to take him off you for a bit.'[70]

He came to regret the offer. He warned Dahlberg, who felt himself neglected by the literary world and wanted Aldington to promote his writing: 'I am old, tired, ill, poor and fighting for my existence against the combination of practically all the periodical writers of England and America. I will do anything I can for you, but it is I who need comfort and succour.'[71] Dahlberg arrived in Montpellier, shortly followed by his wife. 'From the moment he arrived here,' Aldington told Read, 'his purpose was plain – i.e. to engage me to praise his works in print on a reciprocal basis.' Aldington thought that many of Dahlberg's comments in the co-written book were libellous and that Dahlberg's own book was 'as disconnected as the Book of Proverbs, from which indeed it may derive.' Forced to be truthful when asked directly for his opinion, Aldington deeply offended the writer. 'Unluckily,' he told Read, 'E.D. has so much the neurasthenic temperament of the neglected and unpublished writer that he lost his temper, abused me, was furious when I retaliated and went off in a huff.' Looking back on the episode the following March he called it *une jolie bouillotte de poissons*, telling Read that he had done his best but that Dahlberg had 'stayed too long and tried to exact too much'.[72]

The other, even more eccentric, writer whom Aldington tried to help was Geoffrey Potocki de Montalk, a New Zealander of Polish extraction, who had lived in England since 1926. Aldington had first met Potocki at Lowenfels' apartment in Paris in 1928, since when Potocki had attracted attention in the interwar years, serving a prison term for obscenity in 1932 for a collection of poems, and expressing support for Fascism through his editorship of a journal entitled the *Right Review*. In 1949 he moved to a tumbledown cottage in Draguignan, inland from Saint-Tropez. He wrote to Aldington in 1954, seeking advice about publication of his work, and their correspondence continued until the end of Aldington's life. Their letters were long and friendly, and Aldington derived much humour from Potocki's views and writings. The Dahlberg fiasco had clearly taught him to be tactful with struggling writers – although Potocki was a much more engaging (and thick-skinned) character – but he advised him in relation to *My Private War Against England*: 'I am afraid the common publisher will be scared of this text.'[73] Mentioning this book in a letter to Warman, Aldington remarked: 'I don't recollect to have read a modern book so completely aloof from base reality.'[74]

Early in 1956, the impoverished Potocki conceived the idea of starting his own printing press,

Geoffrey Potocki de Montalk in a police photograph taken on his arrest in 1932

Geoffrey Potocki de Montalk in Wellington, New Zealand in1984

although Aldington pointed out that books published and printed outside the UK could not then be imported into Britain. When, in 1959, Potocki decided to go ahead with the idea, Aldington did all he could to raise funds – mostly from Kershaw and Warman, but including money of his own – to enable the Melissa Press to be started. Over the years the two men met on several occasions, to their mutual enjoyment; Aldington would tell Potocki in 1958: 'The energy and zest you put into life are a lesson to us all, especially to me at this time when I am moping with one foot in the grave and the other on a banana skin.'[75]

A friend to whom he was able to return the kindness of over 30 years was Gribble, whom Kershaw brought down from Paris to spend a fortnight at Les Rosiers in January 1953. In his early 70s by now, Gribble had begun to develop dementia and his wife and son had little patience with him, much to Kershaw's fury. Aldington told him after the visit: 'The old George chirruped over his cups and was mightily entertaining. On the other hand I must avow to you in secret that some of his discourses somewhat baffle me,' and he told H.D. that Gribble 'is very active, walks a lot, plays the guitar, drinks his wine, but his memory grows confused'.[76]

Gribble died in September 1956. Frieda Lawrence had died that August. Writing to Edward Nehls, the D.H. Lawrence scholar with whom he had been corresponding since 1952, Aldington said that part of his youth and reason for living had died with her: 'While she lived something of Lawrence lived on.' 'If my life has any value,' he continued, 'it is that since 1926 – and to some extent since 1914 – I felt his superiority and always acknowledged it.'[77] Other deaths followed, of figures less close but still associated with a time when his social and literary lives had been active and fulfilling: Arlen in June, and Lewis in March the following year. Aldington had shared with H.D. Lewis's moving 1951 essay on his blindness, 'The Sea Mists of Winter', and now he told Read how highly he thought of Lewis's work. Read was less charitable, calling Lewis 'a fierce, ugly, unhappy man . . . [without] one drop of the milk of human kindness', but Aldington was more prepared to look for reasons, suggesting that Lewis (like Pound) suffered from paranoia, and seeing in his production of so many books that 'begin with magnificent energy, and gradually peter out' the effect of 'poverty and the need to produce'.[78] This was a subject of which he had more understanding than Read, who in one letter complained of the cost of private schooling for his four children.[79]

The death that hit him hardest – all the more so for its total unexpectedness – was Campbell's. He and his family had moved to a farm near Sintra in Portugal in May 1952 and had initially invited Aldington and Catha to live with them there. The problems of Catha's schooling and the births of children to both Campbell daughters made the plan impracticable, and by 1956 the Campbells had been forced for financial reasons to give up the farm and move to a small cottage. Campbell had been in poor health for some time, suffering principally from diabetes. However, he and Mary drove to Seville in 1957 to attend the Holy Week festivities. On 23 April they were returning home – and only an hour's drive away – when a front tyre burst, the car swerved into a tree and both of them were severely injured. Campbell's neck was broken and he died within minutes. Aldington was heart-broken. He wrote to Williamson: 'Dear, dear Henry, Roy's death has almost knocked us out. I admired, revered, loved him and believed he might a little mourn me, not I shed tears for him. . . . He was a great man and a great poet.'[80] He expressed similar sentiments to H.D.[81]

One of those in whom he confided his sense of loss was a new and important friend – who would come to replace Campbell in the years ahead. Lawrence Durrell had contacted Aldington early in 1957 when he and his French partner, Claude Vincendon, had decided to move to the south of France. They had settled at Sommières, halfway between Montpellier and Nîmes, and the occasional meetings between them and Aldington and Catha were supplemented by regular correspondence. Durrell was about to achieve literary success with the publication of *Justine*, the first volume in his *Alexandria Quartet*, and was sympathetic to Aldington's literary struggles. They shared right-wing and Anglophobic views, although Durrell could not be persuaded to offer support for Potocki, telling Aldington: 'I didn't approve of his affiliation with Mosley and adoration of Adolf.'[82]

Aldington's chief correspondent throughout these years was H.D., to whom by 1957 he was writing at least once a week. In 1953 she consulted him about *Madrigal*, her *roman à clef* about her experiences during the First World War, which she called her 'beautiful, tragic and basically anti-war story' and which would eventually be entitled *Bid Me to Live*.[83] If he was troubled by her revelations of those dramatic and tragic years of their marriage, he did not reveal this to anyone, least of all H.D. 'It is awfully good, Dooley, really good, authentic and concentrated, better than the equivalent chapters in *Aaron's Rod*,' he told her, and he tried – unsuccessfully – to interest Frere in publishing the book: 'She has written a real novel at last . . . about real people, and has a beginning, a middle and an end.'[84] What struck him forcefully, however, was the narrow domestic focus of this novel on a time when he was fighting on the Western Front, something he only hinted at to H.D, telling her that he had thought of sending her *Roads to Glory* 'for the curiosity of seeing how simultaneously in Time there may be such utter contrast of experience in Space'.[85] When he failed to find her a publisher, Bryher wrote to him to stress how important it was for H.D. that the book be published. They corresponded for several months on the issue, until he had to admit that he could do no more.[86] Although he had failed in this matter, he had given Bryher cause to trust his devotion to H.D., in one letter asking Bryher to break the news of Walter Rummel's death to H.D. as he feared it would distress her.[87]

The most ubiquitous topic in his letters to H.D. is health. Although he wrote of his own problems, he became more concerned about hers. In 1953 she had two abdominal operations and after the second one moved into the Klinik Brunner in Küsnacht, where she had been treated for her emotional breakdown in 1946. Once more, he was communicating with Bryher, who kept him informed of her progress. Her residence in the *klinik*, which stretched to almost a year, gave rise to extensive communication between them on Shakespeare and on prosody as H.D.'s doctor and counsellor, Eric Heydt ('a very old head on young shoulders,' she told Aldington), had encouraged her to conduct group readings of Shakespeare among the residents.[88] It is interesting to observe here H.D.'s reliance on Aldington, her former adviser and mentor, even as the influence of a new one came into her life. Her feelings about the sheltered environment of the clinic were ambivalent. She told Aldington in November 1953: 'I am so happy here and staying NOT because I am not well, but because I have a pleasant room and books and time, and time, and time to read. I have such fun.'[89] A year later, however, she moved to a hotel in Lugano, where she had spent the previous six summers, and told him that she was 'so happy to be on [her] own and independent'. His response was heartfelt. He was pleased to hear that she had 'escaped' from Küsnacht to 'the deep peace of Lugano' and told her: 'I look time and again on the last words of your card: "happy to be on my own again". Of course you are! And you must not again be anything else . . . you must be a whole and free person.'[90]

It was a perennial problem for H.D.: the lure of the wise and reassuring (male) mentor and a secure environment versus the attractions of solitude and independence; Aldington, although he slipped comfortably into the mentoring role, paradoxically appreciated her need for autonomy. Their correspondence in these years shows them to have been remarkably in tune with each other's feelings and able to share both pleasures and anxieties. They talked often of Pound and his circumstances but they also exchanged pressed flowers and impressions of nature and the seasons – and he continued to send her the erotic postcard pictures. 'I never knew anyone but you and DHL who really understood flowers and made one feel their beauty,' he told her.[91] In July 1956 she sent him a photograph of herself and he wrote: 'I have your snapshot on my work table. You have changed little and I was very glad to have it.'[92] He was, as he had always been, proud of her achievements, telling his brother that her *Tribute to Freud* was 'beautifully written'.[93] On receiving a copy of her 1957 *Selected Poems*, he wrote: 'You are much more sure of yourself and your art, and so less "taut" without losing any of the wonderful acuity and compression of the first poems.' He could not resist a comparison with Eliot and Pound: 'Eliot is a pedant and a plagiarist, and so is Ezra, compared with this entirely pure and lovely work of yours.'[94]

When she flew to New York in September 1956 to see Perdita and her family, now consisting of three children, she continued to write to him. After returning to Switzerland, she had a fall and broke her hip, and was forced to stay in hospital for four months; when she left in February 1957 it was for the Klinik Brunner once more. 'Dear Dooley, how are you? Are you really getting stronger and better? Piano, piano, must be your motto,' Aldington wrote to her in March, and again in May: 'I worry so much about you, and wish you were up and about again.'[95] Cohen's wife, Léa, had broken her hip shortly after H.D.'s accident and by June he was concerned that H.D. was still immobile while Léa was up and about, and wondered whether H.D.'s doctors had 'taken her for a ride'. He added an intimate observation: 'Certainly you are delicately and sensitively formed – who should know it better than I? – but you have the strength and health of a good stock and a good family.'[96] Such was his concern that he wrote to Bryher for the first time since 1953 and received a full – and reassuring – report.[97]

These were years that found H.D. at the top of her creative powers, while Aldington had little inspiration left.[98] Apart from one or two periods of anxiety – such as when Bryher came up with the idea of selling Kenwin (and thus cutting her ties to Switzerland) or when she felt stifled by the Klinik Brunner – H.D.'s life was tranquil and financially secure; she was also winning a reputation in the United States, chiefly through the efforts of the American academic, Norman Holmes Pearson, who had met H.D. in New York in 1937 and been a frequent visitor at Lowndes Square while serving with American intelligence during the war. In contrast, Aldington's career and reputation were on the wane and his financial circumstances desperate. H.D. had some health crises – her abdominal operations and her broken hip – but her general health was good, while Aldington's was poor. Nevertheless, he rejoiced in her successes and sympathised with her problems without bitterness or envy.

H.D. with Bryher and Norman Holmes Pearson in the US, 1956

By 1957 he was facing a new problem. He had fallen behind on the rent at Les Rosiers on several occasions during his six years' stay and been rescued by Kershaw and Warman. Now, not only was he ten months in arrears but Les Rosiers was to be sold and a block of flats built on the site. Kershaw, who had started a new and well-paid job in December 1956, offered to buy a house in which Aldington and Catha could live rent-free. The Duttons offered £600 to clear the rent arrears but the process of sending this money from Australia was complex and slow. Aldington found himself forced to write frankly to H.D. about his circumstances:

> You will think me very imprudent to have gotten myself and Catha into a state of virtual destitution, but such is the case. ... Any (even five!) dollars you could lend us would be most gratefully received, and I can reply by assignment on US royalties – my Boccaccio and Alcestis still sell there. The Russians and East Germans also promise to pay me, but you know how uncertain they are.[99]

Not only did H.D. send money (although her first cheque had to be returned as it was signed in pencil and misdated) but she called in Bryher, who immediately sent the 800,000 francs needed to settle the rent arrears. Aldington was grateful for Bryher's aid but – perhaps too unwell and anxious – could not avoid self-pity: 'Forgive me if I sound a bit rebellious, but this is a nice way for me to celebrate my 65th birthday after nearly 50 years of hard work, out of which I have been largely cheated by publishers.'[100] 'The boycott of my books and person is only too real, and is not due to anyone's apathy but to vindictive dislike and spite,' he told her in a further letter.[101] Furthermore, his response to Bryher's suggestion that his making an unannounced call on H.D. would lift her spirits immensely was to plead ill health and the need to make the move and find Catha a job. The prospect of coming face-to-face with H.D., after nearly 20 years, had frightened him.[102]

Since Kershaw could not afford a property in the south, one was found at Sury-en-Vaux, near Sancerre in the Cher, only a hundred miles from Paris, where Catha could be found work. Cohen was horrified: 'A man in the sixties can't live alone – it is far too dangerous . . . [also] changing the mild climate of the south in the winter, so beneficial for your chest, for the dreadful and dark damp of the North.'[103] There was no other option. 'It breaks my heart to leave the Midi,' Aldington wrote to H.D.; but on 24 July 1957 he left Montpellier for good.[104]

21. A Solitary Life
1957-1961

Maison Sallé, Aldington's home from July 1957, was an unprepossessing six-roomed modern bungalow, the only building for miles around that was less than a hundred years old, its red-painted exterior a contrast with the half-dozen old stone houses close by, occupied by wine-growing families who had lived in this tiny hamlet outside Sury-en-Vaux for generations. Unlike most of those houses, however, Maison Sallé had electricity, running water, central heating and a bathroom.[1] Aldington came to enjoy living in this remote spot, as Kershaw tells us, for the countryside was beautiful and it was a pleasure to be surrounded by vineyards. He also liked and respected the *vignerons* 'with their sense of hospitality, their readiness to render a service as between equals, their natural dignity and courtesy ... and he was liked and respected by them'.[2] 'The complete quiet and peace of this place are most healing,' he told Warman.[3] When Bryher expressed concern about his isolation, he told her:

> I am not in the least lonely in Sury – I love the silence, and the age-old peasant life of these people, who are not much corrupted or even disturbed by the hyper-nervous mechanical life of to-day. They live with the earth and in their religion, and one wouldn't disturb them for anything.[4]

He gave H.D. an outline of his daily routine:

> I go to bed about 8 pm and stay there whether waking or sleeping until about 10 am, getting up only to stoke the furnace and take in the morning milk from the little girl. I then drive (for I can't walk that far) the mile to Sury P.O., collect mail, newspaper and bread etc., return, and about 11 am take my first meal of brunch, which is simply a good English breakfast of eggs and bacon. I walk

a little when it is not raining or too cold, and about four drive to beautiful old Sancerre, where I usually mail letters and do main shopping either there or at St Satur. About 6 I have a second meal – soup and fish or vegetables. The water here is not safe, but wine is too heating, but one can now get a light bock for about 1/- for rather less than a litre. And with that plus some Evian or Vichy I make out.[5]

What is missing from this schedule, for almost the first time in his life, is work. His health was a source of anxiety to himself and others, and when, towards the end of 1957, he suffered paralysis of his right arm for several weeks, a doctor's examination found him to be run down from overwork and worry. Rest and a simple diet were prescribed. 'Books are out of the question for some time, probably for ever,' he told Warman.[6] He had committed himself to writing a biography of Balzac for Paul Elek, Warman's former partner, so, through Rosica Colin, his literary agent since 1954 (and another Warman contact), Kershaw arranged for the contract to be cancelled. Aldington told Warman: 'If I can get articles, reviews, introductions – it is much better than killing myself with books that are not wanted and which give the highbrows another opportunity to be insulting.'[7] Warman had already given him the job of writing introductions in English and French to a series of four books of photographs, of Italy, France, Switzerland and Austria. In early 1958 he offered him the task of translating the Larousse *Mythologie Générale*. 'I am deeply obliged to you for this job,' Aldington told him. 'It is the kind of work I can do in my present state of body and mind and I found the subject matter extremely interesting and learned a lot.'[8] Quite what he had learned is revealed in a letter written as he finished the work: 'I knew that human beings everywhere and in every age were bloody fools, but this book proves it conclusively. The only race for whom there is anything to be said is the ancient Greek people – they at least believed in grace and beauty.'[9] In the autumn of 1959 Warman commissioned him for another introduction to a book of photographs, this time of Rome. It was a task he performed too assiduously: the introduction had to be simplified for the publication. An amusing postscript to this story is that he decided that the original text might make an appropriate gift for friends and thus gave Potocki a commission for the Melissa Press. The result was so poor in quality that he had to apologise to everyone to whom he sent it.

The even greater service that Warman did for him was to have his own accountant examine Aldington's tax situation; the 42.5% tax he had consistently paid seemed to Warman excessive. Aldington ultimately received a substantial rebate and began to pay tax in France rather than in Britain. '[Y]ou are the only person who has ever helped me here,' he wrote to Warman, 'though I have had agents and bankers and what not. It is clear the damned Brits have been robbing me for years, and you were the only person who suspected it.'[10] Other events helped him to achieve a more positive outlook on his circumstances. The small publishing house Four Square Books negotiated with Collins, who had let *Lawrence of Arabia* go out of print, in order to bring out a paperback edition in 1957, to which Aldington was able to add corroborating material which he had received from several reputable sources following the book's first appearance. Four Square sold 30,000 copies immediately and another 10,000 in a 1958 reprint. The company also reprinted *Death of a Hero* by negotiation with Heinemann, selling 20,000 copies.

Relations with Frere were at an all-time low in this period and were never fully restored. In 1959 Aldington asked his brother to find out which of his post-1945 Heinemann titles had gone out of print, so that he could recover copyright.[11] Frere, he claimed, had personally promised to keep all his work in print, and had done so until 1939, after which time 'the hope of title counselled the scrapping of an author not persona grata at Buck House and similar Establishments'. 'He has mishandled a valuable literary property, through ignorance, snobbery and deferring to British journalism,' he told Tony.[12] It was an intractable problem: there was little demand for most of his Heinemann titles, particularly the post-1945 work, but, if the books were out of print, booksellers could not obtain them or display them; and if – and here Aldington was right – his work was ignored or discounted by the critics, no demand was created. If not a despised writer, as he believed, he had become a forgotten one. The Four Square sales of *Lawrence of Arabia* and *Death of a Hero* and the 10,000 of a Paul Elek edition of *The Decameron* in 1957 demonstrated, however, that there were titles for which popular demand did exist.

Frere's continuing refusal to contemplate publishing *Life for Life's Sake* was a running sore in their relationship, as was Heinemann's holding on to the copyright of *A Dream in the Luxembourg*, which made it impossible for Aldington to publish a *Complete Poems* elsewhere. There was a further problem for him, however, which could not be blamed on Frere – or on Browning at Evans Brothers: if either publishing house had reprinted titles, the royalties would have gone to the Patmores.[13] Frere was both exasperated and sad about the deterioration of his relationship with Aldington, telling Tony Aldington in 1959: 'I hope that I shall always retain whatever shreds of friendship he cares to offer me.'[14] Matters were not helped by an estrangement between the Freres and Kershaw, who had so often mediated between the

Lawrence Durrell and Claude Vincendon at Sommières, 1957

two men; unaware of the circumstances of Kershaw's separation from Patsy, the Freres had seen it as the ruthless abandonment of a mother and baby and had severed their connection with him.

Durrell was convinced that Aldington could restore his reputation, telling him in September 1959:

> [T]he whole problem, as I see it, is that there is an empty chair marked R.A. You may have enemies among the middle-aged, but it is a more serious thing that many of the young do not know your name at all. ... [Y]ou could rectify your whole rapport with your public by three television appearances. ... At a blow you could alter the Aldington image (people seem to think that you are both grumpy and cantankerous and 'superior') – the young I mean. And with your film-star physique you'd have them bowled. Seriously, *please* plan a trip to England to recover the fortress; a carefully planned campaign, well thought out, would put you right back.[15]

It was the advice Campbell had given Aldington eight years earlier, but now – as then – he had not the energy for such a 'campaign' – and no longer anyone in the literary or broadcasting establishments willing and able to mount it. Moreover, his bitterness and cynicism were entrenched:

Your suggestion of personal appearance on TV was made in all kindness, but I am sure that it would be even more disastrous than Aldous's attempt was for him. The sin is not exile (you too are an exile) but Huxley and I have published satirical novels, wherein we laugh consumedly at Brit pretensions, and I have debunked 2 local heroes, old Doug and Colonel Mecca, both sods of high degree. For this there is no pardon. The only way to treat them (Brits) is to kick them again, which I propose to do, if ONLY I can get back health and strength.[16]

Williamson's *The Golden Virgin* was published in 1957 and dedicated to Aldington, who thought its account of the Somme 'simply magnificent; and certainly one of the greatest evocations of battle ever written'.[17] The two men had put their differences behind them, but Williamson still returned occasionally to the issue of Aldington's bitterness, warning him in September 1957: 'Bitter satires are boomerangs. They indicate our inner conditions.'[18] A letter of September 1960 – his first for seventeen months – returned to the T.E. Lawrence affair:

I think that if you could have modified or even omitted certain angry and contemptuous passages ... you would have made a deeper impression. Perhaps you were 'too honest' to say the same things indirectly. I saw your first proof and it did injure you, by vituperative bits here and there: at the same time I saw you as one who was a self-exile and alone. I know also that you had tenderness in you; I was certainly one, in some moments, to whom you revealed concern and affection, and I shall never forget it.[19]

Williamson had set himself a punishing task, producing a volume of *A Chronicle of Ancient Sunlight* every year from 1951 to 1969, and this, along with his infidelities, had taken its toll on his marriage by the early 1960s. The stress under which he had placed himself made him a poor correspondent during those years, sometimes more than a year passing without his writing to Aldington; the latter's letters frequently express concern about the lack of communication.[20] When Williamson did write, it was often in order to seek consolation. Aldington would tell him in April 1959: 'I don't think you are forgotten. You are simply suffering from the boycott and virtual censorship imposed by the Establishment because of your unpopular political views.'[21]

In the early months of Aldington's move, Cohen corresponded regularly, despite being in poor health and wheelchair-bound; but in December 1957 he was viciously attacked and robbed by his young male nurse. He never fully recovered and died in June 1958. News of another death came that year; in January H.D. forwarded a letter from Athol Capper telling her of Jessie's suicide. Aldington could probably not have acknowledged his own role in damaging Capper's life (a fact of which H.D. was well aware), but his haste to blame others was jarring:

> This is a damned business about poor Jessie. Of course she never recovered from that unfortunate fact that her first lover was a pederast. And then Athol had that ghastly wound at Ypres, and in consequence was partially blinded. What will become of him? ... It makes me speechless when I think of good innocent people like the Cappers, in their millions, paying for the spurious *réclame* of Lloyd Georges and Churchills, Haigs and Montgomerys, and all the rest of them.[22]

In July 1958 Aldington heard from MacGreevy – for the first time in twelve years. MacGreevy and Beckett were still close friends and Kershaw had met the latter in Paris and given him Aldington's address. MacGreevy had been Director of the National Gallery of Ireland since 1950 but had suffered heart attacks in 1957 and 1958 and was in poor health. 'I have fallen on evil days,' Aldington told him in turn, explaining that he had overworked for a number of years, and been 'insulted by the brutal Anglo-American press for giving the truth about the national hero.' The quiet of Sury was, however, 'most healing'.[23] MacGreevy insisted on sending him sums of money from time to time, reminding him of how frequently in the 1930s Aldington had given him financial assistance. They made plans for MacGreevy to visit Sury when travelling on the Continent on Gallery business, but each time they did so, MacGreevy was taken ill and had to return home. Aldington told Kershaw that MacGreevy was 'a most agreeable and highly cultivated man' but found it necessary to warn him when he was about to meet up with him in Paris: 'Remember that he is very Catholic and chauvinist Irish.'[24] When a complimentary copy of MacGreevy's book on Poussin arrived at Sury, Aldington found it 'full of religious and political bigotries'. 'Except that the prejudices are different they are so violent they might have come from your dear self,' he told Kershaw.[25]

However, the two men had a genuine affection for each other, built on those years in France and Italy in the 1930s, and MacGreevy mourned the actual loss of Prentice and the virtual one of Frere, writing to Aldington in November 1958: 'Maybe we'll all have a party together in France and be happy again and drink to our Charles.'[26] Aldington was sceptical: 'I fear your dream of a meeting with them [the Freres] and me is indeed a dream. ...

Letters are not answered.' He blamed this on the *Pinorman* controversy: 'In my remoteness and ignorance I just set down cheerfully what we all know and took for granted, and the squawks were terrific.' 'That was followed,' he continued, 'by the bogus prince of Mecca. Apparently as a result of those two books, Frere and Billie Collins will never be peers, and much of that ever climbing up a climbing wave by their wives is a sheer waste.'[27] Despite his continuing poor health, MacGreevy tried to be optimistic, writing a year later: '[M]aybe things will all work out for us yet, you and Frere and I will have a happy party, and say an inward prayer for our Charles. But what I look forward to is a couple of days with yourself.'[28]

Catha had to return to Montpellier in the autumn of 1957, having failed in science and mathematics in the *Baccalauréat Général* in both 1956 and 1957, and she rented a room in order to prepare for the *'Philo-Bac'* in the summer of 1958. By now she had a boyfriend, her future husband, Jacques Guillaume, and continued to be passionate about the Midi and about riding, but had few ideas about a career.[29] Aldington thought that, once she had passed her *baccalauréat*, she could become an interpreter, and asked for help and advice from both Kershaw and Randall, in touch as they were with international organisations. He had been working, before moving to Sury, on a revised two-volume edition of the *Viking Book of Poetry of the English-Speaking World*, which was to be published in 1958, and he sold the publisher his interest in the book in order to pay for Catha's final year at the *lycée*.

In the late summer of 1958, having failed her *Philo-Bac*, Catha went reluctantly to London to visit her mother. Writing to Warman just before she left, Aldington expressed concern about her state of mind: 'Catha is here, very depressed about something. She hasn't confided in me so I don't know.'[30] Warman, who had established a good relationship with Catha on her 1956 visit to London, went to visit her. It was to him – rather than to her mother – that she revealed her suspicion that she was pregnant. A test proved negative, but her physical problems required medical treatment, which Warman tactfully and sympathetically arranged. 'I am deeply grateful to you,' Aldington wrote, 'for helping Catha through this dismal trouble.'[31] Perhaps recognising how the failure of communication between them must have hurt him, Catha wrote from London:

> Dearest Daddy, I am now at 'home' (no comment) and madly trying to get away as soon as possible. . . . I do so much want after these two months of misery to collect a bit of peace before the fight again if you see what I mean. . . . I want to say that I have always known that when everything seems desperate I still have my Daddy, I have very often thought it.[32]

She would tell Bryher after her father's death: '[M]y father never talked to me of my relations with men, so I never asked him what he felt.'[33] This constraint applied to his own sexual history too: Catha was not told that H.D. was Aldington's ex-wife until shortly before she visited Zurich in 1959; and, in 1965, on receiving a cutting from Kershaw of an article by Patmore on her relationship with Aldington ('the greatest love of my life'), she remarked to Bryher: '[Y]ou all seem to have had such a fuller and more actif [sic] life than any I can imagine.'[34]

Because of her enforced extended stay in London, Catha missed the 1958 autumn resit for her examinations and had to return to Montpellier for yet another year, studying shorthand and typing, preparing for her examinations the following summer and taking on part-time work as an English tutor. Aldington was able to tell Warman: 'She recovered her spirits very rapidly on getting back here [and] went off cheerfully to Montpellier,' but the events of that summer had left him anxious.[35] 'Catha, unluckily, doesn't like her mother, and I was perhaps wrong in thinking she ought to try,' he told H.D., and later he confided to Bryher: 'It is almost impossible for a man to be both parents.'[36]

The most surprising – and fortunate – event of these years was Bryher's decision at this point to fund Catha's continuing education. 'I want to get Catha settled – and then to die,' Aldington had told H.D.[37] In January 1959 he could tell her that he had slept all night for the first time in years since getting Bryher's 'overwhelmingly kind letter'.[38] Bryher's move was clearly designed to gratify H.D. ('I was delighted and touched when she told me,' H.D. told him), but her kindness to one who had been an enemy for so many years was remarkable.[39] She and H.D. had already – since the Les Rosiers débacle – been sending Aldington gifts of money, which enabled him to spend an enjoyable 1958 Christmas holiday with his daughter, visiting Toulon, Menton, Monte Carlo, Aix and Avignon, ending up at Les-Saintes-Maries-de-la-Mer in Catha's beloved Camargue, and meeting up with the Temples and the Durrells. In May 1959 Bryher suggested that Catha visit Switzerland after her examinations that summer for a vocational assessment and to discuss her plans for the future. She then provided the money for Catha, once her examinations were over (and passed) to spend a month in the Midi before flying to Zurich in October. 'Bryher is the kindest and most generous of friends – this extra holiday in the Camargue has made Catha wonderfully happy. . . . It is a grand farewell to her childhood and without Bryher's help and yours it could not have been done,' Aldington told H.D.[40]

It had been a wonderful summer for them both, starting in early July with a fleeting visit to Pamplona for the *encierro* at the Saint Fermin Festival – both because Catha loved the bulls and as a commemoration

Richard Aldington, Lawrence Durrell, Henry Miller and Frédéric-Jacques
Temple, Pont de Sommières, July 1959

of Campbell, whom they had both loved – followed by three weeks in
Montpellier where Temple had lent them his flat and where the Durrells
and the Millers attended her 21st birthday party. It was Henry Miller's
first – and only – meeting with Aldington and he later commented:

> He was bigger, bolder, kinder, more sympathetic – and far less
> British – than I had pictured him in my mind. . . . Something in his
> eyes which spelled sadness – not human sadness, but the sadness
> of the animal which knows not why it is sad. Or, as if at some

time or other he had experienced a profound betrayal. . . . And then, later in the day, after we had all had dinner together . . . to my surprise he waxed jovial. He laughed, drank, told stories – as a man might who had been deprived of human companionship for many moons.[41]

As for Aldington's impression of Miller, he would write to H.D: 'He is a good kind of American – they do exist!'[42] While in Montpellier he underwent dentistry and medical examinations, all arranged by the kindness of Temple, so was able to return in a confident state to Sury to welcome the Kershaws for their August holiday.

He asked H.D. tactfully: '[W]hen Catha comes to Suisse would you care to see her, or would you rather not?'[43] She reassured him on the matter, adding: 'I only fear that Catha will find it VERY DULL here, en Suisse.'[44] Aldington told her that Catha was thrilled at the prospect of meeting them both, but privately he wondered what Catha would make of the 'Swiss Cottagers' and told Kershaw that he suspected she would like H.D. and dislike Bryher.[45] In the case of Bryher, he was completely wrong. She and Catha took to each other at once; their friendship – and her support for Catha – would last until Bryher's death in 1983. As for H.D., Aldington told her that Catha had found her 'beautiful and sweet' and 'loved her very much'.[46] H.D. replied that Catha's visit had made her very happy. 'She is very endearing + everyone loved DAS MADCHEN,' she told him, thanking him for letting her come to them.[47] 'Catha,' Aldington told Kershaw, 'seems to have done a veni, vidi, vici in Suisse . . . H.D. is enthusiastic – they seem to have made friends at once – and even Bryher is converted.'[48] H.D. would tell George Plank:

> Can you believe it? Catha Aldington turned up through Bryher's inspiration and bounty. This has been a very strange return to Rye, Sussex, where I knew Richard's two sisters. This girl is so strikingly 'Aldington' and though from Montpellier, she seems to have walked out of a cobbled Cinque Ports village.

Indulging her – and Plank's – perennial interest in gossip, she added: 'We can't find out yet the mystery of Richard's marriage and where and why Netta left him. . . . The girl has no connections of any kind with her mother's family except an old grandmother whom she visited in London and who did not seem in the least interested.'[49]

What H.D. did not know was that Plank (himself a regular recipient of Bryher's generosity) had written spitefully to Bryher:

I detest cads like R.A. who send their responsibilities through Hilda to you. Expect you to unravel all the knots. They can always depend on your kind heart and are not disappointed. . . . What I cannot bear is that some people can casually open their mouths and EXPECT to be fed.

A week later he wrote: '[A] man responsible for so much suffering in others perhaps deserves his own. It is true that the child is innocent, and you make me see that she deserves help, and I can only hope that she will be grateful for it.'[50] He asked H.D: 'Are you sure her mama's name is Netta: – she could be *anybody*, from my intuition.'[51] What he had failed to grasp was the genuine affection that was being expressed in this project: H.D.'s for Aldington and Bryher's for H.D. The latter would remark to Aldington in February 1961: '[Bryher] has an uncannily selfless way of VICARIOUS ENJOYMENT.'[52] Ever looking for ways to please H.D., Bryher now had another project in mind: she asked Aldington to find out whether Flint needed any financial support. Both H.D. and Pound were concerned about his welfare and Aldington obtained his address and tried to contact him but without any success; Flint died in March 1960.[53]

The outcome of Catha's visit to Switzerland was her enrolment on an undergraduate course in '*Sciences Sociales*' at the Sorbonne. She was to have a subsidy of a million francs a year, to be paid on a monthly basis. She remained in Paris for only a year, however, transferring to Aix, where she felt more at home, in the autumn of 1960. In 1961 Bryher bought her a car, enabling her to spend her weekends at Les-Saintes-Maries. She would graduate in 1964 and train subsequently to become a psychologist.

The correspondence between H.D. and Aldington continued to be regular, intimate and sustaining for them both. His continued habit of sending erotic pictures – including current beauties such as Brigit Bardot and Gina Lollobrigida – and initiating discussion of their physical attributes, to which H.D. responded with amusement, gave a frisson to the relationship. More intimately, they regularly reminded each other of their former shared life. 'When I think of what our brief time in Rome has meant to me – I am simply staggered,' he told her in December 1957, adding a few weeks later: 'Forty-five years ago today we were in Rome, and life seemed hopeful, however poor one was.'[54] That idyllic Italian holiday of 1912-1913 crops up often. Concerned about the slowness of H.D.'s recovery after breaking her hip, he asks: 'Is there an (unwaxed) corridor in which you can walk and perhaps look over the lake?' Conceding that she has 'a weight of years', he reminds her, nevertheless, of how 'spry' her father was on their 'never-to-be-forgotten-tour'.[55] H.D. in turn asks whether Aldington remembers standing with her and John Cournos outside Buckingham Palace on 4 August 1914, when 'the family appeared at various lighted windows, like dolls in a dollhouse'. When the crowd shouted 'We want war', she recalls Aldington and Cournos shouting back 'We don't', and her fear that they might get trampled to death.[56] One revealing exchange concerned their participation in Imagism. When Aldington commented: 'How bitterly and deeply do I regret having anything to do with it!' H.D.'s response was: 'How sad I am that you so regret having had to do with the old Imagist saga. . . . At seventy-two, it is part of my youth.'[57] While the one writer had not freed himself from his past – or forgiven it, the other had constantly used hers for creative inspiration and, in doing so, acknowledged its contribution to her fulfilment.

Despite her general contentment and rich creative output, H.D. was as nervous as ever and Aldington gave her constant support, sometimes suggesting courses of action but often simply providing affirmation. In September 1958, when, at the urging of Bryher and Pearson, but with some reluctance, she went to the US Embassy to reinstate her US citizenship, he applauded the move, although telling Warman:

> This, though I don't think she knows it, is because Pearson at Yale wants to make his academic reputation by boosting her up as great American poet. He has the Pulitzer prize all teed up as soon as the news is broken, literary talent being, as we all know, a matter of toeing the line and knowing the right people.[58]

It is important to note that this bitterness was not towards H.D. (who never was awarded the Pulitzer Prize) but towards what he perceived as the self-serving literary establishment.

His feelings towards Pearson, whom he had initially suspected of self-interest in his sponsorship of H.D., softened as he realised how much Pearson genuinely valued her work. He demonstrated a similar change of heart towards Harry T. Moore, whom he had also suspected of espousing D.H. Lawrence simply to boost his own academic career. Moore's visits to him at Sury in the summers of 1958 and 1960 established trust, particularly as Moore agreed to excise letters that libelled H.D. from his 1962 edition of Lawrence's letters and arranged in 1959 for Southern Illinois University Press to publish *Mistral*.[59] Aldington's feelings towards that other American D.H. Lawrence scholar, Edward Nehls, were more consistently positive, although they never met. Nehls dedicated the

H.D. and Perdita
Schaffner on Lake
Lugano during
the 1950s

second volume of his *D.H. Lawrence: A Composite Biography* to Aldington
and asked him to write the foreword to the third volume. 'A very nice
fellow, friend of Moore's, but also of mine,' Aldington told H.D.[60]

When, in April 1959, Heydt suggested H.D. learn to drive in order to
give her more freedom, Aldington was prepared to oppose Bryher, who
felt that H.D. was too old. '[Bryher] has been so staunch and loyal it is
hard for me to argue,' wrote H.D. Aldington's response was to send her a
list of driving terms with their German equivalents and various pieces of
advice on driving.[61] Earlier that month, faced with a visit from Perdita,
H.D. confessed: 'I would love to see her but I do feel so humiliated and
unpresentable. I am sure if I make a supreme effort all will be well – I
KNOW that, and I am grateful not to be forgotten. But I know that you
understand.'[62] He did, telling her that he was sure the visit would be 'great
fun', adding in a later letter: 'You must be as strong as possible for the
meeting at the end of the month, which I'm sure will go off well.'[63] Despite
the difference of opinion on the driving issue, he showed constant respect
for Bryher and appreciation of her support for H.D.[64] In 1960, by which
time he was himself a beneficiary of Bryher's generosity, he would tell
Kershaw, who had sent him a cutting of an article about Bryher:

> Not a word about [her] really vast philanthropy. She lives in four
> rooms of that 'factory', an ascetic sort of life, writing, and attending
> to her 'protégés'. She never gives to 'charitable organisations', only
> to persons, and has done more for literature than the bloody Brit
> guvverment [sic] ever did. (It was she who kept old Norman in his
> dotage.)[65]

No sooner had Bryher settled Catha's future, than she turned her attention to H.D.'s concerns about Aldington's health and suggested that he come to Switzerland for a medical diagnosis. 'She does have marvellous ideas,' H.D. told him, 'but is so far ahead of me in energy.'[66] Both she and Aldington felt nervous at the prospect of a meeting. 'I'm so shabby you'd be ashamed for me to be seen,' he wrote, 'but under Catha's tyranny a corduroy complete is being made in Sancerre.'[67] He asked Bryher to be present when the two of them met: 'Hilda will have kittens at seeing me.'[68] H.D. turned, as she had done in 1929, to Pound, now living in Italy since his release from St Elizabeth's in April 1958: 'I have not seen R.A. for twenty-one years + am terribly apprehensive, I mean, merely physically – will I come unstuck?' Pound's response was identical to that of 1929: to the horror of Bryher, he suggested that he come to Zurich too, a proposal very quickly turned down.[69]

The trip proved a pleasure to them all and the medical results were reassuring: exhaustion and overweight were the chief problems. H.D. told Plank (who had, like Pound, been a confidant during her 1929 reunion with Aldington):

> [I]t was all very strange. His voice seemed more charming than ever.
> ... We gossiped long and easily on the superficial, and that was fun
> too. He is, of course, a little heavy, but he always was. His hair is grey.
> Heydt ... spoke of R. as 'an English gentleman' and R. did seem here
> astonishingly English and, as I say, he was easy or at ease after the
> initial inevitable tension. He spoke of things that happened 40 years
> ago, as if it were yesterday, but you know how the past, the real past,
> is printed or photographed on one's mind or in one's psyche.[70]

They had lunched twice at Aldington's hotel and he had visited her twice for tea at the *klinik*; he had also visited Kenwin. Plank was wilfully misunderstanding: 'I am so shocked by the shock to *you* at Richard turning up and telephoning out of the blue! Thank all the gods and goddesses that Bryher was at hand to be a prop – and a very present help in time of trouble.' 'I pity him with all my heart,' he wrote patronisingly (and insincerely) in a subsequent letter, 'because he has made such a mess of his life, it is tragic.'[71]

Aldington was away a week, using the opportunity to visit Vézelay, Dijon, Bourg and Cluny en route. 'How to thank you and Bryher for all you did I know not,' he wrote, once back at Sury, closing the physical distance between them with the comment: 'My green fields this afternoon are as misty as your lake.' In response, H.D. told him: 'It was good to have you bring a new vibration here – or a new old vibration.'[72]

Ezra Pound, Genoa, 1958

He told Durrell: 'She is 73, crawling about still on crutches . . . lonely in that Klinik,' but still 'a noble-looking woman and bright as sunlight.'[73] His visit had increased his anxiety about her circumstances at the Klinik Brunner. She had moved back there in February 1957 to convalesce after her accident and, despite wistful talk of Lugano, and murmurings about the 'semi-invalid atmosphere' of the *klinik*, had not left, constrained by both her difficulties in walking and her emotional dependence on Heydt.[74] One course of action, recommended by Bryher, Pearson and Perdita, was for her to settle in the United States but she told Aldington in the spring of 1959 that, although she was not sure that she could stand another winter in Switzerland, her 'files and roots' were in Europe.[75]

She had been in fairly constant contact with Pound since his release, and letters also passed intermittently between Pound and Aldington. As always, Aldington's feelings towards his old friend fluctuated. In April 1958 he was pleased to hear from H.D. that Pound's 'long martyrdom' was over and hoped that he would find 'a quiet refuge' in Italy, reflecting on the 'amazing courage and energy' with which Pound had borne his thirteen-year incarceration.[76] However, he was also concerned about H.D. becoming too involved with Pound. This may have been partly out of jealousy, and some of his communications with Bryher around this time would support that notion: he told her that Pound was 'in a very jumpy state, with chips on both shoulders and a great sense of his own importance' and that she should not take him seriously 'even as a poet, and politically it's all bunk'.[77] More importantly, however, he was concerned for H.D.'s emotional stability and also for her public reputation, just as she was becoming a celebrated figure in America; he warned Bryher that H.D. should not link up with Pound, who was 'quite discredited except in the neo-Nazi crowd'.[78]

It was a brief letter from Pound in the summer of 1959 that moved him to greater sympathy: 'Cher R/ amid cumulative fatigue, and much that has gone to muddle. Thinking of early friendships and late. This is to say that I have for you a lasting affection.'[79] Aldington told H.D. how 'shattered' he was to receive this note: 'It upset me greatly – seems to have something valedictory about it. . . . It seems to indicate surrender – although I have never doubted the warmth of his heart.'[80] That warmth was displayed in a comment Pound made to H.D.: 'Not since Brigit, Richard, the 4 of us, has there been any harmony around me.'[81] Writing at the end of 1960 to Charles Norman, whose biography of Pound was published that year in the United States, Aldington told him that he had found Pound's letter 'infinitely touching, a flash of "the real Ezra" so long lost "under the rubble"'. Sadly, he added: 'I responded as warmly as I could, but evidently not enough, as nothing happened; and later letters go unanswered.' He – and H.D. –

approved of Norman's book. He told him: 'You have treated Ezra with the respect and affection the better side of him deserves, and you have had the courage to try to tell the truth, not to acquiesce in his later extravagances, absurdities and worse.' He was struck by Norman's phrase, 'This man could have done anything', which, in his view, 'put the whole tragedy in six words'. 'Those who knew Ezra pre-1914,' he explained, 'would agree that no one else at that time seemed to have a more brilliant future.'[82]

When H.D. sent him *End to Torment*, her memoir of Pound, he told her that he had 'wolfed [it] down with the utmost interest and approval' and was now starting to reread it since it was 'a most subtle text which must be reread and brooded over'.[83] He proceeded to type up the manuscript for her. Given public attitudes about Pound, he advised her not to consider publication for the time being, but there seems to have been no jealousy here.[84] His respect for her creative output never wavered, despite his doubts as to whether it was publishable.

Despite his genuine affection for the Pound who had befriended him nearly 50 years earlier and his pity for the ordeal his friend had undergone, he could not forget that Pound had been a non-combatant in the First World War. Quoting to Durrell the well-known lines from *Hugh Selwyn Mauberley*, 'There died a myriad,/ And of the best, among them,/ For an old bitch gone in the teeth,/ For a botched civilization', he commented:

> We don't want his condescending croc's tears. If he had carried down in stretchers sick, wounded and corpses, if he had lived and slept week in, week out, with wounds and death, stood by open graves as the young men were lowered in their blanket coffins, cursing bloody God and the blasted Government, then perhaps he might humbly – not with his conceit – take his place as mourner. He spent the war keeping out of it, like his mate Eliot; and in the name of five years of mute casualties I spit on that particular effusion of a draft-dodging yank.[85]

His own political outlook remained to the left of Pound's, and he would have no truck with the latter's anti-Semitism. Kershaw became a friend of the Mosleys, finding them 'very intelligent, amusing and charming', and the Mosleys next tried to 'woo' Aldington, inviting him to write for *Action*, their relaunched newspaper.[86] He refused, although he did contribute an article on Campbell to the last issue of Diana Mosley's *European*, before it folded in February 1959. Mosley was standing as a candidate in the 1959 General Election and Aldington told Kershaw, 'He hasn't an earthly chance. He outed himself for ever when he did that pseudo-Hitler stunt in the

1930s.'[87] However, he was happy for Catha to accept an invitation to lunch with the Mosleys while she was studying in Paris. He also came to like Michael Harald, a regular contributor to the Mosley publications, whom Kershaw brought to visit him in Sury and who went to Italy to interview Pound in 1960. Harald, he told Warman, was 'a good lad (ex R.A.F. Bomber Command) but fascinated by Mosley's personal charm and culture'.[88]

He had another reason for staying out of right-wing politics. He would write to his brother in July 1961: 'I got an invite from Lady Mosley to go and stay with her and the Bart at Orsay. Refused, as I didn't want to get entangled with politicos, and thought that it would displease my friends in Moscow.'[89] In the USSR he was now an acclaimed writer, although his popularity went back to the 1930s: *Death of a Hero* had first been translated into Russian in 1932, *The Colonel's Daughter* in 1935 and *All Men Are Enemies* in 1937. In 1959 a new edition of *All Men Are Enemies* was published (225,000 copies), followed in 1961 by a *Death of a Hero* in English (100,000 copies) and a translation of short stories taken from both *Roads to Glory* and *Soft Answers*. In the foreword to the second Russian edition of *Death of a Hero*, published in 1935, the writer Ivan Anisomov had spoken of the novel's 'genuine and very bitter realism', claiming that 'Aldington wrote about the "decline of the West" directly, without reserve, mercilessly'. He had, Anisomov, maintained, 'reached the "limit" attainable by a writer within the confines of bourgeois "respectability"'.

In 1957 Mikhail Urnov, Professor of Literature at the Moscow Institute of Printing Arts and member of the Soviet Union of Writers, had written to invite Aldington to Moscow for his 65th birthday, an invitation he had had to turn down on grounds of ill health and because he had to make the move from Montpellier that summer; but he was also dissuaded from the visit on political grounds by everyone from H.D. and Durrell to Randall. In 1960 he received a copy of the recently published third volume of the Russian History of English Literature. Chapter 14 was devoted to himself – 20 pages, he told Warman.[90] He had also begun to receive Russian royalties and advances, which had previously been blocked. He continued to keep in touch with Urnov and with Professor Dilyara Zhantieva of the Gorky Institute of World Literature, who wrote the preface to the English language edition of *Death of a Hero*.

Explaining his surprising popularity in the Soviet Union to Potocki in 1960, he wrote:

> [A]s you say, they perfectly well know that I am not a Left-wing writer, but I think they dislike parlour pinks much more than Tories. Further, I believe that neither the Writers nor the public

is so 'sold' on communist art as the Party wants. . . . The Writers'
Union gets me past the Comrades by passing me off as a chief
critic of bourgeois decadence, who may one day be converted to
the one true faith.[91]

He told Bird the following year:

From the very warm-hearted and (I am sure) sincere letters I get
from Mikhail Urnov and Mrs Zhantieva, I infer that the writers are
very far from toe-ing the Party Line, but have to go cautiously –
and we must help them. They want peace and culture. What do the
Beaver [Beaverbrook], the Rother [Rothermere], the yanquis [sic]
want, but Cold War and more Money For Them?[92]

He was also impressed that in the USSR it was the Union of Writers, not
publishers, who chose foreign books for translation.

His attitude towards the Cold War had always been sceptical. He had
told Bird back in 1953 that he suspected that Russia and America were
'simply head and tail of the same coin' and that what Russia needed was
'a serious world guarantee against American aggression and further
encirclement'.[93] He was incensed by the American spy plane incident of
May 1960, blaming the United States for: 'put[ting] us back in the evil
days of mutual suspicion and hatred'.[94] 'The Yanks have a myth that
everything said by K. or any other Russian means something else,' he told
his brother. 'I think they mean what they say, which the yanks don't. The
Russ wanted a detante [sic], and the yanks have killed that.'[95]

He was not entirely finished with work. He spent at least three hours a
day over the autumn of 1959 working on the revision of the *Encyclopaedia
Britannica* anthology of poetry of the Western world which he had first
completed before leaving the United States in 1946. It would never be
published. In the spring of 1960 he found it a struggle to produce a
'pocket-book' on D.H. Lawrence for the German publisher, Rowohlt.[96] He
toyed with Moore's suggestion of a biography of Durrell but knew that he
had neither the will nor the stamina for a book. 'I can't go on working – an
article even gives me sleepless nights,' he told Durrell. 'You will find that
50 years of earning a living for self and others are quite enough. There
comes a time when one can no more.'[97] Bryher's decision, in January
1960, to pay him an annuity of a hundred dollars a month so that he need
not work settled the matter. Later that year, with the advent of the Lady
Chatterley trial, he would be reminded of that world of publishing and
readership that had almost ceased to concern him. He chose to stay on

the sidelines, refusing Penguin's request for him to appear as a defence witness, but was gratified by the verdict when it came on 2 November. 'True it would have been pleasant to think of Lane picking oakum in Reading Jail,' he remarked to Warman, 'but doubtless if found guilty he would only have been fined, since he is not a degenerate author of genius but a virtuous money-maker.'[98]

Given greater freedom, he was now able to leave Sury more often. The Duttons arrived in England at the beginning of 1960 with their two-year-old son; Dutton had been given a three-month lectureship at Leeds. As soon as the opportunity arose, the couple drove across to France where Aldington, eager for them to meet his two most admired writers, had planned a trip which would take in a visit to Zurich and then proceed south to Nîmes. On 25 March they dined with H.D. Dutton recalls H.D. appearing at the top of the stairs at the Klinik Brunner, 'tall and majestic . . . and waving her arms and the sticks that supported her when she walked', she and Aldington embracing in tears and '[b]ehind all this drama . . . little Bryher, neat and tidy and anonymous in a tweed suit'. 'In contrast,' writes Dutton, 'H.D.'s long dress was stylish, and she had taken great care in making up her face. . . . She was a fascinating mixture of great dignity and gaiety, dragging on a cigarette as she talked.' He remembers Aldington as so exhausted by this meeting that he slept throughout most of their journey through France the next day. Their next engagement, after 'visiting old haunts', was dinner with the Durrells. Dutton recalls Durrell as 'a little man with a neat head, sparky with humour and word-play' and he adds: 'It was obvious that he venerated Richard.'[99] No sooner was Aldington back at Sury than he had to set off for Zurich once more, to pick Catha up from a visit to H.D. and Bryher.

H.D. had been awarded the Gold Medal of the American Academy of Arts and Letters and was due to travel to New York to receive the award. Additionally, *Bid Me to Live*, for which Aldington had failed to find a publisher five years earlier, was to be published in New York by Grove Press. Aldington was delighted with her success but taken aback when H.D. suggested that he accompany her. '[Y]ou would not have to be on view,' she told him. 'The Stanhope is just opposite the Museum + you could stay there incog., with me, in the middle distance, also incog.'[100] The prospect of being in H.D.'s company without the chaperoning presence of Bryher, Catha or the Duttons, or without such pretexts as seeing doctors, must have frightened him. He wrote back: 'New York. What next! My dear girl . . .'[101]

Fortunately, Bryher came up with an alternative companion: Blanche Brunner, grand-daughter of Dr Brunner, the director of the *klinik*. It seems surprising that Bryher herself did not accompany H.D., as she had on her 1956 US visit. Guest suggests: 'It was H.D.'s moment of triumph and she wanted H.D. to prove to herself that she needed no one to assist her in receiving the tributes that would follow.'[102] H.D. wrote to Aldington from New York, telling him about the ceremony and also of her visit to the Metropolitan Museum, where she had felt 'completely at home with Pompeii and archaic Greece'.[103] Once back at the Klinik Brunner, she was once more uncertain about permanent plans, telling him that she did not want to 'get stuck' there again, but unsure whether she could contemplate going to America permanently.

Aldington was able to spend some of the summer of 1960 with Catha in the Camargue, visiting Pamplona again for her birthday and then returning to France for his. In the autumn he spent three weeks in Aix, to see her settled into her new university course. He was back in Sury by the beginning of November but at the end of the month he returned to the Midi, he and Catha spending a few days with the Durrells before flying to Rome for the last two weeks of December. He told H.D. what a 'tremendous stimulus and "uplift"' the trip had been: '[O]ne forgets how footling and dull this mechanical world is compared with the Ancients and the Renaissance.' H.D. had asked them to locate a group of shepherd musicians by the Spanish Steps and give them some money, which she regretted not having done in 1954; remarkably, they were able to do so.[104] However, although Rome was wonderful for Aldington, Catha was often bored.[105] On their return to Aix, she headed back to the Camargue for New Year's Eve, leaving him to spend the start of the New Year alone in the Hotel Sévigné. His being able to do so at a time when the hotel was closed, was due to his being an associate member of the Félibres, an honour bestowed on him in 1954.[106] His love of the region – and its leading poet – had also been recognised in the award of the Prix Frédéric Mistral in 1959.

Catha had meanwhile confided in H.D. about her emotional life and her wish to become engaged to Jacques. H.D. encouraged her but, aware that he was both French and Catholic, advised her to find out about French law. She later told Aldington in a typically convoluted letter:

> Catha wrote me for confidential 'advice' – I was sure you knew of it – but I wrote her – did not mention it to you and don't say I told you – I said: I agree with the IDEA (romance) (???) but she must beware of TRAP, such as nationality problem or/and religion.[107]

Early in February Aldington returned to Sury, where he was visited by Potocki. He told Kershaw:

H.D., by Islay Lyons, 1961

Our squalid hovel here has been honoured by the King of Poland and one of his illegitimate princesses – the English one, brought up by T F Powys. They arrived unannounced and unheralded about 6.30 looking as hungry as the mungrils on The Estate – and ate up everything, drank all my vine [*sic*], and at breakfast the last of my carefully guarded English Breakfast Tea. They then borrowed 20NF, and departed saying they would call in on the way back to England. Such are the Maoris. No Ozzie acts like that.[108]

Kershaw's own visits to the Maison Sallé had become an increased pleasure to Aldington since the birth of Kershaw's son, Sylvain, in March 1960. Warman was given regular reports on the little boy's progress, Aldington telling him in October 1960:

Sylvain is certainly the most energetic and beautiful boy and will probably be the dictator of New South Wales if Alister doesn't sabotage him. I never saw such a beautiful and attractive young child. Even you would be converted. He struts, sings, whistles, trills, grins and blows raspberries with indefatigable energy in the small hours, thus keeping his parent [sic] miserably awake. Trouble is Alister loves him too much. But what can we do?[109]

Spring came to Sury and Aldington described the violets and the cowslips to H.D., but Bryher, delighted by his accounts of his visit to Rome, had another suggestion to make: Venice. He toyed with the idea of a book on the city to justify the trip but she soon persuaded him that he should just enjoy the break.[110] Catha told Bryher: 'Daddy went off to Venice looking ten years younger. It is a real happiness to me to see him take part in life again after so long.'[111] He wrote to H.D.: 'So beautiful is Venice! I spent the morning in the Accademia – such lovely pictures. I wanted to steal them all for you!' A few days later he told her: 'As France is the last beleaguered citadel of European living, so Venice is the last little fortress of pre-machine times.' With characteristic pessimism he added: 'And the machine men and the money men will destroy it.'[112] She was inundated with letters and postcards, as was Bryher.[113] Remembering 1930, he sent cards to MacGreevy, as well as to Warman, Kershaw and Durrell. On 12 May, he gave H.D. a detailed account of his 'lovely "last day"', saying that he did not know how to thank her and Bryher for 'these enchanting five weeks'. 'Tomorrow,' he finished, 'I shall take the slow boat to Piazzale Roma, for a last, lingering look at the Grand Canal.'[114] Bryher's response was to send him the funds for a further week. It was 18 May before he set off on the journey back to the Midi, to Catha's stone cottage, Mas Dromar, at Les-Saintes-Maries. He told Bryher: 'Venice was an enchantment, and I feel in better health than for years.'[115] However, despite H.D.'s urging, he had been unwilling to contact Pound while in Venice:

Bryher , by Islay Lyons, 1961

After that terrible indictment by Hausner of Eichmann, the
Nazis, the Germans and their admirers, I CAN'T, I just can't.
It is too horrible & I just can't condone it, I am cutting off all
communication with pro-Nazis I know. If this is smug, well it is,
but it isn't vile, cold-hearted torture and murder.[116]

H.D. had meanwhile had a setback. On the death of Dr Brunner, his son had decided to sell the *klinik*. H.D., having contemplated a move on so many occasions, was now terrified at the prospect. Bryher arranged for her to move into the Hotel Sonnenberg in Zurich. Aldington told her: '[S]o glad you have found a refuge in the Hotel Sonnenberg. I KNEW you would – have been putting up candles to saints for you, this morning to Santa Lucia.' She wrote back:

> Br thinks of everything + worked so very hard, bringing bags and books from Verena [her home at the *klinik*]. The last days were, in a way, almost funny, two near-suicides, a girl breaks arm, old lady goes down with double pneumonia. Br said, 'stay in bed – anything might happen'. But I could not let her do the heavy packing alone + here I am with one full, stuffed bookcase, radio, a large bathroom, a large balcony + the galaxy of Z underneath at night + raging song-birds at dawn – all new furniture, but not ultra-modern + two lovely flower-prints + room, a garden, with lilac, muguet, red roses. . . . Telephone by my nice, low bed – I hardly know myself + feel that I have descended from space or up out of the horrendous depth. There are thick woods on one side + the open view ahead across the lake. The candles must have 'worked', thank you + them.[117]

Despite the approving nature of the comments, there is here that breathlessness characteristic of H.D. when in an acutely nervous state.

A month later she told him that she had had 'a siege of sleepless nights, Br said due to suppressed anxiety or ANGST about the Brunner break-up'. 'But I think that I am out of the woods,' she reassured him. A few days later, she told him that she was receiving injections for 'cardiac insufficiency'. Bryher had alerted him to the seriousness of her condition, and he had meanwhile written to say how 'grieved indeed' he was to hear that the delayed shock of 'that sudden and brutal up-rooting from Küsnacht' had made her so ill. He told her that she must not exert herself to write and that he would depend on Bryher for news.[118] On 6 June she had a stroke.

22. From Tragedy to Triumph
1961-1962

Although H.D. recovered her mobility quite soon and could understand what was said to her, she could neither speak, read nor write. Aldington had to correspond with Bryher for news. As the weeks went by, reports fluctuated in their level of optimism. A month after her stroke, he told his brother that she was improving daily, able to eat and to walk with the aid of her nurse's arm, and that speech was beginning to return.[1] Six weeks later, when he realised how serious her condition was, he suggested to Bryher that she be given an advance copy of *Helen in Egypt*, shortly to be published by New Directions: 'If she can read at all her own familiar words might help her to recover language.'[2] Bryher asked him to come to Zurich with Catha for H.D.'s 75th birthday on 10 September.

Meanwhile, he had introduced complications into his life. Writing to Netta from Catha's *mas*, the day after his return from Venice, he had asked: 'Do you want to come down here? It is hideously uncomfortable, but there are hotels. You ought to see the place. . . . I can meet you by appointment at any place you like. . . . Is it possible to fly to Tours?' Then he suggested: 'If we met there, we could run down the Loire a bit, and glimpse one or two chateaux and then turn south to avoid the rush.'[3] That Netta should visit her daughter was a reasonable suggestion; that he and his wife should have a holiday alone together was unprecedented. 'She is a splendid woman,' he had told Gluckman a year earlier, 'sensual and not romantic.'[4] Now Gluckman was regaled with a full account of the 1961 holiday in respect of Netta's physical charms and their sexual practices.[5] He revealed that Netta, though living alone, led a full sexual life. The contact with Gluckman, still living in South Africa, had been re-established in 1955 when she had written to him after the publicity surrounding *Lawrence of Arabia*, but only became regular in 1960, when she sought help for placing articles and he put her in touch with his agents in the UK and the US. His letters quickly took on their former prurient quality, at his instigation and with her compliance.

Richard and Catherine Aldington, 1962

From everyone else the holiday was kept secret. Whether Catha was aware of the revival of her parents' relationship, and, if so, how she viewed this development, is not clear. Aldington told Gluckman that he had kept the contact between mother and daughter down to less than 24 hours, 'to avoid the usual antagonisms'.[6] In July, after successfully completing her *Propédeutique*, Catha came for a short stay at Sury with Jacques.[7] The Kershaws also came for their summer holiday visit that month. Aldington was surprised to find how well Kershaw and Jacques got on with each other but confided to Netta that it was probably because they were both 'Fascists'.[8] This was a time, as the Algerian War came to a crisis, when political opinions in France were as sharply polarised as they had ever been, but it is interesting to note in his ongoing discussions about the war with his brother and with Warman, that Aldington distanced himself completely from the colonialists and the supporters of the *Organisation Armée Secrète*.[9] French politics, however, rarely seemed to stir him as much as British.

The other complications concerned his own family. His relations with his siblings had improved since his mother's death in 1953 and he had expressed concern for Margery (and for Pattie, his younger sister, Margery's dependent) on the death of her husband in January 1960, particularly in relation to the continuation of her late husband's Indian railway pension. His correspondence with his brother shows that he heard quite regularly from her after this and was reassured about her financial circumstances; indeed by November 1961, much to his horror, she was suggesting that he and Catha come to live with her in Rye.[10] He felt compassion for her ('Poor Molly – Life is a lousy business for her') but her intense Catholicism, which must have reminded him of his father, and what he described as 'the awful repressed energy of the unemployed female', reminiscent perhaps of his mother, repelled him.[11] Now she suggested that she come to visit him, and he turned to his brother for help: 'Molly hinted at coming over here in August by car with a female friend. Discourage this in the name of god and his blessed mother. The main French roads are already a pandemonium of tourists and an English car . . . is really dangerous.'[12] His grounds for putting his sister off appear rather disingenuous.

He had also been in contact since 1954 with another branch of the family, his brother's first wife and the two (adult) children of that marriage, Jennifer and Tim.[13] When Jennifer had first written to him he had responded: 'I have always thought that relatives and so on were people better to let alone; your letter changed my ideas on that subject.'[14] Tim Aldington, having trained in Agricultural Engineering, had spent almost three years as an Agricultural Field Officer in Tanganyika and in the summer of 1961 had just returned to Britain. He was 25 years old and his sister, 28. The family had asked if they might visit and Aldington had arranged for them to arrive on 4 September. He took them on a trip to Vézelay one day to see the abbey and to have a restaurant meal, as a change from his home cooking. He and Catha, however, had to reach Zurich on the night of the eleventh: Bryher was to see H.D. on her birthday, the tenth, and he and Catha on the twelfth. He explained to his relatives that he had to visit a 'friend' in Zurich who was seriously ill, and they left in time for him to depart as planned.

He was hugely anxious at the prospect of seeing H.D.: 'I feel that she will not want to see me while this speech difficulty remains,' he told Bryher, and he wrote to Pearson: 'I think Hilda might like to see Catha, but I doubt it would be wise for me to present myself. I think she would not like her ex-husband to see her with these disabilities.' Catha knew her father well enough to know that this was about his own distress; telling Bryher how nervous and upset he was, she commented: 'I suppose that when one's life has been so attached to Hilda's as Daddy's is, it will be painful for him to see her unable to speak.'[15] The visit was made; they stayed in Zurich for two days, but only Catha was permitted by the doctors to see H.D. They returned via Sury to Catha's *mas* at Les-Saintes-Maries and on 2 October moved to Aix so that Aldington could support her as she started her final two years at the university, specialising now in Psychology. He would stay in what had become his usual accommodation, the Hotel Sévigné. 'They have let me have a rather nice room looking over a quiet patio with shrubs, flowers and small trees, with plenty of sun,' he told his brother. 'If I like it, I may stay on for some time.'[16] He would remain there for nearly six months.

H.D. died on 27 September. Bryher sent a telegram and followed it up with a letter, but they were sent to Aix, so it was 2 October before Aldington knew. A copy of *Helen of Egypt* had been placed in her hands the day before she died. 'I dashed over yesterday,' Bryher told him:

> I was able to see her – I have seen many dead – but no one more beautiful and as if she were going to open her eyes and laugh at us and although it had happened eighteen hours before she seemed scarcely cold. I know it must have been a horrible shock for you – I shall miss her terribly but I do feel that in a way it was merciful. She seemed to be getting worse almost every day. But her mind was there and she minded the frustration terribly.

H.D.'s partner and closest friend for over 40 years, she signed her letter to him, 'All my sympathy'.[17] He replied:

> It is a great shock and grief, although I have been trying to prepare for it, but I had hoped it would not be so soon. But after all it is best that she should not have gone on suffering. What more can be said? Only that I hope you will now be able to rest and to recover. It has been a great strain for you.

A few weeks later he told her: 'It has been much more of a shock and loss to me than I had expected. I had got into the habit of noting things to tell her in letters and picking up postcard photographs I thought might interest her. So that I am constantly reminded of the loss.'[18]

The first letter of sympathy he received was from MacGreevy, who had seen the notice in *The Times* on 29 September and written immediately. '[Y]our appreciation of her gifts and your tender thoughts for her,' he wrote, 'have always been amongst the rarest and finest things in your character. And I know enough to realise that she appreciated them and reciprocated them. . . . [A]t the level of poetry, it seems to me that you and she never ceased to belong to each other.' He recalled their meeting in Florence for dinner in 1931: 'Between you, you and HD created an atmosphere that remains a fragrant memory.'[19] It was MacGreevy to whom Aldington would confess several months later: 'The loss of her fills me with a great void.'[20]

Closer to hand, there were the Durrells. With perhaps a little less understanding of the place of H.D. in Aldington's life, Durrell wrote: 'I know what you feel. And yet a poet's death is never wholly sad in the sense of a life unlived – because the work is there, like the after-taste of a wine of high vintage.'[21] It was a comfort to have friends less than two hours away and he would spend Christmas that year with them. Warman was renting the Frere villa at Cap Ferrat in October and drove the 200 kilometres to Aix to take him out for dinner. Aldington had taken his car off the road as an economy – Catha had hers – and was therefore dependent on friends to come to him. Another visitor – and still regular correspondent – was Potocki, who came to see him in December. His loss of H.D. seems to have made him more conscious of the affection and kindness of those around him, including the Durrells, Warman and Bryher, but also his own brother. Over the years his letters had often barely concealed his frustration at Tony's inability to understand and resolve problems which, in some cases, were intractable, certainly for a country solicitor with little experience of the world of publishing: his quarrels with Frere, his debts to the Patmores, his tax affairs and so on. Now he wrote to him: 'Your knowledge of and interest in my books are most heartening.'[22]

He was also visited by someone from his past: Charles Pearce of Duell, Sloan and Pearce, who was hopeful of bringing out a 'Selected Poems'; but the firm had just been bought by the Meredith Publishing Company and nothing would come of the idea. In December he heard from two men (perhaps aware of his bereavement) who had always been firm defenders of his work. C.P. Snow wrote to tell him how much he regretted that they hadn't met for so many years. 'We must meet somewhere and somehow next year,' he concluded, sending his 'affectionate good wishes'.[23] William Haley wrote that he still found Aldington's writings about D.H. Lawrence 'truer than anything'. 'I do not suppose, however, you look much into the past,' he continued:

> Do tell me something about how you spend the present. What are you writing? And do you any longer feel the old Artifex anxiety about the world or have you given it up as hopeless? Probably not. I also suspect that under your pessimism and rage at the folly and futility of modern society there was a tough innate streak of confidence in the future of the ordinary man.[24]

A surprising boost – if a half-hearted one – to Aldington's reputation came with the publication in October 1961 of *Lawrence of Arabia: The Man and the Motive* by the diplomat and Conservative politician Anthony Nutting (historical adviser to Horizon Pictures, the production company for David Lean's 1962 film, *Lawrence of Arabia*). Crawford describes the Nutting biography as 'essentially a paraphrase of *Seven Pillars*'.[25] This is accurate, except in relation to the final chapter, 'The Motive', in which Nutting tries to account for Lawrence's departure from Damascus in September 1918 and his enlistment in the RAF in terms which Aldington would have found acceptable. Nutting even refers to Lawrence's 'silly pretensions' that he had been offered high-ranking positions. This, of course, fired up Liddell Hart ('Diddle Hart, who will go on blustering and bluffing to the end', Aldington told his brother), who responded to the *TLS* critical review of the book with a characteristically disputatious letter; the reviewer responded that, while Liddell Hart 'understandably wished to adhere to the opinions which he formed in the 1920s ... other people must be allowed to revise early judgements in the light of later knowledge'. 'In that process,' he continued, 'Mr Aldington played an undeniable part, although it is common ground that he went much too far.'[26] Aldington told Potocki: 'The Times and TLS came out at least 50% in my favour. And Muggeridge in the New Statesman was witty, and very contemptuous of TEL and Nutting.' Kershaw wrote to him: [Y]ou cannot deny that your tribute to the Colonel has done its job. Ten years ago nobody would have questioned anything about him: now nobody can refer to him without at least conceding that he was 50% phoney. And the rest will follow.'[27] Meanwhile, the production of Terence Rattigan's *Ross* – still playing in the West End after two years – and the publicity surrounding the David Lean film, which would be released at the end of 1962, had vastly increased sales of the Four Square edition of Aldington's book. He told Warman in December 1961 that, while 3,650 copies had been sold in 1960, the first half of 1961 had already seen sales of 7,123.[28]

In February came a letter from wholehearted admirers, the Soviet Union of Writers, conveying once more an invitation to visit the USSR for his birthday – this time his 70th. He and Catha were invited for a three-week visit with all flights and expenses paid; and this time the friends whose counsel he sought – his brother, Bryher, Kershaw and Warman – were encouraging. He returned to Sury in March with his plans for the next few months worked out: a week's touring with Netta in May and his visit to the Soviet Union in June and July. The holiday with Netta, as in the previous year, was a secret. He told his brother: 'I have to take a friend on a 10-day tour round France. In a way it is rather a bore, but it makes a change,' and his niece, Jennifer, was informed that he was going on a ten-day tour of France, 'taking an old friend who spends most of the year in a London office'. On his return both Tony and Bryher were told that he was back from his trip with his 'friend from London.'[29] Williamson had to be kept in the dark about both projects: 'In May I must give up a fortnight to drive an old friend round France during the brief annual escape from London. In July Catha and I have a foreign invite for three weeks which can't be avoided.'[30] It was not merely a desire to avoid a shocked response; after the T.E. Lawrence affair he was not sure how much this particular friend could be trusted to be discreet. Aldington did not want his intentions to reach journalists and commentators before the visit took place.

The peace of Sury – and to be amongst his books again – was a pleasure after the busy atmosphere of Aix. He was reminded of the kindness of his neighbours, who had started the central heating for him before he arrived and left eggs and wine for his first meal.[31] It was also a joy to see the Kershaws again for their Easter holiday – along with their son. 'The little boy is really delightful,' he told his brother, 'not only handsome and quick, but very sensitive. At the age of two he really loves music, not just noise but music. Remarkable.'[32] He wrote to Williamson to obtain a signed copy of *Tarka the Otter* for Sylvain.[33] One sad piece of news came in June: the death of Carl Fallas, who had been virtually an invalid for the previous two and a half years. Aldington wrote immediately to Florence, sending her money, and – more productively – he also wrote to Bryher, who took it upon herself to provide continuing financial support – and affectionate correspondence – until Florence's death in 1965. Florence had never lost her own affection for Aldington, telling him in December 1958: 'I was thinking the other day of all the pleasant memories I have of you in all the years I've known you.'[34]

The tour with Netta in May took in Orléans, Azay-le-Rideau, Brantôme, Les Eyzies, Saint-Bertrand-de-Comminges, Les-Saintes-Maries-de-la-Mer, Nîmes and Montluçon. Catha was preparing for her examinations so the visit to Les-Saintes-Maries was a brief one. Once her examinations were over, she arrived in Sury in time to depart with her father to Paris on 16 June, where they were to obtain their Russian visas. There, at last, Aldington and MacGreevy had their reunion, their first meeting for 24 years. MacGreevy wrote subsequently:

[Richard] looked as young and at least as debonair as he had looked a quarter of a century earlier. And he was as sympathetic as ever. . . . It had been a happy reunion and as we said au revoir and they drove away, waving and smiling, leaving me on the pavement outside my picture gallery, I think we all hoped we should be meeting again soon.[35]

With exquisite timing, Kershaw had also arranged for Aldington to dine with the couple whose acquaintance he had avoided for so long: the Mosleys.

On Friday, 22 June, Aldington and Catha flew to Moscow. They landed at Sheremetyevo Airport after a three-and-a-half-hour flight, to be met by Urnov and his son Dmitri along with an interpreter, journalists and photographers, and were taken to the Peking Hotel, where there were two interviews before dinner and a drive around Moscow. That week they visited the Kremlin, Tolstoy's home, Yasnaya Polyana (where they met his grandson), the Gallery of Western Art and two publishing houses. They visited Zhantieva at her home, lunched in their hotel with Alexei Surkov, the secretary of the Writers' Union, and went to lunch at the Writers' Union Club, where Urnov and Zhantieva questioned Aldington closely about his life and work. ('Tired,' he wrote in his diary, 'but hope and think I made no dangerous statements.') There was also time for gift shopping and for chatting to the large number of ordinary people who came up to him in the streets, shops and museums to talk to him about his books.[36]

On Wednesday, 27 June, they made an overnight train journey to Leningrad and were met by V.M. Moldavsky of the Writers' Union. In a subsequent article about the visit Moldavsky recalled seeing 'a rosy-cheeked, blue-eyed, tall old man ... rather proud of his new slightly crumpled suit-coat'.[37] They were taken to the Hotel European and, after a rest and lunch, to the Museum of Russian Art and then for a drive around the sites of Leningrad. Their five-day stay included visits to the Peterhof Palace, the Summer Garden, the Bronze Horseman, the Voltaire Library – and a modern housing development. At a meeting in the Mayakovsky Writers' Home, they met four writers, including the poet Vsevolod Rozhdestvensky, and Aldington spoke to them about D.H. Lawrence and Robert Louis Stevenson.[38] They attended a performance of Tchaikovsky's *Eugene Onegin* and two performances of folk dancing. For Aldington the high points of the five days in Leningrad were his two visits to the Hermitage Museum, where he surprised Moldavsky with his knowledge of the collection. On Sunday, 1 July, he appeared on Russian television for a 20-minute interview, in which he advised the young people of the Soviet Union to value their cultural heritage and make the most of the opportunities presented to them. On the following day there was an excursion to one of the country homes for writers at Komarovo and then a visit to their guide's *dacha*. At midnight they boarded the train for Moscow: 'Several writers to see us off, one with

Richard Aldington broadcasting in URSS, July 1962

flowers and all friendly, waving as we left.'[39] Moldavsky recalled: 'Richard
Aldington arose before us as the denouncer of the petty bourgeoisie of
all sizes and shapes. We perceived him to be one of the most truthful of
all writers and one who was closest to us.' Moldavsky was not the first
observer, however, to feel that Aldington's calm exterior covered a personal
wound. He guessed that he was a lonely man.[40]

Back in Moscow, having slept badly on the overnight train, they had
to be at the Writers' Union for a lunch hosted by the journalist and
novelist Boris Polevoi: 'a one-eyed man who had fought at the Battle of
Stalingrad, an entertaining and jovial Georgian who drank the better part
of a bottle of vodka and a bottle of wine while he told good stories and
jokes'.[41] Later they attended a reception at the All-Union State Library of
Foreign Literature, where a highlight was meeting Ivy Litvinov.[42] The next
day consisted of visits to Lenin's apartment in the Kremlin ('a puritanical
writer's dwelling, incongruous in all that splendour') and the Cathedral
of the Annunciation.[43] On Thursday, 5 July, they were driven to a holiday
camp of 'Pioneers' and then to the *dacha* of the novelist Konstantin Fedin,

Richard and Catherine Aldington in the Gardens of Peterhof,
June 1962

Chair of the Soviet Writers' Union.[44] There, in a 'literary gathering', they
met Yekaterina Peshkova and were given 'a sumptuous spread'.[45] Aldington
found Fedin, who was the same age as himself, 'amusing and well bred'.

As Friday, 6 July, was Catha's birthday, she was taken to see horses and
to drive a Russian *sulky* (a low, two-wheeled carriage), while Aldington
visited the Gallery of Russian Art. That evening they attended the official
celebration of their visit at the Writers' Club. It was the climax of what
had been throughout a hospitable and gratifying tour. 'There were at least
twenty-five people present,' recorded Aldington, 'including a guitar-player
and one of the best Russian tenors.' It was 'a most friendly and moving
affair with pretty speeches from several people, including Surkov, who is
a member of the Supreme Soviet, and Urnov'.[46] Aldington attempted to
reply, but was 'cut short by emotion'. Later, Urnov recollected that speech:

> Several times in my life I have suffered from the literary fraternity,
> and I am accustomed to shrugging my shoulders in answer to

insults and pinpricks. Here in the Soviet Union, for the first time in my life I have met with extraordinary warmth and attention. This is the happiest day of my life. I shall never forget it.[47]

He was presented with a written address from Pavel Chuvikhov, the Director of the Publishing House of Foreign Literature, which read:

Dear and much respected Richard Aldington

The Publishing House of Foreign Literature warmly congratulate you, a remarkable writer and very dear friend, on the glorious anniversary of your 70th birthday. We are happy to have the opportunity of congratulating you here in the Soviet Union where millions of readers know you and love you. The breadth and youthfulness of your writings, their true humanity and anti-militaristic feelings, bring your books to the hearts of a very wide circle of readers, to the hearts of the whole of progressive mankind.

Your novels, *Death of a Hero*, *The Colonel's Daughter*, *All Men Are Enemies*, are very popular indeed among Soviet readers. We, the staff of this Publishing House, are proud that last year we published a very large edition of your collected stories under the title *Farewell to Memories* – short stories which had not before appeared in Russian. These stories, written like your other works, vividly, with great skill, and great courage, have had an enormous and well-deserved success.

We greatly appreciate your feelings of friendship and sincere goodwill towards our country, where readers love you and your books. We believe that our friendship and understanding will grow and strengthen.

Wishing you, our dear friend and guest, wealth, strength, long and fruitful years of life, and success to all your endeavours.[48]

The letter was signed by the seventeen writers who were present, and Grigori Vladikin, who had published the recent editions of *All Men Are Enemies* and *Death of a Hero*, delivered a eulogy and announced the commissioning of a translation of *Women Must Work*. On Sunday, 8 July, Aldington's 70th birthday, they were driven to Valentin Kataev's *dacha* for 'an excellent lunch', during which Kataev invited him to come and study with him in the coming winter.[49] That evening they had supper in Urnov's home, with his wife and two sons and Zhantieva.

On Tuesday, 10 July, they flew back to Paris. Kershaw wrote subsequently:

Even his letters had not prepared me for the first sight of him on his return. As he got out of the car at the cottage in Maison Sallé where we were waiting for him, he looked younger and happier than I had ever seen him in the fifteen years since we had first met. It seemed impossible that he was seventy years of age and had just completed so long a journey.

Kershaw speaks of the 'inevitable' presents, including ones for all the neighbours. The Kershaws returned to Paris a few days later and their last sight of him was as he waved them goodbye, 'handsome, unbelievably vigorous, full of life'.[50] It had, however, been an exhausting three weeks. 'In spite of every kind consideration for my age,' he told Durrell, 'I did get tired and shall be glad to rest here.'[51]

Catha had to return to the Midi to prepare for resitting her summer examinations. He was alone and spent the next fortnight writing to tell his friends and family about the experience and sending them the gifts he had purchased, as well as sending his friends in the Soviet Union his heartfelt thanks and signed copies of the books in which they had expressed an interest. He told Bryher (whom he had to thank for a birthday gift):

> From several different sources I learned that the three most popular English novelists there are Dickens, H G Wells and Aldington (in that order), closely followed by Maugham and Priestley. They are interested, but less, in Joyce and D H Lawrence, but greatly dislike Virginia Woolf and Tom Eliot whom they consider false talents. To my grief they are very doubtful about Larry Durrell, but may come around. I tried to find out what it was in my novels is liked by what we should call 'working class readers' there, and they agreed that first it was the sincerity and profundity of the emotions, then the vividness of the writing, and then that I so much dislike 'philistines'! So there it is.[52]

He told Durrell that he had found Russians the most cheerful and warm-hearted people he had ever met. 'The interviews as translated to me,' he told his friend, 'were scrupulously exact and the numerous photographs excellent.' 'I knew I was read there,' he continued:

> but didn't know how widely, and I certainly didn't know that I was revered and loved. I was inundated with flowers and letters of good wishes – one elderly woman came a 12-hrs rail journey just

to see me for ten minutes. No matter where I went the mention of my name by the interpreter brought instant attention and smiles and even hand-clapping.

He had received many gifts, the most prized of which was a folio of coloured reproductions of the Eikons.[53]

Thanking Warman for the birthday telegram he had sent to Moscow, he asked whether his friend was coming to France soon and suggested that he might like to call in on him and see some of his Russian photographs and presents. Again, it was the reception he had received from ordinary people that he remarked on: 'Every time the interpreter mentioned my name in a shop or any other public place people instantly thronged round to shake hands and thank me for the books.'[54] His letters to MacGreevy and to his brother were in a similar vein, the one to Tony ending: 'The Russians are really the kindliest and warmest people in the world – such a pity they have to be socialists.'[55]

Bryher received a much more detailed and serious political reflection. He conceded that the press limitations in USSR were 'grotesque' but saw 'no gutter press or strip-tease and libel journalism'. Opera, ballet and theatre were open to everyone and 'always thronged', religion tolerated though not 'State-supported'. He had observed that clothes and food seemed dear, but books and records cheap, and that everyone had television – 'of course a great weapon of propaganda'. 'Everything . . . seems devoted to heavy industry,' he told Bryher:

> The government believes that the old regime was overthrown because it neglected the people, used harsh police methods, persecuted writers and painters, and irritated the factory workers. So the people are daily told that they 'own' everything, the police are the most amiable and gentlest I've seen, writers are protected, paid, but severely controlled, and the factory workers watched.

He described the landscape: '[It] was melancholy even in summer, though a little cheered by beautiful silver birches and wild flowers, particularly yellow iris and wild water-lilies. From the main road the country seemed poorly cultivated, the pastures and gardens weedy, the villages dull, the country people apathetic.'[56]

A surprise visitor arrived at Maison Sallé: his nephew Tim, who was camping in Cosne, on his way home from a holiday in Spain and the south of France. They shared 'the inevitable glass – or two – of wine', but Tim, noting how tired his uncle seemed, declined his invitation to stay for dinner.[57] Meanwhile, his 70th birthday – and his visit to Moscow – had gone unnoticed in the British press, except in *The Sunday Times* where Philip Day, in an article entitled 'Richard Aldington at Seventy', noted that relations between Aldington and his native country were not of the best: 'The climate over here, one might say, does not suit him; neither the weatherwise climate – Aldington's chest has never quite thrown off the effects of gas in the First World War – nor the social and intellectual climate, against which he has been girding for most of his life.' Arguing that Aldington had usually managed to use his biographical subjects 'as a stick for beating his pet hates – selfishness and hypocrisy as exemplified in organised social life', Day commented that what Aldington had said about T.E. Lawrence 'needed saying' although 'perhaps not with such evident relish'. He concluded that Aldington entered his 70s, 'as a vigorous and active man of letters, self-contained as ever, busy with many projects', that his books and translations were appearing and reappearing in the Soviet Union and the United States and that 'he lives cheerfully and works zestfully.'[58] It was hardly praise on the level of Pavel Chuvikhov's encomium, but, with the exception of Haley's articles, it was more positive recognition than Aldington had received from the British press for many years.

On the morning of Saturday, 27 July, he drove into the village, as usual, to collect his mail. Shortly afterwards, his neighbour, Madame Rezard saw him sitting in the garden with his head in his hands. She called two other neighbours, Maxime and Suzanne Gueneau, for help and they assisted him into the house and telephoned for a doctor. He had suffered a heart attack. They stayed with him and towards midday he died. Kershaw and Catha arrived early the following morning, followed shortly by Temple.

Afterwords

The visit to the Soviet Union may have put more strain on Aldington's health than it could take, but it was a fitting end to his career, a triumph – and a contrast with some of the obituaries that appeared in the British press. The *Manchester Guardian* reviewer commented that 'the later Aldington often had a sour style' and found it typical of him that he had gone to the USSR and not Britain for his 70th birthday. He observed that Aldington's 'creative gifts' 'often seemed to work only sporadically' and that, 'like many of the writers of his generation', he had 'found the form and passion of his best work' only when trying to deal with the horrors of the First World War.[1]

The Times published a much fuller and more insightful obituary, almost certainly written by Haley. Conceding that '[t]here were times when [Aldington's] anger betrayed him' so that he 'wrote beneath his true bent', the writer argued that 'the tendency to write him off as a discomfited railer of no consequence' was wrong, that '[h]is anger was directed at the stupidity of mankind' and that '[h]is idea of what human society might be had something fine about it'. *Death of a Hero, All Men Are Enemies, Women Must Work* and *A Dream in the Luxembourg* were praised, as was his critical writing, but *The Colonel's Daughter* was criticised for showing 'some of the crudity and tastelessness which was to mar some of his later work'. After *Women Must Work*, 'it could be said that Aldington's creative writing ceased ... none of his subsequent writings – outside his biographies – fulfil[ling] the promise of his earlier work [and] some books, such as *Pinorman* ... better forgotten'. Nevertheless, the writer concluded, there were many readers who valued his work on D.H. Lawrence, or the charm of *A Dream in the Luxembourg* or the way in which he had inspired them to read French literature.[2]

David Holloway in the *Daily Telegraph* called Aldington a 'brilliant and bitter writer' and remarked that '[h]is talent was great but there was something missing'. 'Whether this was lost in Flanders in 1918 or was a more fundamental flaw, no man can tell,' he added. He nevertheless conceded that: 'Aldington's brilliance in so many fields of literature has been rivalled by few of his generation and is indeed rare at any time.' Anthony Curtis, in the same paper, was more enthusiastic, describing the writer as 'an English literary all-rounder of formidable genius, one of the truly independent minds of the age', and arguing that in none of the genres he attempted 'did he fail to write something brilliant and trenchant that caused many people to stand up and protest'. He was a master of biographical writing, with his 'combination of scholarship and imaginative insight'. 'If the modern "angry young man" cared to learn intellectual discipline,' concluded Curtis, 'he could not do better than to go to the works of Aldington.'[3]

Aldington would not have been surprised to read a letter from Read to Church:

> Poor Richard Aldington has gone. A sad life on the whole. He was destroyed by ressentment [sic] – he could not bear the thought of other people's success. But I liked him very much – something very open and generous in his nature. His great success in the USSR must have been an ironic consolation – he was a Tory at heart, in spite of his hatred of England.[4]

Church's own verdict, in the final volume of his memoirs, was that Aldington was a man 'incapable of finding his way home' – 'a terrible fate'.[5]

Rathbone, a more loyal friend, was shocked to hear of Aldington's death. She wrote to Cunard: 'For years, as you know, Richard and I had not met, not written. Therefore my sorrow may be considered foolish. But I can't somehow bear him not to be in this world.'[6] A year later she was still writing: 'I wish he had not died. That wish is not just selfish. For his own sake I would like him to be still alive.'[7] In the summer of 1964, freed at last, by her mother's death, from her duties as a carer, she travelled to south-west France to stay with Cunard – and then made her way north to Sury to lay flowers on Aldington's grave, before travelling on to Paris at the invitation of the Kershaws and where 'much talk of Richard went on'.[8]

Other devoted friends made their tributes in *Richard Aldington: An Intimate Portrait*, the volume compiled by Kershaw and Temple. Just two may speak for the rest. MacGreevy wrote:

> Most of his values were not mine, yet as a friend I found him one of the most forbearing, most generous, most patient, most devoted and to crown all, most laughter-loving, friends I have

ever had. In his personal relationships he, who could write so angrily of the collective shoddinesses that constitute what the Gospel calls 'the world', was one of the most courteous of men. He enjoyed conversation and as a conversationalist was himself not only interesting but winning. His erudition was immense but it was the erudition of the humanist not of the pedant.[9]

Randall wrote:

I don't think that those writers – English writers, at any rate – who wrote about Richard Aldington after his lamented death could possibly have known him personally. Otherwise they would surely have emphasised his generous nature, his kindliness, his sense of humour, his deep affection, love of children and essentially tolerant, scholarly and civilised outlook which, to those who knew him well, shone through all his disillusionment and frustration.

Randall concluded:

On the whole, it seems to me, Richard had not a happy life; he was so often beset by personal problems and anxieties, and it is no mitigation to say they were sometimes brought upon him by himself [but] the picture of Richard that will always be in my mind is that of a merry, humorous, kindly man. I think that it was this Richard, Richard in a time of happiness and contentment, who was so suddenly taken away from the friends who loved him.[10]

Notes

Repository Symbols

Berkeley:	Special Collections at the Bancroft Library, University of California, Berkeley
British Library:	Manuscripts and Archives Department, British Library
Harvard:	Special Collections, Houghton Library, Harvard University
Leeds:	Special Collections, Brotherton Library, University of Leeds
Reading:	Chatto & Windus Archives of Random House Publishers, University of Reading
Rushden:	William Heinemann Collection, Penguin Random House Archive and Library, Rushden, Northamptonshire
S.I.U.:	Special Collections Research Center at the Morris Library, University of Southern Illinois at Carbondale
TCD:	Manuscripts and Archives at the Library, Trinity College, Dublin
Texas:	Harry Ransom Humanities Research Center at the University of Texas at Austin
U.C.L.A.:	Special Collections at the Charles E. Young Research Library, University of California, Los Angeles
UOI:	Special Collections at the Library of the University of Illinois at Urbana
Victoria:	Special Collections Library at the University of Victoria
Yale:	Beineke Rare Book and Manuscript Library, Yale University

Introduction

1. The five collections of poems were:
    *   *Images: 1910-1915* (London: Poetry Bookshop, 1915); *Images Old and New* (Boston: Four Seas, 1916);
    *   *The Love of Myrrhine and Konallis, and Other Prose Poems* (Cleveland: Clerk's Press, 1917; Chicago: Pascal Covici, 1926);
    *   *Images of War: A Book of Poems* (London: C.W. Beaumont, April 1919); expanded edition (London: Allen & Unwin, December 1919);
    *   *Images of Desire* (London: Elkin Mathews, June 1919);
    *   Other editions used some of the material from *Images of War* and *Images of Desire: Reverie: A Little Book of Poems for H.D.* (Cleveland: Clerk's Press, 1917); *War and Love* (Boston: Four Seas, September 1919);
    *   *Exile and Other Poems* (London: Allen & Unwin, 1923); one poem, *The Berkshire Kennet*, was also published separately by the Curwen Press in 1923.

    Aldington's *Collected Poems* were also published at the end of this period (New York: Covici, Friede, 1928; London: Allen & Unwin, 1929), perhaps an indication of his sense of the closure of his poetic career.

    The three long poems were:
    *   *A Fool i' the Forest: A Phantasmagoria* (London: Allen & Unwin, 1924);
    *   *The Eaten Heart* (La Chapelle-Réanville, Eure, France: Hours Press, 1929);
    *   *A Dream in the Luxembourg* (London: Chatto & Windus, 1930); *Love and the Luxembourg* (New York: Covici, Friede, 1930); although these editions were not published until 1930, the poem had been written in 1928.

    The anthologies were:
    *   *Des Imagistes* (New York: Boni & Liveright; London: The Poetry Bookshop, 1914);
    *   *Some Imagist Poets: An Anthology* (Boston: Houghton Mifflin, 1915, 1916 and 1917);
    *   *New Paths: Verse, Prose, Pictures, 1917-1918*, edited by C.W. Beaumont and M.T.H. Sadler (London: C.W. Beaumont, 1918).

2. *Voltaire* (London: Routledge, 1925; New York: E.P. Dutton, 1925).

    The principal journals to which Aldington contributed as critic, essayist or reviewer in the immediate postwar years were: *Today, Outlook, The Monthly Chapbook, The English Review, The Times Literary Supplement, The Criterion, The Nation and Athenaeum* and *The Spectator*.

    Additionally, he published essays and collections of reviews:
    *   *Literary Studies and Reviews* (London: Allen & Unwin, 1924; New York: Dial Press, 1924);
    *   *French Studies and Reviews* (London: Allen & Unwin, 1926; New York: Dial Press, 1926);

- *D.H. Lawrence: An Indiscretion*, University of Washington Chapbooks, no. 6 (Seattle: University of Washington Book Store, 1927);
- *Remy de Gourmont: A Modern Man of Letters*, University of Washington Chapbooks, no. 13 (Seattle: University of Washington Book Store, 1928).

The published translations were:

- *The Poems of Anyte of Tegea*, Poets' Translation Series, no. 1 (London: The Egoist Press, 1915; Cleveland: Clerk's Press, 1917);
- *Latin Poems of the Renaissance*, Poets' Translation Series, no. 4 (London: The Egoist Press, 1916);
- Folgóre da San Gimignano, *The Garland of Months*, Poets' Translation Series, no. 5 (London: The Egoist Press, 1915; Cleveland: Clerk's Press, 1917);
- *Greek Songs in the Manner of Anacreon*, Poets' Translation Series, Second Set, no. 1 (London: The Egoist Press, 1920);
- *The Poems of Meleager of Gadara*, Poets' Translation Series, Second Set, no. 6 (London: Egoist Press, 1920);
- *The Poems of Anyte of Tegea*, *The Poems of Meleager of Gadara*, *Greek Songs in the Manner of Anacreon* and *Latin Poems of the Renaissance* were also published as *Medallions in Clay* in 1921 (New York: A.A. Knopf) and by Chatto & Windus in 1930;
- Carlo Goldoni, *The Good-Humoured Ladies: A Comedy* (London: C.W. Beaumont, 1922);
- *French Comedies of the XVIII Century* (London: Routledge, 1923; New York: E.P. Dutton, 1923);
- Cyrano de Bergerac, *Voyages to the Moon and the Sun* (London: Routledge & Sons, 1923; New York: E.P. Dutton, 1923);
- Pierre Choderlos de Laclos, *Dangerous Acquaintances* (London: Routledge, 1924; New York: E.P Dutton, 1924);
- Pierre Custot, *Sturly* (London: Jonathan Cape, 1924; Boston: Houghton Mifflin, 1925);
- *A Book of Characters from Theophrastus* (London: Routledge & Sons, 1924; New York: E.P. Dutton, 1924);
- *The Fifteen Joys of Marriage, Ascribed to Antoine de la Sale, c.1388-c.1462* (London: Routledge & Sons, 1926; New York: E.P. Dutton, 1926);
- *Letters of Madame de Sevigné to Her Daughter and Her Friends* (London: Routledge & Sons, 1927);
- *Letters of Voltaire and Frederick the Great* (London: Routledge, 1927; New York: Brentano's, 1927);
- *Letters of Voltaire and Madame du Deffand* (London: Routledge & Sons, 1927; New York: Brentano's, 1927);
- Voltaire, *Candide and Other Romances* (London: Routledge & Sons, 1928; New York: E.P. Dutton, 1928);
- Julien Benda, *The Great Betrayal* (London: Routledge & Sons, 1928) and *The Treason of the Intellectuals* (New York: Crosby Gaige, 1928; London: Chatto & Windus, 1931);

- *Fifty Romance Lyric Poems* (New York: Crosby Gaige, 1928; London: Allan Wingate, 1928; Chatto & Windus, 1931);
- *Remy de Gourmont: Selections from All His Works* (New York: Covici, Friede, 1928);
- *The Decameron of Giovanni Boccaccio* (New York: Covici, Friede, 1930; London: G.P. Putnam's Sons, 1930);
- Euripides, *Alcestis* (London: Chatto & Windus, 1930);
- Remy de Gourmont, *Letters to the Amazon* (London: Chatto & Windus, 1931).

Additionally, the translation of *The Decameron*, on which Aldington had been working throughout 1928 and 1929 was published in the United States by Covici, Friede and in Britain by Putnam's in 1930. *Aurélia* had been commissioned by the Aquila Press, but the company went bankrupt and Chatto & Windus published this translation in 1932. Covici, Friede would also run into financial difficulties – the Wall Street Crash came a month after the publication of *Death of a Hero* – and Aldington's planned Greek drama translation project was abandoned; it was left to Chatto & Windus to publish his translation of *Alcestis* in 1930.

3. Richard Aldington, *Life for Life's Sake: A Book of Reminiscences* (New York: Viking Press, 1941; London: Cassell, 1968) p. 360.
4. The six works reprinted in 1938 were: *Voltaire*; *Death of a Hero*; *The Colonel's Daughter*; *Soft Answers*; *All Men Are Enemies*; and *Very Heaven*. Snow's booklet was entitled *Richard Aldington: An Appreciation*.
5. C.P. Snow, *Richard Aldington: An* Appreciation (London: Heinemann, 1938), reproduced in Alister Kershaw and F.-J. Temple, eds, *Richard Aldington: An Intimate Portrait* (Carbondale: Southern Illinois University Press, 1965) pp. 136-37.

1. A Sociable Life: Travel, Friendship and Patronage, 1930-1931

1. Aldington had known Davray (1873-1944) in his role as editor of the *Anglo-French Review* for a decade and Davray had recently translated *Death of a Hero* into French.
2. Aldington's new agent, Ralph Pinker, had obtained for him an offer of 80 guineas for two 2,500-word articles.
3. Richard Aldington to Charles Prentice, 23 January 1930 (Reading).
4. Richard Aldington, *All Men Are Enemies: A Romance* (London: Chatto & Windus, 1933) pp. 378-79.
5. *Nash's Pall Mall Magazine*, vol. LXXXV, no. 447 (August 1930) pp. 50-52.
6. Thomas MacGreevy was born Thomas *McGreevy*, but this text uses throughout the spelling MacGreevy himself favoured in later life.
7. Samuel Beckett, *Whoroscope* (La Chapelle-Réanville: Hours Press, 1930), 100 signed and 200 unsigned copies. A limit of 100 lines had been imposed in the competition; Beckett's poem ran to 98.

8. Titus, a Polish-American married to the beautician Helena Rubenstein, had been resident in Paris since 1918. Between 1926 and its closure in 1932 his Black Manikin Press published a total of 25 books, including an edition of *Lady Chatterley's Lover*. *This Quarter* also ceased publication in 1932. We noted in Volume One that Dorothy Yorke worked in the Black Manikin bookshop in Paris after her separation from Aldington in 1928.

9. Richard Aldington to Thomas MacGreevy, 22 February 1930 (TCD).

10. Richard Aldington to Charles Prentice, 20 September 1930 (Reading).

11. Richard Aldington to Edward Titus, 1 December 1930 (Texas).

12. *This Quarter*, vol. iv, no. 1 (July-September 1931).

13. The American millionaire and philanthropist Henry Hall Church and his Bavarian wife Barbara, who lived in a Le Corbusier-designed villa near Versailles, became friends of Aldington. Church supported little magazines such as *Mesures*, edited in Paris by Jean Paulhan, and was a collector of modern art. He translated Aldington's *The Eaten Heart* (*Le Coeur Mangé* [Paris: Commerce, 1930]). While Aldington never became close to the Churches, they remained friends with Thomas MacGreevy for the rest of their lives. Why Aldington and Church never became close friends is explained in Aldington's memoir, where Church is referred to as 'William Ernest' (Aldington, *Life for Life's Sake*, pp. 316-18).

14. Quoted in Miriam Benkovitz, 'Nine for Reeves: Letters from Richard Aldington,' *Bulletin of the New York Public Library*, vol. 69, no. 6 (June 1965).

15. Samuel Beckett, *Proust* (London: Chatto & Windus, 1931). The Dolphins were a short-lived series of translations, essays and short stories by important contemporary writers; the plan was to issue them in three formats: a signed, limited edition; a cheaper cloth edition; and a one-shilling paperback. The slump in the book-trade in the early 1930s put paid to the limited edition and the shilling-paperback idea was dropped on the advice of booksellers. It wasn't until 1936 that Allen Lane of Bodley Head demonstrated that there was a market for the cheap paperback book. It is worth noting here that Aldington's distressing experience with Routledge in 1925 (see Vivien Whelpton, *Richard Aldington: Poet, Soldier and Lover* [Cambridge: Lutterworth Press, 2014] pp. 277-78) seems not to have held him back from getting involved in the publishing strategies of Chatto & Windus.

16. MacGreevy never completed a novel but Heinemann published a volume of his poetry in 1934. He continued to write poetry, although no more was published in his lifetime. He became a prominent art critic and was appointed Director of the National Gallery of Ireland in 1950, a post he held until 1963.

17. Aldington, *Life for Life's Sake*, p. 351.

18. Thomas MacGreevy, *T.S. Eliot: A Study* and *Richard Aldington: An Englishman* (both London: Chatto & Windus, 1931).

19. Richard Aldington to Thomas MacGreevy, 10 January 1930 (TCD).

20. Richard Aldington to Alexander Frere, 24 November 1930, in Norman Gates, ed., *Richard Aldington: An Autobiography in Letters* (University Park: Pennsylvania State University Press, 1992) p. 116.
21. Richard Aldington to Thomas MacGreevy, 15 September 1930 (TCD).
22. Richard Aldington to Alexander Frere, 15 August 1934, in Gates, *Richard Aldington: An Autobiography in Letters*, p. 136.
23. Richard Aldington, *Life for Life's Sake*, p. 352.
24. Richard Aldington to Charles Prentice, 18 March 1930 (Reading).
25. 200 signed copies and 300 additional copies (retailing at £2 and 7s 6d respectively); Cunard tells us that the only other Hours Press publication which ran to so many copies was Norman Douglas's *One Day*, see Nancy Cunard, *These Were the Hours* (Carbondale: Southern Illinois University Press, 1969) p. 158.
26. Cunard, *ibid.*, p. 160.
27. Nancy Cunard to Richard Aldington, 8 March 1931 (S.I.U.).
28. Richard Aldington to Brigit Patmore, 9 February 1931 (Texas).
29. Cunard, *These Were the Hours*, p. 53.
30. *Ibid.*, p. 159.

2. A Sociable Life: France, 1930-1933

1. Brigit Patmore to H.D., 11 and 30 May 1930 (Yale). The American violinist Olga Rudge) had been Pound's lover since 1923 and had given birth to their daughter Mary in 1925.
2. In the 1920s and 1930s, Vanessa Bell, Duncan Grant and the Woolfs used to spend summers in Cassis, fifteen miles east of Marseilles.
3. Richard Aldington to Herbert Read, 9 August 1930 (Victoria).
4. Richard Aldington to Herbert Read, 30 May 1931 (Victoria).
5. Richard Aldington to Ralph Pinker, 5 May 1931 (S.I.U.). The 'artist' was the composer Charles Koechlin, whose love of the villa was such that he would be buried in its grounds on his death in 1950.
6. Richard Aldington to Bonamy Dobrée, 27 March 1933 (Leeds). Relations between Aldington and the writer and critic Dobrée, another member of the *Criterion* circle, had been strained since the former had fallen passionately (and unrequitedly) in love with Dobrée's wife, Valentine, in 1928; she was the inspiration for *A Dream in the Luxembourg*. See Whelpton, *Richard Aldington: Poet, Soldier and Lover*, pp. 307-313.
7. T.S. Eliot was the founding editor of *The Criterion*, the quarterly literary review published from October 1922 until January 1939. Aldington had acted as the journal's 'secretary and managing editor' for a period of seven months in 1923; his membership of the close-knit group of critics which Eliot had gathered around him had commenced again in April 1925 but terminated abruptly in August 1927. His friendship with Read had flourished in the context of this group. See Whelpton, *Richard Aldington: Poet, Soldier and Lover*, pp. 269, 275, 293, 300-301, 341.

8. Cyril Connolly, *The Rock Pool* (Paris: Obelisk Press, 1936; Oxford: Oxford University Press, 1981) p. 50. The Castel Sainte-Claire, above Hyères, was Edith Wharton's summer residence from 1927 until her death ten years later; Roy Campbell and his family lived at Martigues, west of Marseilles, from 1928 until 1933, but he and Aldington did not meet at this time; Edward Phillips Oppenheim (1866-1946) was a popular writer of crime fiction who lived for many years inland from Cagnes-sur-Mer, halfway between Antibes and Nice. Cagnes was the model for Connolly's fictional 'Trou-sur-Mer' in *The Rock Pool*.

9. Richard Aldington to H.D., 17 August 1931(Yale).

10. Richard Aldington to Herbert Read, 9 August 1930 (Victoria).

11. Huxley's observation that Lawrence was 'the most extraordinary and impressive human being' he had ever known (Aldous Huxley to Eugene Saxton, 8 March 1930, in Grover Smith, ed., *Letters of Aldous Huxley* [New York: Harper & Row, 1969]) expressed what Aldington himself believed. Both men would devote much time through the 1930s and beyond to ensuring the perpetuation of Lawrence's reputation.

12. See, for example, Huxley's *Do What You Will* (London: Chatto & Windus, 1929).

13. Richard Aldington to Herbert Read, 9 August 1930 (Victoria).

14. Richard Aldington to Charles Prentice, 7 June 1930 (Reading).

15. Aldington, *Life for Life's Sake*, p. 354.

16. J.R. Frere, *The Early Life and Family History of A.S. Frere* (2009, unpublished). The author was given access to the late Jean Raulin Frere's research by Elizabeth Frere-Jones, Frere's daughter.

17. Von Arnim's novel, *Love* (London: Macmillan, 1925), was loosely based on her affair with Frere.

18. Richard Aldington to Alexander Frere, 7 June 1934, in Gates, *Richard Aldington: An Autobiography in Letters*, pp. 133-34.

19. Richard Aldington to Herbert Read, 31 December 1934 (Victoria). We may need to treat this piece of information with caution: Frere's daughter, Elizabeth Frere-Jones, told the current writer in 2017 that her father's migraines only occurred on Christmas Day and that the family associated them with his troubled childhood.

20. Aldington, *Life for Life's Sake*, pp. 352-53.

21. *Ibid.*, pp. 215-16.

22. Richard Aldington to Charles Prentice, 27 May 1931 (Reading).

23. Richard Aldington to Thomas MacGreevy, 13 September 1930 (TCD).

24. Richard Aldington to Charles Prentice, 27 May 1931 (Reading).

25. Gerald Dawe, 'Nocturnes: Thomas MacGreevy and World War One', in Susan Schreibman, ed., *The Life and Work of Thomas MacGreevy* (London: Bloomsbury, 2013) p. 6.

26. MacGreevy, *Richard Aldington: An Englishman*, p. 6.

27. Charles Prentice to Richard Aldington, 19 January and 20 May 1931 (S.I.U.).

28. Richard Aldington to Charles Prentice, 4 August and 13 September 1930 (Reading).

29. Richard Aldington to Charles Prentice, 28 August 1931 (Reading).
30. Richard Aldington to Charles Prentice, 5 September 1931(Reading).
31. Richard Aldington to Charles Prentice, 19 November 1932 (Reading).
32. Richard Aldington to Eunice Black, 20 November 1932 (Yale).

3. A Sociable Life: Italy – Further Friendships, 1930-1932

1. Richard Aldington to Charles Prentice, 30 July 1929 (Reading).
2. See Richard Aldington to Herbert Read, 15 September 1930 (Victoria). Read picked out for this criticism passages in *Meditation on a German Grave* and *At All Costs*.
3. See the correspondence from Richard Aldington to Herbert Read, 30 May and 5 June 1931 and 3, 13 and 24 April 1933 (Victoria).
4. Richard Aldington to Herbert Read, 13 July 1933 (Victoria).
5. *Life Goes On* appeared in *The Yale Review*, vol. 33, no. 2 (December 1933), and was published in a group of 'New Poems' in *The Poems of Richard Aldington* (New York: Doubleday, Doran, 1934).
6. Richard Aldington to Herbert Read, 22 and 31 December 1934 (Victoria).
7. Richard Aldington to Herbert Read, 25 February 1936 (Victoria).
8. Kershaw and Temple, *Richard Aldington: An Intimate Portrait*. This book was a collection of tributes to Aldington compiled after his death.
9. James King, *The Last Modern: A Life of Herbert Read* (London: Weidenfeld & Nicolson, 1990) pp. 150-51.
10. Herbert Read to Richard Church, 26 October 1943 (Texas). Richard Church was a civil servant, poet, novelist and critic. In the 1920s and 1930s, he and Read were members of Eliot's *Criterion* group, to which Aldington had also belonged in the 1920s.
11. Initially the artists were Henry Moore, Barbara Hepworth and Ben Nicholson and the place, the Mall Studios, off Parkhill Road, Hampstead.
12. Herbert Read to Richard Church, 1 February 1965 (Texas).
13. Herbert Read, 'A Lost Generation', in *The Nation and Athenaeum*, 27 April 1929.
14. Charles Prentice to Richard Aldington, 11 November 1930 (S.I.U.).
15. Brigit Patmore to Thomas MacGreevy, 12 January 1931 (TCD); Thomas MacGreevy to Charles Prentice, 15 January 1931 (Reading).
16. Orioli, a printer and bookseller, had published D.H. Lawrence's *Lady Chatterley's Lover*. He was Norman Douglas's close companion from 1922, when Douglas settled in Italy, until shortly before his own death 20 years later. Frere would have to practise patience: it was not until January 1935 that Martin Secker sold Heinemann the rights to Lawrence's published works.
17. Richard Aldington to Charles Prentice, 17 March 1931 (Reading).
18. Norman Douglas, *Old Calabria* (London: Martin Secker, 1915).
19. Richard Aldington, *Pinorman: Personal Recollections of Norman Douglas, Pino Orioli and Charles Prentice* (London: Heinemann, 1954) p. 89.

20. Aldington was a weekly reviewer for the *Sunday Referee* from 24 November 1929 until 24 April 1932, and then again from 30 April to 23 July 1933. During the earlier period, the only dates on which his reviews did not appear were: 16 February and 24 October 1930; 28 June and 2 August 1931; 10 and 17 January, and 10 April 1932.

21. Aldington, *Pinorman*, p. 94.

22. *Sunday Referee*, 27 March 1932.

23. Charles Prentice to Richard Aldington (quoted in Aldington, *Pinorman*, pp. 91-92).

24. Richard Aldington to Thomas MacGreevy, 1 April 1932 (TCD).

25. Aldington, *Life for Life's Sake*, p. 373.

26. Giuseppe Orioli, *Moving Along* (London: Chatto & Windus, 1934) pp. 57 and 123. Aldington dismisses these accounts in *Pinorman*, pp. 100-102.

27. Aldington, *Life for Life's Sake*, p. 365.

28. *Ibid.*, pp. 369-70.

29. Aldington, *Pinorman*, p. 62.

30. Aldington, *Life for Life's Sake*, pp. 366 and 370.

31. Derek Patmore, 'Introduction', in Brigit Patmore, *My Friends When Young* (London: Heinemann, 1968) p. 29.

32. Richard Aldington to Charles Prentice, 2 January 1931 (Reading).

33. Richard Aldington to Thomas MacGreevy, 6 January 1931 (TCD).

34. Richard Aldington to Brigit Patmore, 5 February 1931(Texas).

35. Richard Aldington to Thomas MacGreevy, 17 February 1932 (TCD); Richard Aldington to Charles Prentice, 15 February 1932 (Reading).

36. Mark Holloway, *Norman Douglas* (London: Secker & Warburg, 1976) p. 324.

37. Reginald Turner (1869-1938) was an aesthete and unsuccessful novelist. The character Algy Constable in D.H. Lawrence's *Aaron's Rod* is modelled on Turner. Harold Acton (1904-1994), although also a poet and novelist, was better known as a historian.

38. The meeting with Cunard predated the quarrel of January 1931. Dorothy Wilde (1895-1941) was the niece of Oscar Wilde and the lover, for some time, of Natalie Barney. The poet and translator Edward Storer (1880-1944) had been involved in the earliest experiments of Imagism and had also contributed to Aldington's Poets' Translation Series.

39. Richard Aldington to H.D., 13 December 1930 (Yale).

40. Richard Aldington to Thomas MacGreevy, 17 February 1932 (TCD).

41. Richard Aldington to Charles Prentice, 6 May 1932 (Reading).

42. Richard Aldington to Charles Prentice, 11 May 1932 (Reading).

43. Richard Aldington to Charles Prentice, 31 July 1932 (Reading).

44. Aldington, *Life for Life's Sake*, p. 380.

45. Richard Aldington to Thomas MacGreevy, 21 September 1932 (TCD).

4. The Public Face: Critic and Satirist

1. Ralph Pinker ran the London end of the very successful agency founded by his father, J.B. Pinker, in 1896; his brother Eric ran the New York office.

Aldington went to Pinker in 1930 after the success of *Death of a Hero*. In 1940 the business would collapse when both brothers faced charges of embezzling their clients' funds.

2. Stephen Steele and Heesok Chang, 'Modernism at the Margins: Richard Aldington's Letters to Douglas Goldring (1932-1946)', *Modern Language Studies*, vol. 35, no. 2 (Autumn 2005) pp. 22-55.

3. Book-buying would build up during the 1930s, principally because of the founding of the Book Society in 1929, which supplied members with a pre-selected newly published book to buy each month. Its influence (generally conservative) began to work both on the market (as its choices would be advertised in the press and in libraries and bookshops) and on the content of books, as the judges would see texts at the proofreading stage and advise changes to suit their readership. The early judges were Hugh Walpole, J.B. Priestley, Clemence Dane, Sylvia Lynd and George Stuart Gordon, all members of the Hampstead literary coterie that clustered round the writers and critics Robert and Sylvia Lynd. The traditionalist nature of this group was in strong contrast to the modernism of the Bloomsbury and Sitwell sets.

4. J. Richardson to Harold Raymond, 22 May 1931 (Reading).

5. W. Roy of W.H. Smith to Harold Raymond, 11 May 1931 (Reading).

6. Many stationers also operated their own subscription library service.

7. Blackwell's to Harold Raymond, 13 April 1931 (Reading).

8. Alfred Wilson to Harold Raymond, 9 April 1931(Reading).

9. In *The Criterion: Cultural Politics and Periodical Networks in Inter-War Britain* (Oxford: Oxford University Press, 2002) pp. 83 and 142, Jason Harding, observes that the literary world of 1930s London was characterised not only by the growth of a sharp political divide between right and left but by the existence of a variety of coteries, and speaks of 'the calculatedly embattled nature of the literary marketplace' and 'the incipient tensions between aestheticism, academicism, and religious dogma, not to mention the highly complicated networks of personal loyalty and sentiment'.

10. *Sunday Referee*, 3 May 1931.

11. *Daily Mail*, 12 May 1931.

12. *Daily Express*, 12 May 1931.

13. *The Times*, 1 May 1931.

14. *The Sunday Times*, 3 May and 13 December 1931.

15. *Daily Telegraph*, 5 May 1931.

16. *The Spectator*, 2 May 1931.

17. Richard Aldington to Bonamy Dobrée, 23 May 1931 (Leeds).

18. *John O' London's Weekly*, 9 May 1931.

19. *Life and Letters*, June 1931.

20. *Time and Tide*, 30 May 1931.

21. Richard Aldington to Charles Prentice, 5 June 1931 (Reading). Ervine's review of *Death of a Hero* had appeared in the *Daily Express* on 3 October 1929.

22. *The Times Literary Supplement*, 30 April 1931.

23. *New Statesman and Nation*, 16 May 1931.

24. *Punch*, 20 May 1931.

25. Richard Aldington to Harold Raymond, 14 May 1931 (Reading).

26. Richard Aldington to Thomas MacGreevy, 15 and 19 May 1931 (TCD).

27. Richard Aldington to Charles Prentice, 18 May 1931 (Reading).

28. See Richard Aldington to Herbert Read, 5 June 1931 (Victoria).

29. Richard Aldington to Sydney Schiff, 26 May 1931 (British Library). Schiff, whose own novels were written under the pen-name of Stephen Hudson, and who was a translator of Proust, was a major patron of the arts in the 1920s and 1930s.

30. Richard Aldington to Herbert Read, 5 June 1931 (Victoria).

31. Richard Aldington to Charles Prentice, 30 May 1931 (Reading).

32. Richard Aldington to Herbert Read, 5 June 1931(Victoria).

33. Richard Aldington to Charles Prentice, 5 June 1931 (Reading). The 'Dame Gwynne episode' refers to the objection raised by Helen Gwynne-Vaughan, Controller of the WAAC in France, 1917-1918, to a comment in *Death of a Hero* which had implied that many of the WAAC women in France were pregnant.

34. Richard Aldington to James Reeves, 18 November 1930 (cited in Benkovitz, 'Nine for Reeves').

35. Chris Baldick, *The Oxford English Literary History, Volume 10: The Modern Movement* (Oxford: Oxford University Press, 2004) p. 235.

36. *Ibid.*, pp. 235-40.

37. See Richard Aldington to Charles Prentice, 29 August 1930, in which Aldington pleads his attachment to what was then the Prologue, 30 November 1930, where he begins to share Prentice's doubts, 12 December 1930, where he agrees to omit it, and 9 January 1931, in which, at Frere's suggestion, he strikes a compromise with Prentice by making it an Epilogue (Reading).

38. David Wilkinson, *The Death of a Hero: The Quest for First World War Poet Richard Aldington's Berkshire Retreat* (Barnsley: Pen & Sword, 2016). See especially pp. 240-52.

39. Jessie Capper to H.D., 20 April 1937 (Yale).

40. Richard Aldington, *The Colonel's Daughter* (London: Chatto & Windus, 1931) p. 346.

41. Baldick, *The Modern Movement*, p. 248.

42. Roy Campbell, *The Georgiad* (London: Boriswood, 1931).

43. Percy Wyndham Lewis, *The Apes of God* (London: Arthur Press, 1930). The artist and writer Dick Wyndham (1896-1948) had been one of Lewis's pupils and had subsequently given him financial support, as had the artist Edward Wadsworth (1889-1949). Richard Aldington to Sydney Schiff, 11 February 1932 (British Library).

44. Richard Aldington to Herbert Read, 9 August 1930 (Victoria).

45. Richard Aldington to Herbert Read, 15 September 1930 (Victoria).

46. *Sunday Referee*, 22 June 1930.

47. *Sunday Referee*, 16 November 1930; Osbert Sitwell, *Dumb Animals and Other Stories* (London: Duckworth, 1930).

48. As usual with Aldington's titles, we have a quotation: the allusion is to Proverbs 15:1, 'A soft answer turneth away wrath: but grievous words stir up anger.' Whether the stories are indeed 'soft answers' rather than 'grievous words' is for the reader to decide.

49. Richard Aldington to Charles Prentice, 13 October 1930 (Reading).

50. There were, in fact, two 'mystery' babies: the daughter born to Olga Rudge in July 1925 and the son born to Dorothy Pound in September 1926. Mary Rudge was brought up by a peasant family in Gais in the Italian Tyrol while Omar Pound was placed in a nursery in London.

51. Richard Aldington, *Soft Answers* (London: Chatto & Windus, 1932) p. 133.

52. Richard Aldington to T.S. Eliot, 18 July 1919 (Harvard).

53. Charles Prentice to Richard Aldington, 20 February 1931 (S.I.U.).

54. Richard Aldington to Sydney Schiff, 9 December 1931 (British Library).

55. Richard Aldington to H.D., 21 February 1932 (Yale).

56. Richard Aldington to John Atkins, 5 June 1957 (Texas).

57. *Sunday Referee*, 27 April 1932.

58. *The Sunday Times*, 17 April 1932.

59. *The Times Literary Supplement*, 21 April 1932.

60. *The Times*, 15 April 1932. The critic Orlando Cyprian (Orlo) Williams (1883-1967) was Clerk to the House of Commons and an authority on Italian literature and culture.

5. The Public Face: Elegist and Romantic

1. The collection was to have been entitled *Paths of Glory* but Aldington changed it on discovering that there was an American book with that title: a 1915 non-fiction account by Irvin S. Cobb of his experiences as a journalist in the First World War (not the Humphrey Cobb novel of the same title [adapted for the screen by Stanley Kubrick in 1957] which was not published until 1935). In selecting the new title, he directed Pinker and Prentice to the Tennyson lines, 'Not once or twice in our fair island story/ The path of duty was the road to glory', lines he had already referenced for similarly ironic purposes in *Death of a Hero*: Richard Aldington to Ralph Pinker, 4 March 1930; Aldington, *Death of a Hero* (London: Chatto & Windus, 1929; New York: Penguin Books, 2013) p. 216.

2. Richard Aldington to Charles Prentice, 13 August 1929 (Reading).

3. The stories that appeared in *Nash's Pall Mall Magazine* were: 'Meditation on a German Grave' (January 1930); 'Victory' (February); 'Killed in Action' (March); 'Booby Trap' (April); and 'Of Unsound Mind' (appearing under the title 'And the Verdict Was') (September). Elkin Mathews published 'Deserter' and 'Lads of the Village', in a limited, signed edition, and Frere chose 'At All Costs' for Heinemann.

4. Covici, Friede had been due to publish Aldington's translation of *Alcestis*, which therefore did not appear in the US. Doubleday offered Aldington very attractive terms: an income of £550 for four years and 15% royalties on all fiction, 10% on other works. Covici, Friede pulled round their fortunes when they signed John Steinbeck in 1934; he went with Covici to Viking in 1938. Aldington would leave Doubleday for Viking in 1939.

5. Aldington, 'Meditation on a German Grave', in *Roads to Glory* (London: Chatto & Windus, 1930) p. 17.

6. 'Farewell to Memories', in *ibid.*, p. 264.

7. 'Sacrifice Post', in *ibid.*, pp. 171-72.

8. 'Victory', in *ibid.*, p. 45; see also Cumberland in the closing section of 'Meditation on a German Grave', in *ibid.*, pp. 30-32; Davison in 'Sacrifice Post' comes to similar conclusions but does not live to fulfil his aim.

9. 'Farewell to Memories', in *ibid.*, p. 258.

10. 'Victory', in *ibid.*, p. 39.

11. 'Meditation on a German Grave', in *ibid.*, p. 5.

12. 'Deserter', in *ibid.*, p. 77.

13. 'The Case of Lieutenant Hall', in *ibid.*, p. 245.

14. 'Sacrifice Post', in *ibid.*, p. 179.

15. 'The Case of Lieutenant Hall', in *ibid.*, p. 253. Aldington told Herbert Read, 15 September 1930, that the Coroner's summing up at Hall's inquest, with which the story ends, gave him more satisfaction than anything else in the book.

16. 'Farewell to Memories', in Aldington, *Roads to Glory*, p. 278.

17. MacGreevy, *Richard Aldington: An Englishman*, p. 64.

18. *News Chronicle*, 22 October 1930.

19. *The Times Literary Supplement*, 11 September 1930.

20. *New Statesman*, 27 September 1930.

21. Aldington, *All Men Are Enemies*, pp. v-vi.

22. *Everyman*, 18 March 1933.

23. Aldington, *All Men Are Enemies*, p. 26.

24. *Ibid.*, p. 495.

25. Aldington, *Life for Life's Sake*, p. 383.

26. Richard Aldington to Brigit Patmore, 17 September 1932 (Texas).

27. The current writer attempts to show in Whelpton, *Richard Aldington: Poet, Soldier and Lover*, pp. 18-35, that Aldington's own family and upbringing more closely resembled those of George Winterbourne in *Death of a Hero* (see pp. 28-90); see also Aldington, *Life for Life's Sake*, pp. 37-63.

28. Richard Aldington to Eunice Black, 25 November 1932, then Eunice Gluckman, 10 September 1960, 14 November 1960, 27 April 1961, 7 August 1961.

29. Aldington, *All Men Are Enemies*, p. 84.

30. *Ibid.*, pp. 276-77.

31. *Ibid.*, pp. 280, 295.

32. Elizabeth Vandiver to Vivien Whelpton, 18 May 2018.

33. Aldington, *All Men Are Enemies*, pp. 157, 434 and 495.

34. Charles Prentice to Richard Aldington, 9 September 1932 (S.I.U.).

35. Richard Aldington to Thomas MacGreevy, 27 April 1932 (TCD).

36. Richard Aldington to Charles Prentice, 3 July 1932 (Reading).

37. Aldington, *All Men Are Enemies*, p. 309.

38. *Daily Mail*, 2 March 1933.

39. *The Times Literary Supplement*, 2 March 1933.

40. *New Statesman and Nation*, 15 April 1933.

41. Nelson Doubleday to Richard Aldington, 6 October 1932 (S.I.U.).

42. Alec Waugh, *My Brother Evelyn and Other Profiles* (London: Cassell & Co., 1967) p. 72.

43. See Richard Aldington to Eunice Black, 20 November 1932 (Yale).

44. Charles Prentice to Richard Aldington, 20 December 1932 (S.I.U.).

45. See Richard Aldington to Charles Prentice, 4, 10, 19, 22, 31 December 1932 (Reading) and Charles Prentice to Richard Aldington, 5 and 20 December 1932 (S.I.U.).

46. Richard Aldington to Sydney Schiff, 17 January 1933 (British Library).

47. Charles Prentice to Richard Aldington, 11 April 1933 (S.I.U.); 'the others' refers to Harold Raymond and Ian Parsons, Prentice's fellow directors.

48. Richard Aldington to Henry Slonimsky, 9 April 1933 (S.I.U.).

6. The Social Life Fragments, 1932-1936

1. Richard Aldington to Ralph Pinker, 25 November 1932 (S.I.U.).

2. Richard Aldington to Charles Prentice, 9 October 1933 (Reading); 'he lappitup like mad' is a humorous imitation of Orioli's dialect, a joke that Prentice would share.

3. Richard Aldington to Ralph Pinker, 20 November 1933 (S.I.U.).

4. Richard Aldington to Giuseppe Orioli, 9 May 1934 (Texas); Aldington, *Life for Life's Sake*, p. 388.

5. *Ibid.*, pp. 392-93. The couple in the other car would recover from their injuries, the driver served a short term of imprisonment for dangerous driving and his Austrian insurance company paid Aldington substantial compensation.

6. Aldington, *Life for Life's Sake*, p. 397.

7. *Ibid.*, p. 398.

8. *Ibid.*

9. Richard Aldington to Thomas MacGreevy, 31 January 1935 (TCD).

10. Aldington, *Life for Life's Sake*, p. 406.

11. Aldington, *Artifex: Sketches and Ideas* (London: Chatto & Windus, 1935) p. 41.

12. *Ibid.*, p. 48.

13. Aldington, *D.H. Lawrence: A Complete List of His Works, Together with a Critical Appreciation* (London: Heinemann, 1935). This essay would also be included in *Artifex*.

14. Richard Aldington to Richard Church, 11 May 1935 (Texas).
15. Richard Aldington to Alexander Frere, 11 May 1935, in Gates, *Richard Aldington: An Autobiography in Letters*, p. 140.
16. Richard Aldington to Harold Raymond, 30 May, 7, 10 and 30 June 1935 (Reading).
17. Richard Aldington to Douglas Goldring, 11 July 1935, in Steele and Chang, 'Modernism at the Margins', *Modern Language Studies* vol. 1, no. 2 (Fall, 2005) pp. 45-6.
18. Richard Aldington to Richard Church, 27 June 1935 (Texas).
19. Richard Aldington to Thomas MacGreevy, 6 August 1935 (TCD).
20. Richard Aldington to Harold Raymond, 17 July 1935 (Reading).
21. Richard Aldington to Harold Raymond, 7 September 1935 (Reading).
22. Richard Aldington to Henry Slonimsky, 23 September 1935 (S.I.U.).
23. Brigit Patmore to Derek Patmore, 4 July 1936, in Derek Patmore, 'Introduction', in Brigit Patmore, *My Friends When Young*, p. 37.
24. Richard Aldington to Harold Raymond, 20 April 1936 (Reading).
25. Aldington, *Life for Life's Sake*, p. 386.
26. Richard Aldington to Eric Warman, 18 September 1936 (S.I.U.). Aldington and Eric Warman had met in London in 1932, when Warman was 28 and Aldington 40 years old. Warman went on to be a very successful publisher and a lifelong friend. He wrote to Aldington and Patmore in the early days of the friendship: 'I have never known two people so completely human and so understanding of how life should be lived', 12 May 1934 (S.I.U.).
27. Richard Aldington to Ian Parsons, 5 September 1936 (Rushden).
28. Malcolm Johnson to Richard Aldington, 17 September 1936 (Reading).

7. The Public Face: Reviewer, Philosopher and Essayist

1. *Sunday Referee*, 30 April 1933.
2. *Ibid.*, 15 June 1930.
3. *Ibid.*, 25 May 1930.
4. *Ibid.*, 23 February 1930.
5. *Ibid.*, 6 December 1931.
6. *Ibid.*, 15 December 1929 and 25 May 1930. Of *Brave New World*, however, Aldington was critical. He told Prentice in a letter dated 22 January 1932 (Reading) that he would not review it, but he must have felt on reflection that this was an evasion of responsibility. In the event he castigated it for its 'squeamish, squirming contempt'.
7. *Sunday Referee*, 14 September 1930.
8. *Ibid.*, 5 April 1931.
9. *Ibid.*, 4 October 1931.
10. *Ibid.*, 21 June 1931.
11. *Ibid.*, 7 April 1930.
12. *Ibid.*, 9 November 1930. The three books under review were: Vernon Bartlett, *No Man's Land* (London: G. Allen & Unwin Ltd, 1930), Coningsby William

Dawson, *The Test of Scarlet* (London: Hutchinson & Co., 1930) and Ronald Gurner, *Pass Guard at Ypres* (London: J.M. Dent & Sons Ltd, 1930).

13. *Sunday Referee*, 2 March 1930; Ex-Private X (Alfred McClelland Burrage), *War is War* (London: Victor Gollancz, 1930).

14. *Ibid.*, 4 May 1930. 'Honour's Easy' appeared in a collection of Montague's short stories entitled *Fiery Particles* (London: Chatto & Windus, 1923).

15. *Sunday Referee*, 8 December 1929, 10 August 1930.

16. *Ibid.*, 25 June 1933; Paul Alverdes, *Changed Men* (London: Martin Secker, 1933).

17. *Ibid.*, 31 May 1931; Erich Remarque, *The Road Back* (London: G.P. Putnam's Sons, 1931).

18. *Ibid.*, 20 April 1930.

19. *Ibid.*, 14 February 1932; Pollard's *Memoirs of a V.C.* (Hutchinson) and Crozier's *Five Years Hard* (Jonathan Cape) were both published in London in 1932.

20. This poem first appeared in the 1933 Chatto & Windus edition of *The Eaten Heart*.

21. *Sunday Referee*, 14 May 1933.

22. *Ibid.*, 3 January 1932. W.K. Rose was the editor of the Routledge Republic of Letters imprint under which Aldington's *Voltaire* was published. For the 1925 controversy surrounding this imprint (which involved both Aldington and Eliot) see Whelpton, *Richard Aldington: Poet, Soldier and Lover*, pp. 277-278.

23. *Sunday Referee*, 27 December 1931; Ezra Pound, *How to Read* (London: Desmond Harmsworth, 1931).

24. Aldington had already published one literary biography, his *Voltaire* in 1925.

25. *Sunday Referee*, 2 November 1930; Carswell's *Life of Robert Burns* was published in London by Chatto & Windus in 1930.

26. *Sunday Referee*, 21 December 1930 and 22 October 1931. Muir's *John Knox: Portrait of a Calvinist* was published by Jonathan Cape in 1930 and Carr's *Dostoevsky, 1821-1881: A New Biography* by George Allen & Unwin in 1931.

27. *Evening Standard*, 2 February 1933. West's *St Augustine* was published by Davies Ltd in 1933.

28. *Sunday Referee*, 26 August, 2 and 9 September 1934.

29. Once again, the title is a quotation: this time from Charles Kingsley's 1851 tragic ballad 'The Three Fishers':
    Men must work and women must weep
    And the sooner it's over, the sooner to sleep.

30. Richard Aldington, *Women Must Work: A Novel* (London: Chatto & Windus, 1934) p. 25.

31. *Ibid.*, p. 142.

32. *Ibid.*, p. 380.

33. *Sunday Referee*, 30 September 1934.

34. *The Times Literary Supplement*, 20 September 1934.

35. *The Times*, 21 September and *The Observer* and *The Sunday Times*, 23 September 1934.

36. G. Eliot Smith, *Human History* (London: Jonathan Cape, 1930, 1934) pp. 25-34.
37. Aldington, *Death of a Hero*, p. 335.
38. *Apocalypse* was edited by Aldington and published in Florence by Orioli in 1931 and in London (with an introduction by Aldington) by Martin Secker the following year. *Last Poems* was edited by Aldington and Orioli and published by Orioli in Florence in 1932 and, with an introduction by Aldington, by Secker in London in 1933.
39. D.H. Lawrence, *Apocalypse*, p. 307. Aldington not only quoted this passage in his introduction to the work, but would use it to close his biography of Lawrence, *Portrait of a Genius, But ...* (New York: Duell, Sloan and Pearce, 1949; London: Heinemann, 1950) p. 354.
40. D.H. Lawrence, *Phoenix: The Posthumous Papers* (New York: Penguin Books, 1972) p. 147.
41. Richard Aldington to Thomas MacGreevy, 11 August 1935 (TCD).
42. *The Spectator*, 31 May 1935.
43. Richard Aldington, ed., *The Spirit of Place: An Anthology Compiled from the Prose of D.H. Lawrence* (London: Heinemann, 1935).
44. Lawrence had also been an earlier subject: *D.H. Lawrence: An Indiscretion* had been published by Glenn Hughes as a University of Washington Chapbook (no. 6) (Seattle: University of Washington Book Store, 1927) and re-issued by Chatto & Windus in 1930.
45. Aldington, *Artifex*, pp. 10, 16.
46. *Ibid.*, pp. 27-28.
47. *Ibid.*, p. 48.
48. *Ibid.*, p. 95.
49. *Ibid.*, pp. 158-59.
50. *Ibid.*, pp. 185-91.
51. Richard Aldington to Eric Warman, 18 September 1936 (S.I.U.).

8. The Private Life: Leading a Double Life, 1930-1936

1. Charles Prentice to Richard Aldington, 10 February 1931 (S.I.U.); 'the two Florentine members' refers to Douglas and Orioli, 'members' of the 'Canterbury Literary Society' – see p. 29 above.
2. Charles Prentice to Richard Aldington, 7 November 1932 (S.I.U.).
3. Richard Aldington to Brigit Patmore, 30 March 1930 (Texas).
4. Richard Aldington to Brigit Patmore, 'Tuesday [1 April] 1930' (Texas).
5. Richard Aldington to Brigit Patmore, 5 February 1931 (Texas).
6. Richard Aldington to Brigit Patmore, 15 February 1931 (Texas).
7. Richard Aldington to Brigit Patmore, 18 September 1932 (Texas).
8. Brigit Patmore to Thomas MacGreevy, 28 November 1930 (TCD).
9. Richard Aldington to Derek Patmore, 8 March 1931(Texas).
10. Douglas and Orioli never did visit Aldington on the Riviera.
11. Richard Aldington to Thomas MacGreevy, 6 February 1931 (TCD).

12. Thomas MacGreevy to Charles Prentice, 29 July 1931 (Reading).

13. Richard Aldington to Derek Patmore, 15 June 1933 (Texas).

14. Richard Aldington to Thomas MacGreevy, 6 February 1931 (TCD). Orioli had recently been in London with Frieda Lawrence, discussing the publication of Lawrence's work with Martin Secker. For a more detailed account of Aldington's homophobia and its impact on his relationship with Derek Patmore, see Whelpton, *Richard Aldington: Poet, Soldier and Lover*, pp. 369-370.

15. Strenuous and continued attempts on Aldington's part to get the play published or performed – including his first contact with Crosby Gaige for four years – proved unsuccessful, until 1936, when it was published by Doubleday, Doran in New York and G.P. Putnam's Sons in London; it was never performed.

16. Derek Patmore, 'Introduction', in Brigit Patmore, *My Friends When Young*, p. 26.

17. Richard Aldington to Richard Church, 9 February 1933 (Texas).

18. Richard Aldington to Harold Raymond, 29 December 1934 (Reading).

19. Thomas MacGreevy to Charles Prentice, 29 July 1931 (Reading).

20. Richard Aldington to Thomas MacGreevy (undated), probably end November 1931(TCD).

21. Richard Aldington to H.D., 25 May and 26 August 1929 (Yale).

22. H.D. to Glenn Hughes (undated), probably early May 1929 (Yale); H.D. to George Plank, 30 May 1929 (Yale); H.D. to John Cournos, 3 July 1929 (Yale).

23. Richard Aldington to H.D., 17 August 1931(Yale).

24. Richard Aldington to H.D., 21 February 1932 (Yale).

25. For an account of the relationship between D.H. Lawrence and H.D., see Whelpton, *Richard Aldington: Poet, Soldier and Lover*, pp. 109-110, 133-134, 146, 158-161, 171-172, 348.

26. Richard Aldington to H.D. (undated), May 1931 (Yale).

27. *Medallions in Clay*, bringing together all Aldington's translations (*Anyte of Tegea, Meleager of Gadara, the Anacreontea, Latin Poets of the Renaissance*) had first been published in New York by A.A. Knopf in 1921; Chatto brought out their edition in 1930.

28. Richard Aldington to H.D., 5 June 1931 (Yale).

29. Richard Aldington to H.D., 23 February 1930 (Yale).

30. Richard Aldington to H.D., 10 January 1930 (Yale).

31. Caroline Zilboorg, *Richard Aldington and H.D.: Their Lives in Letters, 1918-1961* (Manchester University Press, 2003) p. 232.

32. Richard Aldington to Brigit Patmore (undated), probably 13 May 1929, and 14 May 1929 (Texas). For a discussion of the state of the relationship between H.D. and Aldington after their meetings in Paris in 1929, and of Patmore's response to it, see Whelpton, *Richard Aldington: Poet, Soldier and Lover*, pp. 347-351.

33. Brigit Patmore to H.D., 11 May 1930 (Yale).

34. Brigit Patmore to H.D., 21 July 1930 (Yale).

35. Richard Aldington to H.D., 13 December 1930 (Yale).

36. For the correspondence relating to this incident, see: Richard Aldington to Brigit Patmore, 6, 12, 19 and 20 February 1931 (Texas); Richard Aldington to H.D., 12 and 24 February 1931 (Yale); Richard Aldington to Thomas MacGreevy, 6, 8 and 17 February 1931 (TCD); and Charles Prentice to Thomas MacGreevy, 18 February 1931 (TCD).

37. Richard Aldington to H.D., 17 March 1931 (Yale).

38. Richard Aldington to Derek Patmore, 9 March 1931 (Texas).

39. Zilboorg, *Richard Aldington and H.D.*, p. 227.

40. Richard Aldington to H.D., 5 June, 17 and 21 August 1931 (Yale).

41. H.D. to Charles Prentice, 2 November 1931 (Reading).

42. Richard Aldington to H.D., 21 February 1932 (Yale).

43. Their correspondence resumed in 1955, when Black wrote to Aldington after reading *Lawrence of Arabia*, and continued, with some intermissions, until 1962. Black married the South African poet Vincent Swart in 1939, but they were divorced in 1941; she subsequently remarried and became Eunice Gluckman, giving birth to a daughter in 1948.

44. Aldington's first three lovers were Patmore, H.D. and Florence Fallas.

45. Richard Aldington to Marjorie Pollard, 2 and 16 April, 3, 12 and 13 May, 15 August and 27 November 1933 (S.I.U.). Pollard married the journalist and Catholic commentator John Leonard Beevers in June 1934.

46. Richard Aldington to Eunice Black, 24 June and 3 July 1932 (Yale).

47. Richard Aldington to Eunice Black, 23 July 1932 (Yale).

48. Richard Aldington to Eunice Black, 18 and 20 November 1932 (Yale).

49. Richard Aldington to Eunice Black, 25 November 1932 (Yale).

50. Richard Aldington to Eunice Black, 17 January 1933 (Yale).

51. Richard Aldington to Brigit Patmore, 28 January 1933 (Texas).

52. Richard Aldington to Eunice Black, 15 August 1933 (Yale).

53. Unpublished conversation between David Wilkinson and Eunice Gluckman, 30 December 1982.

54. See Aldington, *Death of a Hero*, pp. 75-76 and 83, and *All Men Are Enemies*, pp. 9-10, 13-14 and 31-37.

55. Richard Aldington to Eunice Gluckman, 10 September and 14 November 1960 (Yale).

56. See Whelpton, *Richard Aldington: Poet, Soldier and Lover*, pp. 28-31 and 35.

57. Aldington, *Death of a Hero*, p. 6; for Ursula Bloom's account, in *Holiday Mood* (London: Hutchinson, 1934), see Whelpton, *Richard Aldington: Poet, Soldier and Lover*, pp. 28-29.

58. Richard Aldington to Eunice Gluckman, 14 November 1960.

59. Unpublished interview between Dorothy Yorke and Walter and Lilian Lowenfels, 1964 (S.I.U.).

60. *Sunday Referee*, 6 September 1931.

61. Irene Rathbone, *Was There a Summer?* (London: Constable & Co. Ltd, 1943).

62. It was *Was There a Summer?* that brought Cunard and Rathbone together. Having read the poem on its publication in 1943, Cunard approached

Rathbone at a PEN Club dinner in London to ask her to contribute to the anthology she was compiling in support of the French resistance. They became close friends. Rathbone's correspondence with Louise Morgan Theis began in response to the latter's critical reviews of her novels; they did not meet in person until 1952.

63. Irene Rathbone to Richard Aldington, 4 May 1931 (Reading).
64. Irene Rathbone, *October* (London: Dent & Sons, 1934) p. 31.
65. Irene Rathbone, *They Call It Peace* (London: Dent & Sons, 1936) p. 543. The novel was dedicated to Aldington. For a detailed discussion of Rathbone's novels and their connections with her personal life, see Caroline Zilboorg, 'Irene Rathbone: The Great War and Its Aftermath', in Patrick Quinn, ed., *Recharting the Thirties* (London: Associated University Presses, 1996) pp. 64-81.
66. The current writer learned this through email exchanges with Lynn Knight in 2016 and a telephone conversation with Nicholas Utechin in 2017.
67. Irene Rathbone to Nancy Cunard, 27 September 1953 (Texas).

9. The Private Life: Meltdown, 1936-1937

1. Philip Snow, *Stranger and Brother: A Portrait of C.P. Snow* (London: Macmillan, 1982) p. 49.
2. Snow's Rede Lecture, 'The Two Cultures', was delivered on 7 May 1959.
3. See *Encounter* vol. 1, no. 9 (December 1938).
4. 'Beachcomber' was (from 1924-1975) the humourist, J.B. Morton.
5. *To-Day*, vol. 6, no. 32 (October 1919) p. 64.
6. William Wordsworth, *The Prelude*, lines 692-93.
7. Richard Aldington, *Very Heaven* (London: Heinemann, 1937) pp. 367 and 376.
8. *Ibid.*, pp. 122 and 322.
9. Richard Aldington to F.S. Flint, 3 May 1921, in Michael Copp, ed., *Imagist Dialogues: Letters Between Aldington, Flint and Others* (Cambridge: Lutterworth Press, 2009).
10. Aldington, *Very Heaven*, p. 73.
11. See Richard Aldington to Eunice Black, 7 April 1936 (Yale), and Richard Aldington to Leonard Bacon, 17 July and 21 August 1936 (Yale). The plan to visit Japan may have been a tentative arrangement with the Glovers. With Hal much recovered since his return to England in July 1935, the couple travelled extensively through Europe and to Japan and the east coast of Africa during 1936 and 1937.
12. Undated entry (circa 1938) in a notebook in the Brigit Patmore archive at Texas.
13. Ralph Pinker to Alexander Frere and Harold Raymond, 1 December 1936 (Reading).
14. Alexander Frere to Harold Raymond, 12 January 1937 (Reading).
15. Harold Raymond to Ralph Pinker, 13 November 1936 (Reading).

16. Harold Raymond to Ralph Pinker, 10 November 1936 (Reading).
17. Harold Raymond to Richard Aldington, 9 November 1935 (S.I.U.).
18. Harold Raymond to Richard Aldington, 20 December 1935 (S.I.U.).
19. Richard Aldington to Harold Raymond, 16 January 1936 (Reading).
20. Richard Aldington to Alister Kershaw, 13 July 1948 (S.I.U.).
21. Richard Aldington to H.D., 15 January 1937 (Yale).
22. H.D. to Jessie Capper, 1 February 1937 (Yale).
23. Richard Aldington to Brigit Patmore, 30 March 1930 (Texas). See page 81 above.
24. Richard Aldington to Alexander and Patricia Frere (undated), probably 5 December 1936, in Gates, *Richard Aldington: An Autobiography in Letters*, p. 144.
25. *Ibid.*
26. Richard Aldington to H.D., 15 January 1937 (Yale).
27. *Ibid.*
28. Netta Patmore to Richard Aldington (undated) (S.I.U.).
29. Richard Aldington to Alexander and Patricia Frere, 21 December 1936, in Gates, *Richard Aldington: An Autobiography in Letters*, pp. 145-47.
30. Ellen Doubleday to Brigit Patmore, 30 January 1937 (Texas).
31. Richard Aldington to Henry Slonimsky, 2 January 1937 (S.I.U.).
32. Richard Aldington to Henry Slonimsky, 7 January 1937 (S.I.U.).
33. Netta Patmore to Richard Aldington, 9, 14 and 15 January 1937 (S.I.U.).
34. Brigit Patmore to Eric and Violet Warman, 12 January 1937 (S.I.U.).
35. Richard Aldington to Alexander and Pat Frere, 20 January 1937, in Gates, *Richard Aldington: An Autobiography in Letters*, pp. 147-49.
36. Richard Aldington to H.D., 15 January 1937 (Yale). See Aldington, *All Men Are Enemies*, p. 495.
37. H.D. to George Plank, 17 January 1937 (Yale).
38. Bryher to H.D., 3 February 1937 (Yale).
39. Richard Aldington to Giuseppe Orioli, 26 January 1937 (S.I.U.). Aldington did not meet up with Prentice in Florence, the latter having been recalled to Scotland because of the death of his father.
40. Unpublished notebook of Brigit Patmore dating from 1938 (Texas).
41. Brigit Patmore to H.G. Wells, 28 January 1937 (UOI).
42. Derek Patmore, 'Introduction', in Brigit Patmore, *When We Were Young*, p. 38.
43. *Ibid.*, pp. 41-42.
44. Patmore was not, of course, a widow; she was still married to Deighton Patmore.
45. Alec Waugh, *My Brother Evelyn*, pp. 65-67.
46. See Richard Aldington, *The Crystal World* (London: Heinemann, 1937).
47. Derek Patmore, in Brigit Patmore, *My Friends When Young*, p. 38. For the circumstances which led to this, see Whelpton, *Richard Aldington: Poet, Soldier and Lover*, p. 55.
48. Jean Warman was born in 1932, Elizabeth Frere (named after Elizabeth von Arnim) in 1937.

49. Brigit Patmore to Louise Morgan Theis, 30 June 1938 (Yale).
50. Richard Aldington to Eunice Gluckman, 27 April 1961 (Yale).

10. Divorce, 1937-1938.

1. H.D. to Jessie Capper, 1 February 1937 (Yale).
2. Untitled and undated account by H.D. (Yale); this appears to be an early draft of her statement.
3. Undated notes by H.D. addressed to Bryher (Yale).
4. H.D. to Jessie Capper, 1 February 1937 (Yale).
5. Barbara Guest, *Herself Defined: The Poet H.D. and Her World* (London: Collins, 1985).
6. H.D. to George Plank, 18 June 1938.

11. A Crystal World? 1937-1939

1. Brigit Patmore to Eric and Violet Warman, 4 February 1937 (S.I.U.).
2. *The Times*, 2 April 1937; *The Times Literary Supplement*, 13 March 1937; *The Sunday Times*, 14 March 1937.
3. *Daily Telegraph*, 16 March 1937.
4. *Daily Mail*, 18 March 1937.
5. *Poetry*, June 1938.
6. Richard Aldington to Alexander Frere, 11 August 1937 (Rushden).
7. Richard Aldington to Giuseppe Orioli, 17 July 1937 (Texas).
8. Richard Aldington, *Seven Against Reeves: A Comedy-Farce* (London: Heinemann, 1938; New York: Doubleday, Doran, 1938) pp. 94-95.
9. *The Times Literary Supplement*, 26 February 1938; *The Times*, 4 March 1938; *The Sunday Times*, 20 February 1938.
10. Charles Seddon Evans to Richard Aldington, 26 August 1937 (Rushden).
11. Richard Aldington to Eric Warman, 18 August 1937, in Gates, *Richard Aldington: An Autobiography in Letters*, p. 151.
12. See Richard Aldington to Giuseppe Orioli, 4 February 1938 (S.I.U.), and 9 February and 12 December 1938 (Texas).
13. Their address was 22 Boulevard de Chamblandes, Pully.
14. Richard Aldington to Eric Warman, 20 May 1938 (S.I.U.).
15. C.P. Snow, *Richard Aldington: An Appreciation* (London: Heinemann, 1938). The re-issued Aldington works were: *Death of a* Hero, *The Colonel's Daughter*, *All Men Are Enemies*, *Very Heaven*, *Voltaire* and *Soft Answers*.
16. Richard Aldington to Eric Warman, 20 May 1938 (S.I.U.).
17. Thomas MacGreevy to Richard Aldington, 21 September 1958 (S.I.U.). MacGreevy had only re-established contact with Aldington (after a silence of nearly 20 years) that summer.
18. Richard Aldington to Eric Warman, 9 November 1938 (S.I.U.).
19. Richard Aldington to Leonard Bacon, 16 November 1938 (Yale).
20. Leonard Bacon to Richard Aldington, 30 November and 23 December 1938 (Yale).

21. Aldington told Bacon on 2 January 1939 that this inheritance amounted to $2,500. (Yale).

12. The New World – Again, 1939-1942

1. The Columbia lectures were on: Housman; Yeats; Lawrence and H.D.; Osbert and Sacheverell Sitwell; and Eliot and Pound. Aldington's *Ezra Pound and T.S. Eliot: A Lecture* and *A.E. Housman and W.B. Yeats: Two Lectures* were published in Hurst, Berkshire by the Peacocks Press in 1954 and 1955, respectively. The Philadelphia lecture was on Yeats.
2. Richard Aldington to Henry Slonimsky, 7 April 1939 (S.I.U.).
3. Richard Aldington to Eric Warman, 5 June 1939 (S.I.U.).
4. James Whitall (1889-1954) was an American author and translator who spent fourteen years in England, working for publishing houses.
5. Richard Aldington, 'Norman Douglas and Calabria', *Atlantic Monthly*, CLXIII (June 1939) pp. 757-60; 'D.H. Lawrence: Ten Years After', *Saturday Review of Literature*, 24 June 1939, pp. 3-4; 'Des Imagistes', *Saturday Review of Literature*, 16 March 1940, pp. 3-4; 'Percy Bysshe Shelley', *Saturday Review of Literature*, 7 December 1940, p. 7; 'Going Native', *Esquire*, February 1940, pp. 56 and 100; 'Errant Knight of Capri', *Esquire*, December 1941, pp. 74 and 230-31.
6. Richard Aldington, *W. Somerset Maugham: An Appreciation* (New York: Doubleday, Doran, 1939).
7. Leonard Bacon, *Semi-Centennial: Some of the Life and Part of the Opinions* (New York: Harper Brothers, 1939).
8. These appeared in the September, October, November and December 1940 issues of the journal.
9. Richard Aldington to Alvin Manuel, 3 May 1940 (U.C.L.A.).
10. Richard Aldington to H.D., 20 July 1939 (Yale).
11. Richard Aldington to H.D., 9 August 1939 (Yale).
12. Richard Aldington to H.D., 20 July and 9 August 1939 (Yale).
13. Quoted in A. David Moody, *Ezra Pound: Poet: A Portrait of the Man and His Work: Volume II: The Epic Years 1921-1939* (Oxford: Oxford University Press, 2014) p. 301.
14. Richard Aldington to Henry Slonimsky, 5 September 1939 (S.I.U.).
15. Richard Aldington to Leonard Bacon, 26 September 1939 (Yale). In New York the Aldington apartment was number 5E at 620 West 115th Street.
16. Richard Aldington to Henry Slonimsky, 26 September 1939 (S.I.U.).
17. H.D. to Richard Aldington, 13 October 1939 (S.I.U.).
18. Richard Aldington to H.D., 29 November 1939 (Yale).
19. *Ibid*.
20. Richard Aldington to Henry Slonimsky, 9 May 1940 (S.I.U.).
21. Richard Aldington to Henry Slonimsky, 12 August 1942.
22. This criticism began during the war itself: perhaps the most explicit literary condemnation was Evelyn Waugh's 1943 portrait of Auden and Isherwood as Parsnip and Pimpernel in *Put Out More Flags* (London: Penguin Books, 1943).

23. Richard Aldington, 'The Horn of Roland' (undated) (S.I.U.).
24. Richard Aldington to Henry Slonimsky, 5 June 1940 (S.I.U.).
25. See letters from Richard Aldington to Eric Warman, 15 June, 15 August, 10 September, 11 November 1940 (S.I.U.).
26. Richard Aldington to Henry Slonimsky, 11 July 1940 (S.I.U.).
27. Richard Aldington to Henry Slonimsky, 23 August 1940 (S.I.U.).
28. The family stayed in the Dupont Circle Apartments on Connecticut Avenue.
29. Richard Aldington to H.D., 30 April 1941(Yale).
30. Richard Aldington to Violet Schiff, 7 February 1949 (British Library). Sydney Schiff had died in October 1944.
31. Richard Aldington to Henry Slonimsky, 8 November and 13 December 1940 (S.I.U.).
32. Richard Aldington to Henry Slonimsky, 11 April 1941 (S.I.U.).
33. Richard Aldington to Henry Slonimsky, 5 June 1940 (S.I.U.).
34. Richard Aldington to Eric Warman, 11 March 1941 (S.I.U.).
35. Richard Aldington to H.D., 30 April 1941 (Yale). This was the first exchange of letters between Aldington and H.D. for nearly eighteen months and his letter does suggest that there may have been correspondence in the intervening period that never reached its destination, a common occurrence during the war.
36. Catherine Aldington, 'Richard Aldington: Souvenir de Mon Père', 1984, in D. Kempton and H.R. Stoneback, eds, *Locations and Dislocations: Proceedings of the Fourth International Richard Aldington Conference* (Les-Saintes-Maries-de-la-Mer, France, and New Palz, NY: Gregau Press and International Richard Aldington Society, 2008).
37. Richard Aldington to Alexander Frere, 14 June 1941, in Gates, *Richard Aldington: An Autobiography in Letters*, p. 182. Frere now had two children, Richard Tobias having been born in 1938.
38. Aldous Huxley, *Ends and Means* (New York: Harper & Brothers, 1937).
39. Richard Aldington, 'Notes in New Mexico', unpublished essay (S.I.U.).
40. D.H. Lawrence, 'New Mexico', in *Phoenix: The Posthumous Papers* (New York: Penguin Books, 1972) pp. 142-43.
41. Richard Aldington to Frieda Lawrence, 1 August 1941 (S.I.U.).
42. Confusingly, Aldington's biography of Wellington was published in the US (by Viking in 1943) under the title *The Duke*, but in the UK (by Heinemann in 1946) as *Wellington*. This was due to the fact that Philip Guedalla's 1931 biography had appeared in the UK as *The Duke* (Hodder & Stoughton, 1931) and in the US as *Wellington* (Harper & Brothers, 1931).
43. Richard Aldington, *Wellington: Being an Account of the Life & Achievements of Arthur Wellesley, 1ˢᵗ Duke of Wellington* (London: Heinemann, 1946) p. 4.
44. *Ibid*., pp. 8-9.
45. *Ibid*., p. 240.
46. *Ibid*., p. 8.
47. *Ibid*., p. 242.
48. Richard Aldington to Leonard Bacon, 26 May 1942 (Yale).
49. Richard Aldington to Leonard Bacon, 4 July 1942 (Yale).

50. Richard Aldington to Marshall Best, 10 July 1942 (Viking).
51. Richard Aldington, 'Notes in Florida', unpublished essay (S.I.U.).
52. Richard Aldington to Leonard Bacon, 2 March 1942 (Yale).
53. Richard Aldington to Henry Slonimsky, 19 October 1941 (S.I.U.). An indictment for treason would be issued against Pound in July 1943 on account of his pro-Fascist broadcasts from Italy.
54. Richard Aldington to Leonard Bacon, 6 August 1942 (Yale).
55. Richard Aldington to Eric Warman, 6 August 1942 (S.I.U.).

13. A New Life – Hollywood, 1942-1946

1. Richard Aldington to Alvin Manuel, 26 July 1942 (U.C.L.A.).
2. Richard Aldington to Bertram Eskell, 29 December 1942 (private collection of Simon Hewett).
3. W. Somerset Maugham, *The Hour Before the Dawn* (New York: Doubleday, Doran, 1942). The film would be made in 1944, with a different writer, directed by Frank Tuttle and starring Veronica Lake.
4. Richard Aldington to Eric Warman, 30 December 1942 (S.I.U.).
5. Richard Aldington to Bertram Eskell, 29 December 1942 (private collection of Simon Hewett).
6. Richard Aldington to Leonard Bacon, 1 January 1943 (Yale).
7. Richard Aldington to Henry Slonimsky, 15 January 1943 (S.I.U.).
8. Richard Aldington to Henry Slonimsky, 10 February 1943 (S.I.U.).
9. Richard Aldington to Henry Slonimsky, 14 April 1943 (S.I.U.); Richard Aldington to Bertram Eskell, 29 December 1942 (private collection of Simon Hewett).
10. Richard Aldington to Leonard Bacon, 12 June 1943 (Yale).
11. Richard Aldington to Alvin Manuel, 7 July 1943 (U.C.L.A.).
12. The *Chicago Daily News* article, 'Liberty Is Won for a Nation by Courage Against Fear', appeared on 1 December 1943.
13. This film, too, would not be made until 1948, directed by William Dieterle and starring Jennifer Jones. In the intervening period, five more screenwriters were hired.
14. Richard Aldington to Leonard Bacon, 19 December 1943 (Yale).
15. Richard Aldington to Eric Warman, 12 February 1944 (S.I.U.).
16. Richard Aldington to Leonard Bacon, 17 February 1944 (Yale).
17. Richard Aldington to Henry Slonimsky, 18 March 1944 (S.I.U.).
18. Richard Aldington to Leonard Bacon, 9 April 1944 (Yale).
19. *The Miracle* was not released until 1959. The screenplay used was by Frank Butler and the film was directed by Irving Rapper and starred Carroll Baker and Roger Moore.
20. Richard Aldington to Eric Warman, 11 April 1944 (S.I.U.).
21. Robert Easton, *Max Brand: The Big 'Westerner'* (Norman, OK: University of Oklahoma Press, 1970) p. 146.
22. *Ibid.*, pp. 229-30.

23. Frederick Faust to Dorothy Faust, 8 April 1944 (Berkeley).

24. Jane Easton to Robert Easton, 19 November 1944, in Robert and Jane Easton, *Love and War: Pearl Harbor Through V-J Day* (Norman, OK: University of Oklahoma Press, 1991) pp. 258-60.

25. Richard Aldington to Henry Slonimsky, 13 September 1944 (S.I.U.).

26. Richard Aldington to Henry Slonimsky, 13 August, 1 and 13 September 1944 (S.I.U.).

27. May Aldington to Richard Aldington, 9 November 1944 (S.I.U.).

28. Richard Aldington to Alvin Manuel, 28 September 1944 (U.C.L.A.).

29. Richard Aldington to Leonard Bacon, 4 March 1945 (Yale).

30. Richard Aldington to Henry Slonimsky, 15 April 1945 (S.I.U.).

31. Richard Aldington to Leonard Bacon, 15 May 1945 (Yale); Richard Aldington to Henry Slonimsky, 19 May 1945 (S.I.U.). Aldington worked intermittently on the *Encyclopaedia Britannica* project for many years but it was never published. The four French romances were *La Princesse de Clèves* by Madame de La Fayette, *Manon Lescaut* by Abbé Prévost, *Les Liaisons Dangereuses* by Choderlos de Laclos and *La Duchesse de Langeais* by Honoré de Balzac. (One of the translations, that of *Les Liaisons Dangereuses*, was Aldington's own, published by Routledge in 1924.) The book was also published by Duell, Sloan and Pearce in the US.

32. Richard Aldington to P.A.G. Aldington, 22 April 1946 (S.I.U.).

33. Richard Aldington to Leonard Bacon, 13 July 1945 (Yale).

34. Richard Aldington to Eric Warman, 10 and 25 August 1945 (S.I.U.).

35. Richard Aldington to Leonard Bacon, 24 May 1945 (Yale).

36. The book would not appear in England until six years after Aldington's death, when it was published by Cassell.

37. Richard Aldington to Herbert Read, 19 January 1946 (Victoria).

38. Richard Aldington to H.D., 23 January 1946 (Yale).

39. Richard Aldington to P.A.G. Aldington, 5 April 1946 (S.I.U.).

40. Richard Aldington to Leonard Bacon, 7 March 1946; Richard Aldington to Eric Warman, 10 April 1946 (S.I.U.); Richard Aldington to P.A.G. Aldington, 19 March 1946 (S.I.U.).

41. Richard Aldington to H.D., 24 April 1951 (Yale).

42. Richard Aldington to Eric Warman, 8 June 1946 (S.I.U.).

43. Richard Aldington to Eric Warman, 17 June 1946 (S.I.U.).

44. Richard Aldington to Lawrence Clark Powell, 28 July 1946, in Gates, *Richard Aldington: An Autobiography in Letters*, pp. 214-216.

45. Richard Aldington to Leonard Bacon, 14 August 1946 (Yale); Richard Aldington to Henry Slonimsky, 14 August 1946 (S.I.U.).

14. The Public Face: Novelist, Biographer, Memoirist and Anthologist

1. Richard Aldington to Martin Secker, 6 March 1949 (S.I.U.).

2. The third stanza of Shelley's *The World's Wanderers* reads:

> Weary Wind, who wanderest
> Like the world's rejected guest,
> Hast thou still some secret nest
> On the tree or billow?

3. Richard Aldington, *Rejected Guest: A Novel* (New York: Viking Press, 1939) p. 289.

4. *Ibid.*, pp. 285 and 294.

5. May Aldington became Watkins on her second marriage.

6. Aldington, *Rejected Guest*, p. 288.

7. *Ibid.*, pp. 5, 23, 109, 163 and 296.

8. *The Times Literary Supplement*, 28 October 1939.

9. *The Times*, 30 October 1939.

10. Aldington, *Life for Life's Sake*, p. 61.

11. *Ibid.*, pp. 104 and 156.

12. *Ibid.*, p. 217.

13. *Ibid.*, p. 306.

14. *Ibid.*, pp. 375-76.

15. *Ibid.*, pp. 204-206 and 215.

16. *Ibid.*, pp. 206-207.

17. *Ibid.*, p. 320.

18. *Ibid.*, pp. 404 and 410-11. The two occasions on which Aldington returned from the US to Europe were in October 1935, when he and Patmore left Connecticut, and January 1937 when he was summoned back by Netta.

19. *The New York Times*, 12 January 1941.

20. The book was published by Cassell in 1967.

21. *Manchester Evening News*, 2 January 1948. The anthology appeared in the UK as *Poetry of the English-Speaking World* (London: Heinemann, 1947).

22. *The Times Literary Supplement*, 14 December 1947.

23. Richard Aldington, ed., *Great French Romances* (London: The Pilot Press, 1946; New York: Duell, Sloan and Pearce, 1946); *The Portable Oscar Wilde* (New York: Viking Press, 1946); *Oscar Wilde: Selected Works, with 12 Unpublished Letters* (London: Heinemann, 1946); *Walter Pater: Selected Works* (London: Heinemann, 1948; New York: Duell, Sloan and Pearce, 1948); *The Religion of Beauty: Selections from the Aesthetes* (London: Heinemann, 1950).

24. Selwyn Kittredge, *The Literary Career of Richard Aldington* (PhD. dissertation, two vols) (Ann Arbor, MI: New York University Press, 1976) pp. 508-509.

25. *The Times Literary Supplement*, 19 October 1946.

26. Graeme Cooper to Vivien Whelpton, March 2018.

27. Richard Aldington, *Wellington*, p. 254.

28. *Ibid.*, p. 258.

29. *Ibid.*, p. 261.

30. *The Sunday Times*, 15 September 1946.

31. *Daily Telegraph*, 4 October 1946.

32. *The Times Literary Supplement*, 25 January 1947.

33. *The Manchester Guardian*, 24 January 1947.

15. Back to the Old World, 1946-1947

1. Richard Aldington to Arnold Gyde, 21 August 1946 (Rushden).
2. Irene Rathbone to Nancy Cunard, 14 and 29 November 1946 (Texas).
3. Richard Aldington to Nancy Cunard, 2 September 1946 (Texas).
4. Rathbone quotes Cunard's comment in her own letter to Cunard, 29 November 1946 (Texas).
5. Richard Aldington to Alexander Frere, 6 September 1946 (Rushden).
6. Alexander Frere to Richard Aldington, 24 August 1946 (Rushden).
7. Richard Aldington to P.A.G. Aldington, 18 September 1946 (S.I.U.).
8. Alexander Frere to Richard Aldington, 3 April 1947 (Rushden).
9. Richard Aldington to Leonard Bacon, 14 September 1946 (Yale).
10. Richard Aldington to Henry Slonimsky, 15 September 1946 (S.I.U.).
11. Richard Aldington to Alexander Frere, 6 October 1946 (Rushden).
12. Richard Aldington to P.A.G. Aldington, 8 October 1946 (S.I.U.).
13. Richard Aldington to Richard Church, 2 December 1946 (Texas).
14. Richard Aldington to Douglas Goldring, 21 September 1946, in Steele and Chang, 'Modernism at the Margins', p. 53.
15. Aldington shared his anxieties about the Glovers in a letter to Richard Church on 2 December: 'Hal and Etta seem to be wearying of Colwyn and talk of coming back to Paris. This is excellent news for us but I am frankly a little troubled by the idea of their trying to do it on too little money.' (Texas)
16. Richard Aldington to Thomas MacGreevy, 30 November 1946 (TCD).
17. Richard Aldington to H.D., 2 September 1946 (Yale).
18. Bryher to H.D., 29 September 1946 (Yale).
19. Richard Aldington to H.D., 25 September 1946 (Yale).
20. Richard Aldington to H.D., 7 December 1946 (Yale). May Aldington was 73 years old.
21. H.D. to Richard Aldington, 13 December 1946 (S.I.U.).
22. Richard Aldington to H.D., 26 October 1946 (Yale).
23. Richard Aldington to H.D., 9 and 26 October and 4 November 1946 (Yale).
24. Richard Aldington to H.D., 4 November 1946 (Yale).
25. Guest, *Herself Defined*, p. 284.
26. Richard Aldington to H.D., 22 December 1946 (Yale).
27. Richard Aldington to H.D., 18 January 1947 (Yale).
28. Richard Aldington to H.D., 8 March 1947 (Yale).
29. Richard Aldington to H.D., 2 May 1947 (Yale).
30. H.D. to Richard Aldington, 5 May 1947 (S.I.U.).
31. The specified books were Euripides and Aristotle's *Poetics* for H.D, and Rabelais and Aeschylus (along with Sinclair's ink-stand) for Aldington.
32. Richard Aldington to H.D., 26 April 1947 (Yale). Sinclair had been diagnosed with Parkinson's Disease in the late 1920s and moved with a companion to Buckinghamshire in 1932. She died on 14 November 1946.
33. Richard Aldington to H.D., 15 and 23 May 1947 (Yale).
34. Richard Aldington to H.D., 25 January 1948 (Yale).

35. Richard Aldington to H.D., 18 April 1947 (Yale).
36. Richard Aldington to H.D., 14 May 1947 (Yale).
37. Richard Aldington to P.A.G. Aldington, 5 May 1947 (S.I.U.).
38. H.D. to Richard Aldington, 6 June 1947 (S.I.U.).
39. See Guest, *Herself Defined*, p. 285. The novel was eventually published by the University of Florida Press in 2007.
40. Richard Aldington to H.D., 10 June 1947 (Yale).
41. H.D. to Richard Aldington, 22 June 1947 (S.I.U.).
42. Richard Aldington to H.D., 11 June and 15 July 1947 (Yale).
43. See page 160 above.
44. Alister Kershaw to Richard Aldington, 9 May 1947 (S.I.U.).
45. Netta Aldington to Eric Warman, 9 July 1947 (S.I.U.).
46. Alister Kershaw, *The Pleasure of Their Company* (Brisbane: University of Queensland Press, 1986) pp. 93-95.
47. Richard Aldington to Alister Kershaw, 16 July 1947 (S.I.U.).
48. Richard Aldington to Alister Kershaw, 22 July 1947 (S.I.U.). *Talking Bronco* was published by Faber & Faber in 1946. Campbell did indeed 'knock [Spender's] block off' two years later, on 14 April 1949, when he punched Spender on the nose at a reading that the latter was giving for the Poetry Society in the crypt of the Ethical Church in Bayswater.
49. Albatross was the German-based publisher of English language books in paperback editions for the European market. Under John Holroyd-Reece's management they had published *Soft Answers*, *All Men Are Enemies*, *Women Must Work*, *Very Heaven* and *Seven Against Reeves* between 1935 and 1938. *Rejected Guest* was added to their list in 1947.
50. Richard Aldington to H.D., 11 and 20 June and 22 July 1947 (Yale).
51. Richard Aldington to Henry Slonimsky, 8 July 1947 (S.I.U.).
52. Richard Aldington to H.D., 20 June 1947 (Yale).

16. The Sociable Life: Paradise Regained – and Lost, 1947-1949

1. Richard Aldington to H.D., 7 August and 13 October 1947 (Yale).
2. W.D. Deasey, 'Lunch at the Villa', *The Bulletin Literary Supplement* (Sydney), no. 23, 30 December 1980, pp. 177-80.
3. Alister Kershaw to Norman Gates (undated), 1980 (S.I.U.).
4. The third Frere child, Henry, was born in 1945.
5. Richard Aldington to Alister Kershaw, 18 August 1947 (S.I.U.).
6. Richard Aldington to H.D., 31 August 1947 (Yale).
7. Alister Kershaw to Richard Aldington, 27 July 1947 (S.I.U.).
8. From a projected (but discarded) preface for Norman Gates's 1992 selection of Aldington's letters (S.I.U.).
9. Etta Glover died from cardiac problems in June 1947, aged 80.
10. Richard Aldington to H.D., 10 November 1947 (Yale).
11. Richard Church, *The Voyage Home* (London: Heinemann, 1964) p. 75.
12. Richard Aldington to Richard Church, 6 October 1946 (Texas).

13. For examples of Church's lack of charity towards Aldington, see *The Voyage Home*, pp. 72-76, which includes several inaccurate assertions about Aldington's personal life and written works, and his half-hearted review of Aldington's *Walter Pater* in *John O' London's Weekly* on 3 September 1948.
14. Richard Aldington to Alexander Frere, 23 April 1948 (Rushden).
15. Kershaw, *The Pleasure of Their Company*, p. 103.
16. Deasey had never been into combat, but his service as a commando had involved him for six months of 1942 in a training experiment in isolated conditions in the North West Territories that was a horrific and prolonged physical and mental ordeal. His subsequent health problems may well have been triggered by this experience.
17. Geoffrey Dutton, *The Mortal and the Marble* (London: Chapman & Hall, 1950).
18. Geoffrey Dutton, *Out in the Open: An Autobiography* (Brisbane: University of Queensland Press, 1994) pp. 170-71.
19. Alister Kershaw to Richard Aldington, 7 March 1949 (S.I.U.).
20. Alister Kershaw to Richard Aldington, 16 January 1950 (S.I.U.).
21. Alister Kershaw to Richard Aldington, 23 February 1950 (S.I.U.).
22. For an account of her holiday in Rye with Patmore, H.D. and Aldington in 1912, see Whelpton, *Richard Aldington: Poet, Soldier and Lover*, pp. 42.
23. Aldington, *The Religion of Beauty*, p. 5.
24. Alister Kershaw to Richard Aldington, 3 October 1949 (S.I.U.).
25. See Roy Campbell, *Adamastor* (London: Faber & Faber, 1930).
26. Kershaw, *The Pleasure of Their Company*, pp. 48-54.
27. See Campbell, *The Georgiad*, and Aldington's *Death of a Hero* and *Soft Answers*.
28. *The Times Literary Supplement*, 26 February 1949; Ross's review appeared in the 5 February issue. Campbell's essay appeared in *Poetry Review* XL (April-May 1949) and is reproduced in Kershaw and Temple, *Richard Aldington: An Intimate Portrait*, pp. 4-11.
29. Richard Aldington to H.D., 10 June 1948 (Yale).
30. Richard Aldington to Alister Kershaw, 18 June 1948 (S.I.U.).
31. Alister Kershaw to Richard Aldington, 21 July 1948 (S.I.U.).
32. Richard Aldington to William Dibben, 8 August 1948 (S.I.U.).
33. Richard Aldington to Alister Kershaw, 5 October 1948 (S.I.U.).
34. Richard Aldington to Alister Kershaw, 12 October 1948 (S.I.U.).
35. Richard Aldington to Alister Kershaw, 29 December 1948 (S.I.U.).
36. Richard Aldington to Alister Kershaw, 12 October 1948 (S.I.U.).
37. Richard Aldington to Alister Kershaw, 12 October 1948 (S.I.U.). What Aldington could not foresee was that Muggeridge would become a supportive reviewer of his work and a much-needed ally in the years to come.
38. Alister Kershaw to Richard Aldington, 5, 8 and 29 October and 1 November 1948 (S.I.U.).
39. In the event, and not entirely to Aldington's satisfaction, the Penguin poetry selection was chosen and introduced by William Emrys Williams, Penguin's chief editor, while the letters, although selected by Aldington,

were introduced by Huxley. However, Aldington chose and introduced the Penguin selection of Lawrence's essays and wrote introductions for their editions of *The White Peacock*, *Aaron's Rod*, *Kangaroo*, *Etruscan Places*, *The Lost Girl*, *The Plumed Serpent*, *St Mawr*, *The Virgin and the Gipsy* and *The Woman Who Rode Away and Other Stories*. (*Sons and Lovers* and *The Rainbow* were already in print in Penguin editions.) Aldington's introductions were also used for the Heinemann editions of *The White Peacock*, *Kangaroo*, *The Plumed Serpent*, *The Lost Girl* and *The Woman Who Rode Away and Other Stories*, while he wrote further introductions for their editions of *Mornings in Mexico*, *The Trespasser*, *The Man Who Died*, *Twilight in Italy*, *The Rainbow*, *Sea in Sardinia* and *England, My England and Other Stories*. Heinemann published *Women in Love* with an Aldington introduction in 1954. He thus wrote a total of seventeen introductions, as well as selecting the material for the *Selected Letters* and *Selected Essays* and writing a monograph for the Penguin series and the Heinemann biography.

40. Norman Gates archives at S.I.U..

41. Allan Wingate was publishing the *Complete Poems*, a new edition of *Fifty Romance Lyric Poems* and the Chawton edition of Jane Austen's novels, with an introduction by Aldington; Arthur Barker was bringing out a new edition of *All Men Are Enemies*, under licence from Heinemann; and Evans Brothers was publishing *Four English Portraits* and *The Strange History of Charles Waterton*.

42. Richard Aldington to Alvin Manuel, 31 August and 7 November 1948 (U.C.L.A.).

43. Henry Williamson, *The Story of a Norfolk Farm* (London: Faber & Faber, 1941).

44. Kershaw, *The Pleasure of Their Company*, pp. 75 and 80.

45. See Aldington's *Death of a Hero* and Williamson's *The Patriot's Progress* (London: Geoffrey Bles, 1930).

46. *The Wet Flanders Plain* (London: Faber & Faber, 1929) was Williamson's account of his return visits to the battlefields in 1925 and 1927.

47. Richard Aldington to H.D., 8 May 1949 (Yale). The current writer has not been able to establish the identity of the American visitors to whom Aldington refers.

48. John Holroyd-Reece was nicknamed 'the Bird' because of his company's name: Albatross.

49. Richard Aldington to Alister Kershaw, 15 May 1949 (S.I.U.).

50. Henry Williamson, in Kershaw and Temple, *Richard Aldington: An Intimate Portrait*, pp. 166-67.

51. Richard Aldington to Alister Kershaw, 20 January 1949 (S.I.U.).

52. Richard Aldington to H.D., 11 May 1948 (Yale).

53. Richard Aldington to Alister Kershaw, 20 May 1949 (S.I.U.).

54. Richard Aldington to Leonard Bacon, 20 September 1949 (Yale).

55. Richard Aldington to Alister Kershaw, 4 October 1949 (S.I.U.).

56. Dutton, *Out in the Open*, pp. 170-71.

57. Alister Kershaw to Richard Aldington, 22 September 1949 (S.I.U.).

58. Richard Aldington to Alister Kershaw, 20 October 1949 (S.I.U.).

59. Richard Aldington to Alister Kershaw, 13 November 1949 (S.I.U.).

60. Alister Kershaw to Richard Aldington, 18 November 1949 (S.I.U.).

61. *The Mint* would appear before Aldington's T.E. Lawrence biography; it was published by Jonathan Cape in 1955.

62. Richard Aldington to William Dibben, 22 November 1948 (S.I.U.).

63. Richard Aldington to Martin Secker, 4 February and 6 March 1949 (S.I.U.).

64. Richard Aldington to Alister Kershaw, 13 and 24 September 1949 (S.I.U.).

65. Richard Aldington to William Dibben, 5 November 1949. The American poet, Witter Bynner had been a close friend of the Lawrences in New Mexico. His book, *Journey with Genius: Recollections and Reflections Concerning the D.H. Lawrences*, was published in New York by John Day Co. in 1951.

66. Richard Aldington to Alister Kershaw, 20 December 1949 (S.I.U.).

17. The Public Face: The Old Loyalties

1. For an account of this episode in H.D.'s life, see Whelpton, *Richard Aldington: Poet, Soldier and Lover*, pp. 156-161 and 348.

2. Richard Aldington to H.D., 29 April 1948 (Yale).

3. Ada Lawrence, Middleton Murry, Catherine Carswell, Dorothy Brett, Helen Corke, Mabel Dodge Luhan, Jessie Chambers and Frieda herself had all published their own reminiscences.

4. H.D. to Richard Aldington, 20 June 1948 (S.I.U.). Zilboorg concludes that the reference here is to the Odyssey Press edition of *Lady Chatterley's Lover* (Leipzig, 1933), which carried a brief introduction by Frieda Lawrence (Zilboorg, *Richard Aldington and H.D.*, p. 290).

5. See H.D., *Bid Me to Live* (New York: Dial Press, 1960) pp. 163-84.

6. Richard Aldington to H.D., 27 June 1948 (Yale).

7. Richard Aldington to Martin Secker, 6 March 1949 (S.I.U.).

8. Richard Aldington to Alister Kershaw, 9 October 1948 (S.I.U.).

9. Richard Aldington to Alister Kershaw, 22 October 1948 (S.I.U.).

10. Alister Kershaw to Richard Aldington, 6 February 1949 (S.I.U.).

11. Richard Aldington to Alexander Frere, 22 October 1949 (Rushden).

12. Richard Aldington to Alexander Frere, 15 and 22 October 1949 (Rushden).

13. Richard Aldington, *D.H. Lawrence: Portrait of a Genius, But . . .*, p. 163.

14. *Ibid.*, p. 111.

15. *Ibid.*, p. 76.

16. *Ibid.*, p. 131.

17. *Ibid.*, p. 269.

18. *Ibid.*, p. 170.

19. *Ibid.*, p. 24.

20. *Ibid.*, p. 32.

21. *Ibid.*, pp. 80, 210.

22. *Ibid.*, pp. 95 and 329.

23. *Ibid.*, pp. 290.
24. *The Observer*, 2 April 1950.
25. See: Richard Aldington to *The Observer*, 29 March 1950; Assistant Editor of *The Observer* to Richard Aldington, 8 April 1950; Alexander Frere to *The Observer*, 12 April 1950; Richard Aldington to *The Observer*, 13 and 14 April 1950; Alexander Frere to Richard Aldington, 17 April 1950; Richard Aldington to Alexander Frere, 21 April 1950 (all at Rushden).
26. Richard Aldington to David Garnett, 19 May, 5 and 22 June 1950 (Texas).
27. *The Times Literary Supplement*, 31 March 1950. Muggeridge also wrote the *Daily Telegraph* review of the same date.
28. *New Statesman and Nation*, 29 April 1950; *Daily Mail*, 1 April 1950.
29. Richard Aldington to Alister Kershaw, 2/3 April 1950 (S.I.U.).
30. Frieda Lawrence to Richard Aldington, [*ante* 26] April 1950 (S.I.U.).
31. *The Sunday Times*, 2 April 1950.
32. Herbert Read, 'An Irregular Genius: The Significance of D.H. Lawrence', *World Review*, no. 17 (July 1950) pp. 50-56.
33. Aldington, *D.H. Lawrence: Portrait of a Genius, But . . .* , p. 130.
34. *Saturday Review of Literature*, 29 April 1950.
35. Moore's first Lawrence biography, *The Life and Works of D.H. Lawrence*, was published in 1950 by George Allen & Unwin in London and by Twayne in New York; his second, *The Intelligent Heart*, was published by Heinemann in London in 1953 and by Farrar, Straus and Young in New York in 1954; his third, *The Priest of Love* was published by Heinemann in London, and by Farrar, Straus and Giroux in Gordonsville, Virginia in 1974.
36. Richard Aldington to Leonard Bacon, 16 May 1950.
37. Richard Aldington, 'Introduction', in D.H. Lawrence, *The Trespasser* (London: Heinemann, 1950); 'Introduction', in D.H. Lawrence, *Twilight in Italy* (London: Heinemann, 1950). For a list of the Penguin and Heinemann titles, see note 39 to chapter 16.
38. Richard Aldington to Leonard Bacon, 19 October 1950 (Yale).
39. Kittredge, *The Literary Career of Richard Aldington*, p. 564.
40. Aldington, *Life for Life's Sake*, p. 42.
41. *The Sunday Times*, 20 August 1950.
42. Aldington, *The Religion of Beauty*, pp. 1, 5, 22, 23 and 43.
43. *The Times Literary Supplement*, 1 September 1950.
44. *The Sunday Times*, 27 October 1946. The selection consisted of *The Picture of Dorian Gray*, *Salome*, *The Importance of Being Earnest*, *De Profundis*, *The Critic as Artist*, *Phrases and Philosophies for the Use of the Very Young* and selections from *A Woman of No Importance*, *Lady Windermere's Fan* and *An Ideal Husband* as well as a selection of letters, poems and reviews.
45. Richard Aldington, 'Oscar Wilde', reproduced in Alister Kershaw, ed., *Richard Aldington: Selected Critical Writings, 1928-1960* (Carbondale: Southern Illinois University Press, 1970) pp. 47, 52, 54, 56, 64 and 69
46. *Ibid.*, pp. 42-43.
47. *Ibid.*, pp. 43 and 70.

48. Richard Aldington, 'Walter Pater', reproduced in Kershaw, *Selected Critical Writings*, p. 72.
49. *Ibid.*, p. 79.
50. *Ibid.*, pp. 83.
51. *Ibid.*, p. 88.
52. *Ibid.*, pp. 94 and 101.
53. *New Statesman and Nation*, 13 November 1948.
54. *John O' London's Weekly*, 3 September 1948.
55. Richard Aldington, 'Jane Austen', reproduced in Kershaw, *Selected Critical Writings*, pp. 110-11, 105 and 107-108. Aldington notes that the Cinderella in *Emma* is not the eponymous heroine, but Jane Fairfax.
56. *Ibid.*, pp. 110 and 113.
57. Richard Aldington, 'Laurent Tailhade', *Egoist*, vol. 2, no. 10 (1 October 1915) pp. 159-61.
58. Richard Aldington, *Four English Portraits* (London: Evans Brothers, 1948) p. 171.
59. *Ibid.*, p. 189.
60. *Ibid.*, p. 173.
61. *Ibid.*, p. 149.
62. *Ibid.*, pp. 147 and 180-81.
63. *Ibid.*, p. 177.
64. While both Disraeli and Dickens lived well into the second half of the century, Aldington focuses in both cases on their early lives and achievements.
65. Aldington, *Four English Portraits*, p. 143. Aldington's essay-length account of Waterton's life appeared first in *The Times Literary Supplement*, 29 December 1932, and was subsequently published by Heinemann in a limited private edition in 1934. It also appeared in the *Virginia Quarterly Review*, no. 10 (October 1934) and was included in Aldington, *Artifex* in 1935.
66. *Ibid.*, pp. 11, 16 and 26.
67. *Ibid.*, pp. 8 and 14.
68. *Ibid.*, pp. 57 and 59.
69. *Ibid.*, p. 76.
70. Richard Aldington, *The Strange Life of Charles Waterton, 1782-1865* (London: Evans Brothers, 1949) pp. 170-171; Norman Douglas, 'A Mad Englishman', in *Experiments* (London: Chapman and Hall, 1926); Edith Sitwell, 'Charles Waterton: the South American Wanderer', in *The English Eccentrics* (London: Faber & Faber, 1933); Philip Gosse, *The Squire of Walton Hall* (London: Cassell & Co., 1940).
71. Aldington, *The Strange Life of Charles Waterton*, p. 11.
72. *Ibid.*, p. 12.
73. Aldington, *Four English Portraits*, p. 102. Both these feats were allegedly accomplished by Waterton.
74. *The Times Literary Supplement*, 26 August 1949; Richard Hobson, *Charles Waterton: His Home, Habits and Handiwork* (London: Whittaker & Co., 1867).
75. *The Times Literary Supplement*, 8 September 1949.

76. Richard Aldington to William Dibben, 1 September 1949 (S.I.U.). It is worth noting that, when *The Times Literary Supplement* published Muggeridge's favourable review of *Portrait of a Genius, But ...* some six months later, Aldington did register his surprise, telling Kershaw that it was 'a defeat for Eliot-Sitwellism': Richard Aldington to Alister Kershaw, 2/3 April 1950 (S.I.U.).
77. Richard Aldington to William Dibben, 7 September 1949 (S.I.U.).

18. The Private Life: Crisis, 1950

1. Richard Aldington to Lawrence Clarke Powell, 8 January 1950, in Gates, *Richard Aldington: An Autobiography in Letters*, p. 244. If this figure was correct, either no Patmore payments, income tax or otherwise, had been paid for the whole thirteen years since the settlement (and this does not appear to be the case), or the unpaid portion had accrued interest at a very high rate. Kershaw told Tony Aldington on 17 April: 'There seems to be no doubt that Richard agreed to a tax-free payment and is therefore up for some £1,200 quid in retrospective taxation. Also, of course, it doubles the sum which must be paid hereafter' (S.I.U.).
2. Alister Kershaw to Richard Aldington, 16 January 1950 (S.I.U.).
3. Richard Aldington to Alister Kershaw, 18 January 1950 (S.I.U.).
4. Richard Aldington to Leonard Bacon, 17 January 1950 (Yale).
5. Richard Aldington to Alister Kershaw, 13 January 1950 (S.I.U.). In the General Election of 23 February 1950, the Labour Party did win an overall majority, but only of five seats. They were forced to call another election in October 1951, in which, despite gaining the popular vote, they were defeated by Winston Churchill's Conservative Party. This would be the beginning of a thirteen-year period of Conservative government.
6. T.S. Eliot was awarded the Order of Merit and the Nobel Prize for Literature in 1948.
7. Richard Aldington to William Dibben, 19 January 1950 (S.I.U.).
8. Richard Aldington to H.D., 8 January 1950 (Yale).
9. Richard Aldington to Alister Kershaw, 8 February 1950 (S.I.U.).
10. Richard Aldington to Alister Kershaw, 24 February 1950 (S.I.U.).
11. Richard Aldington to Alexander Frere, 1 March 1950, in Gates, *Richard Aldington: An Autobiography in Letters*, p. 245.
12. Dutton, *Out in the Open*, p. 171.
13. *Ibid.*, pp. 162-63.
14. John Arlott, *Basingstoke Boy* (London: Collins, 1990).
15. Richard Aldington to H.D., 26 October 1946 (Yale).
16. Richard Aldington to Eunice Gluckman, 8 August 1960 (Yale).
17. Nesta Macdonald to Charles Doyle, 27 March 1990 (Victoria).
18. The address of the first flat was Flat 5, 37 Ennismore Gardens, SW17. The arrangement is referred to in Richard Aldington to Alister Kershaw, 13 April 1951(S.I.U.). The second address was 1A Bramerton Street, SW3. See Richard Aldington to Alister Kershaw, 19 December 1952 (S.I.U.).

19. Richard Aldington to Alister Kershaw, 3 and 27 August 1954 (S.I.U.).
20. Richard Aldington to Eunice Gluckman, 8 August 1960 (Yale).
21. Frieda Lawrence to Richard Aldington, 23 May 1950 (S.I.U.).
22. Richard Aldington to Leonard Bacon, 5 May 1950 (Yale).
23. Richard Aldington to Leonard Bacon, 23 September 1950 (Yale).
24. Richard Aldington to Miriam Slonimsky, 12 December 1951 (S.I.U.).
25. Richard Aldington to H.D., 23 May 1950 (Yale). Perdita was married to the American literary agent John Schaffner on 24 June 1950.
26. Richard Aldington to H.D., 2 October 1950 (Yale).
27. Richard Aldington to Alister Kershaw, 24/25 March 1950 (S.I.U.).
28. Richard Aldington to Leonard Bacon, 19 June 1950 (Yale).
29. Richard Aldington to Alister Kershaw, 5 July 1950, and to William Dibben, 7 July 1950 (S.I.U.).
30. Richard Aldington to Denison Deasey, 18 November 1950.
31. Richard Aldington to William Dibben, 5 December 1950 (S.I.U.).
32. Richard Aldington to Alister Kershaw, 22 December 1950 (S.I.U.).
33. Charles Prentice to Richard Aldington, 7 March 1948 (S.I.U.).
34. Charles Prentice to Richard Aldington, 24 April 1948 (S.I.U.).
35. Charles Prentice to Richard Aldington, 11 July and 11 November 1948 (S.I.U.).
36. Charles Prentice to Richard Aldington, 30 January 1949 (S.I.U.).
37. Charles Prentice to Richard Aldington, 20 March 1949 (S.I.U.).
38. Charles Prentice to Richard Aldington, 10 May 1949 (S.I.U.).
39. Richard Aldington to Leonard Bacon, 16 May 1950.
40. Richard Aldington to H.D., 8 January 1947 (Yale).
41. Richard Aldington to Alister Kershaw, 14 August 1952 (S.I.U.).
42. Richard Aldington to Miriam Slonimsky, 15 August 1952 (S.I.U.).
43. Richard Aldington to Miriam Slonimsky, 11 March 1954 (S.I.U.).
44. Arlott, *Basingstoke Boy*, p. 188.
45. Richard Aldington to William Dibben, 22 March 1955 (S.I.U.).
46. Richard Aldington to Alister Kershaw, 22 February 1957 (S.I.U.).
47. Richard Aldington, trans., *The Mystery of the Nativity* (London: Allen & Unwin, 1924). The original text, the fragment of a longer play, the remainder of which is lost, appears in Cohen's *Mystères et Moralités du MS. 617 de Chantilly* (Paris: Champion, 1920).
48. Richard Aldington to Eric Warman, 15 August 1956 (S.I.U.).
49. *Un Songe dans le Jardin du Luxembourg* was published by La Table Ronde in October 1957.
50. Gustave Cohen to Richard Aldington, 30 April 1956 (S.I.U.).
51. Aldington, Patmore and the Freres had stayed at Bormes in the summer of 1932 when Aldington was working on *All Men Are Enemies*.
52. Richard Aldington to H.D., 28 June 1950 (Yale).
53. Richard Aldington to Henry Williamson, 13 February 1953 (S.I.U.).
54. Denison Deasey to Norman Gates, (undated) 1980 (S.I.U.).
55. Richard Aldington to Alan Bird, 15 June 1956, in Miriam Benkovitz, ed., *A Passionate Prodigality: Letters to Alan Bird from Richard Aldington* (New York: New York Public Library, 1975) p. 235.
56. Richard Emeny, *Roy Campbell: Poet of Two Wars* (London: Cecil Woolf, 2014).

57. Peter Alexander, *Roy Campbell: A Political Biography* (Oxford: Oxford University Press, 1982).
58. Richard Aldington, *Introduction to Mistral* (London: Heinemann, 1956) p. 131.
59. Richard Aldington to P.A.G. Aldington, 10 October 1955 (S.I.U.).
60. Roy Campbell to Richard Aldington, 24 February 1951 (S.I.U.).
61. Richard Aldington to Rob Lyle, 19 March 1955 (NYPL). The 'civil servants' included many of the *Criterion* set. Frankie Birrell (1899-1935) was a journalist and critic and one-time lover of David Garnett; Raymond Mortimer (1895-1980), who conducted a long-term relationship with Harold Nicolson (husband of Vita Sackville-West) in the 1920s, was literary editor of the *New Statesman and Nation* from 1935-1947 and lead reviewer at *The Sunday Times* from 1947 onwards.
62. Roy Campbell to Richard Aldington, 24 February 1951 (S.I.U.).
63. Richard Aldington to Henry Williamson, 7 February 1951 (S.I.U.).
64. Richard Aldington to Leonard Bacon, 6 October 1949 (Yale). The award of the prize to Pound in its first year caused such a furore that Congress ended the Library of Congress's involvement in the programme. The unused portion of the grant was returned to the Bollingen Foundation who handed over the future administration of the prize to the Beinecke Library at Yale.
65. Richard Aldington to H.D., 25 November and 16 December 1950 (Yale).
66. Richard Aldington to H.D., 17 June 1951(Yale).
67. Richard Aldington to H.D., 21 July 1951 (Yale).
68. Richard Aldington to H.D., 9 August 1951 (Yale).
69. Richard Aldington to H.D., 26 August 1951 (Yale).
70. Ezra Pound to Richard Aldington, 19 January 1952 (S.I.U.).
71. Ezra Pound to Richard Aldington, 3 February 1952 (S.I.U.).
72. Richard Aldington to Leonard Bacon, 21 March 1952 (Yale).
73. Richard Aldington to H.D., 23 February 1952 (Yale).
74. Richard Aldington to H.D., 24 April 1952 (Yale).
75. Richard Aldington to H.D., 28 June 1950 (Yale).
76. Richard Aldington to H.D., 12 October 1952 (Yale).
77. Richard Aldington to P.A.G. Aldington, 16 November 1950 (S.I.U.).
78. Richard Aldington to Alister Kershaw, 16 November 1951, and to P.A.G. Aldington, 12 January 1952 (S.I.U.). May Aldington died in March 1954.
79. Zilboorg, *Richard Aldington and H.D.*, p. 411.
80. Richard Aldington to H.D., 16 December 1950 (Yale).
81. Richard Aldington to Denison Deasey, 20 January 1955 (Canberra).
82. Richard Aldington to Leonard Bacon, 19 October 1950 (Yale).
83. Richard Aldington to H.D., 29 November 1950 (Yale).
84. Alexander Frere to Richard Aldington, 17 December 1950 (Rushden).

19. The Public Face: Disaster

1. Fred D. Crawford, *Richard Aldington and Lawrence of Arabia: A Cautionary Tale* (Carbondale: University of Southern Illinois Press, 1998).
2. Richard Aldington to Alister Kershaw, 2 January 1951 (S.I.U.).

3. Richard Aldington to Henry Williamson, 4 January 1951 (S.I.U.).

4. In fact, the truth had already been revealed in Léon Bussard's *Le Secret du Colonel Lawrence* (Clermont-Ferrand: Mont-Louis, 1941), a text Kershaw had attempted to obtain for Aldington without success. It would also be stated in a 1954 book, *A Diary with Letters 1931-1950* (Oxford University Press) by Thomas Jones, who had served on the War Cabinet Secretariat during the First World War.

5. Richard Aldington, *Lawrence of Arabia: A Biographical Enquiry* (London: Collins, 1955) p. 40.

6. *Ibid.*, pp. 22 and 36.

7. *Ibid.*, p. 23.

8. *Ibid.*, p. 24.

9. T.E. Lawrence, *The Seven Pillars of Wisdom*. Eight copies of the book were privately printed in 1922 (known as the 'Oxford Text'); an abridged version was published in a subscription of 200 copies (the 'Subscribers' Text') in 1926; a much more stringently abridged version appeared as *Revolt in the Desert* (London: Jonathan Cape) in 1927. The 'Subscribers' Text' was republished by Jonathan Cape in 1935 after Lawrence's death and the original unabridged 'Oxford Text', edited by Jeremy Wilson, appeared in editions of 1997 and 2003 (Fordingbridge: Castle Hill Press).

10. See: Lowell Thomas, *With Lawrence in Arabia* (New York: Century Press, 1924); Robert Graves, *Lawrence and the Arabs* (London: Jonathan Cape, 1927); Basil H. Liddell Hart, *T.E. Lawrence in Arabia and After* (London: Jonathan Cape, 1934); Vyvyan Richards, *Portrait of T.E. Lawrence* (London: Jonathan Cape, 1936).

11. See: *T.E. Lawrence to His Biographer, Robert Graves* (London: Faber & Faber, 1938); *T.E. Lawrence to His Biographer, Liddell Hart* (London: Faber & Faber, 1938). The two publications were brought together in 1963 (London: Cassell).

12. Richard Aldington to Alister Kershaw, 24 July 1951 (S.I.U.). *Secret Despatches from Arabia* (London: Golden Cockerel Press, 1939) was a selection collated by Professor A.W. Lawrence, Lawrence's brother (and manager of Lawrence's literary estate), of articles contributed by Lawrence to the Arab Bureau's Bulletin, issued in Cairo between June 1916 and December 1918 and intended as information and intelligence for the British authorities in the Near and Middle East, the Foreign Office, the War Office and the Admiralty. The relevant official history was Cyril Falls, *Military Operations: Egypt and Palestine* (two volumes) (London: HMSO, 1928). Archibald Wavell (later Field Marshall Sir Archibald Wavell) (1883-1950) was (as a lieutenant colonel) a staff officer with the Egyptian Expeditionary Force from June 1917. His books on the Palestine campaign were: *The Palestine Campaign* (London: Constable, 1933) and *Allenby: A Study in Generalship* (London: Harrap, 1940). General (later Sir) George de Symons Barrow (1864-1959) served as commander of the Yeomanry Mounted Division and the 4th Cavalry Division in Palestine in 1917 and 1918. His account of his experiences is entitled *The*

Fire of Life (London: Hutchinson, 1942). General Edouard Brémond (1868-1948) was head of the French Military Mission in Egypt and the Hejaz from August 1916 to December 1917. He published his account, *Le Hedjaz dans la Guerre Mondiale* (Paris: Payot) in 1931. It was Major N.N.E. Bray (1886-1962), an intelligence officer seconded to Palestine from the India Office in 1916, who recommended to the British government in November 1916 that Britain support an Arab guerrilla campaign. His memoir of events is entitled *Shifting Sands* (London: Unicorn Press, 1934); he also wrote a biography of Lieutenant Colonel G.E. Leachman, an important figure in the Arab Revolt, who was murdered in 1920, *A Paladin of Arabia* (London: The Unicorn Press, 1936). Major Hubert Young (later Sir Hubert Young) (1885-1950) was staff officer with the Hejaz Regular Army in 1918. His memoir, *The Independent Arab* (London: John Murray) was published in 1933.

13. Richard Aldington to Alister Kershaw, 23 August 1954 (S.I.U.). George Antonius (1891-1942) was a Lebanese-Egyptian diplomat whose *The Arab Awakening* (London: Hamish Hamilton, 1938) was, as Aldington acknowledges (calling him 'the special-pleading advocate of "the Arabs"'), an account of events from the Arab perspective. King Abdullah, Emir of Transjordan from 1921 until 1946 and King of Jordan until his assassination in 1951, published his own memoirs in 1951 (London: Jonathan Cape). The diplomat Ronald Storrs (later Sir Ronald Storrs) (1881-1955) had been a friend of Lawrence when they were both attached to the Arab Bureau in Cairo. He was political officer to the Egyptian Expeditionary Force in 1917 and 1918 and a participant in the organisation of the Arab Revolt. He was appointed Governor of Jerusalem in December 1918. His memoirs, *Orientations*, were published by Nicholson & Watson in 1937. Colonel Robert Buxton (1883-1953), an officer in the Imperial Camel Corps, decorated for his part in the seizing of the Muddawara Railway Station in August 1918, is quoted in Graves's book. General (later Field Marshall and Viscount) Edmund Allenby (1861-1936) led the Egyptian Expeditionary Force from June 1917 onwards. He supported the Arab Revolt but Aldington's adverse quotations from Allenby about Lawrence are taken from the books by Barrow and Wavell. Captain Rosario Pisani was a member of the French forces who participated in most of the attacks on the Turkish Railway, with his French-Algerian mountain and machine gun company; his accounts were recorded in the official French history, *Les Armées Françaises dans la Grande Guerre*. Colonel Walter Stirling (1880-1958) was an intelligence officer at the Arab Bureau throughout the Palestine Campaign. As his autobiography, *Safety Last* (London: Hollis & Carter), was not published until 1953, Aldington is probably here referring to quotations from him in other works.

14. Andrew MacPhail, *Three Persons* (London: John Murray, 1929). Sir Andrew MacPhail (1864-1938) was a Canadian doctor and writer who had served in the First World War. His book is a critical review of the memoirs of 'Colonel' House (adviser to President Wilson), Field Marshall Sir Henry Wilson (Chief of the Imperial General Staff in 1918) and T.E. Lawrence.

15. Aldington, *Lawrence of Arabia*, pp. 13-14.

16. *Ibid.*, pp. 59-60.

17. A.W. Lawrence, ed., *T.E. Lawrence by His Friends* (London: Jonathan Cape, 1937) p. 199. It is worth noting that in 1954, anticipating some of Aldington's criticisms, Lawrence's brother had Jonathan Cape issue a new and abridged edition of this book.

18. Aldington, *Lawrence of Arabia*, pp. 381-85.

19. See Henry Williamson to Richard Aldington, 4 January 1956 (S.I.U.).

20. In fact, Lawrence had not written this *Who's Who* entry, but had, the publishers revealed, amplified the entry for the 1921 edition and frequently modified it in subsequent years.

21. Henry Williamson to Richard Aldington, 31 March 1951 (S.I.U.).

22. Henry Williamson, 'Threnos to T.E. Lawrence', *The European*, May and June 1954.

23. *The European* was published between 1953 and 1959 by Diana Mosley and was a cultural magazine and platform for Oswald Mosley's political views. Quotations from *The European* are taken from Anne Williamson, 'The Genius of Friendship: Part Two: Richard Aldington', *Henry Williamson Society Journal*, no. 28 (September 1993) p. 14. *The Home Letters of T.E. Lawrence and His Brothers* was published in Oxford by Basil Blackwell in 1954, almost certainly as part of a campaign by the Seven Pillars of Wisdom Trust and the 'Lawrence Bureau' to put positive representations of Lawrence in front of the public in advance of the Aldington biography.

24. Henry Williamson to David Garnett, 8 February 1955, quoted in Anne Williamson, 'The Genius of Friendship'. Garnett's review appeared in the *New Statesman and Nation* on 5 February 1955.

25. Anne Williamson, 'The Genius of Friendship', pp. 16-18.

26. Richard Aldington to Henry Williamson, 12 February 1955 (S.I.U.).

27. Alister Kershaw to Richard Aldington, 23 March 1951 (S.I.U.).

28. Alister Kershaw to Richard Aldington, 8 July 1951 (S.I.U.).

29. Alister Kershaw to Richard Aldington, 27 April 1952 (S.I.U.).

30. Quoted in Crawford, *Richard Aldington and Lawrence of Arabia*, p. 1.

31. *Ibid.*, p. 44.

32. Richard Aldington to Alister Kershaw, 7 April 1952 (S.I.U.).

33. Richard Aldington to Alan Bird, 8 October 1952, in Benkovitz, *A Passionate Prodigality*, p. 59.

34. Richard Aldington to Netta Aldington, 11 September 1953 (BL).

35. Richard Aldington to Alister Kershaw, 11 September 1953 (S.I.U.).

36. Quoted in Crawford, *Richard Aldington and Lawrence of Arabia*, p. 108.

37. Richard Aldington to William Dibben, 13 November 1954 (S.I.U.).

38. Alister Kershaw to Richard Aldington, 28 May 1954 (S.I.U.).

39. Richard Aldington to Alister Kershaw, 1 June 1954 (S.I.U.).

40. *Evening Standard*, 19 January 1954.

41. Basil Liddell Hart to W.F. Stirling, 20 June 1955, quoted in Crawford, *Richard Aldington and Lawrence of Arabia*, p. 130.

42. Liddell Hart, *T.E. Lawrence in Arabia and After*, p. 384.
43. Brian Bond to the author, 11 August 2018.
44. Peter Simkins to the author, 13 August 2018.
45. Winston Churchill to Basil Liddell Hart, 12 March 1954 (Texas).
46. Maurice Hankey to Basil Liddell Hart, 24 February 1954 (Texas).
47. Winston Churchill to Basil Liddell Hart, 17 July 1954 (Texas). Liddell Hart did not receive permission from Churchill to show this letter to Collins until 22 August. However, before publication, Collins added a paraphrase of this letter as a footnote to Aldington's discussion of the issue: see Aldington, *Lawrence of Arabia*, p. 385.
48. Basil Liddell Hart to various correspondents, 9 April 1954 (Texas).
49. Mark Bonham Carter to Basil Liddell Hart, 18 January 1955 (Texas).
50. William Collins to Basil Liddell Hart, 15 June 1954 (Texas).
51. A.W. Lawrence to Basil Liddell Hart, 24 March 1954 (Texas).
52. Basil Liddell Hart to Eric Kennington, 18 October 1954 (Texas).
53. Celandine Kennington to Basil Liddell Hart, 5 May 1954 (Texas).
54. Celandine Kennington to Basil Liddell Hart, 28 July 1954 (Texas).
55. Celandine Kennington to Basil Liddell Hart, 14 August 1954 (Texas).
56. Basil Liddell Hart to William Collins, 25 January 1954 (Texas).
57. Celandine Kennington to Basil Liddell Hart, 18 August and 17 October 1954 (Texas).
58. See Basil Liddell Hart to Eric Kennington *et al.*, 21 April 1954 (Texas). Wright's book was entitled *Portraits and Criticisms* and was published in London by Nash & Grayson in 1925.
59. The most famous – and unsuccessful – case of this kind was Oscar Wilde's libel case against the Marquis of Queensberry in 1895.
60. A.W. Lawrence to Basil Liddell Hart, 15 June 1954 (Texas). The story of T.E. Lawrence's masochistic activities was finally revealed in *The Sunday Times*, 23 June 1968.
61. Celandine Kennington to Basil Liddell Hart, 17 October 1954 (Texas).
62. Richard Church to Richard Aldington, 12 December 1954 (S.I.U.).
63. Richard Aldington to Alister Kershaw, 9 March 1953 (S.I.U.).
64. The *Sunday Chronicle* had absorbed the *Sunday Referee* in 1939, thus depriving Aldington of a newspaper well-disposed towards him.
65. Celandine Kennington to Basil Liddell Hart, 28 January 1955 (Texas).
66. The quotation comes from *The Manchester Guardian* review of 31 January 1955.
67. *The Times*, 2 February 1955.
68. Basil Liddell Hart to Charles Carrington, 7 February 1955 (Texas). Copies of all the letters written by Liddell Hart to reviewers are also to be found in the archive.
69. Basil Liddell Hart to Lord Vansittart, 7 February 1955, and Lord Vansittart to Basil Liddell Hart, 9 February 1955 (Texas). Lord Vansittart (1888-1957) was a diplomat who, having served in the Middle East, was attached to the Foreign Office from 1911 and was private secretary to Lord Curzon, the Foreign Secretary, from 1920 to 1924. His review appeared in the *Daily Telegraph* on 31 January 1955.

70. Burnham had fought with the Royal Buckinghamshire Hussars and then (as Acting Lieutenant Colonel) in the 1st Middlesex Yeomanry in Palestine.

71. Breese had been the adjutant at Uxbridge when Lawrence enlisted in the RAF in 1922; Dening had been Deputy Assistant Adjutant General for 4th Cavalry Division in Palestine in 1918. The interview with Aldington, entitled 'Why I Debunked the Lawrence Legend', appeared in *Illustrated* on 5 February 1955.

72. 'Why I Decided to Debunk a Hero: Richard Aldington talks to Sydney Smith', *Daily Express*, 28 January 1955; 'The Big Lie Is Not Proved, Randolph Churchill Finds Lawrence a Liar', *Evening Standard*, 31 January 1955; 'Hero or Fake', Charles Curran in the *Daily Mirror*, 27 January 1955; 'Lawrence of Arabia, Now a Book Debunks Him', by Deryck Winterton in the *Daily Herald*, 28 January 1955; 'The Battle over Lawrence of Arabia: Richard Aldington Defends His Book', *Daily Mail*, 1 February 1955.

73. The *London Magazine*, no. 2 (April 1955).

74. The 25-year-old Lyle was a poet and the heir to the Tate & Lyle fortune. He would later marry Anna, Campbell's younger daughter.

75. Aldington, *Lawrence of Arabia*, p. 183.

76. *Ibid.*, p. 317.

77. *Ibid.*, p. 349.

78. *Ibid.*, p. 379.

79. Richard Aldington to Alan Bird, 11 February 1953, in Benkovitz, *A Passionate Prodigality*, p. 81.

80. Aldington, *Lawrence of Arabia*, p. 381.

81. *Ibid.*, p. 247.

82. *The New Republic*, 21 March 1955.

83. *Introduction to Mistral* (London: Heinemann, 1956); *Frauds* (London: Heinemann, 1957); *Portrait of a Rebel: The Life and Works of Robert Louis Stevenson* (London: Evans Brothers, 1957).

84. Crawford, *Richard Aldington and Lawrence of Arabia*, p. 206.

20. Private and Public Lives: Trials of Endurance, 1951-1957

1. Richard Aldington diary for 1951 (S.I.U.).

2. Richard Aldington to H.D., 9 March 1951 (Yale).

3. Richard Aldington to Henry Williamson, 26 January 1951 (S.I.U.).

4. Richard Aldington to Alister Kershaw, 16 April 1951(S.I.U.).

5. Richard Aldington to H.D., 29 May 1951 (Yale).

6. Kershaw, *The Pleasure of Their Company*, pp. 112-13.

7. Dutton, *Out in the Open*, p. 196.

8. Richard Aldington to Henry Williamson, 7 February 1955 (S.I.U.).

9. Richard Aldington to Denison Deasey, quoted in Dutton, *Out in the Open*, p. 200.

10. Kershaw and Temple, *Richard Aldington: An Intimate Portrait*, pp. 142-43.

11. Richard Aldington to William Dibben, 3 June 1952 (S.I.U.).

12. Richard Aldington to Alister Kershaw, 1 May 1952 (S.I.U.).

13. Bryher was Douglas's patron and it was at her request – and expense – that Douglas spent his final years in the villa on Capri which Bryher had bought for MacPherson and his partner, the photographer Islay de Courcy Lyons.

14. Aldington, *Pinorman*, p. vii; *Lawrence of Arabia*, p. 14.

15. Aldington, *Pinorman*, p. 120.

16. *Ibid.*, p. 172. For details of the 'Magnus affair', see p. 165-166 above.

17. Richard Aldington to Rob Lyle, 24 January 1955 (NYPL).

18. Anne Chisholm, *Nancy Cunard* (London: Sidgwick & Jackson, 1979) p. 385. The Fitzgibbon review appeared in *The Times Literary Supplement* of 7 May 1954.

19. Nancy Cunard, *Grand Man: Memories of Norman Douglas* (London: Secker & Warburg, 1954).

20. Nancy Cunard, '"Bonbons" of Gall', *Time and Tide*, 17 April 1954.

21. Nancy Cunard's April 1954 letter to Heinemann is quoted in Benkovitz, *A Passionate Prodigality*, p. 137.

22. William King (1894-1958) was Keeper of Ceramics at the British Museum and a literary critic who befriended Douglas when the latter returned to England during the Second World War; he became Douglas's literary executor for a short period. The writer Harold Acton (1904-1994) was part of Douglas's circle in Florence. Like King, the Irish writer Charles Duff (1894-1966) became a friend of Douglas's during the Second World War. Arthur Johnson was an international lawyer and art collector, who owned a villa at Anacapri and came to know Douglas in his final years.

23. *Time and Tide*, 29 May 1954. Cunard responded in turn on 5 June 1954.

24. Frieda Ravagli to Richard Aldington, 29 March and (27?) May 1954 (S.I.U.). Three months later, Frieda modified her recollections of Douglas, writing to Aldington: 'Now about the Norman thing. After getting rid of my indignation, I feel milder about him. In one way he had a fine idea of hospitality. He was not small beer . . . I don't go back for a moment on what I said, but I think perhaps you are more effective if you give the devil his due.' Frieda Ravagli to Richard Aldington, 29 August 1954 (S.I.U.).

25. Eric Warman to Richard Aldington, 4 May 1954 (S.I.U.).

26. Roy Campbell to Richard Aldington, 31 May 1954 (NYPL).

27. Richard Aldington to Rob Lyle, 20 October 1954 (NYPL).

28. Richard Aldington to Herbert Read, 9 May 1956 (Victoria).

29. Richard Aldington to H.D., 29 April 1957 (Yale).

30. Aldington, *Introduction to Mistral*, p. 55.

31. Richard Aldington to Alan Bird, 13 May 1955, in Benkovitz, *A Passionate Prodigality*, p. 171.

32. Richard Aldington to Eric Warman, 11 May 1957 (S.I.U.).

33. Alexander Frere to Richard Aldington, 20 November 1956 (Rushden). William Haley was Editor of *The Times* from 1952 until 1966. Given Haley's admiration for much of Aldington's earlier work, it is perhaps surprising to see Frere attributing the hostile tone of the *Times Literary Supplement's Pinorman* and *Lawrence* reviews to Haley's influence.

34. *The Times Literary Supplement*, 8 March 1957.

35. *New Statesman and Nation*, 4 May 1957.

36. Richard Aldington to Herbert Read, 12 March 1957 (Victoria).

37. Richard Aldington to H.D., 27 February 1960 (Yale).

38. Aldington to Alan Bird, 30 September 1956, in Benkovitz, *A Passionate Prodigality*, p. 243.

39. Richard Aldington to Alan Bird, 7 July 1955, in Benkovitz, *ibid.*, p. 188.

40. Richard Aldington to Alister Kershaw, 13 March and 9 April 1956 (S.I.U.).

41. Richard Aldington to William Dibben, 8 September 1956 (S.I.U.).

42. See Aldington, *Portrait of a Rebel*, p. 21, for the phrases quoted here.

43. *Ibid.*, p. 42.

44. *Ibid.*, p. 89.

45. *Ibid.*, pp. 50, 92 and 94.

46. *Ibid.*, p. 66.

47. *Ibid.*, p. 110. *The Amateur Emigrant*, Stevenson's account of his voyage to America in 1879, was published in London by Eveleigh Nash & Grayson in 1895.

48. Aldington, *Portrait of a Rebel*, p. 178. 'The Day After Tomorrow' appeared in *The Contemporary Review*, April 1887.

49. Robert Louis Stevenson, 'Some Aspects of Robert Burns', *Cornhill Magazine*, October 1879, quoted in Aldington, *Portrait of a Rebel*, p. 104.

50. Aldington, *Portrait of a Rebel*, p. 95.

51. *Ibid.*, p. 169.

52. *Ibid.*, p. 207.

53. *Ibid.*, p. 110.

54. *The Times Literary Supplement*, 4 October 1957.

55. *The Times*, 2 January 1958.

56. *Daily Telegraph*, 20 September 1957.

57. *The Sunday Times*, 6 October 1957.

58. Richard Aldington to P.A.G. Aldington, 15 October 1954 (S.I.U.).

59. Richard Aldington to Henry Williamson, 18, 25 and 27 January 1956 (S.I.U.).

60. Richard Aldington to Henry Williamson, 14 March 1956 (S.I.U.). *How Dear is Life* is the novel that precedes *A Fox Under My Cloak* in Williamson's *A Chronicle of Ancient Sunlight* sequence.

61. Richard Aldington to Alister Kershaw, 19 May 1956 (S.I.U.).

62. Richard Aldington to P.A.G. Aldington, 2 August 1956 (S.I.U.).

63. Richard Aldington to Eric Warman, 10 November 1956 (S.I.U.).

64. Richard Aldington to P.A.G. Aldington, 14 November 1956 (S.I.U.).

65. Richard Aldington to P.A.G. Aldington, 5 February 1957 (S.I.U.).

66. Richard Aldington to Netta Aldington, 4 April 1955 (British Library).

67. Richard Aldington to Alister Kershaw, 29 July 1956 (S.I.U.).

68. Richard Aldington to Alister Kershaw, 3 November 1956 (S.I.U.).

69. Herbert Read to Richard Aldington, 8 May 1956 (S.I.U.). The co-written book, *Truth is More Sacred: A Critical Exchange on Modern Literature*, would eventually be published by Routledge in 1961. *The Sorrows of Priapus* was published in New York by New Directions in 1957.

70. Richard Aldington to Herbert Read, 9 May 1956 (Victoria).

71. Richard Aldington to Edward Dahlberg, 8 June 1956 (Texas).

72. Richard Aldington to Herbert Read, 9 May and 10 August 1956 and 12 March 1957 (Victoria).

73. Richard Aldington to Geoffrey Potocki, 20 June 1957 (S.I.U.).

74. Richard Aldington to Eric Warman, 25 June 1957 (S.I.U.).

75. Richard Aldington to Geoffrey Potocki, 15 February 1958 (S.I.U.).

76. Richard Aldington to H.D., 3 February 1953 (Yale).

77. Richard Aldington to Edward Nehls, 16 August 1956 (Texas). Nehls's *D.H. Lawrence: A Composite Biography*, consisting of reminiscences of Lawrence by those who knew him, was published in three volumes by the University of Wisconsin Press between 1957 and 1959 and included extracts from all Aldington's writings about Lawrence. The second volume was dedicated to Aldington, who also, at Nehls's invitation, wrote the foreword to the third volume.

78. Herbert Read to Richard Aldington, 10 March 1957 (S.I.U.), and Richard Aldington to Herbert Read, 12 March 1957 (Victoria). See also Richard Aldington to H.D., 17 September 1951 (Yale), and H.D. to Richard Aldington, 3 October 1951 (S.I.U.). 'The Sea Mists of Winter' appeared in *The Listener* on 19 May 1951.

79. Herbert Read to Richard Aldington, 8 May 1956 (S.I.U.).

80. Richard Aldington to Henry Williamson, 27 April 1957 (S.I.U.).

81. Richard Aldington to H.D., 29 April 1957 (Yale).

82. Lawrence Durrell to Richard Aldington, 4-14 August 1958, in Ian S. MacNiven and Harry T. Moore, eds, *Literary Lifelines* (New York: Viking Press, 1981) p. 51.

83. H.D. to Richard Aldington, 31 January 1953 (S.I.U.).

84. Richard Aldington to H.D., 7 January 1953 (Yale); Richard Aldington to Alexander Frere, 12 February 1953 (Rushden).

85. Richard Aldington to H.D., 7 January 1953 (Yale).

86. See Bryher to Richard Aldington and Richard Aldington to Bryher between 10 February and 14 September 1953 (Yale). *Bid Me to Live* was eventually published in New York by the Dial Press in 1960.

87. Richard Aldington to Bryher, 5 May 1953 (Yale).

88. H.D. to Richard Aldington, 28 November 1953 (S.I.U.).

89. H.D. to Richard Aldington, 24 November 1953 (S.I.U.).

90. H.D. to Richard Aldington, 13 July 1954 (S.I.U.); Richard Aldington to H.D., 12 July 1954 (Yale).

91. H.D. to Richard Aldington, 19 May 1957 (Yale).

92. H.D. to Richard Aldington, 11 July 1956 (S.I.U.).

93. Richard Aldington to P.A.G. Aldington, 5 November 1956 (S.I.U.). *Tribute to Freud* was published in New York by Pantheon in 1956.

94. Richard Aldington to H.D., 18 June 1957 (Yale).

95. Richard Aldington to H.D., 15 March and 21 May 1957 (Yale).

96. Richard Aldington to H.D., 8 June 1957 (Yale).

97. Richard Aldington to Bryher, 16 June 1957 (Yale).   ˙

98. H.D. wrote her *Tribute to Freud* in 1954 and 1955, worked on her epic poem *Helen in Egypt* from 1952 to 1954, composed her *roman à clef Magic Mirror* in 1955 and 1956 and started work on the three poems that would eventually be published as *Hermetic Definition* in 1957.

99. Richard Aldington to H.D., 24 May 1957 (Yale).

100. Richard Aldington to Bryher, 8 July 1957 (Yale).

101. Richard Aldington to Bryher, 20 July 1957 (Yale).

102. Richard Aldington to Bryher, 27 June 1957 (Yale).

103. Gustave Cohen to Richard Aldington, 15 May 1957 (S.I.U.).

104. Richard Aldington to H.D., 2 June 1957 (Yale).

21. A Solitary Life, 1957-1961

1. See Alister Kershaw, *Village to Village: Misadventures in France* (Sydney: Angus & Robertson, 1991) pp. 81-83.

2. Kershaw, *The Pleasure of Their Company*, p. 114.

3. Richard Aldington to Eric Warman, 29 January 1958 (S.I.U.).

4. Richard Aldington to Bryher, 31 May 1961(Yale).

5. Richard Aldington to H.D., 10 January 1958 (Yale).

6. Richard Aldington to Eric Warman, 28 December 1957 (S.I.U.).

7. Richard Aldington to Eric Warman, 29 January 1958 (S.I.U.).

8. Richard Aldington to Eric Warman, 21 April 1958 (S.I.U.).

9. Richard Aldington to Eric Warman, 4 June 1958 (S.I.U.).

10. Richard Aldington to Eric Warman, 13 August 1958 (S.I.U.).

11. With the exception of *A Dream in the Luxembourg*, all his pre-1939 UK titles had now reverted to his ownership.

12. Richard Aldington to P.A.G. Aldington, 3 October and 12 November 1959 (S.I.U.).

13. The Patmore solicitors had issued a writ attaching any Heinemann royalties in March 1957 and another attaching Evans royalties in February 1958. They could not access Collins royalties because of the Trust that had been set up but, since Collins had allowed *Lawrence of Arabia* to go out of print, there were none.

14. Alexander Frere to P.A.G. Aldington, 17 November 1959 (Rushden).

15. Lawrence Durrell to Richard Aldington, before 22 September 1959, in MacNiven and Moore, *Literary Lifelines*, p. 102.

16. Richard Aldington to Lawrence Durrell, 2 November 1959, in MacNiven and Moore, *ibid.*, p. 103.

17. Richard Aldington to Henry Williamson, 8 October 1957 (S.I.U.). *The Golden Virgin*, the sixth volume of Williamson's *Chronicle of Ancient Sunlight*, was published in London by MacDonald and Company in 1957.

18. Henry Williamson to Richard Aldington, 16 September 1957 (S.I.U.). With reference to *D.H. Lawrence: Portrait of a Genius, But . . .*, he had told Aldington on 4 March 1951: 'I still think little knocking snips should have been left out'(S.I.U.).

19. Henry Williamson to Richard Aldington, 5 September 1960 (S.I.U.).

20. See, for example, Richard Aldington to Henry Williamson, 3 December 1957 ('You are a bit of a so-and-so not to write but perhaps I said something that annoyed you'), 3 March 1958 ('Where have you disappeared and why?') and 9 September 1960 ('I am very glad to hear from you after this hiatus, which doubtless was my fault for not writing') (S.I.U.).

21. Richard Aldington to Henry Williamson, 14 April 1959 (S.I.U.).

22. Richard Aldington to H.D., 21 January 1958 (Yale). For an account of Aldington's 1927 affair with Jessie Capper, see Whelpton, *Richard Aldington: Poet, Soldier and Lover*, pp. 297-299 and 307.

23. Richard Aldington to Thomas MacGreevy, 27 July 1958 (TCD).

24. Richard Aldington to Alister Kershaw, 15 September 1958 and 9 February 1961 (S.I.U.).

25. Richard Aldington to Alister Kershaw, 8 November 1960 (S.I.U.).

26. Thomas MacGreevy to Richard Aldington, 10 November 1958 (S.I.U.).

27. Thomas MacGreevy to Richard Aldington, 10 November 1958 (S.I.U.), and Richard Aldington to Thomas MacGreevy, 15 November 1958 (TCD).

28. Thomas MacGreevy to Richard Aldington, 1 December 1959 (S.I.U.).

29. Catherine Aldington and Jacques Guillaume would marry in January 1963.

30. Richard Aldington to Eric Warman, 21 August 1958 (S.I.U.).

31. Richard Aldington to Eric Warman, 16 September 1958 (S.I.U.).

32. Catherine Aldington to Richard Aldington, 27 September 1958 (S.I.U.).

33. Catherine Aldington to Bryher, 5 September 1962 (Yale).

34. Catherine Aldington in telephone conversation with the author in July 2009; Catherine Aldington to Bryher, 27 September 1965 (Yale).

35. Richard Aldington to Eric Warman, 14 October 1958 (S.I.U.).

36. Richard Aldington to H.D., 24 September 1958, and to Bryher, 11 May 1959 (Yale).

37. Richard Aldington to H.D., 24 September 1958 (Yale).

38. Richard Aldington to H.D., 15 January 1959 (Yale).

39. H.D. to Richard Aldington, 4 March 1959 (S.I.U.).

40. Richard Aldington to H.D., 18 June 1959 (Yale).

41. Henry Miller, in Kershaw and Temple, *Richard Aldington: An Intimate Portrait*, p. 78.

42. Richard Aldington to H.D., 30 July 1959 (Yale).

43. Richard Aldington to H.D., 7 September 1959 (Yale).

44. H.D. to Richard Aldington, 23 September 1959 (S.I.U.).

45. H.D. to Richard Aldington, 23 September 1959 (S.I.U.), and Richard Aldington to H.D., 25 September 1959 (Yale); Richard Aldington to Alister Kershaw, 29 September 1959 (S.I.U.).

46. Richard Aldington to H.D., 9 and 12 October 1959 (Yale).

47. H.D. to Richard Aldington, 13 October 1959 (S.I.U.).

48. Richard Aldington to Alister Kershaw, 5 October 1959 (S.I.U.).

49. H.D. to George Plank, 3 October 1959 (Yale).

50. George Plank to Bryher, 2 and 8 October 1959 (Yale).

51. George Plank to H.D., 4 October 1959 (Yale).
52. H.D. to Richard Aldington, 11 February 1961 (S.I.U.).
53. See letters from Richard Aldington to Bryher, 23 April 1959 and 25 February 1960, and to H.D., 27 February 1960 (Yale), and Ezra Pound to Richard Aldington (undated) December 1959 (Texas).
54. Richard Aldington to H.D., 10 December 1957 and 21 January 1958 (Yale).
55. Richard Aldington to H.D., 7 September 1959 (Yale). H.D.'s father, Professor Charles Doolittle, was 70 years old at the time of that 1912-1913 tour of Italy.
56. H.D. to Richard Aldington, 30 October 1959 (S.I.U.).
57. Richard Aldington to H.D., 21 November 1958 (Yale), and H.D. to Richard Aldington, 24 November 1958 (S.I.U.).
58. Richard Aldington to Eric Warman, 16 September 1958 (S.I.U.).
59. Aldington had described Moore to Bacon on 16 May 1950 as 'a somewhat brash academic go-getter'. (Yale) For the correspondence with H.D. concerning the Lawrence letters, see Richard Aldington to H.D., 22 and 30 June, 6 July and 27 August 1958 (Yale), and H.D. to Richard Aldington, 4 July 1958 (S.I.U.). The Harry Moore two-volume edition of *The Collected Letters of D.H. Lawrence* was published by Heinemann in 1962.
60. Richard Aldington to H.D., 30 June 1958 (Yale).
61. H.D. to Richard Aldington, 28 April 1959 (S.I.U.), and Richard Aldington to H.D., 30 April 1959 (Yale).
62. H.D. to Richard Aldington, 3 April 1959 (S.I.U.).
63. Richard Aldington to H.D., 6 and 19 April 1959 (Yale).
64. See, for example, the letter of 6 April 1959 above, where he comments on Bryher's thoughtfulness in putting off a trip in order to support H.D. during Perdita's visit.
65. Richard Aldington to Alister Kershaw, 24 August 1960 (S.I.U.).
66. H.D. to Richard Aldington, 4 November 1959 (S.I.U.).
67. Richard Aldington to H.D., 5 November 1959 (Yale).
68. Richard Aldington to Bryher, 10 November 1959 (Yale).
69. H.D. to Ezra Pound, 16 November 1959 (Yale); H.D. to Richard Aldington, 17 November 1959 (S.I.U.).
70. H.D. to George Plank, 1 December 1959 (Yale).
71. George Plank to H.D., 27 November and 3 December 1959 (Yale).
72. Richard Aldington to H.D., 1 December 1959 (Yale); H.D. to Richard Aldington, 4 December 1959 (S.I.U.).
73. Richard Aldington to Lawrence Durrell, 4 December 1959 and 16 February 1960, in MacNiven and Moore, *Literary Lifelines*, pp. 110 and 132.
74. H.D. to Richard Aldington, 18 November 1958 (S.I.U.).
75. H.D. to Richard Aldington, 18 March and 28 April 1959 (S.I.U.).
76. Richard Aldington to H.D., 18 and 24 April 1958 (Yale).
77. Richard Aldington to Bryher, 21 November and 13 December 1958 (Yale).
78. Richard Aldington to Bryher, 4 December 1959 (Yale).
79. Ezra Pound to Richard Aldington, 25 August 1959 (S.I.U.).

80. Richard Aldington to H.D., 7 September 1959 (Yale).

81. H.D. to Richard Aldington, 30 September 1959 (S.I.U.).

82. Richard Aldington to Charles Norman, 5 and 25 November 1960 (Texas). Norman's *Ezra Pound: A Biography* was published in New York by Macmillan in 1960; it was a further nine years before it found a UK publisher: Macdonald & Co. in 1969.

83. Richard Aldington to H.D., 13 November 1958 (Yale).

84. *End to Torment* was not published until 1979 (New York: New Directions).

85. Richard Aldington to Lawrence Durrell, 24 November 1960, in MacNiven and Moore, *Literary Lifelines*, p. 163.

86. Alister Kershaw to Richard Aldington, 13 December 1958, and Richard Aldington to Eric Warman, 22 February 1959 (S.I.U.). The Mosleys were living in Paris in this period.

87. Richard Aldington to Eric Warman, 22 February 1959, and to Alister Kershaw, 23 February 1959 (S.I.U.). Mosley obtained 7.6 per cent of the votes cast in the 1959 General Election in Kensington North.

88. Richard Aldington to Eric Warman, 10 September 1960 (S.I.U.).

89. Richard Aldington to P.A.G. Aldington, 6 July 1961 (S.I.U.).

90. Richard Aldington to Eric Warman, 23 April 1960 (S.I.U.).

91. Richard Aldington to Geoffrey Potocki de Montalk, 8 March 1960 (S.I.U.).

92. Richard Aldington to Alan Bird, 12 February and 6 July 1961, in Benkovitz, *A Passionate Prodigality*, pp. 287 and 288.

93. Richard Aldington to Alan Bird, 23 February and 18 December 1953, in Benkovitz, *ibid.*, pp. 85 and 103.

94. Richard Aldington to Alan Bird, 14 May 1960, in Benkovitz, *ibid.*, p. 280.

95. Richard Aldington to P.A.G. Aldington, 13 May 1960 (S.I.U.).

96. Richard Aldington, *D.H. Lawrence in Selbstzeugnissen und Bilddokumenten* (Reinbek bei Hamburg: Rowohlt Taschenbuch Verlag, 1961).

97. Richard Aldington to Lawrence Durrell, 9 January 1960, in MacNiven and Moore, *Literary Lifelines*, p. 126.

98. Richard Aldington to Eric Warman, 6 November 1960 (S.I.U.).

99. Dutton, *Out in the Open*, p. 235.

100. H.D. to Richard Aldington, 30 December 1959 (S.I.U.).

101. Richard Aldington to H.D., 2 January 1960 (Yale).

102. Guest, *Herself Defined*, p. 325.

103. H.D. to Aldington, 15 and 28 May 1960 (S.I.U.).

104. H.D. to Richard Aldington, 18 December 1960 (S.I.U.); Richard Aldington to H.D., 30 December 1960 (Yale).

105. Richard Aldington to Lawrence Durrell, 1 January 1961, in MacNiven and Moore, *Literary Lifelines*, p. 167.

106. *Ibid. Les Félibres* was a society founded in 1854 to promote the literature and culture of Provence. Membership was by invitation. Campbell had also been a member.

107. H.D. to Catherine Aldington, 29 December 1960 (Yale), and to Richard Aldington, 12 January 1961 (S.I.U.).

108. Richard Aldington to Alister Kershaw, 22 February 1961 (S.I.U.). Potocki's daughter, Theodora, had been adopted as a baby by T.F. Powys and his wife; Potocki himself had been a prisoner in Wormwood Scrubs at the time of her birth in 1932. Her mother was Sally Powys, wife of T.F. Powys's second son, Francis. Theodora did not meet Potocki until 1960 and for a time he moved to Dorset to be near her and her adoptive mother.

109. Richard Aldington to Eric Warman, 3 October 1960 (S.I.U.). It is clear from Aldington's next letter to Warman, 6 November 1960 (S.I.U.), that the latter had informed him that his own little granddaughter was equally accomplished!

110. Richard Aldington to H.D., 4 and 7 March 1961 (Yale).

111. Catherine Aldington to Bryher, 23 April 1961 (Yale).

112. Richard Aldington to H.D., 18 and 21 April 1961 (Yale).

113. On 21 April 1961 he told her: 'One gets such lovely cards here now – I long to buy you MILLIONS' (Yale).

114. Richard Aldington to H.D., 12 May 1961 (Yale).

115. Richard Aldington to Bryher, 31 May 1961(Yale).

116. Richard Aldington to H.D., 21 April 1961(Yale). The Eichmann trial had opened in Israel on 11 April 1961.

117. Richard Aldington to H.D., 25 April 1961 (Yale), and H.D. to Richard Aldington, 28 April 1961 (S.I.U.).

118. H.D. to Richard Aldington, 28 May and 4 June 1961 (S.I.U.), and Richard Aldington to H.D., 1 June 1961 (Yale).

22. From Tragedy to Triumph, 1961-1962

1. Richard Aldington to P.A.G. Aldington, 6 July 1961 (S.I.U.).

2. Richard Aldington to Bryher, 25 August 2018 (Yale).

3. Richard Aldington to Netta Aldington, 19 May 1961 (British Library).

4. Richard Aldington to Eunice Gluckman, 1 October 1960 (Yale).

5. Richard Aldington to Eunice Gluckman, 13 July and 7 and 9 August 1961 (Yale).

6. Richard Aldington to Eunice Gluckman, 9 August 1961 (Yale).

7. The *Propédeutique* was, until educational reforms in 1966, the intermediate stage in the progress towards a bachelor's degree.

8. Richard Aldington to Netta Aldington, 17 August 1961 (British Library).

9. See, for example, his letters to Warman on 29 January 1960 and 8 February and 30 May 1962, and to P.A.G. Aldington, 17 January and 28 March 1962 (S.I.U.).

10. Richard Aldington to P.A.G. Aldington, 13 January, 1 March and 15 July 1960 and 2 November 1961 (S.I.U.).

11. Richard Aldington to P.A.G. Aldington, 21 December 1961 and 17 January 1962 (S.I.U.).

12. Richard Aldington to P.A.G. Aldington, 6 and 19 July 1961 (S.I.U.).

13. Tony Aldington had left his first wife, Moira Osborne, in 1941 when his daughter was eight years old and his son, five; they were brought up by

their mother and grandmother. Tony had three further children by his second wife, Daphne Bird, whom he married in 1946.

14. Richard Aldington to Jennifer Aldington, 30 September 1954 (private collection of Jennifer Aldington Emous).

15. Richard Aldington to Bryher, 14 and 19 August 1961, and to Norman Pearson, 29 August 1961; Catherine Aldington to Bryher, 16 August 1961 (Yale).

16. Richard Aldington to P.A.G. Aldington, 25 September 1961 (S.I.U.).

17. Bryher to Richard Aldington, 29 September 1961 (Yale).

18. Richard Aldington to Bryher, 2 and 21 October 1961 (Yale).

19. Thomas MacGreevy to Richard Aldington, 29 September 1961(S.I.U.).

20. Richard Aldington to Thomas MacGreevy, 11 February 1962 (TCD).

21. Lawrence Durrell to Richard Aldington, 4 October 1961, in MacNiven and Moore, *Literary Lifelines*, p. 190.

22. Richard Aldington to P.A.G. Aldington, 10 February 1962 (S.I.U.).

23. C.P. Snow to Richard Aldington, 22 December 1961 (S.I.U.).

24. William Haley to Richard Aldington, 5 December 1961 (S.I.U.).

25. Crawford, *Richard Aldington and Lawrence of Arabia*, p. 139.

26. The *Times Literary Supplement* review appeared on 20 October 1961 and Liddell Hart's letter, and the reviewer's response, on 3 November 1961. Richard Aldington to P.A.G. Aldington, 17 April 1962 (S.I.U.).

27. Richard Aldington to Geoffrey Potocki de Montalk, 19 November 1961, and Alister Kershaw to Richard Aldington, 3 November 1961 (S.I.U.).

28. Richard Aldington to Eric Warman, 4 December 1961 (S.I.U.).

29. Richard Aldington to P.A.G. Aldington, 3 and 15 May 1962 (S.I.U.); Richard Aldington to Jennifer Aldington, 3 May 1962 (private collection of Jennifer Aldington Emous); Richard Aldington to Bryher, 16 May 1962 (Yale).

30. Richard Aldington to Henry Williamson, 4 March 1962 (S.I.U.).

31. See letter from Richard Aldington to Netta Aldington, 7 March 1962 (British Library).

32. Richard Aldington to P.A.G. Aldington, 8 April 1962 (S.I.U.).

33. Richard Aldington to Henry Williamson, 17 April 1962 (S.I.U.).

34. Florence Fallas to Richard Aldington, 7 December 1958 (S.I.U.).

35. MacGreevy, in Kershaw and Temple, *Richard Aldington: An Intimate Portrait*, p. 62.

36. Richard Aldington's Russian Diary (S.I.U.).

37. V.M. Moldavsky, 'Richard Aldington in Leningrad', *Neva*, no. 5 (1963) pp. 164-67 (translated by Robert J. Winter). In a letter to his brother the day before he left Sury, Aldington had written: 'After some meditation I determined to use my dress as a first mute declaration to the Russ. They are accustomed to comrade-sympathisers and road-squatters turning up in baggy pants and turtle-neck sweaters or such like proletarian garb. I have had made for me here a mild imitation of the British pseudo-gent, i.e. a would-be immaculate black jacket with small check trousers and a dark blue jacket with plain grey. The first, worn with a nylon shirt and a severe but expensive tie, should strike the right note', 15 June 1962 (S.I.U.).

38. Vsevolod Rozhdestvensky (1895-1977) was a Russian poet, who served as a war correspondent during the Second World War.
39. Richard Aldington's Russian Diary (S.I.U.).
40. Moldavsky, 'Richard Aldington in Leningrad'.
41. Richard Aldington's Russian Diary (S.I.U.). Boris Polevoi (1908-1981) was a member of the Supreme Soviet.
42. Ivy Litvinov (1899-1977) was the widow of the Russian diplomat Maxim Litvinov. A novelist and translator, she was an admirer of D.H. Lawrence and had visited Lawrence and Frieda in Tuscany in 1914.
43. Richard Aldington's Russian Diary (S.I.U.).
44. Konstantin Fedin (1892-1977) was a novelist and served as Chair of the Soviet Union of Writers from 1959 until his death in 1977.
45. Richard Aldington's Russian Diary (S.I.U.). Yekaterina Peshkova (1887-1965) was Maxim Gorky's first wife and a human rights activist during the Stalin regime.
46. Richard Aldington's Russian Diary (S.I.U.). Alexy Surkov (1899-1983) was a poet, editor and literary critic and Chair of the Soviet Writers' Union from 1953 to 1959.
47. Mikhail Urnov, in Kershaw and Temple, *Richard Aldington: An Intimate Portrait*, pp. 158-59.
48. Quoted in Kershaw and Temple, *ibid.*, pp. 17-18.
49. Valentin Kataev (1897-1986) was a Russian novelist and playwright.
50. Kershaw and Temple, *Richard Aldington: An Intimate Portrait*, pp. 49-50.
51. Richard Aldington to Lawrence Durrell, 14 July 1962, in MacNiven and Moore, *Literary Lifelines*, pp. 217-18.
52. Richard Aldington to Bryher, 17 and 21 July 1962 (Yale).
53. Richard Aldington to Lawrence Durrell, 14 and 19 July 1962, in MacNiven and Moore, *Literary Lifelines*, pp. 217-19.
54. Richard Aldington to Eric Warman, 25 July 1962 (S.I.U.).
55. Richard Aldington to P.A.G. Aldington, 15 July 1962, and to Thomas MacGreevy, 18 July 1962 (S.I.U.).
56. Richard Aldington to Bryher, 13 and 21 July 1962 (Yale).
57. Tim Aldington to Vivien Whelpton, 26 September 2018.
58. *The Sunday Times*, 8 July 1962.

Afterwords

1. *The Manchester Guardian*, 30 July 1962.
2. *The Times*, 30 July 1962.
3. *Daily Telegraph*, 30 and 29 July 1962.
4. Herbert Read to Richard Church (undated) July 1962 (Texas).
5. Church, *The Voyage Home*, p. 76.
6. Irene Rathbone to Nancy Cunard, 6 August 1962 (Texas).
7. Irene Rathbone to Nancy Cunard, 3 August 1963 (Texas).
8. Irene Rathbone to Nancy Cunard, 30 September 1964 (Texas).
9. MacGreevy, in Kershaw and Temple, *Richard Aldington: An Intimate Portrait*, p. 55.
10. Randall, in *ibid.*, pp. 110-11, 121.

Bibliography

Works by Richard Aldington, 1930-1962
(in chronological order)

Poetry

A Dream in the Luxembourg (London: Chatto & Windus, 1930; London: Heinemann, 1946); *Love and the Luxembourg* (New York: Covici, Friede, 1930)

Movietones: Invented and Set Down by Richard Aldington, 1928-1929 (Privately printed, 1932)

The Eaten Heart (London: Chatto & Windus, 1933)

Collected Poems, 1915-1923 (London: Allen & Unwin, 1933)

The Poems of Richard Aldington (New York: Doubleday, Doran, 1934)

Life Quest (London: Chatto & Windus, 1935; New York: Doubleday, Doran, 1935)

The Crystal World (London: Heinemann, 1937; New York: Doubleday, Doran, 1938)

The Complete Poems of Richard Aldington (London: Allan Wingate, 1948)

Anthologies

Imagist Anthology, 1930 (London: Chatto & Windus, 1930)

Prose works

Two Stories ('Deserter' and 'Lads of the Village') (London: Elkin Mathews & Marrot, 1930)

At All Costs (London: Heinemann, 1930)

Last Straws (Paris: The Hours Press, 1930)

Roads to Glory (London: Chatto & Windus, 1930; New York: Doubleday, Doran and Co., 1930; London: Imperial War Museum, 1992); *Farewell to Memories* (Moscow: Foreign Languages Publishing House, 1963)

The Colonel's Daughter: A Novel (London: Chatto & Windus, 1931; New York: Doubleday, Doran, 1931; London: Penguin, 1939; London: The Hogarth Press, 1986)

Stepping Heavenward: A Record (Florence: G. Orioli, 1931; London: Chatto & Windus, 1931)

Soft Answers (London: Chatto Windus, 1932; New York: Doubleday, Doran, 1932; Hamburg: The Albatross, 1935; London: Penguin, 1949; Carbondale: Southern Illinois University Press, 1967)

All Men Are Enemies: A Romance (London: Chatto & Windus, 1933; New York: Doubleday, Doran, 1933; Hamburg: The Albatross, 1934; London: Heinemann, 1934; London: Arthur Barker, 1948)

Women Must Work: A Novel (London: Chatto & Windus, 1934; New York: Doubleday, Doran, 1934; Hamburg: The Albatross, 1935)

Life of a Lady: A Play by Richard Aldington and Derek Patmore (New York: Doubleday, Doran, 1936; London: G.P. Putnam's Sons, 1936)

Very Heaven (London: Heinemann, 1937; New York: Doubleday, Doran, 1937; Hamburg: The Albatross, 1937)

Seven Against Reeves: A Comedy-Farce (London: Heinemann, 1938; New York: Doubleday, Doran, 1938; Hamburg: The Albatross, 1938; London: Penguin, 1950)

Rejected Guest: A Novel (New York: Viking Press, 1939; London: Heinemann, 1939; Hamburg: The Albatross, 1947)

The Romance of Casanova: A Novel (New York: Duell, Sloan and Pearce, 1946; London: Heinemann, 1947)

Biographies, Essays and Memoirs

Balls and Another Book for Suppression (London: E. Lahr, 1930; Privately printed, 1932)

The Squire (London: Heinemann, 1934)

D.H. Lawrence: A Complete List of His Works, Together with a Critical Appreciation (London: Heinemann, 1935)

Artifex: Sketches and Ideas (London: Chatto & Windus, 1935; New York: Doubleday, Doran, 1936)

W. Somerset Maugham: An Appreciation by Richard Aldington. In *Sixty-Five*, by W. Somerset Maugham (New York: Doubleday, Doran, 1939); also published under the title *Sixty-five Short Stories* (London: Heinemann, 1976)

Life for Life's Sake: A Book of Reminiscences (New York: Viking Press, 1941; London: Cassell, 1968)

The Duke: Being an Account of the Life & Achievements of Arthur Wellesley, 1ˢᵗ Duke of Wellington (New York: Viking, 1943); *Wellington: Being an Account of the Life & Achievements of Arthur Wellesley, 1ˢᵗ Duke of Wellington* (London: Heinemann, 1946)

Four English Portraits, 1801-1851 (London: Evans Bros, 1948)

The Strange Life of Charles Waterton, 1782-1865 (London: Evans Bros, 1949; New York: Duell, Sloan and Pearce, 1949)

D.H. Lawrence: Portrait of a Genius, But . . . (New York: Duell, Sloan and Pearce, 1949; New York: Crowell-Collier, 1961)

Portrait of a Genius, But . . . : The Life of D.H. Lawrence, 1885-1930 (London: Heinemann, 1950)

D.H. Lawrence: An Appreciation (Harmondsworth: Penguin, 1950)

Pinorman: Personal Recollections of Norman Douglas, Pino Orioli and Charles Prentice (London: Heinemann, 1954)

Ezra Pound and T.S. Eliot: A Lecture (Hurst, Berkshire: Peacocks Press, 1954).

A.E. Housman and W.B. Yeats: Two Lectures (Hurst, Berkshire: Peacocks Press, 1955)

Lawrence l'Imposteur: T.E. Lawrence, the Legend and the Man (Paris: Amiot-Dumont, 1954); *Lawrence of Arabia: A Biographical Inquiry* (London: William Collins, 1955; Chicago: Henry Regnery, 1955; London: Four Square Books, 1957: Harmondsworth: Penguin, 1971)

Introduction to Mistral (London: Heinemann, 1956; Carbondale: Southern Illinois University Press, 1960)

Frauds (London: Heinemann, 1957)

Portrait of a Rebel: The Life and Work of Robert Louis Stevenson (London: Evans Bros, 1957)

A Tourist's Rome (Draguignan: Melissa Press, 1961)

D.H. Lawrence in Selbstzeugnissen und Bilddokumenten (Reinbek bei Hamburg: Rowohlt Taschenbuch Verlag, 1961)

A Letter from Richard Aldington and a Summary Bibliography of Count Potocki's Published Works (Draguignan: Melissa Press, 1962)

Translations

The Decameron of Giovanni Boccaccio (New York: Covici, Friede, 1930; London: G.P. Putnam's Sons, 1930; New York: Doubleday, Doran, 1949; London: Folio Society, 1954; London: Paul Elek 1957; New York: Laurel, Dell, 1962)

Alcestis, by Euripides (London: Chatto & Windus, 1930)

Letters to the Amazon by Remy de Gourmont (London: Chatto & Windus, 1931)

Fifty Romance Lyric Poems (New York: Crosby Gaige, 1928; London: Chatto & Windus, 1931; London: Allan Wingate, 1948)

Aurélia, by Gérard de Nerval (London: Chatto & Windus, 1932)

A Wreath for San Gemignano (New York: Duell, Sloan and Pearce, 1945; London: Heinemann, 1946)

Dangerous Acquaintances by Choderlos de Laclos (New York: New Directions, 1952; London: Four Square, 1962; London: Folio Society, 1962) (Aldington's translation first published, London: Routledge, 1924: New York: Dutton, 1924)

New Larousse Encyclopedia of Mythology (with Ames, Delano) (London: Hamlyn Publishing Group, 1959)

Works Edited and/or Introduced

The German Prisoner, Hanley, James (Privately printed, 1930)

The Last Voyage, Hanley, James (London: William Jackson Ltd, 1931)

Apocalypse, Lawrence, D.H. (Florence: G. Orioli, 1931; New York: Viking Press, 1932; London: Martin Secker, 1932; Hamburg: The Albatross, 1932; London: Heinemann, 1972; Harmondsworth: Penguin, 1974; New York: Penguin, 1976)

Last Poems, Lawrence, D.H. (Florence: G.Orioli, 1932; New York: Viking Press, 1933; London: Martin Secker, 1933; London: Heinemann, 1935)

Selected Poems, Lawrence, D.H. (London: Martin Secker, 1934)

The Spirit of Place: An Anthology Compiled from the Prose of D.H. Lawrence (London: Heinemann, 1935, 1944)

The Viking Book of Poetry of the English-Speaking World (New York: Viking Press, 1941, 1958, 1962)

Great French Romances (New York: Duell, Sloan and Pearce, 1946; London: The Pilot Press, 1946)

The Portable Oscar Wilde (New York: Viking Press, 1946; Harmondsworth: Penguin, 1977)

Selected Works of Oscar Wilde, with 12 Unpublished Letters (London: Heinemann, 1946)

Poetry of the English-Speaking World (London: Heinemann, 1947)

Selected Works of Walter Pater (London: Heinemann, 1948; New York: Duell, Sloan and Pearce, 1948)

The first Chawton edition of the novels of Jane Austen (London: Allan Wingate, 1948) (Introduction also published separately in Pasadena by Ampersand Press, 1948)

The Religion of Beauty: Selections from the Aesthetes (London: Heinemann, 1950)

Sea and Sardinia, Lawrence, D.H. (London, Heinemann, 1950; Harmondsworth: Penguin, 1953; New York: Viking Press, 1963)

Mornings in Mexico, Lawrence, D.H. (London: Heinemann, 1950)

Twilight in Italy, Lawrence, D.H. (London: Heinemann, 1950)

The White Peacock, Lawrence, D.H. (Harmondsworth: Penguin, 1950; London: Heinemann, 1950)

Aaron's Rod, Lawrence, D.H. (Harmondsworth: Penguin, 1950)

Kangaroo, Lawrence, D.H. (Harmondsworth: Penguin, 1950; London: Heinemann, 1950)

Selected Letters of D.H. Lawrence (Harmondsworth: Penguin, 1950)

Selected Essays of D.H. Lawrence (Harmondsworth: Penguin, 1950)

Etruscan Places, Lawrence, D.H. (Harmondsworth: Penguin, 1950)

The Lost Girl, Lawrence, D.H. (Harmondsworth: Penguin, 1950; London: Heinemann, 1950)

The Plumed Serpent, Lawrence, D.H. (Harmondsworth: Penguin, 1950; London: Heinemann, 1950)

The Trespasser (London: Heinemann, 1950; Harmondsworth: Penguin, 1960)

St Mawr and *The Virgin and the Gypsy*, Lawrence, D.H. (Harmondsworth: Penguin, 1950)

The Woman Who Rode Away and Other Stories, Lawrence, D.H. (Harmondsworth: Penguin, 1950; London: Heinemann, 1950)

England, My England, Lawrence, D.H. (London: Heinemann, 1950)

The Man Who Died (London: Heinemann, 1950)

The Rainbow, Lawrence, D.H. (London: Heinemann, 1950; New York: Viking Press, 1961; Harmondsworth: Penguin, 1976)

Women in Love, Lawrence, D.H. (London: Heinemann, 1954; New York: Viking Press, 1950; Harmondsworth: Penguin, 1976)

Austria: A Book of Photographs (London: Anglo-Italian Publication, 1958)

Switzerland: A Book of Photographs (London: Anglo-Italian Publication, 1958)

France: A Book of Photographs (London: Anglo-Italian Publication, (1958)

Italy: A Book of Photographs (London: Anglo-Italian Publication, 1958)

D.H. Lawrence: A Composite Biography, vol. 3, Nehls, Edward (ed.) (Madison: University of Wisconsin Press, 1959)

Famous Cities of the World: Rome (London: Hamlyn, 1960); *Rome: A Book of Photographs* (London: Spring Books, 1960)

Eugénie Grandet by Honoré de Balzac, trans. by Ellen Marriage (New York: Limited Editions Club, 1960; London: Curwen Press, 1960; New York: Heritage Press, 1961)

D.H. Lawrence: L'Oeuvre et la Vie, Temple, F.-J. (Paris: Seghers, 1960)

Editions of Letters

Benkovitz, Miriam, ed., *A Passionate Prodigality: Letters to Alan Bird from Richard Aldington, 1949-1962* (New York: New York Public Library, 1975)

Gates, Norman, ed., *Richard Aldington: An Autobiography in Letters* (Philadelphia: Pennsylvania University Press, 1992)

MacNiven, I.S., and Moore, H.T., eds, *Literary Lifelines: The Richard Aldington-Lawrence Durrell Correspondence* (New York: Viking Press, 1981)

Zilboorg, Caroline, ed. with an introduction and commentary, *Richard Aldington and H.D.: Their Lives in Letters* (Manchester and New York: Manchester University Press, 2003)

Editions of Others' Letters

Hollenberg, Donna Krolik, ed., *Between History and Poetry: The letters of H.D. and Norman Holmes Pearson* (Iowa City: University of Iowa Press, 1997)

Lawrence, T.E., *T.E. Lawrence: Letters to His Biographers Robert Graves and Liddell Hart* (London: Cassell, 1963)

Primary Sources

Arlott, John, *Basingstoke Boy* (London: Willow Books, 1990)

Church, Richard, *The Voyage Home* (London: Heinemann, 1964)

Cole, Margaret Postgate, *Growing Up into Revolution* (London: Longmans, 1949)

Connolly, Cyril, *The Rock Pool* (Paris: Obelisk Press, 1936; Oxford University Press, 1981)

Cunard, Nancy, *These Were the Hours* (Carbondale: Southern Illinois University Press, 1969)

Doolittle, Hilda, *Tribute to Freud* (New York: Pantheon, 1956; Manchester: Carcanet Press, 1985)

———, *End to Torment* (New York: New Directions, 1979)

Dutton, Geoffrey, *Out in the Open: An Autobiography* (Brisbane: University of Queensland Press, 1994)

Dutton, Ninette, *Firing* (Sydney: Harper Collins, 1995)

Easton, Robert, and Easton, Jane, *Love and War: Pearl Harbour Through V-J Day* (Norman: University of Oklahoma Press, 1991)

Kershaw, Alister, *The Pleasure of Their Company* (Brisbane: University of Queensland Press, 1990)

———, *Heydays* (Sydney: Angus & Robertson, 1991)

———, *Village to Village: Misadventures in France* (Sydney: Angus & Robertson, 1993)

Kershaw, Alister, and Temple, F.-J., eds, *Richard Aldington: An Intimate Portrait* (Carbondale: Southern Illinois University Press, 1965)

Lawrence, T.E., *Seven Pillars of Wisdom* (London: Jonathan Cape, 1935)

Orioli, Giuseppe, *Adventures of a Bookseller*, (London: Chatto & Windus, 1938)

Patmore, Brigit, *My Friends When Young* (London: William Heinemann, 1968)

Patmore, Derek, *Private History: An Autobiography of the Years 1919-1939* (London: Hogarth Press, 1967)

Rathbone, Irene, *Was There a Summer?* (London: Constable and Co. Ltd, 1943)

Rumbold, Richard, *My Father's Son* (London: Jonathan Cape, 1949)

Snow, Philip, *Stranger and Brother: A Portrait of C.P. Snow* (London: Macmillan, 1982)

Waugh, Alec, *My Brother Evelyn and Other Profiles* (London: Cassell & Co., 1967)

Secondary Sources

Alexander, Peter, *Roy Campbell: A Critical Biography* (Oxford University Press, 1982)

Asher, Michael, *Lawrence, the Uncrowned King of Arabia* (London: Viking, 1998)

Baldick, Chris, *The Oxford English Literary History, Volume 10: The Modern Movement* (Oxford University Press, 2005)

Blayac, Alain, and Zilboorg, Caroline, eds, *Richard Aldington: Essays in Honour of His Birth*, Papers from the Richard Aldington International Conference (Montpellier: Université Paul Valéry, 1992)

Brown, Malcolm, and Cave, Julia, *A Touch of Genius: The Life of T.E. Lawrence* (London: J.M. Dent & Sons, 1988)

Chapman, Robert T., *Wyndham Lewis: Fictions and Satires* (London: Vision Press, 1973)

Chisholm, Anne, *Nancy Cunard* (London: Sidgwick & Jackson, 1979)

Conover, Anne, *Olga Rudge and Ezra Pound:"What Thou Lovest Well . . ."* (Newhaven: Yale University Press, 2001)

Crawford, Fred D., *Richard Aldington and Lawrence of Arabia: A Cautionary Tale* (Carbondale: University of Southern Illinois Press, 1998)

Cunard, Nancy, *Grand Man: Memories of Norman Douglas* (London: Secker & Warburg, 1954)

Cunningham, Valentine, *British Writers of the Thirties* (Oxford: Oxford University Press, 1988)

Deasey, Louisa, *A Letter from Paris* (London: Scribe Publications, 2018)

Doyle, Charles, *Richard Aldington: A Biography* (Basingstoke: Macmillan, 1989)

———, ed., *Richard Aldington: Reappraisals* (Victoria: University of Victoria Press, 1990)

Easton, Robert, *Max Brand, The Big 'Westerner'* (Norman: University of Oklahoma Press, 1970)

Emeny, Richard, *Roy Campbell: Poet of Two Wars* (London: Cecil Woolf, 2014)

Frere, J.R., *The Early Life and Family History of A.S. Frere* (2009, unpublished)

Gates, Norman T., *A Checklist of the Letters of Richard Aldington* (Carbondale: Southern Illinois University Press, 1977)

———, ed., *Richard Aldington: An Autobiography in Letters* (Philadelphia: Pennsylvania State University Press, 1992)

———, *The Poetry of Richard Aldington: A Critical Evaluation and an Anthology of Uncollected Poems* (Philadelphia: Pennsylvania State University Press, 1975)

Gindin, James, *British Fiction in the 1930s: The Dispiriting Decade* (London: Macmillan, 1992)

Graves, Robert, *Lawrence and the Arabs* (London: Jonathan Cape, 1927)

Guest, Barbara, *Herself Defined: The Poet H.D. and Her World* (London: Collins, 1985)

Harding, Jason, *The Criterion: Cultural Politics and Periodical Networks in Inter-War Britain* (Oxford: Oxford University Press, 2002)

Harrison, John, *The Reactionaries* (London: Gollancz, 1966)

Hynes, Samuel, *The Auden Generation: Literature and Politics in England in the 1930s* (London: Bodley Head, 1976; London: Pimlico, 1992)

Kelly, Lionel, ed., *Richard Aldington: Papers from the Reading SympoS.I.U.m* (Reading: University of Reading, 1987)

Kempton, Daniel, and Stoneback, H.R., eds, *Writers in Provence: Proceedings of the First and Second International Richard Aldington Conference* (2003)

———, *New Places: Proceedings of the Third International Richard Aldington Conference* (2005)

———, *Locations and Dislocations: Proceedings of the Fourth International Richard Aldington Conference* (2008)

———, *Aldington, Pound and the Imagists at Brunnenburg: Selected Essays from the Sixth International Richard Aldington/Second International Imagism Conference* (2012)

(All published at Les-Saintes-Maries-de-la-Mer and New Paltz: Gregau Press and International Richard Aldington Society)

Kershaw, Alister, ed., *Richard Aldington: Selected Critical Writings, 1928-1960* (Carbondale: Southern Illinois University Press, 1970)

Kershaw, Alister, and Temple, F.-J., eds, *Richard Aldington, An Intimate Portrait* (Carbondale: Southern Illinois University Press, 1965)

King, James, *The Last Modern: A Life of Herbert Read* (London: Weidenfeld & Nicolson, 1990)

Kittredge, Selwyn, *The Literary Career of Richard Aldington* (dissertation, 2 volumes) (Ann Arbor: University of Michigan Press, 1976)

Klaidman, Stephen, *Sydney and Violet: Their Life with T.S. Eliot, Proust, Joyce and the Excruciatingly Irascible Wyndham Lewis* (New York: Nan A. Talese/Doubleday, 2013)

Korda, Michael, *Hero: The Life and Legend of Lawrence of Arabia* (London: J.R. Books, 2011)

Liddell Hart, B.H., *T.E. Lawrence in Arabia and After* (London: Jonathan Cape, 1934)

Lucas, F.L., 'English Literature', in Wright, Harold, ed., *University Studies, Cambridge 1933* (London: Ivor Nicholson & Watson, 1933)

MacGreevy, *Richard Aldington: An Englishman* (London: Chatto & Windus, 1931)

MacPhail, Andrew, *Three Persons* (London: John Murray, 1929)

Moody, A. David, *Ezra Pound: Poet: A Portrait of the Man and his Work: Volume II: The Epic Years, 1921-1939* (Oxford University Press, 2014)

———, *Ezra Pound: Poet: A Portrait of the Man and his Work: Volume III: The Tragic Years, 1939-1972* (Oxford University Press, 2015)

Morgan, Louise, *Writers at Work*, (London: Chatto & Windus, 1931)

Nash, Andrew, 'Literary Culture and Literary Publishing in Interwar Britain: A View from Chatto and Windus', in Eliot, Simon, Nash, Andrew, and Willison, Ian, eds, *Literary Culture and the Material Book* (London: British Library, 2007) pp. 323-42

Nutting, Anthony, *Lawrence of Arabia* (London: Hollis & Carter, 1961)

O'Keeffe, Paul, *Some Sort of Genius: A Life of Wyndham Lewis* (London: Jonathan Cape, 2000)

Richards, Vyvyan, *Portrait of T.E. Lawrence* (London: Jonathan Cape, 1936)

Schreibman, Susan, ed., *The Life and Work of Thomas MacGreevy* (London: Bloomsbury, 2013)

Smith, G. Eliot, *Human History* (London: Jonathan Cape, 1930)

Smith, R., *Richard Aldington* (London: Twayne, 1977)

Snow, C.P., *Richard Aldington: An Appreciation* (London: Heinemann, 1938)

Swinnerton, Frank, *The Georgian Literary Scene, 1910-1935* (London: Radius/ Hutchinson, 1935)

Symons, Julian, *Makers of the New: The Revolution in Literature, 1912-1939* (London: André Deutsch, 1987)

Usborne, Karen, *Elizabeth: The Author of 'Elizabeth and Her German Garden'* (London: Bodley Head, 1986)

Wilkinson, David, *The Death of a Hero: The Quest for First World War Poet Richard Aldington's Berkshire Retreat* (Barnsley: Pen & Sword, 2016)

Zilboorg, Caroline: 'Irene Rathbone: The Great War and Its Aftermath', in Quinn, Patrick, ed., *Recharting the Thirties* (London: Associated University Presses, 1996)

Journal Articles

Benkowitz, Miriam, 'Nine for Reeves: Letters from Richard Aldington', *Bulletin of the New York Public Library*, vol. 69, no. 6 (June 1965)

Crawford, Fred D., 'Misleading Accounts of Aldington and H.D.', *English Literature in Transition, 1880-1920*, vol. 30, no. 1 (1987) pp. 49-67

Fox, C.J., 'On the Line: Aldington of the Referee', *London Magazine*, vol. 25, nos. 9 and 10 (December 1985/January 1986) pp. 72-81

Moldavsky, V. M., 'Richard Aldington in Leningrad', *Neva*, no. 5 (1963) pp. 164-67, trans. by Robert J. Winter

Steele, Stephen, and Chang, Heesok, 'Modernism at the Margins: Richard Aldington's Letters to Douglas Goldring (1932-1946)', *Modern Language Studies*, vol. 35, no. 2 (Autumn 2005) pp. 22-55

Thatcher, David S., 'Richard Aldington's Letters to Herbert Read', *The Malahat Review*, no. 15 (July 1970) pp. 5-44

Index

Also by Vivien Whelpton:

RICHARD ALDINGTON
Poet, Soldier and Lover
1911-1929

Revised Edition

The story of Richard Aldington, outstanding Imagist poet and author of the bestselling war novel, *Death of a Hero* (1929), takes place against the backdrop of some of the most turbulent and creative years of the twentieth century.

Vivien Whelpton provides a remarkably detailed and sensitive portrayal of the writer from early adolescence. His life as a stalwart of the pre-war London literary scene, as a soldier, and in the difficult aftermath of the First World War is deftly rendered through a careful and detailed analysis of the novels, poems and letters of the writer himself and his close circle of acquaintance. The complexities of London's Bohemia, with its scandalous relationships, social grandstanding and incredible creative output, are masterfully untangled, and the spotlight placed firmly on the talented group of poets christened by Ezra Pound as 'Imagistes'. The author demonstrates profound psychological insight into Aldington's character and childhood in her nuanced analysis of his post-war survivor's guilt, and consideration of the three most influential women in his life: his wife, the gifted American poet, H.D. (Hilda Doolittle); Dorothy Yorke, the woman he left her for; and Brigit Patmore, his brilliant and fascinating older mistress.

Richard Aldington: Poet, Soldier and Lover vividly reveals Aldington's warm and passionate nature and the vitality which characterised his life and works, concluding with his triumphant personal and literary resurrection with the publication of *Death of a Hero*.

234x156mm / 471pp / Published: January 2014
Paperback ISBN: 978 0 7188 9546 4 / ePub ISBN: 978 0 7188 4797 5
Kindle ISBN: 978 0 7188 4798 2 / PDF ISBN: 978 0 7188 4796 8

BV - #0016 - 240522 - C0 - 234/156/22 - PB - 9780718894771 - Gloss Lamination